Cartier

Hans Nadelhoffer

Thames & Hudson

half-title page

1 Detail from a catalogue of Cartier
New York, 1914

frontispiece

2 Autochrome plate of a ruby and pearl
necklace made for Sir Bhupindra Singh,
Maharaja of Patiala, in 1928

For Ralph Esmerian

First published in the United Kingdom in 2007 by
Thames & Hudson Ltd, 181A High Holborn,
London WC1V 7QX
www.thamesandhudson.com

Cartier
© 2007 Thames & Hudson Ltd, London
Original text © 1984 Hans Nadelhoffer,
© 2007 Estate of Hans Nadelhoffer
New material © 2007 Cartier

Art direction and design by Andersen M Studio
www.andersenm.com

British Library Cataloguing-in-Publication Data
A catalogue record for this book is available from
the British Library

ISBN 978-0-500-51361-3

Printed and bound in Singapore by C S Graphics

NOTES TO THE READER

Sizes Unless otherwise stated, pieces reproduced in colour are
actual size, and pieces reproduced in black and white – from
photographs in the Cartier Archives – are half actual size.

Dates Dates in captions are those of the year of manufacture.
When the archives do not permit exact dating of a piece, either
no date is given or reference is made to similar datable pieces.

Carats Around 1900 the carat weight for precious stones was
not yet standardized: it varied between the equivalent of 188.5
and 213.5 mg in different parts of the world. The old carat gave
subdivisions as fractions from ½ to 1/64; and the weight was
expressed as a series of fractions – e.g. ½ ¼ 1/32 – rather than
as a unit and unreduced fraction.

A first attempt to standardize the carat at 205 mg, made by
Paris merchants in 1871, did not gain international recognition.
In 1907 the Comité International des Poids et Mesures proposed
a metric carat of 200 mg. This was accepted, and became legal
in Switzerland in 1909, Italy in 1910, France in 1912, the United
States in 1913, and the United Kingdom in 1914.

Documents in the Cartier Archives use the new metric carat
from 1911. Before that they use the old confusing system, where
the weight in France varied between 205.5 and 205.9 mg – greater
than the corresponding official metric weight (thus '10 carats'
would mean 2055 or 2059 mg, not 2000). In this book early
carat references have been left unchanged.

Pearls All pearls are natural unless otherwise stated.

CONTENTS

3 Alfred Cartier and his three sons – from left to
right Pierre (in charge of Cartier New York), Louis
(in charge of Cartier Paris) and Jacques (in charge
of Cartier London) – in 1922

INTRODUCTION

When Louis-François Cartier (1819–1904) [8] established his first, somewhat modest, business in 1847, there were few indications that greatness lay ahead. The period between the abdication of Louis-Philippe and the setting up of the Second Empire was fraught with difficulties for all the luxury trades: competition was severe, and the district round the church of Saint-Eustache in Paris was scarcely one to encourage the growth of a business. Half a century later, however, Cartier's name was to be found in resplendent letters adorning the world's leading shopping street, drawing within its orbit the wealthiest of international customers. Branches in London and New York soon became the fixed points in a strategic game of international business politics. Cartier's was a firm of worldwide reputation; it had become an institution.

Following the industrialization of the nineteenth century, the years between 1900 and 1915 witnessed a period of unprecedented economic growth. Communications were opened up, the wealth of the colonies flooded into Europe, and technical inventions strengthened men's faith in the future. Like the great industrialists, international bankers built up their empires, becoming the confidential advisers of governments and kings. Business tycoons who had acquired their wealth through speculation and pioneering enterprise chose the etiquette of an aristocratic élite as the model on which to base their own lifestyles. Although they lacked the aristocracy's pedigree, their financial dealings were sufficient to ensure them access to the highest circles of court society.

It was in the service of this as yet unspoilt consumer society that Cartier's scored its most triumphant successes, though commissions from royalty were certainly not lacking: between 1904 and 1939 the firm received fifteen letters patent appointing it official supplier to various royal households, from that of King Edward VII of Great Britain and Ireland to those of King Paramindr Maha Chulalongkorn of Siam and King Zog of Albania.

From a sociological point of view, one of Cartier's jewels might well guarantee entry into a society which depended for its survival upon imitation and plagiarism. On the eve of society weddings the firm would deliver its *corbeilles de mariage* – one thinks of the extravagance lavished on that of Marie Bonaparte (pp. 51–52) – as status symbols which complemented trousseaux from the great fashion houses.

For all their diverse backgrounds, Cartier's clients had one thing in common – unlimited wealth, which justified the firm's keeping in stock what, by today's standards, must seem an inconceivably costly range of precious stones. As the stock attracted clients from all over the world, language barriers often gave rise to situations of subtle humour, attested to by countless anecdotes:

> The interpreter of the King of Siam said that the King wished to see some bracelets, whereupon the sales assistant, Jules Glaenzer, showed him one tray after another, glittering with precious stones. But the King simply shook his head. Finally Glaenzer went over to the safe and brought out a tray containing the rarest and costliest bracelets. The King gave his interpreter a sign, and the latter turned to Glaenzer. 'His Majesty has chosen this one.' 'Which one?' asked Glaenzer. 'The whole tray', was the haughty reply.

Thus in 1907 the King of Siam became the owner of bracelets to the value of $450,000.[1] (By way of comparison, in 1910 the 'Hope' diamond was sold for $180,000.)

Coming as it did from a pre-war era of luxury and affluence, the name of Cartier, like that of Ritz, was divorced from its context and turned into one of the few lasting symbols of a lifestyle and a philosophy that were acted out with exemplary taste. 'Dickens in a Cartier setting' was how Edward VIII described Christmas at Sandringham, conjuring up the glittering atmosphere which illuminated the house like a precious jewel.[2]

But perfection provokes imitators. Cartier's ideas, which were to have such an impact on twentieth-century jewelry design, were eagerly taken up by competitors, robbed of their

overleaf, left

4 Louis Cartier (1875–1942)

5 Pierre Cartier (1878–1965)

overleaf, right

6 Jeanne Toussaint (1887–1978)

7 Jacques Cartier (1884–1942)

value and beauty, and often returned to the market in the form of mass-produced trivia.

The Cartier phenomenon was the achievement of three brothers, who built an empire and divided it up among themselves between Paris, New York and London. They were the grandsons of Louis-François [8]; their father, Alfred [3], had carried on the business.

Preeminent among them – and not only for reasons of age – was the eldest, Louis Cartier (1875–1942) [3, 4]. Born four years after Marcel Proust, he was nineteen when the Dreyfus Case burst upon the world, and thirty-nine at the outbreak of the First World War. In Louis Cartier we meet that rare combination of aesthete and instinctive market tactician. As an aesthete, he became a collector, influenced by the taste of the *fin-de-siècle* which embraced all ages and cultures. He found a kindred spirit in his friend, the eccentric bon vivant Boni de Castellane, who for years officiated as a social observer in Cartier's service.

Louis Cartier admired eighteenth-century France for its painting and its elegant and decorative craftsmanship. Not content, however, with the role of a mere arbiter of taste, he developed an understanding of Islamic and Far Eastern art, incorporating their refined ideas into his firm's range of products. It was thanks to him that the Orient came to play so important a role in the firm's Art Deco designs.

Also typical of the *fin-de-siècle* mentality was Louis Cartier's interest in contemporary philosophical and scientific ideas – theories about matter, the atom and radioactivity which were by no means irreconcilable with his poetic awareness of the infinite. 'The grandiose contemplation of our planet's remotest past, this proof of God's existence in the structure of an atom, fills me with a sense of awe', he wrote to his father in an undated letter.

Pierre Cartier (1878–1965) [3, 5, 129], on the other hand, was a born businessman who might have achieved much of value in any field. That he felt the need, as a man of great pragmatic skills, to go to the United States and run the firm's New York branch [23] according to the rules of the New World was entirely in character. Whereas Louis cultivated links with the old aristocracy of Europe, marrying Countess Almassy of Hungary *en secondes noces*, Pierre grew up dreaming of a career as an ambassador, surrounded by the leading families of America who opened their doors to him following his marriage to Elma Rumsey, the daughter of a rich industrialist from St Louis, Missouri. Many of Pierre's important decisions were reached in consultation with Jules Glaenzer, the son of an antique dealer, who was in charge of the firm's Fifth Avenue branch, entertaining Hollywood stars to dinner and contributing to Cartier's image in America in the same way that Jeanne Toussaint did in Paris.

The youngest member of the family, Jacques Cartier (1884–1942) [3, 7, 140, 179], was only fifteen when the firm moved to the rue de la Paix. He was probably the most sensitive and introverted of the three brothers. When his father, Alfred, divided up the family empire, the London branch [27] fell to him. After London broke away from the parent company in 1919, and the political conditions of the 1930s obliged it to adopt a more independent policy in artistic matters, it was Jacques who provided increasingly valuable suggestions for the design studios and whose purchase of gemstones showed a sure understanding. Together with his wife, Nelly Harjes, a member of a well-known banking family which had connections with Morgan in America, he built up his social contacts so that by the time he died they had come to include all the leading princes of the Indian subcontinent.

The triumvirate of brothers was joined in Paris by Jeanne Toussaint (1887–1978) [6, 282]. According to the English court photographer Cecil Beaton, she was a woman 'of small bird-like stature' (one thinks of the countless allusions to birds in descriptions of the American socialite Emerald Cunard). Beaton was struck by her 'almost male contempt for trivialities' and by her sixth sense, the famous 'goût Toussaint'. It was an acid test to which the firm's most sophisticated products were mercilessly subjected. She never designed anything herself: 'My inability to draw qualifies me to assess the work of others.' From the distance of this self-imposed limitation she watched over the firm's designs for four decades, offering splendid suggestions and brilliant analyses.

Jeanne Toussaint saw jewels as an aspect of fashion. The most sophisticated creations of Elsa Schiaparelli, Christian Dior, Coco Chanel and Cristobal Balenciaga provided endlessly changing backgrounds for her jewelry. Painted by Helleu, Boldini, Sem, Iribe and Bérard, she conveyed the impression of a magician even in her daily routine. 'You perfume diamonds!' Princess Bibesco cried out in amazement.

Although she was committed to the aesthetic taste of the 1930s and 1940s, Jeanne Toussaint was one of the first to recognize the originality of Cartier's products from earlier periods, and in 1934 she advised a return to 'the sources of inspiration', namely the ideas that had been formulated around 1906.

Cartier's most original creations stopped short at nothing, especially during the Cocktail Age of the 1930s: tin-openers with a crowned monogram, gold yoyos (W. K. Vanderbilt bought ten of them), and a diamond belt for the actress Polaire, not to mention gold toothpicks made for King Farouk, and a silver shoe which it took Cartier's master craftsman Ferdinand Albouze 180 hours to complete in the firm's workshop. It was an amusing line of work which helped to tide the firm over at a time when, because of the economic situation following the Wall Street crash of 1929, major commissions were relatively few.

At the end of the 1940s Pierre Cartier handed over the New York branch to Louis' son Claude, and devoted himself to the parent firm in Paris. He died in 1965, the last surviving member of the Cartier brothers. The New York branch had been sold three years previously, and the firm was fragmented and sold off in a series of further transactions, before passing into the hands of a financial syndicate organized by Joseph Kanouï and headed by Robert Hocq in 1972. With the reunion of the three Cartier branches foremost in his mind, Hocq once more built up the firm to international preeminence. Apart from carrying on its repu-tation for gems and jewelry, Cartier's in 1972 witnessed the birth of 'Les Must de Cartier', a worldwide marketing concept selling high-fashion items of jewelry and gifts which, under changed social circumstances, once again carry the name of Cartier to every country on earth.

CHAPTER ONE

FROM APPRENTICE TO COURT JEWELLER

The history of Cartier's begins with an incident which, according to family tradition, took place in 1808 in Saragossa at the time of the Napoleonic Wars in Spain: Pierre Cartier (1787–1865), a young and inexperienced infantry soldier, had just been taken prisoner, but was saved from being lined up and shot along with other soldiers by the bravery of a baker's wife, who hid him in the baker's oven and then helped him to escape, dressed as a woman. Wellington's English soldiers, however, soon saw through his disguise and he was transported by ship to Plymouth. It was long before he saw his homeland again, and not until 1815 that he married Elisabeth Gérardin, a washerwoman,[1] and began to earn an honest living as a manufacturer of powder-horns. Pierre had scarcely known his father, Louis-François (1755–93/94), who had been a metal turner in a small workshop in the Louvre, producing items for the royal household. Suspicion had fallen upon Louis-François at the time of the Revolution, as it did on so many others, forcing him to leave Paris. He died at the early age of thirty-nine on his small property near Saint-Denis.

It was Pierre's son, Louis-François (1819–1904) [8], named after his grandfather, who was to point the way to his family's later calling. He was employed in the workshop of the jeweller Adolphe Picard,[2] at 29 rue Montorgueil, close to the great oyster market near the church of Saint-Eustache. Louis-François was a capable assistant, and when in 1847 Picard moved to 29 rue de Richelieu, he put his business in the younger man's hands. Louis-François' entry in the *Almanach du Commerce* describes him as the 'successor to M. Picard, manufacturer of *joaillerie* [gem-set jewels] and *bijouterie* [gold and enamel jewelry], fancy decorations and novelties'.

Another neighbourhood where jewellers had established themselves was the Palais-Royal, where fashionable society went shopping and where the beautiful women of Paris were to be seen driving around in their carriages. Louis-François' ambition to settle near the vast palace of the Orléans family was achieved in 1853, when with Picard's help he set himself up at 5 rue Neuve-des-Petits-Champs as a jeweller and gem-setter, also selling direct to the public. The thirty-four-year-old Cartier not only made his own jewelry but, in accordance with contemporary practice, received supplies from a number of other workshops, including that of Picard, to whom he remained contractually bound.

The business quickly prospered. Cartier's first pre-tax profits amounted to Fr. 9,252, and the firm's proximity to the Palais-Royal began to pay handsome dividends. But how was he to succeed in attracting the attention of the imperial family and its circle? The Emperor Napoleon III had married Eugénie de Montijo, Countess of Teba, in the same year that Cartier had moved his business. The Emperor had chosen several firms to rework various pieces of jewelry: Lemonnier, Baugrand, Mellerio, and Ouizille-Lemoine, in the rue du Bac, who was one of the jewellers whose workshops supplied Cartier. Couturiers and jewellers hoped that the arrival of the beautiful Spanish Countess would bring an increase in business; after all, the Paris City Council had agreed to spend Fr. 600,000 on a necklace with a 23-carat heart-shaped diamond as a wedding present. The Empress, however, wisely foreseeing malicious criticism, declined the generous gift, much to the disappointment of the Parisian jewellers.

Cartier was to achieve his goal by indirect means. His first important female customer was the Comtesse de Nieuwerkerke, who bought some fifty-five items between 1855 and 1858. The time was not yet ripe for large pieces of jewelry: it was a transitional period during which the prevailing fashion was determined by the puritanical bourgeois taste of the age of Louis-Philippe. The great fashion for cameos, which had started under Napoleon I, had not yet died out, and so the Countess began by ordering a cameo necklace, together with six buttons set with antique cameos. The Comte de Nieuwerkerke was well known in his day as a sculptor in bronze: he had produced an equestrian statue of Napoleon III which had won the Emperor's approval. More important, however, as far as Cartier was concerned, was the Count's friendship with Princess Mathilde, through which he had attained his appointment as Superintendent of Fine Art. The Princess, who was the daughter of Napoleon's brother Jérôme, had left St Petersburg in 1845 to settle in Paris, following the failure of her marriage to the Russian Prince Demidov di San Donato. She maintained a salon, first in the Palais de l'Elysée and later in the rue de Courcelles and on her estate at Saint-Gratien, which attracted scholars, politicians and artists and which formed a striking contrast to the frivolity of the Tuileries court. It was through

11 Bracelet. Cartier Paris, *c.* 1899. Gold, silver; rose-cut diamonds, six cushion-shaped rubies (75% actual size)

Nieuwerkerke that Cartier received commissions from the Princess, and an imperial eagle which Nieuwerkerke ordered in 1857 was undoubtedly destined for her jewel casket. The commissions of Princess Mathilde herself, intended for her own use or as gifts, included four Medusa-head cameos, seven amethyst plaque brooches, a turquoise scarab brooch, an opal bracelet, a ruby and pearl necklace, earrings in the Egyptian style, and a parasol. In all there were more than two hundred items, which fill several pages in Cartier's sales ledgers.[3] Louis-François' most ardent wish was to be fulfilled in 1859 when the Empress herself, possibly at the instigation of the Princess, ordered a silver tea-service.

The rue Neuve-des-Petits-Champs had definitely become too small for the supplier to the imperial household. His eye was caught by the business of the jeweller Gillion at 9 boulevard des Italiens, for which offers were being invited. Louis-François took over the lease in 1859 and paid Fr. 40,000 for the existing stock.

Over the years, the area around the Palais-Royal had lost some of its splendour, but this was more than made up for by the bustle of the boulevard des Italiens, which took its name from the nearby Théâtre des Italiens: barouches, landaus and omnibuses jostled along the shady tree-lined street, crinolines billowed over the pavements, flower girls offered their wares to passers-by, and the crowded coffee-shops of Tortoni, the Grand Balcon and the Café Anglais attracted regular customers and tourists alike. In the past no. 9 had housed a confectioner, 'Au Fidèle Berger', and a fashion-house, 'Aux Bayadères', before Gillion acquired it in 1847. We do not know how Cartier initially designed the interior of the shop, but in 1873 the marble interior was renovated; the front of the building was faced with marble in 1891 and at the same time electric lighting was installed; a telephone followed in 1898.

At the new address, the stream of eminent customers continued unabated. They included Prince Bibesco, Prince Saltykov and Prince Belgiojoso, a member of the family of Princess Cristina Belgiojoso, who was politically active in support of her Italian homeland.[4] Cartier's jewels remained of modest size – small emeralds, amethysts, pearls and garnets set in silver and gold. The firm also offered everything from simple silver objects, ivories and bronzes to the varied bric-a-brac of an antique dealer. The business was run on patriarchal principles, with Louis-François enthroned 'like Zeus on Olympus', while his son Alfred (1841–1925) [3] looked after the gemstones, and a general factotum by the name of Prosper was employed both as a designer and to arrange the displays.

Louis-François had the refined taste of a man who enjoys life: both father and son ordered their shirts from the exclusive firm of Charvet, their cellar contained the finest French wines, and the pastry-cook Boissier provided them with a regular supply of *marrons glacés* and similar delicacies. Louis-François also found time to play a musical instrument, which he did immediately on rising; and in later life, following his retirement, he became an expert in ancient and Oriental languages. The garden of his country house at Roanne revealed him to be a modest disciple of Jean-Jacques Rousseau, whose shining example enticed him to the Swiss Alps in 1869. Ever since 1729, when the doctor-poet Albrecht von Haller had praised them in verse, the once-feared Alps had become the shrine for a picturesque and poetical communion with nature. Louis-François' brief account of his journey is full of the magic of an unspoilt tourism, as when he was rowed across Lake Brienz to the Giessbach Falls and came unexpectedly upon Frédéric Boucheron and Jean-Paul Robin from Paris, with whom he marvelled at the natural wonder of the Falls. In Fribourg he trembled beneath the waves of sound produced by the cathedral organ, and he completed his journey by setting out on the back of a mule for the traditional ascent of Mont Blanc. In 1868 he had travelled to Germany, a visit which may have taken him to the gemstone dealers in Idar-Oberstein.

Following the French defeat by the Prussians at Sedan in 1870 and the abdication of Napoleon III, the disruptive policies of the Commune undermined all hopes of a trade revival and economic recovery. The couturier Charles Worth, who was important for Cartier's future survival (see p. 50), temporarily closed down, and in 1871 Alfred sought refuge in England, as the Empress herself had done. His period of exile, which lasted until 1873 and brought Cartier's their first letters patent as suppliers to the Court of St James, had a very firm foundation. The celebrated Italian courtesan Giulia Beneni, better known as La Barucci, had died of tuberculosis in Paris in 1870, like the *Dame aux Camélias*. (During the Second Empire *cocottes* had enjoyed all the material advantages of a socially ambiguous reputation. The example set by the Emperor or the Duc de Morny raised the Parisian *demi-monde* into spheres where, on the arm of some wealthy admirer, these women exercised an equal influence on fashion and on politics.) La Barucci's jewel case was famous for its separate compartments of coloured stones and diamonds.[5] Alfred Cartier was assigned the sale of these jewels, including a ten-row pearl necklace. In London he raised the huge sum of Fr. 800,000 for La Barucci's heirs, who were of simple Italian peasant stock, and he himself kept 5 per cent of the proceeds.

A further event of this period in London was Alfred's meeting with Léonide Leblanc (1842–94), a latterday Ninon de Lenclos, who had been a great success both as a courtesan and as an actress at the Paris Odéon. In 1870–71 she appeared in various English theatres giving benefit performances for French prisoners-of-war, and momentary financial worries brought her into contact with Alfred. It was a debt of gratitude which, upon her return to France, she was never to forget, and as the mistress of Henri d'Orléans, the Duc d'Aumale, she became one of Cartier's leading patrons,[6] comparable to the later Mrs Keppel, who came from a different social background, and Lady de Grey.

When Alfred Cartier took over his father's business in Paris in 1874 circumstances were difficult. In 1866, for example, when Napoleon III had been at the height of his power, the year's profits had amounted to Fr. 48,244, whereas it was only by dint of considerable effort that, following the economic decline which had set in with the Commune, Alfred was able to maintain profits at Fr. 39,200 in 1875, when the Third Republic was proclaimed. Liquid capital then amounted to only Fr. 186,630 – a sum which had increased to Fr. 500,000 by 1890.

Cartier's continued to sell all manner of things: fans, bronze busts of Louis XV, Wedgwood medallions, ivory statuettes, silverware, Sèvres porcelain, and, of course, jewelry and watches. The firm's clientele was made up of the well-to-do families of France, including the Prince de Wagram, the Comtesse de Montesquiou and even the Comte de Paris, who bought six silver-gilt frames adorned with the fleur-de-lys. But the sales ledgers were becoming increasingly filled with the names of well-to-do members of the middle classes, including bankers and industrialists, all of whom had acquired their wealth in often risky speculations during the Second Empire. Their patronage of Cartier and the ostentation with which they flaunted their jewelry were intended to confirm their social respectability. One new customer which Cartier's acquired at this time and which they were able to keep for many years to come was the City of Bordeaux: from 1878 onwards hundreds of bronze medallions were ordered which bore the City's coat-of-arms and which were distributed on numerous occasions, including the university's commemorative celebrations.

Following the economic upheaval of the 1870s, which witnessed the growth of trade unions under a socialist government and which was characterized by constant power struggles between royalists and republicans and between clerical and anticlerical factions, there was a brief period of economic prosperity from 1880 to 1882: banks were liberal in offering credit, new companies were founded, and the French railway network grew; but this was soon followed by a collapse of the market, spectacular bankruptcies, and renewed economic uncertainty. Forces hostile to the parliamentary republic banded into the phalanx of General Georges Boulanger. Alfred Cartier enjoyed the patronage not only of this popular general but also of the latter's companion, the Vicomtesse de Bonnemain, who festooned herself with Cartier silver and Cartier jewelry. The diamond aigrette which she received in 1887 must be one of the earliest Cartier jewels to be recognizable in a contemporary photograph. Daniel Wilson's fraudulent dealings in counterfeit decorations led to the fall of the cabinet. It was an affair whose progress may be charted in Cartier's records, for whereas the profits for 1882–83 still amounted to Fr. 93,365, they fell in 1886 to Fr. 63,904 and did not return to their former high levels until 1888–89, when profits of Fr. 93,725 were recorded (total sales in 1888 amounted to Fr. 399,529). In 1890–91 the figure of Fr. 100,000 was exceeded for the first time, and in 1899–1900, the year following the move to the rue de la Paix, the million-franc barrier was crossed with Fr. 1,776,785.

The sales ledgers for 1886–87 contain insignificant entries, as well as numerous purchases from private individuals who found themselves in financial difficulties: Prince Friedrich of Saxe-Coburg bought miniatures, while a certain Mr Brunswick[7] sold diamonds

FOURNISSEUR
DE LA FAMILLE ROYALE d'ANGLETERRE

CARTIER & FILS

BIJOUTERIE
JOAILLERIE
ORFEVRERIE

12 Cartier's official letterhead recording their royal warrant as suppliers to King Edward VII, *c.* 1904

13 Watch on châtelaine. Cartier Paris, 1874. Châtelaine of pink gold chains with chased and enamelled decoration; two plaques of pink gold and polychrome enamel showing bucolic scenes on front and back, framed by blue enamel and pearls; baskets of gold and enamel with pendant pearls. Round watch-case of enamelled pink gold bearing the portrait of a young woman, rimmed in half-pearls on front and back; round dial of white enamel with Arabic numerals ringed by a minute track and Arabic numerals at the quarter-hours; gold-plated Breguet hands weighing 95 7/8 carats. From 1890 onwards Cartier's enjoyed the patronage of the family of the former Brazilian Emperor Dom Pedro II, who had abdicated in 1889 and now lived in exile in Europe. Although the ex-Emperor died in 1891, his grandson, Prince Pedro, continued to visit Cartier's shop in the boulevard des Italiens.

The stock of a business like Cartier's brought together the products of three different professional groups which, ever since the Middle Ages, had jointly formed one of the most distinguished of guilds: the goldsmith, who made silver and gold vessels; the *bijoutier-orfèvre*, who manufactured gold and enamel jewelry and snuff boxes; and the *joaillier*, who worked with gemstones. It is difficult to gain a clear overall picture of these individual specializations since, following a long-established tradition, the individual firms employed workshops which were scattered across Paris, and which in their turn handed on work to subsidiary workshops. Jules Fossin the Younger, who worked for Cartier's in the rue de Richelieu, was himself in charge of three other workshops, with the result that a single commissioned item was often produced by several workshops in collaboration. What is additionally confusing is the fact that firms which to an outsider looked like rivals supplied each other with items. Not only did the workshop of Alexis Falize produce items for Boucheron and for Cartier's, but Boucheron himself supplied Cartier's in 1858 and 1863, as did Gideon T. F. Reed, who was in charge of the Paris branch of Tiffany's.

As a rule, the manufacturer's or master's mark entered in the register of the state-controlled 'Garantie' was the only indication of who had produced a particular jewel. Cartier's had their first mark in 1846: it showed an ace of hearts set in a lozenge. The pieces of jewelry which the firm made in the nineteenth century are nowadays rarely identifiable, although they ought to bear either Cartier's own mark or that of the workshop from which they had been commissioned. On the whole, French jewels were only rarely marked in the nineteenth century. The practice was generally restricted to particularly impressive three-dimensional pieces, such as those exhibited at world fairs. For purely technical reasons, the gold and silver alloy used in jewelry was based on 14-carat gold, which was in fact illegal. Because of this jewellers preferred not to mark or to sign pieces, which often passed straight from the workshop into the hands of the buyer, since in that way they were able to avoid State controls. Cartier's had already begun to mark items of silver during the final years in the boulevard des Italiens, but jewelry was not marked until after the move to the rue de la Paix. Specially trained engravers traced the signature by hand, without the aid of machinery, using italic script.

14 Bow brooch. Cartier Paris, 1898. Gold, silver; old and rose-cut diamonds

15 Brooch. Cartier Paris, after 1912. Gold, steel; rose-cut diamonds; white and pink enamel.

A further difficulty which faces attempts to recognize items produced during the nineteenth century in Cartier's own workshop and elsewhere is that, unlike Boucheron and Chaumet, almost no drawings unequivocally identifiable as Cartier's have survived. We do know, however, that the then much-respected Eugène Julienne (1808–75), who had begun his career as a draughtsman in the Sèvres porcelain factory, and who later gave drawing lessons to Princess Mathilde, instructed Cartier, as well as various other jewellers, in ornamental drawing.[8] Another draughtsman who was well known at the time was Félix Duval, who published lithographs of jewelry designs in Paris around 1861, basing them on cubes, discs, cylinders and spheres. He, too, worked for Cartier as a graphic artist.

While scarcely any of Cartier's original jewelry drawings from the second half of the nineteenth century are known, later copies dating from around 1900, which may be in Alfred Cartier's hand,[9] are to be found in Cartier's stock books. These provide information about the numerous forms of jewelry then being made.

The earliest articles of jewelry produced by the firm can be dated to the period between 1850 and 1855, when the business operated from the rue Neuve-des-Petits-Champs. They are agate and obsidian cameos, and articles of jasper, pearl, malachite and onyx. The workshop of Pierre Caillot in the rue de la Grande-Truanderie supplied similar items, as did Adolphe Picard, Louis-François Cartier's former master. The first workshop of general importance in Paris to act as supplier for Cartier's was that of Jules Fossin the Younger in the rue de Richelieu, who continued the tradition started by the great Marie-Etienne Nitot. In 1853, for example, Fossin supplied Cartier with a 'Byzantine' bracelet. Especially famous were his naturalistic flower brooches, which prepared the way for those of the more important figure of Oscar Massin in the second half of the century.

16 Black ink sketches from the stock register, including a brooch in the form of an anchor, dolphin and sword supplied by Alphonse Fouquet, 1880

Equally important as suppliers were the two firms of Daux and Delamare, both of which were located in the Palais-Royal, together with Guillaume Falize (1820–1906), brother of the even more famous Alexis Falize, Désiré Froment-Meurice (1802–55), and Jules Chaise, whose pupils were later to include Frédéric Boucheron. Another supplier, Alexandre Gueyton, has gone down in history as the inventor of the 'galvanoplastic' process for electroplating jewelry, which differed from that of Charles Christofle.[10] Christofle devoted himself from 1849 to an exclusive study of electrochemistry, although in later years his firm supplied Cartier's with silver tableware. In the nineteenth century this side of the Cartier business was almost as important quantitatively as the section devoted to jewelry. It was supplied principally by the Paris workshop of Queille; Wolfers in Brussels and, at a later date, Robert Linzeler in the rue d'Argenson were temporary suppliers.

The types of jewelry made by Cartier's in the 1860s that provide the most interesting clues to contemporary styles and fashions are bracelets, necklaces, earrings and brooches. The first three types were mainly designed in a very linear classical form, which shows the influence of a major cultural event: the exhibition of the Campana Collection at the Louvre from 1861 onward. Napoleon III had bought the collection, numbering over one thousand items, formerly owned by the Italian Marchese di Campana, who had run foul of the law. With its Greek, Roman and Etruscan jewelry, and its classical ceramics, bronzes and glass, it offered a complete cross-section of the arts and crafts of the Mediterranean cultures in Antiquity. The impression which the exhibition made upon Paris jewellers, and especially on Fontenay and Christofle, was immediate, whereas the Italian jeweller Fortunato Pio Castellani and his two sons (Alessandro was in Paris at the time of the Campana exhibition) had already been exposed for some time to the influence of classical goldsmiths' work.[11] Inspired by the Campana jewels, Eugène Fontenay (1823–87) created necklaces using amphora and wheat-ear motifs. Pieces that Fontenay had begun to supply to Louis-François Cartier as early as 1850 show that even at that date his work embraced a style which was indebted to classical Antiquity for its decorative meanders and palmettes, such as are to be seen in the paintings of Ingres or the German artist Anselm Feuerbach.

This classical style did not achieve its fullest expression in Cartier's work until the 1870s. Whereas it exercised a dominant influence on bracelets, necklaces and earrings, châtelaines remained in the eighteenth-century style. Brooches, on the other hand, show an unlimited choice of motifs. In necklaces and bracelets the neo-Antique style replaced the naturalistic snakes, wood and fruit motifs in bright enamel colours of the 1850s and 1860s. Popular at a later date, around 1880, were golden chain bracelets (*gourmettes*) studded with rose-cut diamonds and turquoises. Three bracelets above all stand out from those which Cartier's produced during this later period – a silver bracelet made in 1887 with a representation of 'Dance' based on the sculpture by Jean-Baptiste Carpeaux,[12] a 'Celtic' bracelet made in 1893 with a horse medallion and mistletoe motifs, and a steel bracelet dating from 1895 with Gothic arabesques in gold.

In the case of earrings, however, the classical influence led to pendant motifs of long matt gold drops,[13] or to girandoles of lapis lazuli or coral drops.[14] These were followed after 1875–76 by round, concentric forms: simple pearls fastened by screws, diamond solitaires in silver settings (*dormeuses*), or diamond-surrounded pearls. The mineral tiger's-eye was launched in Paris around 1882, and Cartier's made a pair of earrings with the new stone in 1883.

The greatest variety of styles between the years 1850 and 1880 was to be found in brooches, which, together with bracelets, proved to be the most popular of all the various types of jewelry. From the time of Cartier's move to the rue Neuve-des-Petits-Champs in 1853 we find records of brooches consisting initially simply of gold or else decorated with mosaic work, cameos or Limoges enamel. From around 1870 the dominant motifs, not only in Cartier's work but throughout the whole of Paris, were animals and flowers. The fashion for animals led to depictions of horses' heads, horseshoes and stirrups in yellow gold and enamel, which are evidence of the popularity of horse-racing during the Second Empire (the racecourse at Longchamp was inaugurated in 1857) and which point to English influence. The *genre anglais* very much set the tone at the time in the manufacture of jewelry in France.[15]

A second type of animal, again influenced by Victorian England, included small reptiles, crabs, bees and dragonflies and led directly to the style of Art Nouveau.[16] Cartier's rival, Oscar Massin, had popularized these motifs as early as about 1863. Cartier himself introduced dragonfly, salamander and turtle brooches after 1870. Snake heads became popular as hat-pins around 1890, carrying baroque pearls in their gaping jaws. The menagerie was completed by flies and butterflies [16] made of translucent *plique-à-jour* enamel. Two butterfly brooches, for example, were acquired by Princess Mathilde in 1880.

The third variant on the animal motif moved into the realm of pure fantasy and produced the macabre chimaeras and griffins which achieved popularity in Paris above all through the work of Alphonse Fouquet (1828–1911), who was based from 1879 in the avenue de l'Opéra and who at that date was undoubtedly the most interesting of Cartier's suppliers. He had exhibited his dragons, sphinxes and chimaera brooches at the Paris Exposition of 1878. Similar designs first began to appear from Cartier's in 1883 [17], though produced by other workshops. The most original item that Fouquet supplied to Cartier's was a brooch with an interlaced anchor, dolphin and sword (1880) [16]. The dolphin in particular made frequent appearances in Fouquet's work.[17]

Birds occupied a special position among the various animals on brooches. The fashion for birds, especially hummingbirds, had been started by Cartier's rival, Rouvenat. Cartier's preference was for birds of paradise, storks, cockerels and owls. With the lovebird motif, two birds sitting together on a branch, the firm invented an image which retained its appeal well into the twentieth century. To these may be added five bird brooches, forming a flight of swallows made of rose-cut diamonds, which were supplied by René Lalique in 1887. They may well be the model that Henri Vever described as having been sold to Boucheron: 'In 1887 Lalique had the idea of a large set of jewelry *en joaillerie*, representing an entire flight of swallows; he hoped to give them a sense of perspective by means of the decreasing size of the birds.'[18] Dove brooches, a further variant, appeared in 1893 to celebrate the Franco-Russian alliance of that year.

Flowers were as popular as animals. Whereas animal motifs ran the risk of becoming anecdotally sentimental (such as the motif of 'Three Cats as Musicians'), flowers, which lent themselves to naturalistic representation in diamonds, could be turned into *haute joaillerie* whose fame spread far beyond the confines of France. The most famous floral brooches, in the shape of three-dimensional wild roses, were produced by Oscar Massin. His forms are characterized by greater virtuosity than those of his rivals, and his products show a reworking of English models, together with those of eighteenth-century France. Among the blossoms in Cartier's lavish displays were wild roses, narcissi, Parma violets, poppies and marguerites. After 1895 these floral motifs were to be eagerly taken up by Art Nouveau in miniature and using different techniques.

17 Black ink sketches from the stock register, including a chimaera by Fleuret and pieces by Fontenay and Charpentier, 1883

CHAPTER TWO

RUE DE LA PAIX,
NEW BOND STREET, FIFTH AVENUE

The history of Cartier's in the boulevard des Italiens shows clearly the irresistible rise of a family business in which father and son complemented each other in ideal fashion. Contacts with the court and with a bourgeoisie which owed its wealth to speculative dealings on the stock market ensured that even during the crisis-ridden 1880s the firm enjoyed ever-increasing support and patronage. An American customer was noted as early as 1854, but it was really only after Alfred Cartier's return from London in 1873 that the firm's clientele assumed an international profile. It would be incorrect to claim that only following the move to the rue de la Paix in 1899 did Cartier's begin to attract the big spenders of the Belle Epoque, such as J. P. Morgan [21], or those who formed the fun-loving entourage of the Prince of Wales. A letter which Alfred Cartier wrote from the boulevard des Italiens to Lady de Grey in 1898, when plans were temporarily being formulated for the marriage of Princess Victoria and Prince George of Greece, contains a request that the English lady might use her influence to recommend the firm of Cartier for the wedding presents.[1]

Nevertheless, there were differences in size and style between the items on display in the boulevard des Italiens and the later ones: the jewelry bought by customers in the older shop was thoroughly bourgeois and essentially the same as that being made by Cartier's rivals. It was only as a result of the discovery of the great diamond deposits in South Africa in the late 1860s and diamond sales made by the De Beers Mining Company that the French jewelry industry took on a new dimension. A young international clientele made up of bankers, industrialists and speculators now competed with the long-established aristocracy. They came for the most part from North and South America, England and Germany, and ordered jewelry worthy of a Napoleon, which would indeed have placed the jewels of the Empress Eugénie herself in the shade. One of the main reasons for Cartier's move to 13 rue de la Paix in 1899 was to satisfy the pretensions of these inordinately wealthy customers. Here at no. 7 were the premises of the world's most famous couturiers, Jean-Philippe and Gaston Worth, patronized by this international set who were prepared to pay the same prices for clothes as for works of art and who wished to complement their wardrobes with matching jewelry. Friendship and marriage brought the two firms of Worth and Cartier into the closest contact, so that their policies and spheres of influence now became inextricably linked: Cartier profited from Worth's clientele and this liaison turned the rue de la Paix into the leading shopping street of the age.

Rue de la Paix

Then as now, the rue de la Paix formed an indivisible whole with the adjacent Place Vendôme, whose central column provides its crowning monument. The square and the street, however, had come into being under different circumstances. The all-powerful minister Louvois had persuaded Louis XIV to lay out a square which would impress foreign ambassadors on their way to Saint-Germain and Versailles. The King accordingly acquired the Hôtel Vendôme in 1685 and commissioned the architect Jules Hardouin-Mansart to design a square which would be closed on three sides. By the time the square was completed in 1699 Louvois had died and the plans had been altered: the Place Louis-le-Grand was rectangular with canted corners, and at its centre stood Girardon's equestrian statue of the King. Like Bouchardon's statue in the later Place de la Concorde, this became a victim of the French Revolution. For its site, on Napoleon's orders, in 1806–10 a giant column was created – made from the bronze of 1,200 cannon captured from the Austrians and Russians at the battle of Austerlitz – crowned by a statue of the Emperor. Also in 1806 Napoleon ordered the demolition of the Capuchin monastery to the north of the square, with its church in whose crypt the remains of Madame de Pompadour had rested. In this way a new street was created, known initially as the rue Napoléon and, from 1814, as the rue de la Paix.

Whereas the Place Vendôme remained the preferred seat of the City authorities, the rue de la Paix took on a commercial character with remarkable speed: by 1823 it already had six or seven hotels, two or three *limonadiers*, a couturier and a bootmaker. But it was only when Baron Haussmann, the prefect of Napoleon III, created broad new arterial roads and redesigned the capital that the rue de la Paix became strategically important. In 1833 Balzac may have preferred the rue Royale, but by 1856 the rue de la Paix was described as 'broad, cold, correct, straight, level, bordered by superb houses; together with the rue Royale . . . the finest specimen of a street which any capital city might pride itself on owning'.[2]

All the trades which catered to the contemporary taste for luxury were to become established in the rue de la Paix in the course of the following decades, and, just as in the old guild pageants the goldsmiths marched at the head of the procession in token of their superior rank, so the jewellers were among the first to settle in there.

When the firm was still in the boulevard des Italiens, Cartier's had maintained regular contact with those who had already established themselves in the rue de la Paix. They included the firm of François Mellerio (1772–1843), whose family had emigrated from Lombardy in the sixteenth century: some time around 1815 he moved the family business to no. 22, then to no. 5, and finally to no. 9. Another of the famous jewellers in the street was Jean-Benoît Martial Bernard (1784–1846), who had established himself at no. 1 in 1826 and had become jeweller to the royal court and to the Duc d'Orléans. His son, Charles Martial Bernard (1824–96), was a founder member of the jewellers' design classes in which Louis-François Cartier also took part. The firm moved to 12 rue des Pyramides in 1890.

No. 19 had been occupied since 1834 by the firm of Charles Marret, who also had a subsidiary branch in New York from 1848 to 1857. In Paris the Marret brothers worked in association with the far more important figure of Gustave Baugrand (1826–70), and the shop, established in 1861, was long regarded as the very height of fashion. Following Baugrand's death the firm was taken over by Ernest Vever (1823–84) and subsequently by the latter's sons Paul (1851–1915) and Henri (1854–1942). Henri Vever was the author of one of the standard works on the history of jewelry, *La Bijouterie française au 19ème siècle*, published in 1906. Vever moved to 14 rue de la Paix in 1904 and there is evidence of Cartier's links with the family from as early as 1853.

One of the most famous European gold- and silversmiths of the day was Aucoc, at 6 rue de la Paix. Louis Aucoc the Elder took over the business in 1854, adding to it a further range of *bijouterie* and *joaillerie*. André Aucoc (1884–1911) produced silver and silver-gilt in the style of the eighteenth century, as well as dealing in antique silver. In 1912 Cartier's bought from the firm a silver tureen, made in Augsburg in the eighteenth century.

From 1848 Eugène Jacta (1815–93) carried on his business at 17 rue de la Paix. Like Louis-François Cartier, he enjoyed the patronage of Princess Mathilde and the Empress, in addition to that of the tsarist court. His firm was taken over in 1868 by Eugène Bassot and in 1886 by Edgar Morgan. In 1867 Cartier's, at that date still in the boulevard des Italiens, received silver lighters from Jacta and, later on, golden *bonbonnières*, bottles, and silver-gilt and gold snuffboxes in Louis XVI style.

Jules Debut, who had previously worked with Boucheron, joined forces with Léon Coulon at 12 rue de la Paix prior to setting up in business on his own at no. 1 in 1890. In the house of Worth, the famous no. 7, was the jeweller Fontana, who like so many others had left the Palais-Royal for the rue de la Paix. An additional branch of the same family of jewellers was established in 1896 in the rue Royale, where it provided the same sort of attraction as that offered by the premises of Georges Fouquet.

These jewellers, to name only the most important, turned the rue de la Paix into the most expensive street in the world. It was not only their wares that were costly but also the ground rents, which turned the shops into valuable objects of speculation that were almost impossible to come by after 1890. In 1893, for example, Boucheron attempted to find suitable rooms for his business in the rue de la Paix, but had to settle in the end for the Place Vendôme. Much the same thing happened to René Lalique at a later date: he found it impossible to move from the Cours de la Reine to the rue de la Paix, and so he, too, transferred his business to the Place Vendôme.[3]

All the same, the rue de la Paix was not just a bastion of jewellers. Whereas the neighbouring Place Vendôme served as headquarters for the Commune following the collapse of the Second Empire, a circumstance that led to the destruction of the great column, the rue de la Paix was spared such ideological disputations. True to its calling, it offered for sale in the smallest available space all that the *grande dame* of Paris or the most widely travelled globe-trotter might need by way of jewelry or finery. Visitors were accommodated at the Hôtel Mirabeau (no. 8), or the more pretentious Hôtel de Hollande (no. 20), and, at a somewhat later date, the Hôtel des Iles Britanniques (no. 22) and the Hôtel Westminster, the latter mentioned in Cartier's archives from 1860. At no. 17 there was Siraudin's coffee-shop, lit by modern gaslight, where in the late afternoon elegant barouches were to be seen drawing up and discharging their occupants. From 1898, when César Ritz opened his hotel, the focus of social attention shifted to the Place Vendôme.

But what really turned the rue de la Paix into a latter-day Vanity Fair were the couturiers, shirtmakers, hat- and glovemakers and perfume manufacturers.[4] The Empress herself set a fashion reflecting her own personal taste, which became the style of the time and with which neither the Court of St James nor those of Madrid or Rome were able to compete. She now found all the purveyors of fashion assembled together in the rue de la Paix, at their head the fashion house of Worth, her shoemaker Viault, her corsetière Mme Gringoire, and the perfume manufacturer Guerlain, who concocted his 'Bouquet de l'Impératrice' especially for her.

Close proximity to the international fashion houses had given Cartier a creative incentive even while he was in the boulevard des Italiens, with the result that jewelry became an integral part of the image of a person of fashion. The relationship between Cartier's and the various couture houses was that of professional colleagues, neighbours, suppliers and buyers. A good example of this was Alfred Cartier's dealings with the gentlemen's shirtmaker Charvet, who had initially been in the rue de Richelieu and later moved to the Place Vendôme, where he shared his first customers, including the Prince of Wales, with Cartier's. Around 1860 Charvet ordered from Cartier's shirt buttons and cuff-links, including the famous *boutons hongrois*. The Maison Doucet, at 21 rue de la Paix, which specialized in men's and women's fashions, was another influential neighbour.[5]

In 1898, when Alfred Cartier began to cast around for suitable new premises, the rue de la Paix was clearly the most desirable location. His shop in the boulevard des Italiens was no longer adequate. Additional pressure for a quick move came from the twenty-three-year-old Louis, who had become a partner in his father's firm that same year. In 1897 the Hôtel Westminster had been auctioned off to a joint-stock company for half a million francs. It occupied nos. 11 and 13, and Alfred Cartier expressed an interest in one of the shops of no. 13; the other was rented by the lingerie business of Martial et Armand.[6] No. 11 was occupied by the handkerchief shop of Chapron and the porcelain business of Le Rosey.

The new Cartier premises were formally inaugurated in November 1899. The move coincided with the introduction of a new kind of platinum jewelry in the then fashionable garland style, and the young Louis Cartier and his brother Pierre used this as a pretext for drawing the attention of the world's aristocracy to the firm's new premises. They sent charming, handwritten invitations to the Duchess of Sutherland, who was then staying at the Hôtel Bristol, to Countess von Fels, Baron Hottinger and Baroness Edmond de Rothschild. The architect Gauthier was commissioned to redesign the interior of the shop, but no records have survived describing its appearance. The front of the building is recorded in a photograph taken on the occasion of one of Edward VII's frequent visits: the façade is already decorated with the first of the royal coats-of-arms which began to arrive from the English court in 1904. The King is seen leaving the shop through the main entrance, which was then still at the left-hand side of the building.

In 1912 Cartier's took over no. 11 and had the new wider shopfront designed in a unified style, with four display windows flanking the main entrance and forming that magnificent frontage of black marble which continues to excite the world's admiration even today [19]. Like Cartier's own creations in eighteenth-century style, this late classical façade breathes the spirit of France's great château architecture.

At the time of the shop's expansion in 1912 Louis Cartier was in Russia. Even at a distance, however, he continued to take an interest in the smallest details and gave his father Alfred affectionate advice and precise instructions which were passed on to the interior designer Boulanger and to Houdot, who supplied the marble. What emerged was a room-plan that remained unaltered until 1927, when it was redesigned by Carlhian.

The main room was the *Grande Galerie* with a coffered ceiling, allegorical paintings, walls decorated with arrows, lances and masks, and a new type of indirect lighting which was also to be found at the Ritz Hotel. The customer was received in the entrance hall and then escorted, according to his particular wishes, to the Jewel Salon, or the White, Green or English Salon, all of which glittered in the light of Baguès's chandeliers. A separate room for pearls was set aside to the left of the entrance, since 60 per cent of the firm's turnover continued to come from the sale of pearls right up to the end of the 1920s. In addition, the ritual of trying on the pearls frequently involved the presence of Madame Visage, who was in charge of stringing them, and the ceremony required its own setting. With the exception of the *Grande Galerie*, the oak walls were all carved with the vase and garland motifs which were a hallmark of Cartier's jewelry at that time [18].[7] Beyond the Pearl Room was the office of René Prieur, who was employed as Louis Cartier's secretary from 1901; he became one of the firm's leading salesmen in 1911 and spent the years of the First World War in New York. It was in this office in 1921 that he negotiated the sale of a great sapphire necklace with Prince Stirbey on behalf of King Ferdinand of Romania.

Prieur was one of Cartier's star salesmen who had originally worked for Worth; another was Alfred Buisson. They refined and polished their style in their daily dealings with crowned heads of state and the international nouveaux riches, and themselves appeared in the role of *grands seigneurs*. Countless anecdotes circulated about Buisson, who arrived at Cartier's every morning in his chauffeur-driven Delaunay-Belleville, the door of which was opened for him by a sales assistant wearing white gloves.

Beyond Prieur's office lay that of Louis Cartier [4], in whose hands all the threads of the firm were gathered. Here, in private, he received Grand Duchess Vladimir [128], the Aga Khan and the Queen of Spain [74]. Since 1902, Alfred Cartier had had his own office on the other side of the street at no. 4, and it was there that he transacted the purchase of diamonds and coloured stones; until the First World War the draughtsmen were also housed there.

21 Photograph of J. P. Morgan, the American banker, in a blue and green enamel and gold frame which he commissioned from Cartier Paris in 1907

opposite
22 Cartier London: the shop in New Bond Street, opened in 1909

New Bond Street: Cartier London
The earliest plans to expand the Paris business were the result of a suggestion made by the Prince of Wales: a branch in London had been a strong possibility ever since the English high nobility had begun crowding into the rooms in the rue de la Paix and, back in London, had been forced to wait impatiently for their orders to be delivered from France. Cartier's in Paris were regularly visited by Lillie Langtry (1853–1929), the actress and later baroness, whom Millais had painted with a lily (an illusion to her name rather than her lifestyle); by Louisa, Duchess of Manchester (popularly known as the 'double duchess' following her second marriage to the Duke of Devonshire), who in later years frequented the casinos of Monte Carlo under the close watch of distrustful private detectives; and above all there was Gladys, Lady de Grey, whom Sir Osbert Sitwell described, full of admiration, as 'the most striking individual to look at in any room she enters'.

Queen Victoria died on 22 January 1901. Following the obligatory period of mourning at court, England's leading families began their preparations for the ensuing coronation of Edward VII in 1902 and the attendant celebrations. Jewelry was feverishly remodelled, and Cartier's workshops were scarcely able to meet the demand for tiaras, necklaces and breast ornaments. Pierre Cartier and Alfred Buisson used the Cecil Hotel as their base of operations in London. They visited Buckingham Palace, where they received orders from Queen Alexandra, and they looked around the West End for a likely site for their new premises. They were helped in their search by Alice, the Hon. Mrs George Keppel, wife of the younger brother of the Earl of Albemarle, and the King's lifelong friend. She first drew their attention to Old Bond Street, but both Pierre Cartier and Gaston Worth finally chose 4 New Burlington Street, where a shop was opened in 1902. From 1906 the firm was managed by Jacques Cartier [7], the youngest scion of the family, and Arthur Fraser, who was the sales director. They moved to 175 New Bond Street in 1909, five years after having been appointed official suppliers to the court of King Edward VII.

Cartier's new jewelry from Paris created a sensation in England, which at that time was still relatively conservative. Admittedly, the Countess of Warwick wrote in a letter of 'all these silly women, including Gladys de Grey, all thinking life is bounded on one side by Worth and Cartier and on the other by King Edward VII's court and bridge';[8] but the Countess, who invested her money in agricultural schools and who met with the socialist Jean Jaurès in Paris, was not averse to wearing a magnificent emerald tiara bought, naturally, from Cartier's.

Fifth Avenue: Cartier New York

The business in England had scarcely been established when America began to beckon. Reconnaissance trips were undertaken in 1903 and 1907, and the sixty-seven-year-old Alfred Cartier [3] did not hesitate to cross the Atlantic. Financially, New York was the only possible choice for a branch which would be the culmination of Cartier's empire. In 1901 the United States Steel Company had been sold to J. P. Morgan [21] for a billion dollars and in the wake of this economic boom more than a thousand Americans, of whom three hundred lived in New York, acquired vast fortunes in excess of one million dollars each. An outward sign of this affluence was the society balls held by Mrs August Belmont, Mrs Cornelius Vanderbilt [27], Mrs Herman Oelrich and Mrs Ogden Mills, who together had inherited the social sceptre from the retiring Mrs William Astor and who strove to outdo each other in almost vulgar displays of magnificence. Diamonds and emeralds were brought into action in the campaigns waged by the most ambitious hostesses of the day and used as coefficients to determine their individual standing in a constantly shifting social hierarchy. Gemstones glittered not only in the mansions along Fifth Avenue and (from July to September) in fashionable Newport, but also in the thirty-five boxes of the Metropolitan Opera House (opened in 1883), where the same ostentation was flaunted before the public, causing them to be called 'the Diamond Horseshoe'.

23 Cartier New York: 653 Fifth Avenue. Watercolour by Alexandre Genaille, 1917

On 1 November 1909 Pierre Cartier [5] opened the firm's American branch, on the fourth floor of 712 Fifth Avenue. The antique dealer Alavoine had supplied the wood panelling which generally reproduced the decor of the rue de la Paix. The firm's neighbours were the jewellers Schumann at no. 716 and Coty's perfume shop at no. 714, which had been furnished by René Lalique. At no. 560 was Dreicer, the most feared of Cartier's rivals, who did not shrink from copying models from the rue de la Paix and putting them on sale faster than Cartier's American branch could import them.[9] Just as the London branch was supported by Mrs Keppel and Lady de Grey, and the St Petersburg branch (opened in 1908: see pp. 102–13) by Grand Duchess Vladimir, so in New York Pierre Cartier enjoyed the custom of Mrs Clarence Mackay and Mrs Rita Lydig who, with Mrs Stuyvesant Fish, were accounted among the social avant-garde and who provided him with introductions to the houses of Mesdames Blumenthal, Gould, Widener and Stotesbury.

Initially the New York establishment had all its jewels sent over from the rue de la Paix, but the firm's own workshop, which employed forty goldsmiths, including eleven stone-setters, was soon in a position to produce jewelry on American soil.[10] The business of manufacturing this jewelry, which never attempted to deny its Parisian origins, was in the hands of the two masters Paul Maîtrejean and Bouquet, the latter trained in Charpentier's Paris workshop.[11] The draughtsmen, recruited in Paris, were Alexandre Genaille, the young Maurice Duvallet, and, from 1912, Emile Faure.[12] Paul Muffat and, at a somewhat later date, Jules Glaenzer were in charge of the sales staff, who often spent the winter months in the American branch and the summer in France. It was not uncommon for them to find the same customers in Paris as in Fifth Avenue. Each time the great ocean liners crossed the Atlantic in May, telegrams prepared Louis Cartier for the arrival of Mrs George Gould on the *Lusitania*, Mrs Clarence Mackay on the *Kronprinzessin Cäcilie*, and Mrs Rita Lydig and Mrs Vincent Astor on the *Mauretania*.

In 1917 Cartier moved to 653 Fifth Avenue [23], the house of Morton F. Plant: it was exchanged, almost symbolically, for a famous two-row pearl necklace (see p. 121). The Rockefeller family architect, Welles Bosworth, supervised the transformation of the interior of the former patrician residence into an international business establishment, although a touch of the private mansion remained. The Wedgwood Room displayed priceless clocks from Paris, gemstone snuffboxes, plants and miniature hardstone animals. The most expensive jewels were to be found glittering in the Blue Room, where in 1931 fifteen sales assistants were employed, as against eight in London. The displays in the Pearl Room, where the pearl expert Etcheberry officiated, surpassed even those of the rue de la Paix. The Silver Room was dominated by a resplendent porcelain arbour, and in the former family chapel, which was kept intact, religious jewelry and chalices awaited buyers.

As Pierre once remarked to Louis Cartier, the addition of the New York branch turned the firm into a worldwide institution; but what remained of paramount importance to the customers was the close connection between fashion and jewelry, a link symbolized by the rue de la Paix. The photograph which had the greatest impact upon the public of New York in 1914 was one of the rue de la Paix garlanded with flowers on the occasion of a state visit by the King and Queen of England.

Whenever visiting heads of state came to Paris and were officially received at Cartier's, crowds would gather on the pavement outside [19, 24], jostling to see what was going on and withdrawing to a respectful distance as the royal visitors left the building. The state visit of King Haakon VII and Queen Maud of Norway took place in 1907. The Paris City Council's official gift to the Queen, a daughter of Edward VII, was a turquoise and diamond necklace from Cartier's. In 1909, the year in which Guerlain named a perfume 'Rue de la Paix', the city was presented with the spectacle of a visit from King Manuel of Portugal, and in 1910 the King and Queen of Spain passed through Paris on their way to England. Following a banquet in the château of Rambouillet, the Spanish Queen drove to see her godmother, the Empress Eugénie, at the Hôtel Continental, and then had Cartier's show her their latest creations. The following year it was King George of Greece. The list of visitors could easily be extended right down to the 1930s. The street and what it stood for were by then so famous that in 1912 a play entitled *Rue de la Paix* was staged, with costumes by Paquin after designs by Paul Iribe.[13]

24 Adoring fans of 'Le Prince Charmant' – the Prince of Wales, future Edward VIII – outside the shop at 11–13 rue de la Paix. Cartoon by Sem

CHAPTER THREE

THE GARLAND STYLE

Throughout the nineteenth century a series of historical styles had coloured the various arts, beginning with the Gothic Revival of around 1820 and passing through neo-Renaissance and neo-Baroque influences before culminating in a resurgence of the Louis XVI style in the 1890s. This latter style was to retain its appeal until shortly before the First World War, and around 1900 was one of the spurs for the vigorous counter-offensive of Art Nouveau, a style which was directed against the sterile resuscitation of a taste associated with an aristocratic and moneyed élite.

Art Nouveau artists such as Grasset and Lalique took their inspiration directly from nature, whereas the painter, architect or interior designer who was committed to the Louis XVI style remained bound within the framework of an eighteenth-century theatrical setting. The court of Versailles was the inspiration which motivated his customers, whose unique desire was for pomp and splendour. They were generally entrepreneurs who had grown rich through industry or financial speculation and who, behind the imposing façade of their private Trianons or Bagatelles, lived in a world of theatrical pretence. Those who moved within this realm of sophisticated illusion, whether Mrs Cornelius Vanderbilt [27], Mrs Nancy Leeds [77] or Sir Ernest Cassel, were unwitting adherents of a fin-de-siècle aesthetic whose origins may be traced back to Ruskin, Oscar Wilde and D'Annunzio. Thus the English court, the French aristocracy and the moneyed classes of America indulged in the ceremonial of a past century which they used as a pretext for masquerades, hunting parties and balls in New York, Paris, St Petersburg, London or Venice. The hostess received her guests like some lady of the manor, a modern Madame de Pompadour or Madame du Barry; and the portrait which she had painted of herself by one of the much sought-after artists of the day – Antonio de la Gandara, Philip de László or Giovanni Boldini – showed her striking attitudes reminiscent of Velásquez, Largillière and Reynolds.

Interiors were traditionally eighteenth-century in style; dress and jewelry, too, were adapted to match them, and it was precisely this style of jewelry that Cartier's used from 1895 onward to captivate the discriminating taste of contemporary high society. What came into existence in this way was delicate garland-style jewels which Cartier's, though not the first to reintroduce them, handled with greater virtuosity and elegance than, say, Hamelin, Falize or Vever. The latter often added writhing Art Nouveau plant forms which turned the jewels into strange hybrid shapes lacking the playful ease of Cartier's confections.

The new Louis XVI style had been apparent in the work of French jewellers for some time, since the 1850s to be exact, when the Empress Eugénie had had her jewelry reset by Bapst and Lemonnier in the style of Marie Antoinette. The Queen's celebrated necklace [cf. 66] was the model for this work, and with the appearance of crinolines at the Tuileries court there came a revival of the unsurpassed elegance of the eighteenth century, recorded in the work of Winterhalter, the official court portrait painter.

This borrowing of motifs from earlier centuries was made easier for the jeweller by the existence of pictorial records and pattern books. Ever since the time of the young Albrecht Dürer, woodcuts and the then recently invented copperplate engravings ensured the spread of motifs from Italian, French and German designers and goldsmiths across the whole of Europe. In the nineteenth century jewellers continued to use Renaissance sources until around 1870:[1] the work of a leading jeweller such as Désiré Froment-Meurice simply cannot be understood without some knowledge of the influence of Renaissance artists like Etienne Delaune, Théodore de Bry or René Boyvin. In England pendants based on designs by Hans Holbein the Younger were being made around 1870. It must be added that the jeweller used whatever motifs he thought necessary, including interlace, sinuous plant-forms and grotesques, which he freely mingled with later ornaments, generally borrowing them not directly from pattern books of the Renaissance but from popular compendia of the nineteenth century. These provided a summary of fifteenth- and sixteenth-century sources for professional groups such as goldsmiths, interior designers, cabinetmakers and so on.[2]

Pattern books of eighteenth-century motifs, which are of special interest in the present context, began to circulate in the 1850s. Original Louis XV and Louis XVI printed texts were reproduced, with the particular encouragement of the French imperial court.

28 Brooch-pendant from a necklace [27, 37]. Cartier Paris, commissioned in 1909 by Mrs Cornelius Vanderbilt. Platinum; pear-shaped and round old-cut diamonds; millegrain setting

Unlike the Renaissance designs, they displayed flowers, wreaths, garlands and vases. The most important works of this type which Louis Cartier owned and which were at the disposal of his draughtsmen are:[3]

[Auguste] Péquégnot: *Ornements, vases et décorations d'après les maîtres*, 1872. A compendium of interior art, including vases, columns, bouquets and friezes

Théodore Bertren: *Ouvrages de bijouterie & gravure; médaillons, trophées, vases et autres sujets nouveaux*. A reprint of fourteen fascicles of copperplate engravings dating from 1771. This provided Cartier chiefly with motifs for frames, table clocks and floral garlands

Jean-François Forty: a collection of engravings from the age of Louis XVI, reprinted in Paris in 1896, containing, in eight fascicles, motifs for goldsmiths including candelabra, latticework, chalices, clocks, barometers, figurative motifs, acanthus leaves and garlands. This provided Cartier with the inspiration for *objets d'art* and jewelry, as well as plaques for chokers

Pouget Fils [J. H.]: *Traité des pierres précieuses*, 1762. A work containing models for bows, clasps and flowers

L. Vander Cruysen: *Nouveau Livre de desseins*, 1770. Reprinted in Paris, this provided models for bouquets, girandole earrings, aigrettes, breast ornaments and bows

Maria & Babel: a copperplate-engraved text of the age of Louis XVI, reprinted, which includes châtelaines, pommels for walking-sticks, girandole earrings, breast ornaments, boxes, fans and bows

J. H. von Hefner-Halteneck: *Eisenwerke oder Ornamentik der Schmiedekunst des Mittelalters und der Renaissance*, 1885. This includes eighteenth-century grilles. Grilles, developed into rinceaux with tendril-like forms, inspired partly by European wrought ironwork and partly by Islamic lattice motifs, were important in Cartier's jewelry around 1900.[4]

There were a number of specialist works devoted to flowers, especially the rose and lily, which in the decorative art of the Louis XVI style had almost taken on the character of a leitmotif. The following are among those used by Cartier:

Eugène Grasset (ed.), *La Plante et ses applications ornementales*, 1896–1900

J. Foord, *Decorative Plant and Flower Studies*, 1906

M. P. Verneuil, *Etude de la plante*, n.d. Contains motifs such as oak leaves and wheat-ears, which were used particularly in tiaras

P. Plauszewski, *Encyclopédie florale*, n.d.

Pattern books, however, were not the only source of inspiration in this field. Louis Cartier constantly encouraged his draughtsmen to wander through Paris with their sketchbooks and to note down details of seventeenth- and eighteenth-century architecture. In this way drawings were made of patrician houses in the Faubourg Saint-Germain; and the pediments above the doors at Fontainebleau and the garlands of fruit on the Petit Trianon also found their way into Cartier's sketchbooks, where they were transformed by some process of alchemy to reappear in transmuted form on various articles of jewelry.

The ornamental motifs borrowed from the seventeenth and eighteenth centuries, and in rare instances from the Renaissance, produced a canonical style of jewelry around 1900 which was closely dependent upon the contemporary fashion in clothes. Its essential components were tiaras, chokers and bodice jewelry. Other genres, such as bracelets, generally faded into the background as a result of the fashion for long sleeves, in spite of attempts to popularize them by such magazines as *Femina* and *Vogue*.

Chokers were tight-fitting necklaces which first appeared in France around 1865 and in England around 1880; they remained popular until the outbreak of the First World War

[**29-35, 59**]. Edgar Degas painted his ballet-dancers wearing black velvet ribbons, and similar textile models dating back to the eighteenth century may well have started a fashion which was by no means limited to aristocratic circles or to evening wear. Cartier's retained the black moiré or velvet base, which gave an extra dimension to the openwork diamond or pearl motifs. The stylized patterns of these plaques placed them among the earliest geometrical designs of the new century. Some of them were given fanciful names such as 'Byzantine', while others took up traditional floral motifs from the eighteenth century, including some found on snuffboxes.

The jeweller was naturally tempted to give up the traditional fabric ribbon and replace it entirely with gemstones: diamond plaques were held together with strings of pearls (as many as twenty strands together), or else a pearl band in a kind of beadwork based on old lace patterns was created by laborious and detailed work which took weeks to complete [**30**].[5] The most important example of the former type is the Russian double-eagle pearl choker made in 1900 for Grand Duchess Vladimir [**136**]. Before sending it to St Petersburg, Louis and Pierre Cartier invited friends and customers to view it in the rue de la Paix.

Occasionally pearls were dispensed with and chokers were made entirely of diamonds, in refined wavy bands which reproduced the reflections of shot moiré silk [**32**] and which may be seen as early examples of a stylization typical of Art Deco. In other cases the entire necklace was made as a continuous diamond garland, the centre of which was accentuated by an additional motif such as a pendant bow [**35**]. Entirely in keeping with the playful style of the eighteenth century was the *lacet de bergère* motif, an interlaced design recalling bodice ribbons, whose name revived memories of Marie Antoinette's rustic idylls in the park at Versailles.

Chokers and breast ornaments together left very little space for large necklaces. For this reason only isolated examples of that type are to be found at the beginning of the century, such as those ordered by Grand Duchess Vladimir or the German banker Bleichroeder in the form of drop diamond cascades. Chokers were, on the other hand, frequently worn with several ropes of pearls ending in geometrical pendants. A special form of necklace produced around 1900 was the 'lavallière' – an imaginative allusion to a fashion associated with the actress Eve Lavallière[6] – with two conjoined pendants, generally of different lengths [**36, 40**]. The necklace itself often consisted of a simple silk cord with diamond slides, ending in imaginative interlinked ends. Princess George of Greece – née Marie Bonaparte [**62**] – received a lavallière with two diamond fir cones, the Tsarina of Russia one with amethyst acorns.

One of the most original pendants was the motif of two doves beside a well. A single dove had been popular in northern France and Flanders in the seventeenth and eighteenth centuries as an allusion to the dove of the Holy Ghost, while Marie Antoinette harbored a less exalted predilection for pairs of doves as attributes of Venus, which are found on snuffboxes, in painting and in interior decoration, as well as in the pattern book of Théodore Bertren mentioned above. Cartier made a Louis XVI châtelaine in 1874 with the motif of two doves. The later motif of two doves dipping their beaks in a crystal fountain (with moonstone inlay to represent the water) was fashionable as a charming transitional design leading the way to Art Deco. Lovebirds, two birds sitting on a branch, are found on brooches up to the present day.[7]

There is no doubt that, tiaras apart, the greatest variety of traditional motifs was to be found on the breast ornament [**26, 44-46, 48-53, 60, 61, 66, 71**], ultimately derived from the historic stomacher. No form of jewelry was as dependent upon costume as this, which often reproduced the shape of the bodice. No other form so obviously embodies the ostentation of the Belle Epoque, a mode it recaptures far more effectively than the tiara, which obeyed the strict rules of court etiquette and thus survived the passing fashion in clothes. The new, freely articulated platinum settings produced breast ornaments that could harmonize with changes in fashion. The various types of material used provided Cartier's with a background onto which the ornaments were fixed directly by means of eyelets, in the eighteenth-century manner. Motifs found on breast ornaments include acanthus leaves, laurel wreaths and garlands of lilies and roses, as well as abstract lattices. They were all used unrestrictedly and are often built up symmetrically.

below

29 Choker. Cartier Paris, special order, 1906. Platinum; round old-cut diamonds; millegrain setting

opposite

30 Choker. Cartier Paris, commissioned in 1908 by the Princesse de Ganay. Platinum; diamonds and seed pearls, the centre of stylized sun design with four rubies

31 Choker. Cartier Paris, 1910. *Résille* in platinum and circular-cut diamonds

32 Choker. Cartier Paris, 1909. Floral design in platinum and circular-cut diamonds

33 Choker. Cartier Paris, 1906. Intertwined circle and laurel leaf design in platinum and circular-cut diamonds

34 Choker. Cartier Paris, special order, 1912. Linked circular design in platinum with pendant pear-shaped diamonds

30

31

32

33

34

35

36

38

37

opposite

35 Choker. Cartier Paris, commissioned in 1907 by Mrs H. Payne Whitney. Lily and scroll design in platinum, circular-cut diamonds, and two amethysts

36 Lavallière. Cartier Paris, 1911. Platinum; navette-, circular- and triangular-cut diamonds; a drop-shaped pearl of 102 grains; and a faceted emerald drop of 31.8 carats

37 Necklace. Cartier Paris, commissioned in 1909 by Mrs Cornelius Vanderbilt [**27, 28**]. Platinum; three hexagonal diamond pendants with round and pear-shaped drops

38 Chain and pendant. Cartier Paris, 1907. Platinum; pearl and diamond chain, from which a spiral-patterned rose- and circular-cut diamond sphere and drop-shaped pendant are suspended

right

39 Medusa-head pendant. Cartier Paris, 1906. Platinum; pink coral within green enamel, three natural pearls, a pink coral drop and rose-cut diamonds

overleaf, left

40 Lavallière. Cartier Paris, 1912, sold to the Duke of Westminster. Platinum; designed as two flexible circular-cut diamond and pearl pinecones, on pearl and diamond chain

41 Ribbon bow pendant brooch. Cartier Paris, 1911. Platinum; circular-cut and drop-shaped diamonds, with a square-cut diamond in the bow

42 'Arabic' pendant. Cartier Paris, 1910. Platinum; circular- and rose-cut diamonds

43 Pendant of 'Persian' design and ribbon. Cartier Paris, 1909. Platinum; the flowerhead pendant with circular-cut diamonds; the ribbon with seed pearls and diamonds

overleaf, right

44 Ribbon bow breast ornament. Cartier Paris, 1905. Platinum; circular- and rose-cut and pear-shaped diamonds, with cushion-shaped diamond of 15.21 carats

45 Breast ornament of hexagonal flower trellis design. Cartier Paris, commissioned in 1909 by Caroline Otéro. Platinum; diamonds; two grey pearls of 57 and 45 grains

46 Breast ornament. Cartier Paris, commissioned in 1908 by Countess Hohenfelsen [see **61**]. Platinum; circular- and square-cut diamonds, mounted with three button pearls of 247 grains, from which are suspended pear-shaped pearls of 285 grains and an egg-shaped pearl of 145 grains

44

45

46

A portrait of Queen Charlotte of England painted by Alan Ramsay in 1762 shows her wearing a stomacher similar to a piece made by Cartier in 1905 which reproduces the severe triangular lines of the bodice. The latter's affinity with the eighteenth-century designs of Vander Cruysen and Lucotte is clear. Of similar geometrical shape was a breast ornament consisting of ten bows tapering towards the lower end [52], as well as a model acquired by Mrs W. K. Vanderbilt with rhomb motifs.

The luxuriantly expansive forms of bodice jewelry became a thing of the past when, thanks to the influence of Paul Poiret, the bodice disappeared around 1910 and was replaced by new fashions, emphasizing vertical lines. Breast ornaments became unwearable, and in most cases they were broken up. In 1907 Cartier's had begun creating new models with perpendicular strands of diamonds attached to two lateral points. Curving lines and sinuous plant-forms were relegated to the border areas, which led by a process of gradual assimilation to the oblong pendant of the 1920s. Length came to dominate fashion, and it was this feature that was accentuated around 1910 by the new type of epaulette,[8] fastened at the shoulder and generally consisting of two parallel pendant diamond cascades. The epaulette often ended in motifs tapering towards the base known as aiguillettes, a term used interchangeably with the epaulette itself. The latter might also assume the shape of a diamond band up to 35 cm in length, similar to the *régence*, except that the latter also included a pendant watch [e.g. 360]. The most important type of epaulette, however, covered the breast rather like a diagonally draped sash made of several articulated strands of diamonds and pearls, fastened at one shoulder and often ending in aiguillettes. Symmetry was rigorously avoided. Important examples include those made in 1909 for Mrs Frederick Vanderbilt, in 1910 for Mrs W. K. Vanderbilt [56], and the magnificent epaulette made in 1912 for Nancy Leeds, widow of the American tin magnate William B. Leeds, which culminated in a 70-carat emerald.[9]

Apart from the garland and laurel wreath, there were three motifs in the garland style which recurred almost like leitmotifs: the bow, tassel, and lace. The bow and tassel had been essential components of festive Baroque dress since the seventeenth century and, fashioned in velvet or silk, enlivened the surface of the object they adorned. The workshops of the leading jewellers of the time soon began to supply refined imitations in metal, enamel and gemstones.

Bow brooches had been popular since the seventeenth century as far afield as Spain. The most elegant models were designed around 1670 by the French jeweller Gilles Légaré.[10] They were the Baroque bodice ornament par excellence, and at a later date became known simply as 'sévignés',[11] after Madame de Sévigné (1626–96), the most famous letter-writer of her time. During the age of Marie Antoinette, the fashion for bows spread to England, and strictly symmetrical models henceforth maintained their place in the repertoire of the best European jewellers. The Russian crown jewels[12] and the Grünes Gewölbe in Dresden preserve important examples from the eighteenth century. The sale by auction of the French crown jewels in 1887 included not only a bow with pendant tassels (No. 38) but, above all, two shoulder bows from Bapst's workshop (No. 2), used by the Empress Eugénie to fasten the robe of state. Curiously enough, these two shoulder bows passed into Cartier's hands shortly before 1900, as attested by some undated photographs in the firm's archives. They inspired the creation of further bow brooches around 1900. Cartier's earliest experiments with bows date from 1895: 'Shoulder bow with tassel' runs an early entry, followed by another in 1897. Most of the bows were entrusted to Naudet's workshop.[13] They came in large and small versions. The former could measure up to 12 cm in width and was thus a proper breast ornament, unlike the small brooch. An example of the large bow brooch was acquired by the King of Spain in

opposite

47 Lace bow brooch. Cartier Paris, 1906. Platinum, gold; cushion-shaped, marquise-cut, round old- and rose-cut diamonds; millegrain setting and collet setting

this page

48 Breast ornament. Cartier Paris, special order, 1907. Platinum; one pear-shaped sapphire; seven cushion-shaped sapphires; round old- and rose-cut diamonds. Total weight of the sapphires approximately 51 carats

1902; four more followed in 1904, while three small bow brooches went to the Aga Khan. Cartier's designers produced countless variations on the same motif: the Empress Eugénie's brooch provided the inspiration for a brooch made for Lady de Grey, while eighteenth-century engravings by Maria & Babel inspired bow brooches for Mrs Goelet and Mrs Lydig. This last item was made in Picq's workshop in 1909 and measured 16 x 14 cm. The smaller of the two models was backed with velvet, recalling the textile origin of the bow. When velvet temporarily went out of fashion around 1910, the same colour contrast was achieved by means of black onyx.

The second motif, the tassel, generally appeared in conjunction with the bow, but also as a separate pendant motif. French engravings, such as those of Vander Cruysen, influenced the models that have survived in the Russian crown jewels, which date from around 1780.[14] Initially tassels were only slightly curved in form. The motif remained popular until around 1910 in Russia: at fancy dress and masked balls, fully curved three-dimensional tassels dangled from long strings of pearls, linking the traditional head ornaments with the costume. The ballet *Schéhérazade* brought the motif to Western European attention around 1910, reinforced by memories of the Indian turban tassel. This was the source of the Art Deco tassel of onyx, coral and pearls, a central motif of 1920s jewelry.

The third motif, an openwork lace pattern, inspired the jeweller to a degree of illusionistic imitation comparable to the Baroque art of trompe-l'oeil.[15] Lace and braid were a feature of the annual Paris salons, and in 1909 the Musée des Arts Décoratifs organized a special exhibition which evoked widespread interest and which fascinated Louis Cartier. He incorporated the sinuous lines and symmetrical bird-and-plant motifs of lacework into the garland style, presenting his draughtsmen with pattern books which the firm's resident photographer copied for despatch to Cartier's London and New York designers.

The impression of lace, Islamic grilles and European wrought ironwork produced the transparent, articulated, insubstantial background that is characteristic of pieces in the garland style. This was one of the reasons why traditional gold and silver settings were slowly abandoned and platinum was favoured instead.[16] Silver had the great disadvantage of requiring massive settings for stones, because of its softness, and dampening the fire of diamonds because it tarnished.[17] In the eighteenth century, when large diamonds were still relatively rare and jewels worn on festive occasions at court shone in the glimmer of flickering candlelight, the illusion of sparkling jewelry could be preserved. But now the time was not far off when the newly discovered electric light would expose those same jewels to a relentless glare.

Although platinum had been used in ancient Egypt, it had not been recognized as such, and it was really not until the sixteenth century that it began to be mined in Colombia.[18] As late as 1748 the Spanish mathematician Don Antonio de Ulloa (1716–95) reported from New Grenada (Colombia) that a new metal, *platina* (literally 'lesser silver'), had been found, which could be distinguished only with difficulty from gold. Although platinum was soon recognized as a separate chemical element, it was still being described in 1785 by the great French naturalist Buffon in his *Histoire naturelle des minéraux* as an alloy of gold and iron. At the same time, however, platinum was beginning to enjoy its earliest popularity in the Paris of Louis XVI: the German scholar F. C. Achard (1753–1821) had succeeded in alloying platinum and arsenic and thereby lowering the mineral's very high melting point of 1769 °C.[19] Marc-Etienne Jannetti began making platinum salt-shakers, boxes and candelabras in Paris in 1792; the standard metre and standard kilogram were made of platinum. At the same time, new platinum deposits were discovered in the Urals, and the chemist P. G. Sobolevsky invented a new and efficient process for obtaining it. Y. F. Kankrin, the Russian minister of finance (1775–1845), minted a limited series of platinum coins. The German scholar Alexander von Humboldt issued vain warnings about the dangers of such an experiment, and it proved indeed to be a lamentable failure. As a nonprecious metal which was valued for its softness and conductivity, platinum continued to be used on a regular basis in industry.[20] At the 1855 Paris Exposition, the jeweller Eugène Fontenay caused a sensation with a blackberry blossom tiara of which the setting was partly made of platinum.

Cartier's records contain an entry for 1853, when the firm moved to the rue Neuve-des-Petits-Champs, which reads: 'Sale of platinum 142.50 francs'; and that same

this page

54 Necklace. Cartier Paris, 1911. Platinum; collet design, with tied ribbon centre and flexible navette and pear-shaped diamond tassels

opposite

55 Bracelet. Cartier Paris, commissioned in 1912 by Baroness Henri de Rothschild. Platinum; designed as two circular-cut diamond snakes holding a pearl and diamond panel

56 'Echarpe'. Cartier Paris, commissioned in 1910 by Mrs W. K. Vanderbilt. Platinum; round and pear-shaped diamonds

57 'Persian' pendant. Cartier Paris, special order, 1910. Platinum; circular-cut diamonds

58 Pendant of festoon design. Cartier Paris, 1910. Platinum; circular-cut diamonds, with framed cushion-shaped diamond centre

59 Choker. Cartier Paris, commissioned in 1913 by Queen Amelia of Portugal. Platinum; diamonds; eleven rubies of 14.55 carats

55

56

57

58

59

year Cartier ordered from Fossin's workshop a seal made of gold and platinum.[21] But unlimited use of the mineral was still prevented by the technical difficulties of obtaining a pure enough form, difficulties which the German researcher Wilhelm Carl Heraeus finally solved in Hanau, shortly before 1900, with his invention of a new melting process. Platinum first appeared in Cartier's work not on large surfaces but on small buttons, needles and rings, and it was only the technically unnecessary backing with gold that increased the value of platinum so that it came to be regarded as a precious metal. A partial summary of the Cartier archives shows platinum being used as follows:

1859ff.	Shirt buttons (perhaps the model that Cartier supplied to the shirtmaker Charvet)
1874	Cufflinks edged in platinum Lead pencils of gold and platinum
1886	Tie pins, buttons and earrings A sapphire and diamond ring of gold and platinum The year includes an entry for white gold
1894	Diamond necklace with platinum setting Link bracelet
1899	Butterfly brooch *en tremblant* (from Robin's workshop) Also 'maternity' brooches (in the form of safety pins), rings, and a heart-shaped watch

This takes us up to the year in which the firm moved to the rue de la Paix, when its stock increased dramatically and platinum settings were very much a novelty. In the intervening years platinum had slowly come to be regarded as a precious metal, equal in value to gold. In 1903 world consumption reached 7,525 kilograms.[22] But it was not entirely the rising price of platinum that persuaded Cartier's to retain traditional gold and silver settings and to sell them alongside platinum jewelry: the large and small Louis XVI bow brooches made in 1900 were of platinum, while those made in 1902 and 1904 were of silver. Since the purchasers in the last two instances were the King of Spain and Mrs W. K. Vanderbilt, the choice of material is likely to have been due not to the wish for a lower price, but to the fact that individual craftsmen strove tenaciously to maintain traditional nineteenth-century techniques. Price may nevertheless have played a role in the case of certain commissions: in 1901 Pierre Cartier left the final decision between platinum and silver to the Countess of Killarney but drew her attention to the lower price of silver.[23]

Cartier's was said to use the best platinum in Paris. Renowned for its white, shimmering surface, it was an alloy of which the Picq workshop was especially proud. The stone to be set was surrounded by a platinum girdle whose surface was knurled with a regular series of indentations in a manner known as 'millegrain' or 'serti perlé' [e.g. **26**, **28**, **29**, **60**]. In this way the platinum was 'demetallized' and broken up into shimmering reflections of light. Later the stone was set from behind into a delicate platinum bezel, and held in place by four or six claws; the cold white shimmering surface of the bezel was intended to enhance the reflective properties of the diamond. The most delicate platinum setting in the garland style was what was known as 'serti muguet', or 'lily-of-the valley setting', which reproduced the outline of the flower's calyx [**51**, **80**, **403**].[24]

As a result of the new technical freedom of form created by the use of platinum, the garland style, in spite of its eighteenth-century origins, came to be seen as a 'new style' and as an alternative to Art Nouveau. And so, when the firm moved premises, customers such as Lady de Grey were shown 'nouveaux modèles' or 'bijoux entièrement nouveaux', whose much-lauded characteristics included mobility and transformability. Items of jewelry with a multiple purpose were less common in the nineteenth century but were now once more the current fashion, as is clear from a letter written by Louis Cartier to Countess Orlov in Nice: 'The breast ornament is articulated by removal of the lower part and in that way may be worn on the shoulder. On the other hand, it may be attached to a velvet ribbon and worn as a choker.'

60 Flower basket breast ornament. Cartier New York, 1918. Platinum; hexagonal, half-moon, square, round old- and single-cut diamonds; natural pearls; millegrain setting for the basket

Apart from the use of platinum, what was also of importance for the form of this new type of jewelry was the jeweller's intimate familiarity not only with textiles but with fashion as a whole. The move to the rue de la Paix had brought Alfred Cartier and his family into the closest contact with Worth's worldwide couture enterprise.

The second half of the nineteenth century has been called the 'époque Worth'. Charles Frederick Worth (1825–95) had left London for Paris at the age of twenty. Soon he was to revolutionize costume design, just as Louis Cartier was to revolutionize the world of jewelry forty years later. Whether Worth was really the first to introduce the crinoline may be difficult to establish today; but the new fashion, which turned women into unattainable objects of luxury, was taken up and adapted by Worth in numerous commissions for the Empress Eugénie and Princess Metternich, reaching its climax around 1865. He was certainly the first to promote the *tournure*, a style of dress which was straight at the front but had a bustle at the back. The Franco-Prussian War in 1870 was the great turning-point for Worth. Louis-François Cartier could not bear 'to watch the Prussians parading up and down the boulevard in front of my window' and went into self-imposed exile in San Sebastian, from where he sympathized at a distance with his son Alfred, who, before emigrating to London, was living in Paris 'on horsemeat, dogs and rats'; Worth, on the other hand, closed his business and set up a field hospital in his premises in the rue de la Paix, reopening in 1871, this time without his former partner, Otto Bobergh of Sweden. When the war was over and Cartier complained from Etretat of the general absence of jewelry, the hour of the great couturier had finally come. 'Dress', wrote Cartier, 'is becoming more magnificent by the day; on the beach at Etretat at eight o'clock this morning, women from the demi-monde spread out more silk, satin and lace than a queen herself would need for her entire trousseau.'

61 Olga, the wife of Grand Duke Paul of Russia, created Countess Hohenfelsen (and later Princess Paley), wearing her diamond and pearl breast ornament of 1908 [46] as a hat brooch and her tiara of pear-shaped diamonds, of 1911, as a breast ornament. Her dress is by Worth. Photograph by Boissonas & Taponier, 1912

The successful Worth, who was half businessman and half Venetian doge, and whose style of dress, like Richard Wagner's, was inspired by Rembrandt, encouraged Louis-François Cartier in their joint mission 'to live through and for luxury'. It was Worth who drew Cartier's attention to American hostesses who, especially since the time of the 1876 Philadelphia Exhibition, had undertaken regular pilgrimages to Worth's establishment in the rue de la Paix, much to the annoyance of his longstanding French customers who henceforth avoided him, giving credence to a mocking remark in *Harper's Bazaar* that 'not a word of French could be heard' at Worth's. Cartier used a display window at Worth's to attract the attention of the international élite from Russia,[25] Germany, England and America; and, following the death of Charles Frederick Worth in 1895, the friendship of his sons Gaston and Jean-Philippe was transferred to Alfred Cartier's sons, Louis and Pierre. Whereas Gaston was the more commercially minded of the two, Jean-Philippe, who had studied painting with Corot and who continued his father's creative tradition, was as great an aesthete as Louis Cartier [4]. In addition, Louis Cartier married Jean-Philippe Worth's daughter, Andrée, in 1898, and Louis' sister, Suzanne, later became the wife of Gaston's son, Jacques. By 1900 the Worth brothers were the uncrowned kings of Parisian haute couture. The silk factories at

Lyon were ruled by their dictates, and every week the horse-races at Longchamp stimulated Worth and his rivals, Doeuillet, Redfern, Laferrière and Beer, to feats of fashionable achievement.

From 1900 there were striking parallels in the ranges of the couturier on the one hand and the jeweller, now related, on the other: although formal dress had passed through a number of stylistic phases in its development between 1880 and 1900, and although by 1900 it was clearly being influenced by the sinuous curves of the Art Nouveau aesthetic (the Gibson Girl), the Louis XVI style of Marie Antoinette and the Directoire style[26] of Joséphine de Beauharnais continued in turn to provide the inspiration for both costume and jewelry, the ideal silhouette of the period being topped off by a 'Récamier' hairstyle.[27] Fashionable materials – heavy velvet from Genoa, lightweight satins, chiffon and crêpe de chine – were embroidered with the familiar roses and lilies of the garland style, each dress being turned into a precious gem with the addition of silver and gold trimmings. Cartier bought velvet and moiré silk from the couturier to be used as a black, grey or white background for jewelry, and the articles made in this way were placed on display at Worth's. In 1899, for example, two months before Cartier's moved to the rue de la Paix, there were eighteen items, including belt buckles, buttons, combs and clasps. The coronation fever accompanying the accession of Edward VII in 1902 saw Cartier busily producing tiaras while Worth was kept fully occupied for three months making coronation trains. Influenced by Whistler, the fashionable pastel shades around 1900 were *cuisse de nymphe*, lilac, mauve, straw, hydrangea blue and maize; and so Cartier produced monochromatic jewelry to match, in diamonds and pearls discreetly relieved by amethysts and turquoises.[28] When the fashion for strongly contrasting colours returned under the influence of Worth's pupil Paul Poiret, the jeweller was ready with a corresponding colour palette.

62 Princess Marie Bonaparte wearing her olive-leaf diamond and emerald tiara

The affinities between the two arts were so close that a Worth dress made in 1900 for the soprano Lillian Nordica included shoulder motifs in the form of Cartier 'cravats',[29] and on another occasion Boucheron designed diamond sleeves. The most successful blurring of the distinction between jeweller and couturier was achieved in 1901 with the creation of the 'bolero' for Caroline Otéro, known as 'la belle Otéro'. This was a sleeveless jacket of diamonds and coloured cabochons made by the jeweller Paul Hamelin with an openwork lattice design or *résille* (literally, 'hairnet'). Cartier used this same netlike technique to produce a series of some ten necklaces which fitted snugly round the neck like a second skin, banishing all thought of rigid metal [**31**, **65**]. Was it surprising that Mademoiselle Otéro quickly tired of Hamelin's bolero, with its many synthetic stones, and commissioned Cartier to rework it as a *résille* necklace with real diamonds [**66**]? The model on this occasion was Marie Antoinette's famous necklace with its tasselled ribbons crossing over the breast. The most magnificent of *résille* necklaces was one ordered for Queen Alexandra from Pierre Cartier in 1904, an ethereal web of superimposed diamond drops and bows; she wears it in her portrait by the French painter François Flameng [**25**].

When Princess Marie Bonaparte [**62**], the illustrious descendant of Lucien Bonaparte and heiress of the wealthy Blanc family of Monte Carlo, married Prince George of Greece in 1907,[30] Cartier held a special exhibition to show off the wedding gifts, jewels in the garland style which had been produced for the occasion [**63**]. The sumptuous trousseau was the subject of a similar exhibition at the 'Hôtel des Modes'. American *Vogue* observed

63 Cartier's window display on the occasion of the marriage of Princess Marie Bonaparte to Prince George of Greece in 1907. The various pieces of jewelry were commissioned for the event

opposite

64 Necklace. Cartier Paris, 1904. Platinum; round and pear-shaped diamonds

65 *Résille* necklace. Cartier Paris, 1904. Platinum; circular- and rose-cut diamonds and diamond tassel border

that, just as the actress Cécile Sorel embodied the style of Louis XV, so Louis XVI and the Empire were the style of Marie Bonaparte, an analogy confirmed by Cartier's breast ornament, epaulette and olive-leaf tiara in the austere style of her Napoleonic ancestor.

The relationship between fashion and jewelry also appears in a branch of jewelry which it is impossible to appreciate nowadays, namely mourning jewelry. Until the 1920s bereavements dictated a strict ritual, which in the nineteenth century had been lived to the letter by Queen Victoria and the Empress Eugénie. The materials, colour and cut of the clothes which were worn in mourning and half-mourning were all clearly prescribed. Not only the clothes, but also the shoes, umbrella and purse, whose clasp had to be made of browned steel or more precious materials, were subject to the protocol of mourning, and it was only to be expected that jewelry would conform to the same rules: black pearls and jet had been the official expressions of mourning since the nineteenth century. When, around 1910, the fashionable use of black and white as a colour contrast led to the creation of onyx and diamond jewelry, that immediately became an acceptable form of mourning jewelry and as such was often newly set,[31] in forms launched by *Vogue* as 'new models for smart mourning' – an echo of 'Black Ascot' following the death of Edward VII. When the *Titanic* sank in 1912,[32] models such as these inspired Cartier's of New York with the idea of discreetly advertising onyx and diamond jewelry.

As was to be expected, the customers for Cartier's garland-style jewelry were among the most famous names of the day: royal houses, the international aristocracy, trade, and the theatre. According to the taste of the individual buyer, traditional forms alternated with more fashionable designs borrowed from the Orient: a breast ornament in the shape of a lambrequin was produced at the same time as a piece with twenty-nine cabochon emeralds composed like a medallion in a Persian carpet. Mrs Walter Burns, née Evelyn Cavendish-Bentinck, who was a cousin of the Duke of Portland and daughter-in-law of J. P. Morgan, wore this particular jewel on a number of occasions, including the coronation celebrations of George V in London.

The *demi-monde* of the courtesans was every bit as fond of jewelry and ostentation as the very best circles of society. Caroline Otéro bought from Cartier's not only the *résille* necklace mentioned above [66] but a breast ornament in the form of a six-sided floral grille with pendant drop pearls [45]. As one of the most famous representatives of the new genre

64

65

of 'vamp' which had begun with Sarah Bernhardt, she continued to be seen at Cartier's as late as 1919 when, at the age of fifty-one, she ordered a ten-strand pearl sash made of 1,015 pearls and diamonds.[33]

Less clear is the background of Adolph and Olga de Meyer, who were enthusiasts for Cartier's new aesthetic (breast ornament and bow tiara in 1901,[34] laurel tiara in 1905, and a vanity case in 1925). Olga Caracciolo, godchild and possibly also illegitimate off-spring of the Prince of Wales, was painted by Whistler and Boldini as a somewhat lesser Misia Sert. As Mrs Adolph de Meyer she was counted among the social élite, both after 1900 (the couple were raised to the peerage to enable them to attend the coronation of Edward VII) and during the post-war café-society years of Elsie de Wolfe, Elsa Maxwell and Cole Porter. Adolph de Meyer's work as a photographer was influenced by the aesthetic of Ruskin and Whistler. As a supporter of the Ballets Russes (his work on *L'Après-midi d'un faune* was published by Iribe in 1914[35]), as a contributor to *Vogue* [100], *Vanity Fair* and, from 1923, *Harper's Bazaar*, de Meyer became the leading pictorial chronicler of the war years and of an aesthetic which Cartier had helped to mould. His technique of using diffused lighting and groupings reminiscent of still-life paintings remained influential until the late 1920s. Not until the 1930s was de Meyer's work made to seem dated by the photographic techniques of Hoyningen-Huene, Horst and Beaton [205, 407], who celebrated sport and movement with a new sense of colour.

The tiaras and breast ornaments that Cartier's made not to order but for stock frequently contained a lavish variety of large stones and represented a considerable capital investment which was tied up for months. What frequently happened, therefore, was that the most expensive stones were removed and set in a new jewel – not uncommonly as the result of an unexpected order from New York or London. The following diagram traces the odyssey of one series of large drop diamonds between 1904 and 1905:

opposite

66 *Résille* necklace with bow tassel breast ornament. Cartier Paris, commissioned in 1903 by Caroline Otéro. Platinum; circular- and rose-cut diamonds, re-using stones from her famous bolero in a design inspired by Marie Antoinette's necklace (the 'Collier de la Reine')

67 Pair of aiguillettes. Cartier Paris, 1907, sold separately to A. Vanderbilt and Vincenzo Florio. Platinum; circular- and rose-cut diamonds

68 'Egyptian Pylon' pendant. Cartier Paris, 1920. Platinum; onyx and diamonds with circular-cut diamond central motif, suspended from a pearl ribbon necklace

69 Brooch. Cartier Paris, commissioned in 1913. Platinum; oval diamond, onyx and engraved rock crystal

70 Shrimp brooch. Cartier Paris, special order, 1913. Platinum; circular-and rose-cut diamonds; cabochon ruby eye

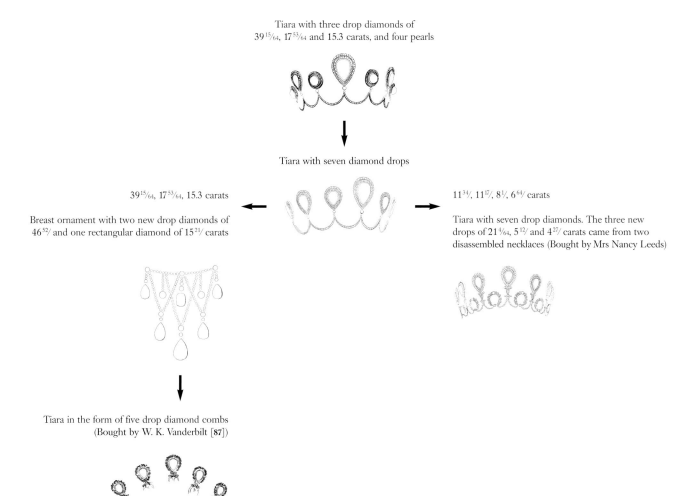

Tiara with three drop diamonds of
39 15/64, 17 53/64 and 15.3 carats, and four pearls

Tiara with seven diamond drops

39 15/64, 17 53/64, 15.3 carats

11 34/, 11 17/, 8 1/, 6 64/ carats

Breast ornament with two new drop diamonds of 46 52/ and one rectangular diamond of 15 21/ carats

Tiara with seven drop diamonds. The three new drops of 21 4/64, 5 12/ and 4 27/ carats came from two disassembled necklaces (Bought by Mrs Nancy Leeds)

Tiara in the form of five drop diamond combs
(Bought by W. K. Vanderbilt [87])

Thus a diamond tiara of 1904 produced two new pieces, both of which went to American buyers: Nancy Leeds and Mrs W. K. Vanderbilt. Increasing numbers of items in the garland style found a market in America as a consequence. Around 1917, when the First World War discouraged the production of large jewels in Europe, *Vogue* sent out a patriotic appeal to all American women, asking them to contribute to national morale by means of beauty and elegance. ('The American woman realizes that she can do this by looking her loveliest. She is a true patriot.') The de Meyer photographs accompanying the article display the garland-style tiara and breast ornament such as had been fashionable ten years earlier in Europe ('the American woman is really just beginning to realize the possibilities of the diamond tiara').[36]

An 1863 photograph shows women alpinists dressed in crinolines for their ascent of a Swiss glacier. However, by the end of the nineteenth century, women's clothes had begun to be adapted to the practical needs of female labour and sport. In 1880 Viscountess Harberton founded her Rational Dress Society which, encouraged by similar movements in Germany, attempted to simplify fashion in favour of comfort and hygiene. Women were taught how to mount a bicycle decently; they began to play hockey around 1900, and they were advised by their couturier to protect themselves from dust while driving by using a *voilette d'automobile*. In 1907 Mademoiselle Bayeux climbed the Matterhorn and two years later the Comtesse de Lambert clambered aboard Wilbur Wright's aeroplane. In the meantime, Paul Poiret had left the couturier Doucet in order to work for Worth, for whom he designed simple dresses suitable for riding on buses and walking. The reform of day and evening wear had begun, and with it the heyday of garland-style jewelry drew gently to a close.

opposite

71 Designs in the garland style. From top to bottom: wheat-ear tiara designed by Charles Jacqueau for execution in platinum and diamonds, 1911; three diamond chokers; laurel leaf tiara and breast ornament, *c.* 1909

CHAPTER FOUR
TIARAS

Thousands of curious visitors flocked to Bond Street in London during the first week of April 1911 to witness a spectacular exhibition at Cartier's [75] There, in return for a guinea admission – the proceeds of which went to the Prince Francis of Teck Foundation (named after Queen Mary's brother who had died the previous year) – they were able to admire at close quarters nineteen tiaras which two months later would be visible to them only at a distance during the coronation celebrations of George V. The Duchess of Marlborough, Princess Alexander of Teck, Lady Desborough, the Marchioness of Cholmondeley, and the Duchesses of Norfolk and Beaufort were all brought together in this display of their jewelry. Presenting as it did tiaras lent by great British aristocrats, the exhibition provided a foretaste of the coronation balls and of performances at Covent Garden with Caruso, Nijinsky and Melba.

In the typology of jewelry the tiara occupied a special place, inasmuch as it was reserved for a hereditary and moneyed élite who wore it at ceremonies and on festive occasions as an outward sign of their privileged status. The woman who wears a tiara towers above all around her; she is identifiable from afar and the glittering aureole around her head turns her into the Queen of the Night. At the same time, the tiara can convey every mood from the sublime to the merely theatrical – theatrical as in the case of the Vicomtesse de Janzé, a pillar of Parisian society around 1910, who seemed to brush the crystal chandeliers with her pagoda-like headdress of flashing diamonds; or sublime like the Comtesse de Haussonville who, even when not wearing a head ornament, always appeared to be 'crowned by an invisible tiara'.[1] Like the eighteenth-century minuet, the traditional tiara symbolized the prerogatives of a society which in Paris and London had essentially outlived itself by the late 1920s. The economic troubles of the time led to the disappearance of the tiara as the leading type of jewelry, a development that happened earlier in Paris than in London. Tiaras, for which Worth and Paquin created their magnificent gowns and which were the subject of glittering parades every Monday and Friday at the Paris Opéra, had really gone out of fashion by 1910. 'Soirées de diadèmes' had been the name given to those astonishing processions of jewels which, at the end of each performance, wended their way to Durand's, the fashionable restaurant in the Place de la Madeleine. There are reports of a 'surging sea of tiaras' at official receptions held in the Russian Embassy in Paris, when orchids were shipped in specially from the distant Crimea and the Grand Duchess Vladimir showed off her latest masterpiece from Cartier's. But even before the outbreak of the First World War, the Orientalizing aigrette and then the simple bandeau supplanted the classic tiara and came to be numbered among the favourite items which Poiret and Vionnet established as part of the prevailing image of what women should wear.

In Paris great aigrette balls were organized by aristocratic families who were proud of their name and their past, such as the Duchesse de Gramont with her 'Crinoline Ball' and Princesse Jacques de Broglie with her 'Gemstone Ball' of 1914. In distant New York, Philadelphia and Newport, on the other hand, Mrs William Astor, Mrs George J. Gould, Mrs W. K. Vanderbilt and Eva (Mrs Edward) Stotesbury entertained with a degree of magnificence which made European balls appear almost insignificant. The moneyed classes of the United States, who had originally raised themselves above their bourgeois origins through their own hard work, set out to rival the historical aristocracy of Europe. In friendly competition with her rivals, the well-to-do American woman refused to forego any of the attributes sanctioned by society. These accessories included country houses imported from Europe, complete with ancestral portraits and furnishing, as well as tiaras ordered from Cartier's in Paris and later New York. Like the grandiose palaces modelled on Blois and Versailles, tiaras revealed the financial power that made luxury possible, and could therefore never be too expensive. The emerald tiara that Cartier's made for Eva Stotesbury was so heavy that she got a stiff neck wearing it; she was advised 'to attach a few helium balloons to it, or wear it without complaining'.[2] Although the First World War did not have the same socially disruptive effect in America as it did in Europe, it seemed like the swan song of an era when, at an advanced age, Caroline Astor stood at the

75 Invitation card to Cartier's tiara exhibition in London, 1911

entrance to her ballroom, wearing a tiara and breast ornament and 'greeting imaginary guests long dead, exchanging pleasantries with ghosts of the utmost social distinction'.[3]

Even after they had gone out of fashion in Paris and New York, tiaras continued to set the tone in London. The fact that in 1923, on the occasion of a reception at Bath House, Lady Lucknow 'wore her enormous Cartier tiara which, with its flashing diamonds, made one think of a halo' was something that struck only the fashion reporter as being in any way excessive. Private detectives kept an eye on the bejewelled guests in the dining room of the Savoy Hotel, and the Court of St James even included the wearing of tiaras in its rules of protocol. Edward VII made his displeasure felt when guests arrived without a tiara. In later years, Consuelo, Duchess of Marlborough, recalled

> a dinner in honour of the Prince and Princess of Wales to which I wore a diamond crescent instead of the prescribed tiara. The Prince with a severe glance at my crescent observed 'The Princess has taken the trouble to wear a tiara, why have you not done so?' Luckily I could truthfully answer that I had been delayed by some charitable function in the country and that I had found the bank in which I kept my tiara closed on my arrival in London.[4]

As late as 1953 Queen Elizabeth the Queen Mother received a tiara from Cartier's [76]: the strict rules of court etiquette remained unaltered, although many members of the nobility, including Princess Marina, Duchess of Kent, regarded the tiara as a nuisance and out of keeping with the times: 'Soon after the Queen left, the Duchess of Kent removed her tiara and handed it to the bandleader, Tommy Kinsman, complaining that it was far too heavy. Kinsman placed the tiara on the piano while the Royal Duchess danced with her old friend Chips Channon.'[5]

Since tiaras were specially made in Paris, London and New York for important occasions and in association with expensive dresses, Cartier's photographic records not only help us to identify specific fashions, but their chronology reveals a most fascinating chapter in the social history of the twentieth century.

The word ' tiara' comes from the Greek for a peaked cap worn by the Persians. The French *diadème*, diadem, comes from the Greek *diadeo*, 'I bind together'; originally it meant a helmet band worn by a military commander, but then it became any secular or sacred head ornament denoting high office.[6] It was the Renaissance painters who finally became the chroniclers of its modern meaning – one thinks, for example, of Titian's *Girl with a Dish of Fruit*, in which the tiara appears as the crowning attribute of a magnificent evening gown. Cartier's tiaras, which belong to the final stage of this change in function, may be divided into various groups according to their form and style.

The 'kokoshnik' or 'Russian tiara'

The term, derived from the Russian word *kokosh*, meaning 'cock's comb', initially described a head ornament based on the form of a cock's comb worn in Russian folk-dances. Originally made of cloth in the form of a pelta and fastened at the side with ribbons, it was taken up by the Russian court during the sixteenth/seventeenth centuries and reproduced in expensive materials. The kokoshnik was accentuated at the centre by a slight swelling and was placed around the head like the disc-shaped halo of a Byzantine madonna. A portrait of Catherine the Great dating from about 1775 shows her wearing a crescent-shaped kokoshnik studded with precious stones. In a portrait of Tsarina Maria Feodorovna of around 1830, it has grown into a huge fan-shaped halo. After 1800 the kokoshnik became fashionable in Western Europe, too. When Cartier's took up the motif around 1900 [78–82, 85], memories of its Russian origins were still so vivid that the archival records of the rue de la Paix consistently use the terms 'kokoshnik', 'Russian tiara' or 'in the Russian style'.

To relieve the static impression produced by its solidity of form, Cartier's turned to one of the purest inspirations of the First Empire and created a group of kokoshniks with diamond drops freely suspended from a gallery within the openwork mount [80, 82]. Every movement on the part of the wearer was gently transmitted to the stones, which increased in size towards the centre. This group was followed by other models with a lozenge-shaped grille pattern, each opening of which was ornamented with a pendant diamond.

76 Queen Elizabeth the Queen Mother wearing her diamond tiara designed by Frederick A. Mew, Cartier London, 1953

opposite

77 Mrs Nancy Leeds – Princess Anastasia of Greece since her marriage to Prince Christopher in 1920 – wearing her emerald and diamond kokoshnik and her emerald and diamond necklace of 1921. Painting by Philip de László

An additional series of kokoshniks, designed in Louis XV style, was reminiscent of tiaras among the French crown jewels made by Bapst around 1820. They included a tiara for Elisabeth, Queen of the Belgians, in 1912, by the Cartier designer Henri Chenaud, and one made for the opera singer Lina Cavalieri, who first appeared with Caruso in Paris in 1905 and who was celebrated as the most beautiful woman of her day.

In 1912 Charles Jacqueau designed a flat kokoshnik with rock crystal trimmings and diamonds. The sinuous plant forms engraved on the crystal owed their inspiration to Renaissance pattern books, but the geometrical diamond motifs show the piece to be an early example of revolutionary Art Deco stylization. The tiara that Princess Yusupov wore at her wedding in 1914 had been made in a similar style in 1911 [84] and its fame soon spread far beyond Russia's borders. It was seized by the Soviets in 1925 and has not been heard of since. We should also include in this group a small series of kokoshniks of much less expensive design: their background of blackened metal [105] or grey and green copper was decorated with diamond stars and sinuous vine-shoots. The boldest piece in the series showed a symmetrically stylized Art Deco tree with black onyx leaves on a diamond background; pearls set at rhythmic intervals enlivened its unbroken contour [79].

Although *Vogue* predicted a revival of the 'Russian tiara' in 1923, very few women in Parisian society seemed inclined to wear huge tiaras with the latest creations of Lanvin and Vionnet; they regarded the bandeau as more in keeping with the time and easier to wear. In London, on the other hand, Cartier's workshops designed a special kokoshnik as late as 1928: rounded at the bottom, it covered the back of the head and at the front ended in a delicate ribbon. It found no imitators. The last great buyer of kokoshniks in London was the American Lady Granard, daughter of Ogden Mills. In 1922 she ordered a delicately wrought model made of 435 seed pearls with diamond embroidery in the centre, and a year later another which, with its sixteen aquamarine beads, sapphires and pearls, achieved what for the time was a novel effect of colour. One wonders whether it was the very last of Lady Granard's kokoshniks, with its priceless diamond drops and heavy helmet-like form, that Chips Channon had in mind when, in 1937 (the year it was ordered), he confided to his diary that 'Lady Granard could scarcely walk for jewels'. The Granard kokoshniks mark the end of a tradition which was fatally checked by the Second World War.

The bandeau

The bandeau is a ribbon-shaped tiara whose centre is not accentuated, as was that of the kokoshnik. It is the most timeless form of head ornament, and gives us a clear idea of what the tiara must have looked like in early civilizations, when it was still worn as a headband.

Cartier's records include an entry dated 1854 describing a hair ornament of two blue enamel flowers and pearls, but the firm's first verifiable tiara is a silver-gilt bandeau recorded in 1859. Plain narrow headbands or *ferronnières* had been popular during the reign of Charles X and were typical of the late bourgeois phase of Neoclassicism.[7]

The bandeaux which Cartier created in the garland style around 1900 met the requirements of court protocol in spite of their simple appearance. The Australian soprano Nellie Melba (1861–1931), who was one of Cartier's regular clients, ordered a 'Greek' bandeau in 1908, presumably with a meander design. Two of the most original bandeaux from the period before the First World War show Cartier's intimate knowledge of Worth's fashions and of textiles and embroidery in general. Nancy Leeds bought the first of these [88], in the form of a 28-cm-long embroidered tapestry; platinum threads formed a transparent base, the 'web' onto which the diamond plant tendrils were embroidered. It is interesting to note that two years later, in 1914, Fabergé used a similar type of 'platinum embroidery' on his 'Mosaic Egg', and Cartier's original idea was taken up again by LaCloche in 1925. The second tiara used black moiré silk as a background on which elongated concentric diamond ellipses reproduced the shimmering surface structure of silk. This fabric trompe-l'oeil bandeau found its way into the collection of Princess Bibesco. At the same time bandeaux were beginning to be worn with aigrettes [97], a fashion which was launched by Paul Poiret. In New York Cartier sold Mrs Eva Stotesbury a bandeau with a 23.40-carat drop diamond projecting upwards as its central peak. He also attached the historic 'Star of the East' diamond to a similar mount for Mrs Evalyn Walsh McLean [397], and in 1914 he designed a simpler model for Nancy Leeds, surmounted by a single drop pearl.

79 Small kokoshnik. Cartier Paris, 1914.
Platinum; onyx, circular-cut diamond mount,
pearl crest border

opposite

80 Kokoshnik. Cartier Paris, 1908. Platinum; fifteen pear-shaped diamonds, weighing approximately 19 carats in total.; round old-cut diamonds;. pearls; 'lily-of-the-valley' setting for the swinging pear-shaped diamonds

below

81 Kokoshnik. Cartier Paris, special order, 1911. Platinum; round old-, single- and rose-cut diamonds; millegrain setting

82

83

84

85

86

87

88

preceding pages, left

82 Kokoshnik. Cartier Paris, commissioned in 1913 by Mrs Nancy Leeds. Platinum; alternate pear-shaped diamonds and pearls suspended in interlinked diamond and pearl hoops. Weights of diamonds: 21.60, 15.35, 11.82, 11.54, 9.85 carats. Weights of pearls: 64.60, 62.72, 49.60, 45.04, 35.76, 35 grains

83 Tiara. Cartier Paris, commissioned in 1912 by Baron de Gunzburg. Platinum; the scroll-engraved rock crystal band with rose-cut diamond base, navette-cut diamond centre, circular-cut diamond gallery

84 Tiara. Cartier Paris, 1911, sold to Princess Yusupov in 1914 for her wedding. Platinum; mounted with engraved rock crystal bars below a circular-cut diamond gallery; central diamond of 3.66 carats

85 Kokoshnik. Cartier Paris, commissioned in 1909 by Grand Duchess Vladimir. Platinum; a cushion-shaped sapphire of 137.20 carats flanked by six cabochon sapphires weighing 102.16 carats, on circular-cut diamond mount

preceding pages, right

86 Bandeau. Cartier Paris, commissioned in 1909 by Mrs W. K. Vanderbilt. Platinum; designed as an intertwined 'Byzantine' circular- and rose-cut diamond plaque with triangular ends, on pearl and diamond band

87 Bandeau. Cartier Paris, transformed in 1909 for Mrs W. K. Vanderbilt from five combs of 1905 [*ill. p. 55*]. Platinum; mounted with five pear-shaped diamonds weighing $39^{60}/_{64}$, $24^{44}/$, $22^{8}/_{64}$, $15^{3}/_{64}$ and $17^{53}/$ carats within laurel leaf surrounds

88 Stomacher/bandeau. Cartier Paris, 1912, sold to Mrs Nancy Leeds. Designed as a platinum canvas studded with circular-cut diamonds

89 Bandeau. Cartier Paris, 1912. Platinum; concentric diamond moiré effect. Shown at the 1912 Canadian Exhibition as the most precious item ($10,080), sold to Princess Antoine Bibesco

this page

90 Bandeau. Cartier New York, 1924. Platinum; two pear-shaped diamonds, and old European-cut diamonds; pearl weighing approximately 51 grains

The bandeaux of the 1920s [**90, 207, 208**] show the geometric wealth of invention that characterizes Art Deco forms: openwork honeycomb patterns, star shapes of Islamic origin, and lozenges which were fully developed in Cartier's work from 1913/14 and which recurred in identical form on bracelets and necklaces. In keeping with the fashion for multi-purpose jewelry, these bandeaux could easily be dismantled and turned into bracelets, brooches and earclips. As late as 1938 a multipurpose bandeau was made for Barbara Hutton (then Countess Haugwitz-Reventlow); its diamond drops were removable, so that it could be worn as a bracelet, while its star and half-moon motifs could be used as brooches.

Occasional excursions into exotic regions enlivened the simple silhouette of the bandeau. An onyx and diamond bandeau of Egyptian character, surmounted by stylized lotus blossoms inspired by tomb frescoes at Deir al Bersha, was created in 1923 [**158**]. Another model was based on a simple diamond bandeau which was bought back from a customer in London in 1929 and felicitously enhanced by the addition of engraved turquoise palmettes, a Greek design from the third century BC. In 1931 Viscountess Astor ordered a diamond 'Peacock Bandeau': its openwork band was made up of lozenge shapes and its central pearl was flanked by two peacocks made of diamond drops, while a stylized peacock tail crowned the motif like a canopy.

The linear form of the bandeau matched the geometrical style of Art Deco, and was also an ideal complement for bobbed hair, the *garçonne* hairstyle which had begun to catch on around 1917 [**238**]. Colette and Polaire wore their hair in this way as early as 1903, when it was considered a revolutionary thing to do, and at a somewhat later date the revue dancer Caryathis launched the alternative Joan-of-Arc cut. Worn low on the forehead below a bobbed hairstyle, the bandeau, like the long cigarette-holder and hip-length pearl sautoir, embodied the chic and eroticism of the 1920s vamp.

In 1925 Cartier's London workshops produced a bandeau which the designer Charles Jacqueau had developed in Paris: crossed by a single arch, it was indebted in form to the barred crown of the Middle Ages and enclosed the bobbed hair like a helmet. It must also have been influenced by the hair ornament worn by Lina Cavalieri in Massenet's opera *Thaïs*, set in Early Christian Alexandria. Jacqueau took over its lateral motif, which in a bandeau made for Queen Marie of Romania gave the embarrassing impression of earflaps [**78**].

Meander tiaras

The word 'meander' is derived from the small river Maiandros in Phrygia. In ancient Greece the river's serpentine curves inspired the motif of an ornamental band of regular lines set at right-angles to each other. It was a popular design in both architecture and vase-painting. When Cartier's workshops began using the meander in 1902 on tiaras and breast ornaments, there were no doubt people who could still remember the most famous of all nineteenth-century meander tiaras, that of the Empress Eugénie. She had ordered it from Bapst in 1867 and for two years wore the famous 'Regent' diamond as part of it. During this same period Princess Mathilde was often to be seen wearing two meander bracelets.

In the classical phase which preceded Art Deco and which produced a profusion of new ideas in Cartier's designs, the adoption of the meander was almost *de rigueur*, and it may be seen on a number of tiaras, especially those in the form of a kokoshnik. One meander tiara was made in 1907 for Baroness Henri de Rothschild, with a circular floral motif at its centre; and the following year a meander kokoshnik was sent to Princess Shakovskoy in Russia. In 1912 Countess von Fels and Madame Larivière of Argentina both chose almost identical meander tiaras from Cartier's.

Sun tiaras

The sun tiara too was based on the form of the kokoshnik. 'Sunbeams' made of diamond radiate from a central point close to the hairline, most of them circumscribed within a flat ellipse called a 'sun'. Several of these ellipses may be placed on top of each other, in which case one speaks of several 'suns'.

The sun tiara may well have originated in the mythological tradition of the Baroque theatre, where goddesses and demons would appear wearing a radial glittering head ornament. The Queen of the Night in Mozart's *Magic Flute* was one of the last representatives of this pagan spirit-world to be seen on a stage in the Enlightenment era.

Sun tiaras are recorded from the beginning of the nineteenth century. At the 1889 Paris Exposition the jeweller Vever exhibited a model containing a 54-carat diamond. A Russian photograph taken in 1914 of the wedding presents of Princess Yusupov clearly shows the family's sun tiara.

Cartier's first sun tiaras date from 1904 and were delivered to J. P. Morgan in New York and the Countess of Suffolk in London. In London Cartier's were still designing sun tiaras in the 1920s, some of which were set with a large cabochon sapphire or emerald at the centre. The last one was ordered in 1926 by the daughter of Mrs Cavendish-Bentinck.

Winged tiaras

In Greek mythology, Hermes, the messenger of the gods, was depicted wearing a winged helmet and shoes. He remained a popular figure in pictorial representations right down to the nineteenth century, including, for example, a statue by Bertel Thorvaldsen in Copenhagen (1818). In the second half of the nineteenth century the winged motif made its appearance on stage in Richard Wagner's operas: Germanic winged helmets were worn by such acclaimed singers as the Croatian soprano Milka Ternina as Brünnhilde or, much later, the Danish *Heldentenor* Lauritz Melchior as Siegfried. Cartier's Valkyrie aigrette of 1899 is evidence of the Wagner mania which gripped Paris when the soprano Lucienne Bréval performed. The winged motif passed quickly from the theatre to fancy-dress balls and thereafter became fashionable in the form of a winged tiara.

The jeweller Alphonse Fouquet had designed a winged tiara in 1883 and six years later the firm of Boucheron's former colleague Debut (Debut & Coulon) exhibited a tiara in the form of doves' wings.

At Cartier's it was once again J. P. Morgan who sparked off the new fashion. In 1901 Cartier produced a winged tiara which was made in Charpentier's workshop. It had ten wings arranged to create a lively interplay of lines, and the American banker liked it. In 1909 Cartier had an expensive model manufactured for him in Lavabre's workshop with a fancy-brown 33-carat diamond at its centre; this, too, found its way to America. In contrast to the earlier models, the winged tiara made for Lady Ross of England was a naturalistic imitation of elongated birds' wings. Years later, in 1935, Cartier's in London were to receive a final order for a winged tiara, this time from the Duchess of Roxburghe.

Foliage and floral tiaras

Like the bandeau, the wreath of classical antiquity is regarded as a forebear of the tiara. It was originally worn in the service of fertility rites and subsequently awarded as a distinction on the occasion of victory celebrations and other cultic festivals. In Rome an oak wreath was the reward for Augustus's service to the state, whereas a golden laurel wreath honoured the victorious general. At the time of the Renaissance, great poets were crowned with a laurel wreath to signify them as princes among poets, and in 1804 Napoleon crowned himself emperor in much the same way.

Cartier's began producing foliage and floral tiaras shortly after 1900. The majority were laurel- or olive-leaf tiaras in the form of a wreath; an example of the latter was to be seen in 1907 in the wedding jewelry made for Marie Bonaparte [62, 63]. Laurel motifs continued to appear in garland-style wreaths, independently of tiaras, and it would certainly not be wide of the mark to claim that Cartier's garlands were based in general on the laurel leaf and acanthus leaves.

Mrs Keppel ordered a laurel tiara in Paris in 1903, to be followed in 1904 by Boni de Castellane, husband of Anna Gould, and by Countess Greffulhe. Laurel tiaras enjoyed great popularity in America, as is shown by the models ordered by the two banking families of Drexel and Stotesbury, as well as that of the American Lady Astor. As late as 1927 Queen Victoria Eugenia of Spain [74] ordered a tiara with arching laurel wreaths intertwined around two horizontal garlands of leaves, a thematic invention which, considering the predominant style of Art Deco at this time, can be explained only by reference to the requirements of traditional court etiquette.

In 1902 and 1903 the Paris branch of Cartier's created two fern tiaras, one of which was bought by Sir Ernest Cassel, the private financial adviser and friend of Edward VII. The banker, who had entered the London establishment of Bischoffsheim & Goldschmidt in 1873, later went on to mine ore in Sweden, had an interest in the American railways as well as Egyptian irrigation schemes, and became a regular visitor to the rue de la Paix.

The tiara exhibition organized by Cartier's in London in 1911 included the oak-leaf tiara of the Duchess of Norfolk. Lady Granard, too, frequently wore an oak-leaf tiara that was much admired.

Naturalistic flowers, such as the jeweller Oscar Massin had produced in the nineteenth century, were seldom found in Cartier's range; thus floral tiaras are comparatively rare, although two were to be seen at the 1911 exhibition. (Cartier's only other botanically authentic plants were part of the series of gemstone potted plants influenced by Carl Fabergé [123].) In 1911 Countess von Bredow ordered a trefoil tiara to be sent to her in Germany; it was based on a model of uncertain origin which the German Empress frequently wore in Berlin. In the 1925 Exposition Cartier showed an orchid tiara in diamonds and onyx; with their contrasting tones of black and white, the two flowers linked by a tortoiseshell comb suggested the abstract stylization of the panther motif.

Genuine floral tiaras were, however, produced in the London workshops at this time, although they gave the impression of an anachronistic revival of Massin's rose motifs. Individual rose blooms could be detached from the tiara and worn separately as brooches. As late as 1947, the Nizam of Hyderabad chose a diamond necklace and a rose-blossom tiara from Cartier's in London as wedding presents for Princess Elizabeth.

Wheat-ear tiaras

Demeter was the Greek goddess of agriculture and fertility, and her priestesses wore sacred wheat-ears in their hair. It is doubtful whether complete wheat-ear tiaras were ever produced by Greek and Etruscan goldsmiths, although surviving pieces include a remarkable wheat-ear necklace now in the Hermitage in Leningrad, together with Etruscan hairpins and pendant brooches.

After a brief vogue at the time of the First Empire, the wheat-ear motif returned in the second half of the nineteenth century, when jewellers such as Castellani and Fontenay were influenced by the techniques of Etruscan goldsmiths. The 'Ceres' tiara of Oscar Massin (1861) is one early example of this neo-Etruscan/Roman fashion.

Cartier's first wheat-ear ornament was in the form of an aigrette and dates from 1901. Wheat-ear tiaras consisted either of ears of wheat tied in bundles at their centre, or else of husks of wheat which followed the rhythmic movement of the tiara band [71]. A particularly delicate example consisted of two bundles of wheat with freely moving husks, which produced the illusion of a breath of wind passing through a field of wheat. Cartier's wheat-ear tiaras were available in any combination of stones: one bought by the Ottoman Riffat Pasha combined ears of wheat with diamond drops; and the wheat-ear tiara chosen by the banker Maurice Ephrussi was studded with rare pink pearls.

Tiaras with vertical ornaments

Even in Byzantium the circlet or *stemma*, which had originally developed out of the diadem, had included ornaments projecting vertically upwards from a narrow band. These projections, which were in the form of geometrical motifs, were found only on women's crowns. Not until the Middle Ages were similar ornaments placed on men's crowns, as on the Crown of St Stephen in the Hungarian crown jewels. The motifs varied according to the social rank of the wearer and hence the function of the crown, and they ranged from heraldic lilies to rhythmic dentate motifs.

In Cartier's case, the preferred ornaments consisted of diamond or pearl drops, set with the narrow end pointing downwards, on a kokoshnik or Louis XVI-style garland. A tiara made in 1905 for Nancy Leeds consisted of a continuous series of Louis XVI garlands, surmounted by seven diamond drops [*ill. p. 55*]. Others of similar inspiration had marquise or brilliant diamonds as their vertical ornaments. In 1906 the Charpentier workshop produced the 'Renaissance' tiara of curving tendril-like motifs, surmounted by five rectangular emeralds.

Another group dispensed with any structural base and set seven drop diamonds above a delicate garland. The first such tiara was made in 1904, with a central stone of 39 carats; it could also be worn as a necklace or with alternating pearls. In 1906 a tiara was

91 Tiara. Cartier London, commissioned
by the Begum Andrée Aga Khan III, 1934.
Platinum; round old- and baguette-cut diamonds

92 Tiara. Cartier London, 1937. Platinum; round old- and baguette-cut diamonds; one large octagonal emerald-cut 62.35-carat dark citrine, calibré- and baguette-cut citrines, one hexagonal citrine

93 Tiara. Cartier London, 1937. Platinum; round old-cut diamonds; oval and fancy-cut aquamarines sold to the Berlin banker Bleichroeder with a central stone of 13.50 carats and two years later one with a central stone of 27 carats was chosen by Grand Duke Paul of Russia for his wife, Countess Hohenfelsen.

Tiaras with pendant drops

When the diamond and pearl kokoshnik of Grand Duchess Vladimir [128] – now in the possession of Queen Elizabeth II – was temporarily deposited with Cartier's in Paris, the firm used it as the inspiration for three new tiaras of similar design, all having interlinking circles of diamonds at whose centres hung a pendant gem. The first of these was made in Picq's workshop in 1911 and had eleven diamonds increasing in size towards the centre. The second and more important one was a reworking of the 1908 tiara owned by Countess Hohenfelsen. Those of Cartier's free-moving tiaras which were worked in platinum could generally only be worn on the head with the aid of additional metal fittings. When these metal supports were removed, the tiaras could be turned into necklaces or even breast ornaments. A photograph taken on the occasion of one of Madame de Yturbe's receptions shows the Countess wearing the drop tiara as a breast ornament [61], while the breast ornament of 1908 has become a hat ornament. The third piece in this group was made for Nancy Leeds in 1913 and consisted of alternate drop diamonds and pearls [82].

Between 1906 and 1908 a further series of tiaras was produced at Cartier's with openwork heart motifs, in the centre of each a pendant diamond. Made in the workshops of Harnichard and Bellemans, one of them found its way to Argentina and another came to England, though not until 1919.

Perhaps the most stunningly simple tiara of pendant drop diamonds consisted of a pointed arch to which were attached twenty-one briolette diamonds. It was made in 1905 for the soprano Lillian Nordica from Maine, whose brilliant career took her to Paris, London, St Petersburg and New York before she was killed in a shipwreck off New Guinea in 1914. Lillian Nordica was one of the great operatic primadonnas of her day, together with Nellie Melba, Lina Cavalieri and Mary Garden, all of whom wore their Cartier jewels as much on the stage as in private life. Thus Victor Dautremont, Pierre Cartier's young London assistant, was regularly sent down to Covent Garden with extravagant jewelry for Nellie Melba, which had to be warmed before it could touch the sensitive skin of the artist. These tragediennes of the operatic stage enjoyed the ecstatic worship of a public which was to turn its attention, after 1925, to the more remote idols of Hollywood.

Aigrettes

Ever since aigrettes became important in the seventeenth century as vertically projecting head ornaments, they were subject to cross-fertilization between Eastern and Western cultural influences: the Victoria and Albert Museum in London has sketches of aigrettes by the Danish designer Arnold Lulls, dating from around 1610, which invite comparison with an aigrette worn by the Mughal emperor Shah Jahan in a miniature dated 1616/17. Whether we are dealing here with a piece made in Lulls' workshop or with a Mughal work of the same period may be a matter for conjecture, but it is clear that the East as well as Europe had an interest in the aigrette.

Aigrettes were also popular in the eighteenth century and are preserved in the set of cornelian ornaments which form part of the Saxon crown jewels (pre-1719), as well as in sketches by Augustin Duflos, who made Louis XV's crown. In the reign of Louis XVI, as fashions took on an Oriental look and inspiration was no longer sought in distant India but in Constantinople, the aigrette was the crowning jewel on exotic sultans' turbans. An aigrette of a heron's feather and drop pearls in the Russian crown jewels was in fact called the 'Sultane', and Marie Antoinette had herself painted by Elisabeth Vigée-Lebrun with an Oriental hairstyle crowned by an aigrette. Madame Mère, Napoleon's mother, similarly wore an aigrette on the occasion of her son's coronation in Notre-Dame.

Aigrettes again became fashionable around 1860. Oscar Massin launched them in the form of small posies worn with or without bird-of-paradise feathers. His most famous aigrette was one with five burgeoning diamond posies for the Duchess of Medina Coeli. Tiffany designed a peacock-feather aigrette, set with the 'Brunswick' diamond, which was admired at the Philadelphia Centennial Exhibition of 1876.

opposite

94 Aigrette. Cartier Paris, special order, 1913. Platinum; designed as a scrolling spray in rose-cut diamonds with ruby and circular-cut diamond tips and circular-cut diamond base. Weight of two rubies: 8.54 carats

95 Aigrette. Cartier Paris, commissioned in 1912 by Prince Gortchakov. Platinum; designed as a lobed diamond base with navette-cut diamond tip and pear-shaped diamond of 19.42 carats from which rise two scrolled diamond lines with pear-shaped diamonds weighing 4.55 carats

94

95

96 Aigrette. Cartier Paris, commissioned in 1913 by Grand Duchess Vladimir. Platinum; mounted with two pear-shaped cabochon emeralds on a nineteenth-century diamond leaf motif

opposite

97 Aigrette bandeau. Cartier Paris, 1913. Platinum; designed as a pierced circular-cut diamond band with lancet centre

98

99

In the 1890s aigrettes became the most popular of all forms of head ornament. They complemented Oriental turbans and historical costumes, and at masked balls they became an indispensable accessory. At the great fancy-dress ball held in the Winter Palace in St Petersburg in 1903, Grand Duke Michael and Prince Yusupov appeared dressed as boyars, with aigrettes in their fur hats. In Paris, fancy-dress balls became illustrated broadsheets of history and mythology, in which illusion and reality were mingled in an ingenious game.

Cartier's aigrettes were an essential part of Worth's evening wear. The requisite feathers came from specialist establishments, the most famous of which were Lurot in the rue des Petits-Champs and Judith Barbier in the rue Daunou, who employed 450 women assistants, of whom two were sales assistants at Worth's. The most popular feathers were those of the Egyptian white egret (in French *aigrette*, whence the name of the hair ornament), the bird-of-paradise from New Guinea, the Cape ostrich, the Egyptian ibis and the Central American green-shimmering quetzal. Black feathers, which in Cartier's jewels provided the desired pitch-black contrast with diamonds, were initially dyed. Especially rare feathers were sold individually and by weight.

Worth was not alone in obtaining his feathers from Judith Barbier: so, too, did Worth's former colleague, Paul Poiret, who was shortly to undermine his master's supremacy and appropriate the aigrette as his own symbol. Poiret had opened his own business in the rue Pasquier in 1903, and, together with Raoul Dufy, who continued to design fabrics for him until 1912, he, like Louis Cartier, contributed to shaping the rising Art Deco style. He designed corsetless dresses, the tunic dress and minaret dress and also, in 1910, the narrow skirt or hobble skirt, against which the Pope inveighed. What is important, in the context of tiaras, is Poiret's Oriental style with its turbans and striking aigrettes, a fashion influenced by the Ballets Russes and Persian miniatures. In 1911 Poiret held a magnificent party on the theme of the Thousand and One Nights, at which three hundred invited guests paid court to their host, who received them dressed as a sultan on a golden throne. Poiret's ball was followed in 1912 by the 'Persian Balls' of the Marquise de Chabrillan and the Comtesse de Clermont-Tonnerre, at which frescoes by Bakst provided a background for Oriental tableaux of Hindu slaves, Shiraz dancers, elephants, tigers and peacocks. The heyday of the Cartier aigrette coincided with those years before the First World War when Oriental influences were most clearly felt.

A 'Persian' aigrette appears in the 1899 stock book, and in 1901 a wheat-ear aigrette, together with a lily-of-the-valley aigrette made of eight diamond drops suspended from a platinum thread. This first period, which was dominated by floral motifs, came to a climax in 1908 with the modification by Cartier for Grand Duchess Vladimir of a nineteenth-century aigrette tiara with symmetrically arranged shoots related to the supple wheat-ear tiara and to Massin's aigrette for the Duchess of Medina Coeli: whenever they moved, its three curving clusters, now set with her Indian-cut briolettes like cascades of blossom, suggested dewdrops shaken from a stem. From 1910, when Cartier began making aigrettes in the Oriental style of the Ballets Russes and Poiret, he reproduced Arabian grille motifs and Persian carpet medallions. Two years later, a Chinese gong motif first appeared in the design of an aigrette [101]. Two calyx-shaped radial aigrettes of 1911 and 1912 [95] were based upon an eighteenth-century model in the Grünes Gewölbe in Dresden.

Also dating from 1912 is the first aigrette with an Indian *sarpech* motif. The *sarpech* was a golden feather-shaped ornament studded with gemstones and generally consisting of a disc with a stalk growing out of it, from the end of which dangled a stone. Cartier's *sarpech* aigrettes were not only admired at Oriental balls in Paris and London but were even bought by the Indian potentates with whom Jacques Cartier did business in London. As late as 1937 the Maharaja of Nawanagar [195] commissioned a *sarpech* from Cartier's which was set with the 'Tiger's-Eye' diamond weighing 61.55 carats.

Apart from Oriental aigrettes, Cartier also launched a number of particularly lavish examples which were set with a single gemstone. Thus the heron aigrette ordered by Paul-Louis Weiller consisted of a single 69-carat drop diamond. In general, however, the most popular aigrette, even as late as the 1920s, was one consisting of clustered rays. The designer Paul Iribe and his circle influenced the fanciful arabesques of another type of Cartier's aigrettes; and the fountain, which became a leitmotif of Art Deco, also found

opposite

98 Aigrette. Cartier Paris, special order, 1913. Platinum; designed as a scrolled diamond plume in rose-cut diamonds from which a briolette-cut diamond is suspended. Weights of two diamonds at the base: 8.12 and 16.60 carats

99 Aigrette. Cartier Paris, 1913, sold to Lord Derby. Platinum; designed as a stylized rose-cut diamond plume

100 *right* A Cartier diamond aigrette as a
bridal ornament, from American *Vogue*,
May 1918. Photograph by Baron de Meyer

opposite

101 'Chinese gong' aigrette. Cartier Paris,
sold to Countess Uvarov in 1912.
Platinum; circular-cut diamond mount
with calibré-cut ruby border. Weight of
central diamond 3.37 carats

102 'Pinecone' aigrette. Cartier Paris, 1913.
Platinum; circular- and rose-cut diamonds

103 Aigrette. Cartier Paris, 1912.
Platinum; three pear-shaped diamonds
and one cushion-shaped diamond,
in diamond surround

favour as a head ornament: the vertically rising aigrette needed only to be bent back on
itself, like a jet of water, to create the impression of a spray.

Combs

Combs, with their twofold function of holding the hair in place and decorating it, were
popular throughout the whole of the nineteenth century, but it was only during the Art
Nouveau period that they became a leading fashion accessory, whether made of horn or
tortoiseshell, or decorated with willows and creepers made of enamel and pearls. Cartier
had begun producing combs around 1850 [9]. An invoice dating from 1859 shows the
case-maker Trepat charging Fr. 18 for a large comb-case, and Fr. 30 for two small ones.
Combs and tiaras were often sold together, just as they were often worn together.

Although Art Nouveau was of only marginal importance in Cartier's work,
Charpentier's workshop in the rue de Richelieu produced a comb with an Art Nouveau
snake motif in 1888. The most expensive combs were a series of five dating from 1905 and
sold to W. K. Vanderbilt in New York [*ill. p. 55*]. Set with five garland-framed diamond
drops, the largest of which weighed 39.60 carats, they could be assembled to form a
bandeau [**87**].

Combs once again became sought after in the rue de la Paix during the Art Deco
period, when couturiers such as Callot launched their Spanish fashions. Made of coral,
onyx and diamonds, they were no longer overshadowed by the larger tiara, but often
formed the only head ornament, on which designers lavished all their imagination.

101

102

103

CHAPTER FIVE

ART NOUVEAU
RELIGIOUS THEMES
THE FIRST WORLD WAR

Art Nouveau

At the turn of the century there were two opposing forces in jewelry design. On one side were the entrenched supporters of the elegant garland style, led by Louis Cartier; on the other, the supporters of Art Nouveau, such as René Lalique and Georges Fouquet, who declared war on a style that was lacking in symbolic and figural elements.[1] As devotees of the cult of a new symbolism derived from nature, they propagated the idea of asymmetrical, sinuous lines in ornamentation, seeing them as part of a dynamic field of force charged with life. Goldsmiths and *orfèvres-bijoutiers* already subscribed to the Art Nouveau aesthetic,[2] whereas the jewellers who worked chiefly with gemstones continued to embrace the garland style. On the whole, the latter were not interested in the great variety of new Art Nouveau materials such as enamel, horn and ivory and celluloid synthetics. 'We use very little material and a great many stones', Pierre Cartier remarked to one of his customers.

The Art Nouveau artist aimed at reform, and this aesthetic stance, together with his unusual materials, was bound to ensure him public interest and, unlike the commercial jeweller, might even entitle him to limited State support. Under its president Louis Aucoc, the Chambre Syndicale de la Bijouterie, Joaillerie et Orfèvrerie, founded in 1864, and the Union Centrale des Arts Décoratifs, which was reorganized in 1872, arranged an active programme of competitions, courses and schools. In addition, there were annual exhibitions, or salons, held in the Grand Palais; all of them, practically without exception, propagated the Art Nouveau style. There were some jewellers prepared to entertain a compromise between Art Nouveau and the garland style: Vever, Aucoc and above all Boucheron attempted to combine the garland with the writhing plant forms of Art Nouveau, but they were never able to resolve the conflict between symmetry and asymmetry. Louis Cartier, on the contrary, was decidedly cool to Art Nouveau, which may help to explain why a few years later, between 1906 and 1908, the linear style of Art Deco was able to develop much more naturally and purely out of the geometrical patterns of his own garland style than it could out of the style of those artists who had been exclusively committed to Art Nouveau.

In spite of Cartier's negative attitude, a number of unequivocal examples of Art Nouveau jewelry may be attributed to him in the period shortly before 1900 when there were fruitful contacts with Art Nouveau artists, including the Belgian jeweller Philippe Wolfers (1858–1929), who supplied Cartier with small snake brooches, and Georges Le Turcq who, on the occasion of the one-thousandth performance of Gounod's *Faust* at the Paris Opéra, produced a silver-gilt bracelet depicting scenes from the opera.[3] Le Turcq was also responsible for a number of floral enamel brooches, including a Japanese azalea, an orchid and a red enamel convolvulus. Cartier's records for 1887 include an entry for a brooch by Violard depicting the most popular of all Art Nouveau insects, the dragonfly, and another entry dated 1900 mentions a pearl-studded brooch in enamel on gold depicting a girl's head, by the little-known Zorra, in the 'new style'.[4] The terms 'nouveau style' and 'art moderne' alternate in Cartier's books, in an attempt to distinguish these items from others in the radically different garland style. Most of the Art Nouveau pieces taken up by Cartier were from Charpentier's workshop, which supplied a number of floral brooches in *plique-à-jour*, or translucent enamel, between 1899 and 1901: vine leaves and ivy, thistles and cornflowers were among Charpentier's favourite plant motifs, and were popular for their lively contours. Although the customers who bought these Art Nouveau brooches were largely recruited from bourgeois circles or from the artistic avant-garde, Cartier's was able to interest the fashion-conscious Duchess of Devonshire in one of Charpentier's floral brooches, and Louis Cartier even recommended a set of enamelled Art Nouveau buttons to Prince Lieven of Russia while he was staying at the Hotel Continental.

Another type of jewelry suited to Art Nouveau forms was the hat-pin, some of which were set with pearls of up to 100 grains in weight. During the Renaissance the strangely distorted shapes of baroque pearls had given rise to amusing dwarfs, sea monsters and mythical animals. In Cartier's jewels they became spherical landscapes crawling with frogs and snakes.

Among the most important of Cartier's Art Nouveau products were two necklaces. One of them, from Louis Aucoc's workshop, consisted of a row of daisies from which hung a blue peacock pendant. The peacock motif had been popular during the reign of Napoleon III, although the earliest example in Cartier's jewels is dated 1883. After 1905 it gave its name to the colour contrast of blue and green. The second necklace, which was sold to Hungary, was made of *plique-à-jour* enamel[5] with a design of turquoise-studded fuchsias.

The quintessential Art Nouveau gemstone, the opal, which appears time and time again in the work of such artists as Gaillard and Lalique, was never of much interest to Louis Cartier. Admittedly, a delightful heart-shaped opal pendant was made for Nellie Melba in 1903, but it sounds almost like an excuse when, in a reply to a supplier in Antwerp, Louis justified his reluctance to work with opals by appealing to the superstition concerning them which, he claimed, was particularly pronounced in France.[6]

Religious themes

Restrained echoes of the Art Nouveau style appear in association with neo-Gothic motifs in the numerous religious pendants which were stocked by Louis Cartier's father, Alfred, who was a devout Catholic. In France the years between 1901 and 1906 were marked by a series of power struggles between Church and State, which led to a strict division of their respective spheres of influence. Emile Combes, the socialist minister of the interior and culture minister, threatened congregations and closed down parochial schools. The ecclesiastical opposition, however, succeeded in organizing a patriotically inspired campaign called 'La Ligue de la Patrie française' which met on the steps of barricaded churches and used popular art on religious themes for propaganda purposes. Joseph Chaumet had already caused a stir at the Paris Exposition of 1900 with his allegorical *Christus Vincit*, and four years later, at the international exhibition held in St Louis, Missouri, he showed his monumental sculpture, *Via Vitae* or 'The Way of Life', the symbolism of which embraced all the world's major religions. Cartier's range included not only patriotic themes such as Joan of Arc at the stake (1905) but silver statues of St Anthony of Padua, which numbered Jean-Philippe Worth and King Edward VII of England among their varied purchasers. The most popular line, however, was in medallions on religious themes, based on the work of the French medallion-maker Frédéric Charles Victor de Vernon (winner of the Prix de Rome in 1887), of the sort described as a 'medallion of highly elevated character with a religious sentiment directed at young girls'. Cartier ordered them from Duval in the rue du Louvre. Subjects included Christ and John the Baptist (obtainable at Cartier's from 1885), the Immaculate Conception, the Virgin among Virgins, the *Virgo Purissima*, and St Cecilia.

From the Baroque age onward, poets, painters and sculptors had used the death's-head motif as a reminder of earthly transience, the vanity of vanities. Cartier's shelves contained death's-heads made of coral, and in 1913 Baroness Henri de Rothschild ordered one in diamond to add to her already exemplary collection [106].[7]

Religious miniature art like Vernon's medallions was generally made in *plique-à-jour* enamel, which ultimately derived its mystic appeal from Gothic church windows. When in the course of the First World War the cathedral of Rheims – Jean Cocteau's 'mountain of old lace' – went up in flames, Jacques Cartier suggested buying up fragments of the cathedral's stained glass windows and resetting the angels and saints in articles of jewelry.[8]

The First World War

During the years 1914–18 a new form of patriotic jewelry emerged, based on martial motifs. The firm's leading employees, including the three Cartier brothers – Louis, Pierre and Jacques – were all at the front, so that the workshops shrank and limited themselves to producing small-scale pieces using gemstones of no great size.[9] Just as during the Franco-Prussian War of 1870 there had been a market for items of jewelry made with shrapnel and military emblems, what was now produced, against the background of the battles of the Marne and of Verdun, were pendants and pins from which were suspended aeroplanes, the Red Cross or the Cross of Lorraine, and miniature replicas of the 75-bore cannon, 'notre glorieux 75' [104, 108]. While the pendants with fragments of glass from Rheims Cathedral conveyed the impression of priceless reliquaries [107], the brass rings which were cut from shells fired by the 75-bore guns and which Cartier's sold as armlets, as their contribution to the war effort, were actual trophies of war.[10] The iron jewelry made in Berlin at the time of Prussia's resistance against Napoleon had aroused similar feelings of patriotism. Other traditional ornamental motifs which had previously been free of any martial symbolism were reinterpreted: a minor modification turned the black-and-white

107 Pendant. Cartier Paris, 1920. Platinum, set with a fragment of stained glass from a window in Rheims Cathedral, within rose-cut diamonds and topazes; on silk cord

onyx bow into an aircraft propeller, an item which remained one of Cartier's most popular lines throughout the war years. The illusion of a martial trophy jewel was perfected by Cartier's *étuis* (cases) in the form of military peaked caps, French naval berets and English soldiers' caps. Among these picturesque examples, the 'machine-gun' brooch was admired even by the British Prime Minister David Lloyd George, while the 'Lebel Bayonet' brooch was purchased by Lord Lonsdale. The somewhat eccentric Princess Murat decided in favour of a brooch depicting a Red Cross ambulance, perhaps to remind her of the widely admired Misia Sert, who with Paul Iribe at the wheel had turned delivery vans from the Paris fashion houses into ambulances.

Of all the workshops which supplied Cartier's with such intriguing examples of trophy jewelry between 1915 and 1918, the most important was that of Paul Templier (1866–1944), who at the time was President of the Chamber of Commerce. His work, which was based on drawings by Théodore Lambert, had already attracted attention at the 1901 salon by virtue of its simple linear style. His son, Raymond, was later to transfer the business from the Place des Victoires to the rue du Quatre-Septembre.

The commision which brought Cartier the greatest honour during the First World War related to General Foch. Shortly after the offensive of the 'Battle of France' in July 1918, Foch was appointed commander of the combined allied forces, and on 6 August the title of field marshal was formally conferred on him by the President of the Republic, Raymond Poincaré, and his Prime Minister, Georges Clemenceau. The ceremony was held in the château at Bompon.[11] The marshal's baton, that symbol of authority, was the work of Cartier's. From the sixteenth century onward, the baton had been made of blue velvet (over wood or silver) and was originally adorned with gold fleurs-de-lys. During the First Empire, the decoration was changed to imperial bees, which under Louis-Philippe became stars and under Napoleon III eagles. With its gold and silver-gilt ornamentation, the marshal's baton presented to Foch marked a return to the star pattern of the nineteenth century. It was surmounted by the motto *Terror Belli – Decus Pacis* ('Terror of War – Adornment of Peace'). The same design was used in November of the same year, when a second marshal's baton, again by Cartier's, was presented to Marshal Pétain in Metz. (Both batons are now in the Musée de l'Armée in Paris.)

108 Aeroplane charm. Cartier Paris, 1916. Platinum; rose-cut diamonds

109 1918 charm. Cartier Paris, made in 1917. Platinum; rose-cut diamonds

CHAPTER SIX

UNDER THE SPELL
OF FABERGÉ

110 Desk clock with strut. Cartier Paris, 1913.
Silver surround with translucent periwinkle-
blue enamel and guilloché decoration; three
white enamel fillets. Ivory plaque on the back.
Round gilt case and strut. Round white enamel
dial with Arabic numerals ringed by a minute
track with gilded dots and indices. Hands in
platinum and rose-cut diamonds. Gold bezel
with ring of white enamel beads

111 Desk clock with strut. Cartier Paris, 1914.
Silver surround with scalloped guilloché
decoration and translucent yellow enamel;
three white enamel fillets. Ivory plaque on the
back. Round gilt case and strut. Round white
enamel dial with Arabic numerals ringed by
a minute track with gilded indices and dots.
Hands in platinum and rose-cut diamonds.
Silver bezel with ring of white enamel beads

112 Cigarette case. Cartier Paris, 1907. Royal
blue enamel on a guilloché ground with three
sections continuing round both sides, each
bordered with a white enamel wavy line,
divided by two bands of green and white
enamel circles. Rosette in the centre of the top,
two lids with diamond buttons

113 Desk set. Cartier Paris, 1908. Enamel
clock and inkstand, grey base decorated with
sunray pattern and white fillets, two pen-
holders, two mauve inkwells with green laurel-
leaf dots on top and bottom, covers capped by
cabochon sapphires. In the centre, mauve cube
clock decorated with white fillets, green laurel-
leaf moulding on the bottom, figure in pink
circle above, white bezel, gold hands, white
dial, wooden base with eight silver-gilt feet

At the turn of the century European interior design was a ghost of its former self: gone was the linear order of the eighteenth century, the spare, elegant, expensive furniture carefully accenting classical proportions. Its place had been taken by a dark, inchoate decor; heavy curtains kept out the daylight, and dark furniture heightened the impression of artificial gloom. But this twilit world of shadows was brought to life and illuminated by every kind of object of *virtù*. Photograph frames, plants and animals carved in gemstones, table ornaments and small clocks shone out like brightly coloured points of light. From priceless treasures to the most garish kitsch, such objects were the latest fad in the homes of the aristocracy, the upper classes and the stars of the theatre in London, Paris and New York. The representatives of this society, be they Lady de Grey, Mrs Keppel or Leopold de Rothschild, had discovered the bibelots of Carl Fabergé and his rivals, popularized them as ideal gifts from St Petersburg, and raised them to the height of chic, acceptable to any member of their own circle, up to and including the court itself.

Around 1900 Fabergé was producing what was indisputably the most refined enamel of the day, using a process which remained a closely guarded secret within his predominantly Scandinavian workforce. Most of his enamel ornaments were made using the guilloché or engine-turned technique and designed in the Louis XVI style of the late 1780s. Those that found their way to Europe as gifts gave Parisian craftsmen the idea of reviving their own local eighteenth-century style, transmitted through a Russian intermediary.

Fabergé's great skill lay in applying five or six layers of enamel, chosen from 144 different shades of colour, to a metallic base of silver or 14-carat gold. The metal was engraved with lines and dots to produce a geometric pattern which remained visible, after firing at a temperature of 700–800 ºC, through the translucent enamel, often creating the impression of shot silk.

Cartier's Russian-inspired range contained a similar technical variety of guilloché work: frames and small clocks have a sunray pattern engraved in straight lines radiating from a central point; other items show a moiré silk or scale motif; and the Russian guilloché design might evolve into zigzags.

In 1904 Cartier's wrote to Yahr's workshop in Moscow, which produced items for the goldsmith Ovchinnikov among others, requesting Yahr to send two complete palettes of his enamel colours to the rue de la Paix. As a result Yahr began to manufacture and enamel items for Cartier's, including cigarette cases, frames, table bells, clocks and belt-buckles.[1] Although Cartier's were unable in their Paris workshops to match the variety of enamel colours of their Russian models, they succeeded instead in creating a number of new colour combinations, such as the blue-green or violet-green match which Louis Cartier himself liked. A white enamel border sometimes framed the *en plein* enamelled surface of an object. In a few instances the technique of opalescent enamelling was used for the faces of small clocks, a technique which involved variegating some of the layers as they were successively fired, until the famous iridescent surface effect of the opal was produced. The most precious product of Cartier's experimentation with the technique of guilloché enamelling was undoubtedly the Easter egg made in 1906 and later presented to Tsar Nicholas II (see p. 112) [130, 131], which was followed in 1907 by a second egg, this time in the form of a small clock with a diamond star which showed the time.

A second category of Fabergé's work to find an echo in Cartier's jewels was one which reveals the wealth of the Siberian mineral deposits: gold-mounted, enamelled objects of *virtù* were produced in nephrite, lapis lazuli, agate and serpentine, and there was not one that could not have stood comparison with the most fabulous treasures of Renaissance curiosity cabinets. The fact that these gemstone bibelots were admired in Paris and London may be explained not only by reference to the fascination which the remote Russian lands exercised on cosmopolitan Europeans. Quite apart from their aesthetic perfection, Fabergé's products were intended to be useful: a jade apple might turn out to be a glue-pot, and a garlanded Louis XVI column might conceal a barometer.

Pierre Cartier visited Russia in 1904 [129] and again in 1905, and in the course of his travels got to know the leading workshops in St Petersburg and Moscow. The lapidary Svietchnikov was among those who, as a result, began supplying Cartier's with animals

114 Wristwatch. Cartier Paris, 1909. Case in gold and translucent green enamel with guilloché decoration. Bezel with a ring of millegrain-set rose-cut diamonds in platinum. Winding crown capped with a cabochon sapphire. Lugs with four collet-set cabochon sapphires. Black moiré strap. Gold tongue buckle. Round silver dial with guilloché sunray pattern and Arabic numerals ringed by minute track. Blue steel hands

115 Cigarette case. Cartier Paris, *c.* 1908. Cushion-shaped case in guilloché yellow enamel, decorated with lines of royal blue enamel, cabochon sapphire button. Silver-gilt bar inside, engraved with the words '12 janvier 1909'

116 Propelling pencil. Cartier Paris, 1906.
Pencil in the form of a feather with pink
guilloché enamel on gold, edged with grey
enamel stripes and white beads. rose-cut
diamond push-rod

117 Measuring tape case. Cartier Paris, 1906.
Box in green and white enamel and gold
wire decorated with diamond rose motifs
on yellow gold

118 Powder box. Cartier Paris, 1906. Yellow
gold, platinum and guilloché pink enamel

119 Cigarette case. Cartier, Paris 1910. Pink-
enamelled yellow gold, edged in white enamel,
sapphire button

120 Trump marker. Cartier, 1907. Silver-gilt and enamel with pink quartz base and push-button capped with a moonstone. Stem and disc in blue enamel on a guilloché ground. Four aces in red and black enamel on a white ground

121 Perfume burner. Cartier Paris, 1907. In the form of an urn in silver-gilt and aventurine, with the central part in grey-blue guilloché enamel decorated with circles and white enamel palmettes

opposite

122 Photograph frame. Cartier Paris, 1907. The slanting mount in purple, white and green guilloché enamel over silver-gilt; rose-cut diamond corners; four motifs in enamel surrounded by enamel circles. Ivory back. Portrait of Countess Zubov in the centre made to his own designs or to Cartier's.[2] If the article contained gold and enamel, Svietchnikov had it completed by Yahr before it was sent on to the rue de la Paix. In 1904 there were no fewer than 160 commissions which the by now overworked Yahr was expected to send to Paris. His best craftsmen having enlisted in the war against Japan, he requested reinforcements from Cartier's Paris workshops, but the help never arrived.

Cartier considered Svietchnikov's animals expensive, and it is certainly true that they cost more than those of Karl Woerffel on the Obvodny Canal in St Petersburg, who was Fabergé's supplier.[3] From Woerffel's shop Pierre Cartier ordered an alabaster hen, gemstone fruit, ashtrays, jade bottles and objects of *virtù* coloured with purpurin.[4] The latter substance was a synthetic dye, crimson in colour, generally thought to have been invented by the Italian Alessio Mattioli around 1750; it was taken up again by Petuchov in the nineteenth century for use in the imperial glassworks, and by 1900 had come to be regarded as one of Fabergé's specialities.

A purpurine toad was also supplied by Ovchinnikov, whose firm had been founded in Moscow in 1853. A branch was opened in St Petersburg twenty years later, but the firm really became known in the West only when it exhibited at the 1900 Paris Exposition. As a rival of Fabergé's, Ovchinnikov's business specialized in cloisonné enamelling in the Russo-Byzantine style. Cartier's first orders also included an obsidian elephant and a dog's-head umbrella handle made of jade. The prices of Ovchinnikov's menagerie varied from Fr. 45 ($11) for the elephant to Fr. 265 ($66) for the purpurine toad. Size, type of engraving and stone quality were the decisive factors, though purpurine was treated as substantially more expensive than the different types of natural stone.

The taste of Russian suppliers did not always meet with approval in the rue de la Paix: when a rhodonite desk set arrived from the firm of Denisov-Uralski, which had already supplied Cartier with miniature animals and other objects of *virtù*, exception was taken to the hideous silver mounting. Sarda, Cartier's contact in St Petersburg, approached Denisov on the matter and reported back to Cartier that Denisov had finally removed his 'scrap metal', which he considered to be elegant, artistic and indispensable. Only the inkwell survived what Denisov called the 'massacre'.

In 1910 Cartier bought two animals direct from Fabergé, a little pig made of pink jade and a cornelian fox. But it is safe to assume that many of the animals nowadays attributed to Fabergé were produced in one or other of the French or Russian workshops which supplied Cartier's needs. In view of their stylistic similarity and the absence of any signature, it is often only the signed and individually lined cases which give any information about the firm which sold them. At all events, a number of animals are found only in Cartier's range, including an ostrich emerging from an egg, and a group of three chickens.

In the meantime, French workshops such as those of Varangoz, Fréville and Césard, and the Taillerie de Royat had familiarized themselves remarkably quickly with the popular Russian style, and were soon providing the greater part of Cartier's stock. Suppliers also included the Japanese dealer Yamanaka, who specialized in ivories and bronze animals in the style of *netsukes*, similar to ones which had already served as models in Russia.[5]

The most popular miniature animals in Cartier's menagerie were the ibis, owl, stork, elephant and piglet. Not until 1907, the year in which Fabergé made models of all the animal species at Sandringham as a present for Edward VII, did Louis Cartier begin to fear that the market was being flooded and turn his attention to launching different types of gemstone fruit.[6] Animals had been of little practical use, except as umbrella handles or hand bells, whereas fruit could serve as desk fittings, inkwells or water jugs.

One of Fabergé's specialities which fell on fertile ground and remained popular for many years in Paris, surviving even the passing mania for all things Russian aroused by the Ballets Russes, was his vases of flowers [123]. As late as 1916 *Vogue* wrote of 'Cartier's dainty hothouses in which fairy-tale trees with gold and silver trunks sprout leaves of jade. On a coral branch a bird begins to sing, just like something out of *Schéhérazade*.'[7] Unlike Fabergé's flowers, those that Cartier sold were typically housed in glass cases with an ivory base, the corners of the glass being both protected and decorated by golden stepped motifs. These architectonic shrines allowed the flowers to be arranged inside in stylized groupings. One cannot fail to see here the influence of the traditional Japanese art of flower arrangement, *ikebana*, which inspired the design of a number of Cartier's arrangements of individual sprays of cherry blossom and lilies. Also indebted to Japanese models was the picturesque association of plants and birds, together with the motif of individual blossoms detached from the plant and lying on the ground. This last motif underlined the melancholy charm of transitoriness, just as cabochon moonstones on jade leaves could give the illusion of fresh dew. The propinquity of plant and insect – a grasshopper, for example, or sometimes even a pygmy tortoise – widened the visual range of the floral image, turning it into a still-life.

Cartier's flower vases surpassed those of Fabergé in the number of materials used: carved in agate, lapis lazuli or crystal and decorated with coloured cabochons, their colour was chosen to match the individual flower. New models included flowerpots of jasper or rose quartz for geraniums and cyclamens, some almost as big as buckets, their handles framing the flowers in a geometrical design. A particularly elaborate hollyhock raised its strong stalks out of two pots, its delicate rhodonite blooms intertwining above them like an arbour. Vases and urns made of gemstones alone, and copied by the firm's resident designers from eighteenth- and nineteenth-century models in the Louvre, predate the floral vases in Cartier's output.

Cartier's flowers differed substantially from Fabergé's and included the magnolia, iris, hyacinth, hydrangea, tulip and lily. They could be monumentally large, unlike Fabergé's more delicate, naturalistic flora.[8] Cartier's basic type remained unchanged over the years, except that during the 1920s the principles of Art Deco required a stylized treatment of leaves and blossoms. In 1907 the firm's archives recorded thirty-seven plants, which soon found admirers throughout the world, including J. P. Morgan in New York, Lady de Grey in England, and King Alfonso XIII of Spain. Among the most expensive plants were the Japanese magnolia, which then cost Fr. 1,500 ($300), and orchids, which sold at up to Fr. 2,000 ($400) each. The prices charged during the same period by Fabergé in London ranged from 10 guineas ($50) for pansies to 117 guineas ($585) for a chrysanthemum.

The workshop to which Alfred Cartier entrusted the task of producing these flowers and other gemstone objects was that of Berquin-Varangoz's widow at Saint-Siméon in the *département* of Seine-et-Marne. The firm had been awarded a gold medal in 1904 at the St Louis Exhibition. It was taken over in 1918 by Aristide Fourrier (1875–1941) and subsequently bore his name. Fourrier employed between twenty-five and thirty craftsmen, who were joined in 1922 by his son Roland (1906–83). Although no Russian craftsmen were employed, the firm remained conscious that it was producing a Russian speciality, and to the end of his life Fourrier continued to refer to Fabergé as his mentor.[9] From time to time he undertook journeys to Idar-Oberstein in Germany and to London in order to buy minerals and ivory, as well as the specifically 'Russian materials': lapis lazuli, jade and rhodonite. These served not only for plants but, to a far greater extent, for animals [126, 127], ashtrays, frames and bowls, in addition to the complicated cases of the 'mystery clocks' (see pp. 276–91). One of the most highly respected of Fourrier's craftsmen was the engraver Hubert, who brought to life the birds and flowers which he embellished. On one occasion a cornflower with a wheat-ear motif, bought direct from Fabergé's, served as a model for Fourrier, but as a general rule the latter would make a copper model based on a preliminary sketch provided by Cartier's, who would then forward their approval of the model from the rue de la Paix.[10] In the final product the metal base was made of silver, and enamel in every available colour was fired onto it. Transparent or opaque glass (opaline) produced umbels and blossoms of

123 'Hydrangea' table ornament. Cartier Paris, 1910. Gold, agate, aventurine quartz, moonstone, paste, rose-cut diamonds, ivory, glass, wood

shimmering translucency. Snowdrops were made of chalcedony, chrysanthemums of jade and later of enamel. Leaves were carved from jade or aventurine quartz, the latter used to imitate the rough surface of a geranium leaf.

Whenever enamelled gemstone objects needed additional work, Cartier turned to the workshop of Henri Lavabre in the rue Tiquetonne, where between fifteen and twenty expert craftsmen were employed for up to twelve hours a day. Detailed commissions were carried out in smaller workshops in the Marais, tiny concerns which generally passed from father to son. Lavabre's workshop, in the rue du Quatre-Septembre like Picq's, was Cartier's preferred supplier, although internal problems meant that Lavabre's collaboration with Cartier's failed to survive the crisis of the 1930s.[11]

Berquin-Varangoz and, at a later date, Fourrier also experimented with carved figural pieces. Although the realism of Fabergé's gemstone figurines of peasants, coachmen and sweeps found no imitators in France,[12] Fourrier manufactured agate portrait busts of Roman emperors, including Caesar, Vitellius and Vespasian, based on originals in the Louvre. Buddhas were made of jade, rose quartz and turquoise, and remained popular until the late 1920s. Buddha-like was the comical Billiken, the 'god of things as they ought to be', invented in America in the early years of the century. The figure was made of chalcedony, nephrite or agate and, looking like some Disney creation *avant la lettre*, it sat enthroned on ashtrays, table bells or mystery clocks [**348**].[13] Queen Alexandra was pleased with her Cartier Billiken, and Maxim Gorki presented one to H. G. Wells on the occasion of the latter's visit to Russia.

It was at first by no means certain that all these articles in the Russian style would find favour in Paris and London. At the 1900 Paris Exposition, for example, Fabergé's basket of lilies-of-the-valley, made in 1896, had been criticized for being 'a colour photograph taken from nature'. But the Russian millionaires who had settled in Menton, Nice and Paris and who patronized Cartier's, including Grand Duchess Xenia, Grand Duke Paul and Princess Vera Lobanov-Rostovsky, expected to find the same items on sale in the rue de la Paix as in their native St Petersburg. They repeatedly suggested to Louis Cartier that he should settle in St Petersburg. For a time he considered serving from Paris as the European representative of the imperial stone-polishing factories in Ekaterinburg, as well as the polishing shops in Peterhof, but the project never materialized, any more than did plans for a Cartier agency in Berlin. A year before taking the plunge in America in 1909, however, Cartier finally gave in to the insistent pleas of Grand Duchess Vladimir and established himself in St Petersburg.

opposite

124 Lorgnette. Cartier Paris, 1906. Guilloché gold, platinum, rose-cut diamonds, blue and white enamel

125 Cane knob. Cartier Paris, 1902. Grey-blue enamel, rosette head, roses appliqué on a grey-blue enamel ground, one brilliant-cut diamond in the centre, surround in pink-tinted white enamel, polished pink gold ground, top of roses separated by brilliant green enamel foliage on a pale yellow gold ground, bottom of roses set in platinum, edges in white enamel

above

126 Bulldog, 1912. Dog in two shades of agate. Gold collar with baroque pearl drop, olivine eyes set in gold

127 Bulldog, 1907. Smoked quartz, gold and diamonds

Marie

Souvenir du Belgi...
H. Petersbourg 1900

CHAPTER SEVEN

IN ST PETERSBURG

preceding pages, left

128 Signed portrait of Maria Pavlovna, Grand Duchess Vladimir, wearing her diamond and pearl kokoshnik

preceding pages, right

129 Pierre Cartier in a horse-drawn sleigh on his first visit to Russia in 1904

It was on 2 December 1908 that Louis Cartier's assistant, Paul Cheyrouze, together with his aide Desbaines, climbed aboard the Express du Nord in Paris for the start of a three-day journey that was to take them via Berlin to the imperial city of St Petersburg. Their fellow travellers included Prince Orlov, Count Benckendorff and – a portentous confrontation – Carl Fabergé. We no longer know what had brought Fabergé to Paris, but since his triumphs at the Paris Exposition eight years earlier, he had not allowed the French capital to slip far from his mind. On that occasion the brothers Louis and Pierre Cartier had been confronted in the Esplanade des Invalides by the fairy-tale spectacle of fifteen imperial Easter eggs, dating from 1884 onwards and devised as presents from Alexander III and Nicholas II to the Tsarina and the Dowager Empress Maria Feodorovna. It was the first time these had been exhibited in the West, and alongside them could be seen reduced replicas of the Russian coronation insignia. Admittedly, a French critic had reproached Fabergé's eggs for their lack of 'any clearly defined practical utility'; yet they were proof of the debt that Russian goldsmiths owed their eighteenth-century French counterparts. After all, Fabergé's ancestors themselves had been driven from France following the revocation of the Edict of Nantes in 1689.

Russia had never ceased to be profoundly indebted to French artistic influences, influences that in the mid-nineteenth century ran parallel to efforts aimed at revitalizing Russian art from the wellspring of its Byzantine origins. By the same token – and not only for political reasons – France was making every effort to show the greatest possible appreciation of all things Russian, especially art. On the occasion of the 1867 Paris Exposition, Napoleon III had offered a particularly ceremonial welcome to Alexander II and two of his sons, Grand Duke Alexander and Grand Duke Vladimir, and at the 1878 Paris Exposition the Russian exhibitors had been singled out for special honours: the goldsmiths Ovchinnikov and Sazikov were each awarded a gold medal, and Khlebnikov a silver one. In addition, after the assassination of Alexander II in Moscow in 1881, many rich Russian émigrés had settled in France, making it their second home.

Cartier's earliest dealings with a Russian customer date back to 1860, when Prince Saltykov visited the boulevard des Italiens and chose an emerald bracelet in a black enamelled gold setting. Cartier's jewels soon found their way to Russia, where they were much admired, and the firm's reputation for excellence spread quickly to the Russian imperial court. According to the accounts of Grand Duchess Olga, daughter of Alexander III, the fairy-tale atmosphere that descended upon the palace at Gatchina[1] before each Christmas owed its special charm to the jewels that Cartier used to send. In 1888, when Olga was a mere six years old, her older sister,

> Grand Duchess Xenia, a great favourite with her mother [the Empress Maria Feodorovna], happened to be in the Empress's rooms when two ladies-in-waiting were unpacking cases of jewelry and bibelots sent by Cartier from Paris. Xenia, aged thirteen, had not yet decided what she would give her mother. But suddenly she saw a filigree scent bottle, its stopper studded with sapphires. She snatched at it and begged Countess Stroganov not to give her secret away. That scent bottle must have cost a small fortune and Xenia duly presented it to her mother on Christmas Day. A little later the Empress made it known that boxes arriving from Cartier and other jewellers could be admired by the children and no more.[2]

At a later date Russian aristocrats regularly sought out Cartier's salons each time they were in Paris, spreading the fashion for 'Russian' bibelots from their native St Petersburg and, in return, taking back to Russia jewels from Cartier's which were more elegantly worked than anything they could have obtained at home from Fabergé or Bolin.

In 1899 it was Grand Duke Alexis, First Lord Admiral of the Russian fleet, who came to Paris from St Petersburg to buy jewels from Cartier's. He was followed in 1900 by Grand Duchess Vladimir (see below) and in 1901 by Countess Sherbatov and Grand Duke Paul, who ordered first a pair of opera-glasses with a Wedgwood design and then a necklace with nine drop diamonds and a meander tiara.[3] Louis Cartier later recalled an episode in connection with the Grand Duke which offers a delightfully atmospheric picture of the salons in the rue de la Paix:

The Grand Duke and his wife, the Countess of Hohenfelsen [**61**], were sitting in my office, having ordered a magnificent sapphire tiara for their daughter, the Grand Duchess Maria. To my amazement, the Grand Duke, who was sitting close to the half-open glass door, suddenly called out the name 'Arthur' to somebody. A dignified-looking Englishman turned round in surprise at hearing his name called. It was the Duke of Connaught, brother of Edward VII. The two princes shook hands, delighted at their unexpected meeting.

Another welcome visitor to the rue de la Paix was Princess Vera Lobanov Rostovsky (née Princess Dolgorouky). Her first, somewhat hesitant, purchase was a delightful pansy brooch in amethyst and diamonds, followed by three boa pins. She had married Prince Ivan Lobanov Rostovsky when she was sixteen, but early widowhood had persuaded her to exchange her 'little Hermitage' in Moscow for the Hôtel du Ranelagh in Paris, where her circle of intimate friends included Princess Yurievsky, the widow of Alexander II, and her sister, Countess Georges Berg. Every spring, this miniature princely household would leave Paris and take up residence in a villa in Menton, or else in the Villa Zina at Vevey.

In 1906 Grand Duchess Xenia made her first visit to Cartier's.[4] She had received a number of magnificent jewels in 1894 on the occasion of her marriage to Alexander Mikhailovich, and her black pearls, which she was later able to rescue from Russia in the wake of the Revolution, caused a not inconsiderable stir in the rue de la Paix. In France, both she and her mother, the widowed Empress Maria Feodorovna, stayed in the Villa Espoir in what since the Empress Eugénie's days had been the fashionable resort of Biarritz; from Cartier's she bought a nephrite frame and a *boîte de jeux*. It was on 22 April 1907 that the Empress finally entered Cartier's establishment in the rue de la Paix. Together with her ladies-in-waiting, she had travelled to Paris from Biarritz where she was spending the spring.[5] Admittedly, she bought only small presents – two tie pins and two hardstone rabbits; but Louis Cartier, who had heard of the Empress's passion for jewelry and of her legendary pearls which, with their ten strands, reached down to her waist, placed before her one case after another containing the most luxurious and costly jewels the firm could produce.

As the Empress expressed a wish to be able to buy such jewels in St Petersburg, she was delighted to discover from Louis Cartier that a first exhibition was already being planned for that same year in the Grand Hôtel d'Europe. Cartier's interests in Russia at that time were represented, with justifiable pride, by Désiré Sarda, who, though not a jeweller, was a very shrewd businessman. Sarda knew that a single expedition would not be sufficient for Cartier's to gain a foothold in St Petersburg: 'The Russians do not like changing their supplier.' It was this insight that persuaded Cartier's to send out 562 individual letters of introduction and invitations. Their method of delivery, recorded in the Cartier archives, is worth quoting: 'Cartier's card, with its polite invitation, to be handed in at the house by a clean and intelligent boy. He shall hand it to the doorman and at the same time conceal all his other cards, so as to give the impression that he has come for that purpose alone.' Then, as an entertaining postscript, 'Doormen are very naive. They never fail to pass on the invitation to the maid.' On hearing of these, the firm's Russian rivals did not remain idle for long, and set about spreading rumours of Cartier's fabulous prices.

Sarda travelled to Paris in March 1908 to discuss the forthcoming Christmas season, and it was to prepare for this that first Pierre Cartier and then Paul Cheyrouze went to St Petersburg in December. Upon their arrival, Cheyrouze and his assistant put up at the Grand Hôtel d'Europe, with its famous view of the Neva, and then turned their attention to arranging suitable premises at 28 Quai de la Cour. The astute Grand Duchess Vladimir had first suggested that they should rent premises in another of her buildings, but Sarda preferred the Quai de la Cour, which the Grand Duchess leased to him at 900 roubles for a two-month period. The building was fitted up with feverish haste; throughout the conversion, the Cartier staff led a spartan life, after the example of Alexander II, sleeping on camp beds and wrapped in travelling rugs. The work was completed on 9 December and the name of Cartier was emblazoned in elegant black letters on the front of the building, whose five windows overlooked the quayside. 'I received your letter just as I was on the point of going to Fabergé's. For the time being I'll buy only a trifle [Fr. 400], but I'll recommend you to my friends and I'll certainly be back.' These were the words spoken by Cartier's first customer, the director of the Northern Bank, Westrach. The delivery by hand of 562 invitations had borne its first fruit!

'I was just on the point of going to Fabergé's . . . ': Cartier's could have had no greater satisfaction during these first few days than to be compared to their great rival. The elimination of their competitors became the guiding motive behind all their activities in St Petersburg, so that by the time they left in 1914 they could proudly observe: 'As is fitting, we are now the leading firm in St Petersburg.' Of course, St Petersburg was bound to strike its foreign visitors as provincial, and competition in such a town was not particularly strong, with the exception of Bolin and, naturally, Carl Fabergé. From his magnificent granite-columned premises on the Morskaya, Fabergé had for years concentrated on *objets d'art* rather than jewelry and, besides, made few changes to his models, all of which adhered to a traditional style. Although his enamel colours revealed the most subtle variations in all Russia, the forms he preferred remained restricted to the same basic types, so that a not entirely implausible story began to circulate, to the effect that five regimental officers were dismayed to discover that they were all wearing the same Fabergé buttons!

In the selection of items that Cartier put on display in St Petersburg he took into account both the experience he had gained during a previous journey and the most recent Paris fashions: diamond-studded platinum brooches so delicately worked as to imitate lace; necklaces on black velvet backing; breast ornaments in Renaissance designs; a meander tiara, and a tiara of five interlaced loops; a ruby necklace with diamonds from the French crown jewels;[6] and thirty-five watches and clocks in platinum, enamel and precious stones. One of these clocks was designed in the shape of an Easter egg, as a concession to Russian taste; and fifteen fobs in the shape of eggs were designed with Russian customers in mind.

News of the opening of a branch of Cartier's spread with great speed: among those who appeared in person were Countess Sergei Zubov [122], Countess Bobrinsky, Princess Shakhovskoy and Grand Duke Michael Mikhailovich.[7] In December Cheyrouze travelled to Gatchina, where the Dowager Empress Maria Feodorovna had lived since the death of her husband in 1894; she bought a pair of cufflinks and a belt-buckle in guilloché enamel similar to those which Fabergé had brought into fashion. In addition, she had recently received two jewel-filled caskets from Cartier's in Paris, one of which contained purchases made by her daughter, Grand Duchess Xenia. The Empress was clearly impressed by Cartier's range, for, on her recommendation, an audience with the Tsar, Nicholas II, followed at Tsarskoe Selo. On the frosty morning of 21 December, Paul Cheyrouze was greeted at the station by Prince Putyatin and accompanied to the Alexander Palace, where the imperial family had resided since 1895. He was given no time to admire the palace, but taken at once to the billiard room, where he laid out his jewels for the Tsar and Tsarina to examine. They were engrossed in grave discourse, and it must initially have appeared that Cheyrouze's visit had come at a particularly inopportune moment; but the imperial couple chose a brooch, excusing themselves from further purchases by pointing out that they must first consider their own local jewellers. It was no secret that The Tsarina Alexandra had less time for jewelry than her mother-in-law, the Dowager Empress Maria Feodorovna.[8] Admittedly, she wore her pearls most gracefully, and was fond of light blue sapphires and turquoises, but opulent jewelry did not suit her reserved character, a fact not well understood in Russia. Yet even so trifling a transaction as this, which was of little more than symbolic value, was a significant event for Cartier's. The news was immediately reported back to Paris, as was the conjecture that it would not be long before Cartier's were appointed official suppliers to the imperial court.

On the banks of the Neva, meanwhile, the approach of Christmas could be keenly felt. Paul Muffat, one of Cartier's assistants from Paris, had arrived, and the three employees often worked until two in the morning, while a young Russian kept guard over the safe. Shortly before the holiday period began, Countess Cheremetiev ordered for her niece a pearl choker, each pearl weighing 13½ grains, and for herself a crescent-shaped hair ornament costing 2,000 roubles (Fr. 5,280). Count Moy ordered a diamond tiara of heart-shaped openwork scrolls, for which he supplied his own gemstones. All the orders were sent off to Paris by letter, for there were as yet no telephone links between Russia and France. The items which were ordered from the Paris workshops for a specific date were often awaited with considerable anxiety. Parcels were initially sent by diplomatic courier, and later carried by express train, a journey that took six days. Among the items which made this journey was a tiara for Countess Stolypin, wife of the Prime Minister. The Louis-XVI style tiara with its intertwining garlands of blossom had been ordered for the New Year's Day reception, which was due to take place in the Winter Palace two weeks later. The keenly awaited jewel did not arrive in time and Cheyrouze was forced to come to the rescue of the irate Countess by lending her an item from his stock, which proved no less delightful to look at than the one of her choice.

In spite of their industry, the firm ended the Christmas season with a deficit: total takings had amounted to 29,534 roubles (Fr. 77,970), with expenses of Fr. 94,871. Many deals could not be properly completed during the brief period when the shop was open, so Sarda once again recommended that Alfred Cartier and his three sons establish themselves on a permanent footing in the city, citing as an example the way in which Georges Delavigne acted as Boucheron's representative in Moscow.[9] Alfred Cartier, however, refused to give in even to the entreaties of his sons Louis and Pierre. He was in the process of opening the New York headquarters, and there was not enough staff for yet another branch. He suggested instead that in future there should be two Russian expeditions each year, and during the rest of the year Sarda should be on the spot to maintain the firm's interests.

One of Cartier's most important customers was Maria Pavlovna, Grand Duchess Vladimir [128]. She had been born in 1854 as Princess Marie of Mecklenburg-Schwerin and had married Grand Duke Vladimir, one of Alexander II's sons. On the death of her husband in 1908, she had found herself in possession of an annual pension of one million francs, plus all the allowances to which the Grand Duke had been entitled as commander-in-chief of the army. It was a sum that allowed the Grand Duchess to lead an imperial lifestyle and to assemble a casket of unique jewels.[10] Her decisions, however, often sprang from a momentary whim, and in her role as patron of the arts Maria Pavlovna was feared by many, including Diaghilev, who, after the Grand Duke's death, found himself abruptly deprived of the support previously granted him. The summer days spent on her Orientally magnificent estate at Ropsha near Peterhof passed more cheerfully than those spent at the imperial palace of Gatchina, for which the Grand Duchess rarely had a good word. And on long winter evenings, the rooms of her brown palace in St Petersburg were lit by the glow of thousands of candles, and the most sophisticated members of St Petersburg society amused themselves dancing a quadrille or polonaise. The Christmas bazaar, which she used to organize with great acumen, formed the official start of the St Petersburg winter season.

In the year of her husband's death, the items that the Grand Duchess ordered from Cartier's included a tiara made of rubies, which included the 'Beauharnais' ruby;[11] in 1909 Cartier's made her a sapphire kokoshnik with a 137-carat sapphire at its centre [85]. Sapphires, even cut *en cabochon*, had recently been a source of some distress to her: when her brother-in-law, Grand Duke Alexis, died in 1908, the cabochon sapphire tiara which she coveted had gone instead to the wife of Grand Duke Paul, Countess Hohenfelsen. Her annoyance had been great; but a tiara from Cartier's was soon to help her over her loss. Quite by chance, Cartier's had a similar piece in stock in the rue de la Paix, and its five large diamonds were easily replaced by five cabochon sapphires. There were reservations about sending such an expensive item on the long journey to Russia, so photographs and a copper model were sent on ahead. But then, in spring 1909, Louis Cartier himself travelled to St Petersburg, and at ten o'clock on the evening of 17 March he received a visit from the Grand Duchess, accompanied by three of her children, Helen, Boris and Andrei. Maria Pavlovna was enchanted with her cabochon sapphire tiara. Not only the Grand Duchess herself but the whole of her family delighted in Louis Cartier's company, for he knew how to charm and entertain them with reports of the cosmopolitan life of distant Paris, a city of which the Grand Duchess's children had only dreamt. An invitation followed to the home of Grand Duke Andrei, who was on intimate terms with the dancer Matilda Khessinska and whose friendship with Louis Cartier was to last for many years.

Grand Duke Michael died shortly before Christmas 1909. The whole of St Petersburg was plunged into mourning and, in accordance with court protocol, the Christmas balls were called off, a great loss to all the luxury trades, including Cartier's.

130, 131 Easter egg. Cartier Paris, 1906, presented by the City Council of Paris to Tsar Nicholas II in 1912. Egg in purple and white guilloché enamel over gold, decorated with Nicholas II's monogram and a pearl and diamond crown; fluorite cushion; enamelled base. Within the egg, a photograph of the Tsarevich

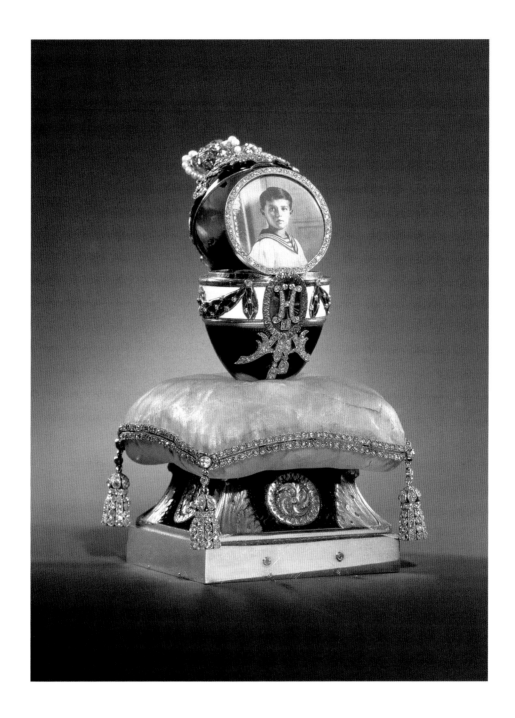

Notwithstanding, Grand Duchess Vladimir could be relied upon to complement her sapphire tiara with a sizable breast ornament sporting a 162-carat sapphire at its centre. Among the highlights of the curtailed winter season was a visit from twenty-five débutantes, who called on Cartier at the suggestion of the Tsarina. Accompanied by maids of honour, they marvelled demurely at the glittering displays of jewels, prevailing upon Cheyrouze to explain to them the unique qualities of each individual piece.

The spring season of 1910 brought few surprises. Grand Duchess Vladimir continued to remain loyal to Cartier's, and in the presence of her sister-in-law, the Duchess of Saxe-Coburg-Gotha, went into raptures over a four-leaf-clover brooch which Louis Cartier had had made for her. He was increasingly conscious of the influence which his powerful patron exercised on St Petersburg society. Countess Cheremetiev, for example, specifically mentioned the Grand Duchess's sapphire tiara when ordering a diamond tiara for herself shortly before the following Christmas, though she asked that it should not be in the same rigid kokoshnik form.

Louis Cartier at that time was having to contend with severe difficulties which threatened to endanger the whole of the 1910 Christmas season: his rivals in St Petersburg, jealous at the growing influence of the French firm, had prevailed upon the customs authorities to impound the goods that Cartier was importing; in that way they hoped to be able to prevent any further sales exhibitions.[12] Forty-four watches and important items of jewelry, without which the exhibition could not open, lay in a bonded warehouse, while Louis Cartier wrote desperate letters to the Ministry of the Interior, requesting an audience. What was the crime of which he stood accused? Gold imported into Russia was taxed at Fr. 343 a kilo, whereas platinum was duty-free, not yet having been recognized as a precious metal. An insignificantly small quantity of the items that Louis Cartier had brought with him were made of yellow gold and had inadvertently not been declared. Thanks to the help of a certain Raffalovich at the Ministry of the Interior and also to the fact that Cartier's had in the meantime been appointed official suppliers to the imperial court, the jewels were released in time to be exhibited at the Grand Duchess's Christmas bazaar, which soon had the whole of St Petersburg talking.

In 1908 Cartier had regarded the bazaar as a serious disruption to business, whereas now, in 1910, the opportunity to participate himself was most welcome. The chance had arisen as a result of an invitation to tea with Count Benckendorff. Dressed in a silk jacket and Russian orders, Cartier had been driven by sleigh to the Benckendorff Palace, where Grand Duchess Vladimir and twenty ladies-in-waiting were gathered. 'The Grand Duchess', Cartier later recalled,

> escorted me into the vast salon where I remained alone with her, feeling somewhat intimidated, while her attendants waited respectfully in the antechamber. I asked her if I might be allowed to take part in a charity sale at the bazaar organized by the Society of Nobles, of which she was president. With her usual generosity she at once agreed and allocated to me two sales assistants from the court, Princess Demidov and Princess Beloselski. In addition, I was encouraged to seek out Mademoiselle Lalive, one of her ladies-in-waiting, and secure for myself the best position.
>
> The next morning I met Mademoiselle Lalive in the palace where the bazaar was to take place. From the stairs I gazed down into the cathedral-like interior and at the vast horseshoe-shaped sales counter over which presided the Grand Duchess together with the flower of St Petersburg's aristocracy. To the right of Maria Pavlovna sat the Duchess of Leuchtenberg. 'Guess whose necklace she's wearing,' the Grand Duchess asked me. It was, would you believe it, the one which Napoleon had given the Empress Josephine. I sat down at a table with Princess Demidov and Princess Beloselski, where we received a visit from the Empress Maria Feodorovna, Grand Duke Mikhail Mikhailovich and many other grand dukes whom I never saw in Paris. In particular I recall Prince Gabriel. Throughout the proceedings the guards' band played plaintive music which filled the vast halls and seemed to rise up out of the depths of history. An old peasant-woman wearing a kokoshnik descended the flight of stairs slowly and solemnly before approaching the Grand Duchess's table, bowing low and kissing her hand. The crowd of onlookers surged every-

where: freedom and order prevailed. At the end we were able to present the Grand Duchess with a sum of between 23,000 and 26,000 roubles, which was distributed among the poor people of St Petersburg.[13]

Although Louis Cartier does not mention them, Grand Dukes Cyril, Andrei, Boris and Dimitri, Counts Fersen, Orlov and Baryatinski, Countesses Shuvalov and Kleinmichel, Dr Emanuel Nobel,[14] and Teliakovsky, the director of the Imperial Theatre, were also present, crowding the stage of a spectacular show which the Grand Duchess had mounted with theatrical brilliance. Reflecting the social importance of the event, Cartier's range contained his choicest items, comprising ninety brooches, nineteen necklaces, including one in Arabian style, thirteen tiaras, including a kokoshnik with seven drop diamonds and a winged tiara, and sixty-nine timepieces of varying sizes, of which twenty-seven were wristwatches.

The turnover since December had amounted to Fr. 1.5 million, an astonishing sum in view of the fact that, in Cartier's experience, the Russians were far more inclined to spend their money abroad, where they could make a great show of it, than at home. 'Outside his own country, the Russian is indecisive and shy. Within three months he may easily spend seven-eighths of his wealth. In Russia, on the other hand, he is distrustful, and only on his third visit does he buy anything' – so runs one of the business reports sent back to the rue de la Paix.

The bazaar had scarcely closed when Louis Cartier set off for Kiev and Moscow, in the company of his designer Charles Jacqueau [145] and sales assistant Farinès. They received prospective customers in Moscow's National Hotel and visited the great art-collector Ivan Morozov. This was the first contact Louis Cartier had had with a collector and patron of the arts who was not a member of St Petersburg's old aristocracy. Morozov had acquired his wealth through industry, and, through his informed purchasing of works by Bonnard, Vuillard, Matisse and Gauguin, he had a noticeable influence on Russian art in the years leading up to the First World War.

Charles Jacqueau, whose talent for drawing had been recognized at an early age by Louis Cartier, was sent to Russia not only to set down on paper the orders placed by important customers, but to take back to Paris fresh creative impulses absorbed from the Orientalism of the imperial capital, from its theatres and from Fabergé's displays. Cartier and Jacqueau visited the Hermitage together countless times, marvelling at harnesses of emeralds and diamonds, priceless enamel clocks from the eighteenth century, and, of course, at Fabergé's eggs, photographs of which Cartier was to take back with him to Paris. Jacqueau also returned home with the memory of a historic collector's piece which Count von Benckendorff had shown him in St Petersburg:

> Following tea with the Grand Duchess, he insisted on showing me a curiosity of great interest, and so we betook ourselves to the home of Prince Lvov, who was later to play an important role in the Kerenski administration. The Prince opened a locked casket and removed from it a large cuirassier's helmet made entirely of gold. It had belonged to King Murat [Joachim Murat, one of Napoleon's generals, who became king of Naples], who had worn it in all his battles, in Smolensk as well as on the Moskva; it is mentioned by General Marbot in his memoirs.

Cartier was soon able to report a new victory over Fabergé: Madame Andreyev ordered a tiara from him, in preference to a design that Fabergé had already produced, which Louis Cartier took back with him to Paris for costing. In spite of his pressing commitments, he found time to congratulate his brother Pierre on the sale of the 'Hope' diamond (pp. 317–18) and – his sense of the need for publicity already being fully developed – to place an announcement of the sale in the international press. 'It is a marvellous advertisement for Cartier's', he said.

It was during the busy Easter exhibition of 1911 that Cartier's received the dreadful news that Boucheron's Moscow representative Georges Delavigne and his son Henri had been murdered on their way back from Baku in the Caucasus, carrying diamonds to the value of 600,000 roubles. Five months later came the death of Prime Minister Stolypin, one of Cartier's faithful customers, who was shot by an assassin following a performance in the

Kiev Theatre, at which Tsar Nicholas II had also been present. A pre-revolutionary, panic-stricken mood gripped the country.

In St Petersburg the approaching Christmas season brought with it the first requests for jewelry made of diamonds and onyx. Grand Duke Andrei bought an onyx bow brooch, as did Grand Duchess Vladimir. She gave it as a present to the Tsarina, and for herself chose simply a lorgnette.[15] On Christmas Day her eldest son, Grand Duke Cyril, bought for his wife Victoria Melita a sapphire necklace from which was suspended an oval star sapphire weighing 311 carats; in its severity of line it reflected craftsmanship at its best in the Empire style.[16]

For Easter 1912 Cartier's produced brooches with arrowhead motifs in onyx, emerald, sapphire and amethyst, one of which was chosen by Princess Zenaida Yusupov. While tortoiseshell combs inlaid with diamonds proved very popular as presents, aigrettes now made their first appearance alongside tiaras, though they had been a traditional element in Russian dress for several decades. Countess Uvarov bought an aigrette in the form of a Chinese gong with diamonds and a calibré-cut ruby border [101]. The most remarkable gem in stock was a blue diamond weighing 11.59 carats, set as a pendant. The rarest, the 'Reine des perles', was presented to the imperial family.

The most significant purchase, however, which brought Cartier into closer contact with the imperial court, was the Easter egg for Tsar Nicholas II [130, 131]. On this occasion, the gift was not from an individual but from the City of Paris. It was intended to have symbolic value and to strengthen the diplomatic ties between the two countries, which were unusually close on the eve of the Great War. Attempts had been made over a number of years to further both countries' interests by means of exhibitions and reciprocal official visits at the highest governmental level. When celebrations were held in 1903 to mark the two-hundredth anniversary of the foundation of St Petersburg, members of the Paris City Council travelled to Russia for the occasion, bringing with them the good wishes of the people of Paris. In 1911 it was the turn of Russia, and the mayor of St Petersburg, Gutchkov, and Alderman Putchkov were given a jubilant reception in Paris, where a gala performance of Wagner's *Valkyrie* was held at the Opéra, specially decorated for the event. The Paris City Council was officially invited to pay a return visit, and the President, Félix Roussel, duly arrived in Moscow on 9 February 1912. Before he left Paris, the Council had turned to Cartier's in their search for a suitable gift. In 1906 the craftsmen of the rue de la Paix had been sufficiently impressed by Fabergé's Easter eggs to produce a similar egg, which Louis Cartier had taken with him as a showpiece to Russia in 1910. The Council was attracted by the idea of honouring the Tsar with a present which, uniquely, symbolized not France but the host country. The presentation took place at Tsarskoe Selo, where the Tsar admired the purple and white enamelled egg which bore both his monogram and a mitre crown of pearls and diamonds, and which opened up to reveal a circular photograph of the Tsarevich.[17]

At least as far as foreign visitors were concerned, the pomp and ceremony of the events which were held in 1913 to mark the three-hundredth anniversary of the Romanovs' rule seemed calculated to drive away the dark storm clouds that were already gathering on the horizon. In spite of the political uncertainty of the times, Cartier's traditional customers remained loyal: Princess Yusupov still preferred to buy her presents at Cartier's, and was particularly taken by some charms bearing a lucky star and the inscription in English, 'I love you'. Another member of her family, Count Elston, bought an emerald and diamond aigrette tiara, a pearl necklace and a Billiken (see p. 101).[18] Only Grand Duchess Vladimir remained undecided, in spite of her initial interest in three large diamond drops of 21.06, 15.46 and 15.15 carats: although Cartier offered to defer payment over a period of three years, in the end she chose only one of them. All the rage during the 1913 season in St Petersburg were Cartier's platinum evening bags, for which the demand was so great that Paris had to insist on twenty-eight days for delivery. Count Alexis Orlov paid Fr. 5,100 for an evening bag made of green gold with a diamond clasp.

Thus began the year 1914, and with it Cartier's final season in Russia. Once again it was Grand Duchess Vladimir who risked a major order, in spite of the adverse conditions which now prevailed, paying 45,600 roubles (Fr. 121,000) for a 39.25-carat drop diamond [240]. Was it through lack of political foresight, or simply through fear of offending so important a customer, that Cartier agreed to her paying the sum in instalments spread over three years? Madame de Balashev chose some miniature hardstone animals in the style of Fabergé, including a piglet and an elephant, as well as two Easter eggs.

The wedding of the year took place in February between Prince Felix Yusupov and Princess Irina, the daughter of Grand Duchess Xenia and niece of Tsar Nicholas II. The family's wealth was immeasurable – greater even than that of the Tsar himself – and the family palace at Archangelskoe outside Moscow housed a collection of paintings surpassed only by that of the Hermitage. Princess Irina chose from Cartier a tiara of rock crystal, a piece of which the Paris workshops were particularly proud [84]. A photograph of the princess wearing her diamond-studded wedding regalia was so coveted in St Petersburg that Sarda was unable to acquire one for his head office in Paris. Further celebrations followed a few months later, this time for the grand wedding of Prince Sherbatov, grandson of the fabulously wealthy Count Stroganov, and the daughter of the late Prime Minister Stolypin. In the face of competition from both Bolin and Fabergé, it was Cartier who was commissioned to design the wedding ring.

Although the outbreak of war brought an end to Cartier's activities in St Petersburg, there was to be an epilogue only a few years later on French soil. Following the murder of the Tsar and his family, the Russian aristocracy and members of the imperial household fled to Monte Carlo, Paris, Cannes, Lausanne and London, quickly establishing themselves in what they came to regard as their second homeland. The Empress Maria Feodorovna eventually returned to her native Denmark, where she died in 1928. Her jewels remained with her till the end, and were then divided up in England. Grand Duchess Vladimir, Cartier's loyal patron, fled from Russia by crossing the Caucasus on her own private railway. She reached Switzerland in 1920, settled in Zurich, and died later that year in Contrexéville. She had entrusted her jewels to an English friend, Albert Stopford, who got them safely out of the country. Following her death, they were shared among her four children: Grand Duke Andrei, who henceforth divided his time between Paris and Cannes, received the rubies; Grand Duchess Helen, the mother of Princess Marina of Kent, the diamonds; Grand Duke Cyril the pearls; and Boris the emeralds. The diamond bow tiara with its drop pearls [128], which the Grand Duchess had treasured more than any other item, went to Queen Mary of England, and the sapphire tiara to Queen Marie of Romania.

The dramatic nature of the exodus of many Russians from their homeland, and their struggles for existence abroad, are the subject of an account by the Paris dealer Léonard Rosenthal, who witnessed many of the sales that circumstances made necessary:

> How many of them risked their lives to escape across the frontier with their jewels, the only thing they still possessed. Only under cover of darkness did they dare advance along the Finnish border, sliding in the snow and desperately clutching the small sacks which contained an entire fortune. How the bullets whistled through the air whenever the Red Guards caught sight of their fleeing countrymen! What tricks they used to protect their precious jewels from the snares of Bolshevik agents! A luxuriant head of hair might serve to conceal jewels worth millions. Others who feared the rigours of persecution swallowed their diamonds, pearls, emeralds and rubies, leaving nature to return them to them. All the great jewellers and dealers in gemstones knew the Russian aristocrats and bourgeois who, before their eyes, threw open cases filled with magnificent jewels, saying, 'Buy these, they're all that stands between me and starvation.'[19]

It was not only the Russian refugees who sold their jewels on the European markets; the Bolsheviks did so too, though in their case the jewels had been robbed from banks, private houses and hiding places. Such was later the fate of the Yusupov treasure (p. 319). These jewels came via Reval on to the London market between 1918 and 1921 and then, following the French government's agreement to such purchases, on to the Paris market, too. Rosenthal calculated that the total value of all the jewels sold by the Soviets amounted to Fr. 300–400 million. An equally large amount accrued from sales which took place privately and which, in the early 1920s, plunged the European jewel market into a crisis that threatened its very survival.

*Diver descending
from Mr. Cartier's boat*

CHAPTER EIGHT

PEARLS

preceding pages, left

132 Illustration from a 1925 catalogue showing a pearl fisher 'descending from Mr. Cartier's boat'

preceding pages, right

133 Necklace. Cartier Paris, special order, 1911. Platinum; round old- and rose-cut diamonds; six pearls; millegrain setting (80% actual size)

this page

134 Brooch-pendant. Cartier Paris, 1913, modified by Cartier London, 1923. Platinum; round old-, single- and rose-cut diamonds, diamond rondelles; one pink conch pearl weighing 111.28 grains; pearls

'Cartier's is the temple of the pink pearl'[1]

When the magazine *Femina* held a competition in 1906 and the lucky winner was offered a choice between an automobile and a pearl necklace, 4,582 readers opted for the former, while only 1,776 decided in favour of the necklace. Was their decision a symptom of the fascination exercised at that time by the novelty and speed of the automobile? Or did it merely reflect the fact that by the turn of the century a pearl necklace was already an obligatory item of jewelry in every privileged household? Two years later there was no mistaking the note of social criticism in the same magazine's condemnation of a pearl-embroidered dress belonging to Mrs George J. Gould, which was valued at one million dollars: the extravagance of the garment 'in no way increased its attractiveness', the writer commented; and 'it tied up vast sums of money which could have been spent in much more useful ways'.

In the ten years leading up to the First World War, Europe rather than the United States witnessed a visible shift in standards of 'morality' as they related to jewels and to lifestyle in general. It was American customers above all who were now buying the largest *parures*, which was one of the main reasons why the Cartier brothers opened their New York branch in 1909 (see p. 28). There and in Philadelphia, Chicago and Washington were to be found vast fortunes that had been accumulated since the time of the Civil War. Marriage ties with the old aristocratic families of Europe,[2] Fifth Avenue palaces modelled on the châteaux of the Loire, and the purchase of foreign family jewels whose age and provenance gave their new owners a spurious pedigree as flattering as the ancestral portraits which the art-dealer Duveen provided for their drawing rooms – all these were intended to legitimize their vast wealth in the eyes of the world and to establish them firmly in the desired cultural context.

At no other time was the demand for historical jewelry as great as it was in the United States at the beginning of the twentieth century. And the greatest demand of all was for pearl necklaces, which, despite their often nebulous origins, were invariably attributed to Catherine the Great, Marie Antoinette or the Empress Eugénie. Mrs Belmont wore Marie Antoinette's pearls; Consuelo Vanderbilt, or, as she then was, the Duchess of Marlborough, wore a strand that had belonged to Catherine the Great and the Empress Eugénie; Mrs Eleanor Whitney, aptly bearing 'Pearle' as a middle name, also wore the French Empress's pearls; and Barbara Hutton later acquired those of Marie Antoinette. The following anecdote of the purchase of a spectacular pearl necklace takes us right to the heart of a society whose characters, motivated by temptation and envy, appear to have stepped straight out of *Vanity Fair*. The actors are the automobile millionaire Horace E. Dodge and his future son-in-law, James Cromwell, son of Eva Stotesbury.[3]

> Not long before the wedding Mr. Dodge took his future son-in-law aside. 'Jim,' he said, 'I'm worried about Mother.' 'What about her?' Cromwell wanted to know. 'Well, Mother doesn't have the kind of pearls your mother has. In the church, people are going to notice that sort of thing. Where does your mother buy 'em?' Cromwell mentioned Cartier. 'Never heard of him,' Dodge said. 'But get me an appointment with this fella.' And so Cromwell arranged a meeting between Pierre Cartier, Horace Dodge, and himself.
>
> At the meeting, Cartier – whom Mr. Dodge persistently called 'Mr. Car-teer' – produced several trays of pearl necklaces. 'No, no, Mr. Car-teer,' said Mr. Dodge. 'I want something bigger than that for Mother. Something to match Mrs. Stotesbury's pearls.'[4] Finally Cartier said, 'Monsieur Dodge, I do have one very fine set. They belonged to the Empress Catherine.' 'Never heard of her,' said Mr. Dodge, 'but let's see 'em.' Cartier then brought out a magnificent strand of pearls the size of robins' eggs. 'That's more like it,' said Mr. Dodge. 'How much?' 'Ah, Monsieur Dodge,' said M. Cartier, 'that necklace is one million dollars.' 'I'll take it,' said Dodge, pulling out his checkbook and writing a check for $1,000,000.[5]

If some pearl necklaces were of dubious pedigree, others appeared on the European market, especially in London and Paris, whose credentials are impeccable:

1872   Sale by auction of the private jewels of the Empress Eugénie: 1 pearl
            necklace consisting of 41 pearls (Christie's, London)[6]

1887	Sale by auction of the French crown jewels: 6 pearl necklaces, 1 pearl tiara by Bapst, the 'Régente' pearl, and 4 pearl brooches
1901	Sale by auction in Paris of the 5-strand pearl necklace of the Comtesse de Castiglione, the famous *intrigante* at the court of Napoleon III
1902	Sale by auction of the famous Dudley pearls (Christie's, London)
1903	Sale by auction in Paris of the stock of the jeweller Paul Hamelin, including 'magnificent' pearls weighing 415¼ grains
1904	Sale by auction in Paris of the 3-strand pearl necklace of Princess Januaria of Braganza
1904	Sale by auction in Paris of the pearls of the late Princess Mathilde, including a 7-strand pearl necklace originally owned by the Queen of Westphalia, and a single-string pearl necklace from Queen Sophie of Holland
1911	Sale by auction in Paris of the pearls of Sultan Abdul Hamid, including a 3-strand necklace of 154 pearls
1916ff.	Four auctions of pearls held by the Red Cross in London, one of which included an enormous sautoir of 4,000 pearls assembled by a commission headed by the Princess Royal. The original plan to hold a lottery was called off following objections by the Archbishop of Canterbury. The sautoir was divided up into separate necklaces and auctioned by Christie's, London
1919	The pearls of the Austrian imperial family acquired by Cartier Paris through a private transaction.[7] Louis Cartier travelled to Prangins in Switzerland for an audience with the last Austrian Emperor, living in exile there
1920	Sale by auction in Paris of the pearls belonging to the revue star Gaby Deslys: 4 pearl necklaces and a necklace of alternate black and white pearls, said to be presents from King Manuel of Portugal
1923	Sale in Doorn, Holland, of the pearls which had been part of the Prussian crown jewels; bought by the dealer A. de Sondheimer, they included 6 pearl necklaces and 13 pearls
1924	Sale by auction in Paris of the pearls of Madame Thiers, an event which the international press (including the *Gazette de Constantinople*) treated as having political significance. Under the terms of her will, Madame Thiers, widow of the first president of the French Republic (1871–77), left her husband's art collection to the Louvre in 1880. Comprising 1,470 separate items, it was ridiculed by the Goncourt brothers as a 'frightful hotchpotch of bourgeois art' and accepted by the Louvre only reluctantly. It did, however, include Madame Thiers' famous pearl necklace, which she had bought pearl by pearl from Germain Bapst.[8] The items were put on display, together with the French crown jewels, in the Galerie d'Apollon, but since, as far as the Louvre was concerned, they had neither 'artistic character' nor 'educational value', a draft bill of 1922 finally allowed the museum to dispose of them. The sale took place in the Salle Denon in the Louvre on 16 June 1924 in the presence of more than one thousand spectators. The three strands of pearls, together with their clasp, were first called out separately and knocked down for Fr. 3,220,000, Fr. 2,680,000 and Fr. 5,030,000, the first two strands being bought by the dealers L. Hemsy and Baron Lopez de Tarragoya, and the third by Oscar Kahn. The clasp went to Paul Esmerian.[9] Immediately afterwards, the sale was annulled, and the necklace was sold via an absentee bid for Fr. 11,280,000 ($2,256,000) to Cartier, who had commissioned Hemsy and Lopez to bid. The necklace was exhibited both in the rue de la Paix and in New York, an entire room being set aside as 'a suitable shrine for the fabulous jewel, which the public came to view as though to a temple'

opposite

135 'Draperie de décolleté'. Cartier Paris, Edwardian. Platinum, mounted with forty-one strings of pearls and rose-cut diamond bars

136 Choker. Cartier Paris, commissioned in 1900 by Grand Duchess Vladimir. Platinum; six-strings of pearls; two diamond imperial eagles

Since the time of Louis XIV it had been diamonds that commanded the highest prices among precious stones, but around 1900 pearls began to enjoy a privileged position in the European and American markets, with prices being paid which seemed almost in the realm of fantasy. In 1908 G. F. Kunz wrote in *The Book of the Pearl*,

135

136

Pearls of 100 grains are even more rare at the present time than are diamonds of 100 carats. Until the middle of the 19th century the diamonds of the world weighing 100 carats or over could be counted on one's fingers, but since the opening of the African mines in 1870 the number of large diamonds has increased at a much greater ratio than have the pearls of one quarter of their weight. It would thus seem that pearls of great size are worth four times as much as diamonds of equal weight.

After 1900, whenever a perfect pearl was found in the Persian Gulf the whole of the European pearl trade was put on a state of alert. Paul Claudel noted: 'their appearance on the market depresses all other values. It alters rates of exchange and causes the banks considerable alarm, since they feel that their operational stability is under threat, once a new and unquantifiable element has been introduced.'[10] Auctioneers and retailers watched in amazement as prices rose above a million francs, and in one case even went beyond the million-dollar barrier. The spectacular prices paid included the following:

1891	Pearls of the actress Léonide Leblanc, 4 strands with 212 pearls weighing 3,300 grains (auction, Paris)	Fr. 181,000 ($36,000)
1895	Pearls of the late Caroline, Duchess of Montrose, 7 strands with 362 pearls (Christie's, London)	11,500 gns ($57,500)
1900	A single pearl weighing 128 grains (sold by the Russian jeweller Koechli at the Paris Exposition)	Fr. 150,000 ($30,000)
1901	Pearls of the Comtesse de Castiglione (auction, Paris)	Fr. 463,500 ($92,600)
	Madame Humbert's pearls, 6 strands with 424 pearls (Christie's, London)	20,000 gns ($100,000)
1902	Earl Dudley's rose-coloured drop pearl weighing 209 grains (Christie's, London)	13,500 gns ($67,500)
	Dudley pearl necklace, 47 pearls weighing 1,090 grains (Christie's, London)	22,200 gns ($111,000)
1904	Pearls of Princess Mathilde (auction, Paris)	Fr. 445,000 ($89,000)
1906	A 5-strand necklace of 285 pearls (auction, London)	10,000 gns ($50,000)
1907	Mrs Lewis-Hill's pearls: 1 strand of 229 pearls (Christie's, London)	16,700 gns ($83,500)
	Mrs Gordon-Lennox's pearls: 5 strands of 287 pearls (Christie's, London)	25,500 gns ($127,500)
1909	Madame Polovstov's pearls: 4 strands weighing 3,852 grains	Fr. 1,003,000 ($200,600)
1910	49 pearls weighing 656 grains (sold to Eva Stotesbury by Cartier New York)	Fr. 810,000 ($162,000)
	Proposed sale by Cartier New York of a pearl necklace to Mrs George D. Widener	$750,000
	39 pearls with diamond roundels weighing 1,122¾ grains (sold to Nancy Leeds by Cartier New York)	Fr. 2,850,000 ($570,000)
1911	Pearls of Sultan Abdul Hamid (auction, Paris)	Fr. 920,000 ($184,000)
1913	1 strand of 59 pearls weighing 1,199.34 grains (sold by Cartier New York)	Fr. 859,117 ($171,822)
1918	Total raised at the four Red Cross pearl auctions since 1916 (Christie's, London)	300,000 gns ($1,500,000)
	Madame de Falbe's pearl necklace (Christie's, London)	47,000 gns
1919	The Austrian imperial pearls (bought by Cartier Paris)	Fr. 1,000,000
1920	A pearl necklace of Russian provenance made up of 188 pearls (Christie's, London)	54,000 gns
	A 3-strand necklace of 171 pearls formerly owned by Tsar Nicholas I (bought by Cartier Paris at the Lobanov sale in Lausanne)	Fr. 553,000

This list, which is necessarily incomplete, can give us no idea of the relationship between price and quality. In the absence of reliable information about the quality of the pearls, it is impossible to say anything about the shape, colour and lustre of the individual pearls, or, in the case of the necklaces, about the graduation of the pearls. An indication of weight in grains (1 carat = 4 grains) simply makes it easier for us to imagine their approximate size. But what the list does show is the enormous potential value of pearls in the jewel market up to the 1920s, an impression confirmed by a comparison with the prices paid at art auctions:

1910	J. M. W. Turner's *Rockets and Blue Lights*	
	bought at auction in New York by Duveen	$129,000
	Frans Hals' *Portrait of a Woman*	
	bought at auction in New York by Knoedler	$137,000
1911	A Gutenberg Bible bought at auction in New York	
	by Huntington (who also bought Gainsborough's	
	Blue Boy from Duveen for $620,000)	$50,000
1927	Rembrandt's *Titus*	
	sold at auction in New York by Parke Bernet	$270,000
1928	Rembrandt's *Young Man with a Harelip*	
	bought at auction in London at Christie's by Knoedler	44,000 gns
	Rembrandt's *Man with a Torah*	
	bought at auction in London at Christie's by Knoedler	48,000 gns

These few examples show that during the 1910s and 1920s pearl necklaces commanded the same prices as the most expensive Rembrandts and similar works by Old Masters.

That there was also a connection between these prices and those being paid at the same time in the fluctuating and unpredictable property market emerges from the now legendary events surrounding Cartier's purchase of the premises at 653 Fifth Avenue in New York [23]. Pierre Cartier had long been searching for an ideal site to replace the arrangement by which he occupied only a single storey of 712 Fifth Avenue. His eye was caught by the splendid six-storey Renaissance palace of Morton F. Plant,[11] which Robert W. Gibson had built on the southeast corner of 52nd Street between 1903 and 1905.[12] With the sure instinct of a businessman and market tactician, Cartier proposed in 1917 to exchange the building for his most valuable two-strand pearl necklace, which he had been assembling over the years and which Mrs Plant was keen to possess. Like the pearl *parure* previously bought from Tiffany's by Mrs George J. Gould, the two strands of fifty-five and seventy-three pearls were valued at one million dollars. The transaction was accepted without hesitation by the shrewd industrialist.[13]

Cartier's, Tiffany's, and Chaumet were the leading firms in the international pearl market. Cartier's made headline news in 1910 when they sold a necklace for Fr. 2.85 million ($570,000) consisting of thirty-nine pearls alternating with diamond roundels. The buyer was Nancy Leeds, one of Cartier's most regular customers up to the First World War. In 1910, however, she was involved in a long-drawn-out court case with the American government about another necklace, which she had bought from Bernard Citroën in Paris in 1906 and which was valued at $220,000.[14] The pearls, which Mrs Leeds had imported loose into the country, were initially taxed at 60 per cent of the purchase price. The case dragged on for years, during which time Mrs Leeds lost her husband, and it was not until 1911 that the customs authorities declared themselves satisfied with a 10 per cent duty, and paid back the disputed sum of $110,335. The newspaper reports provoked by the affair took up almost as many columns as the sale of the 'Hope' diamond which Cartier was then transacting.

The affair came to the ears of Edward VII, who was passing through Paris on his way to Biarritz[15] when Cartier showed him a perfect black pearl. The King hesitated over buying it, and only later learned from Pierre Cartier that it had been sold in the meantime to Nancy Leeds. When, shortly afterwards, King Edward discovered that both he and Mrs Leeds were staying at the Hôtel Bristol in Paris, he sent word via Cartier that he would be flattered by the favour of seeing her pearls. Clearly, Mrs Leeds' own charms were as seductive as those of her jewel casket, for Pierre Cartier was asked to present the sophisticated American woman with the King's dog, 'Caesar', whose silver collar bore the inscription, 'I belong to the king.' The sequel to all this is not recorded, but Mrs Leeds did subsequently become a frequent visitor at the English court.[16]

137 Pendant necklace. Cartier Paris, 1912. Platinum; a pink pearl of 83.36 grains suspended from a baton diamond of 2.17 carats and rose-cut diamond links

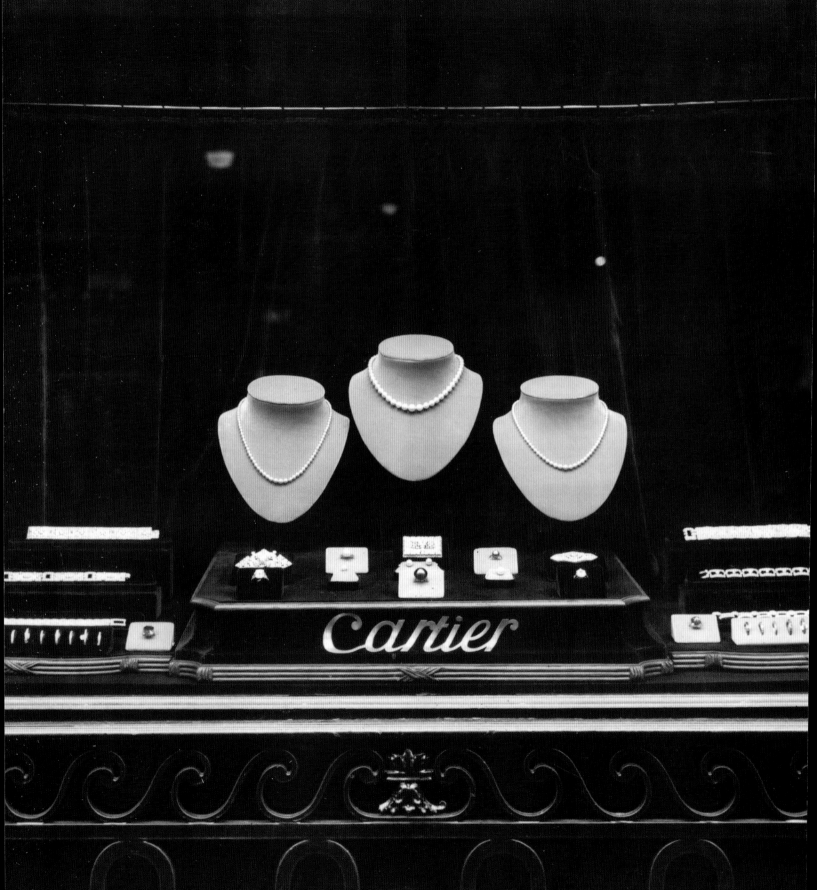

opposite

138 The window of the shop in the rue de la Paix displaying a selection of pearl necklaces, *c.* 1925

139 Necklace. Cartier Paris, 1910. Platinum; single-, round old- and rose-cut diamonds; faceted and calibré-cut sapphires; pearls; millegrain setting

In 1922 Prince Felix Yusupov made his first contact with Pierre Cartier in New York. Once the owner of Russia's largest private fortune, he had engaged, since fleeing the Revolution, in reckless speculations which were to trouble him for the remainder of his life and which were often to try Cartier's patience throughout the twelve years of their relationship. Yusupov, too, had had problems with the American customs: on entering the country, he had been carrying with him the items of jewelry that he had managed to salvage from Russia and which the authorities immediately seized. There was also litigation with the Widener family over two paintings by Rembrandt, and then an unsuccessful attempt to sell parts of his collection of snuffboxes to Elsie de Wolfe for her New York gallery. Before the Revolution, Felix's mother, Princess Zenaida, had so frequently paraded her historic jewels in Paris and Rome that no-one could say there was not tangible proof that they actually existed. In 1887, for example, on the occasion of the sale by auction of the French crown jewels, Fabergé had successfully bid for the 'Régente' pearl on behalf of the Yusupovs, and it was later worn by the Princess as a hair ornament.[17] Her jewel casket also contained the black drop pearl 'Azra',[18] the pearl known as 'La Pelegrina', and a black pearl necklace. Her daughter-in-law, Irina, wife of Prince Felix, was given on the occasion of her marriage in 1914 a pair of pearl ear pendants, together with a two-strand pearl necklace presented to her by the Tsar and a diamond necklace with a pink pearl drop, given her by Grand Duke Nicholas.

When Prince Yusupov turned to Pierre Cartier for financial help, the first pledge he laid before the astonished jeweller was his mother's black pearl necklace, once owned by Catherine the Great.[19] Black pearls[20] – those 'drops of liquid rose-beetle-coloured darkness' – had always had a sinister significance to superstitious minds, more so, certainly, than white pearls, a fact which the Empress Eugénie discovered on her wedding day, when she was advised against wearing the black pearls that she owned. Cartier did not succeed in selling Prince Yusupov's black pearls until 1924, when Mrs Peter Goelet Gerry of Washington acquired them for $400,000. In the meantime, the Prince had received an advance from Cartier of $75,000, and, as an additional pledge, deposited with the jeweller a second necklace of thirty-one pearls.

Further negotiations involving the Yusupovs' jewels began in London in 1927, when the participants were Jacques Cartier and Felix and Irina Yusupov. The Princess, whose 'severe beauty would have suited an icon, while her classically perfect profile recalled a cameo',[21] attended the negotiations dressed in black, in mourning for her relatives killed in Russia. The couple offered Cartier button pearl earstuds weighing 130 grains; two drop pearls weighing 184 grains; the 'La Pelegrina' pearl, weighing 133.20 grains; a pearl necklace of 151 pearls, weighing 1,380.80 grains; a necklace of 35 pearls, weighing 911 grains; and a necklace with three strands made up of 276 pearls and seven pendants comprising 83 pearls, with a clasp of red stone and diamond (formerly owned by Count Branicki of Poland).

The collection was repeatedly mortgaged by the Prince between 1927 and 1929, Cartier's and the firm of T. M. Sutton operating jointly and advancing the by no means inconsiderable sum of £37,807. Not until 1934 did Cartier buy the pearls, long after the family's diamonds had found new owners. But the crisis which by then gripped the world's economies had so weakened the market that the proceeds from their subsequent sale were considerably less than the original advance in 1927. 'La Pelegrina', whose history has always been mysterious, was the only jewel Prince Yusupov seemed reluctant to part with, and not until 1953 did he finally sell it.[22] The buyer was the jeweller Jean Lombard of Geneva.

A single perfect pearl may inspire awe and amazement, as is clear from the hymn of praise written by Paul Claudel following a visit to Cartier's: 'I turned it between my fingers on the point of a needle, and observed how it shone from every angle! But not like the diamond, that geometric pentacle with its hard, penetrating fire; no, the pearl is something attractive, charming, delicate, one might almost say – human.'[23] In describing the kingdom of Heaven, the Bible tells of a merchant who sold all he had in exchange for a 'goodly pearl'; and it can hardly surprise us to hear it said, in a far more prosaic context, of the American silver millionaire Clarence Mackay, that one of Cartier's pearls weighing 130 grains was 'the only thing in the world that had ever impressed him in his life.'[24]

In 1933 the 'wedding of the year' took place in Paris, when the heiress Barbara Hutton and Prince Mdivani were married in the city's Russian Church. The witnesses included the artist José Maria Sert;[25] the Maharaja of Mysore appeared wearing a picturesque turban, the Polish opera singer Ganna Walska (Mrs Harold McCormick) wore her sapphire and emerald jewels bought at Cartier's, and Daisy Fellowes her two Indian-inspired Cartier cuffs. The bride's engagement ring was also from Cartier's and consisted of a single black pearl weighing 105 grains. She had recently returned from Bali, where she had admired the natives' traditional wooden headdresses, and prevailed on Louis Cartier to design a Balinese wedding tiara made of tortoiseshell, with a diamond pattern identical to the blossoms of her wedding veil. But Cartier's most substantial commission came from the bride's father – a necklace of fifty-three pearls that had formerly been worn by Marie Antoinette. It was described in the press as 'one of the rarest strands of pearls ever sold by Cartier'. But even the most awe-inspiring piece of jewelry was not spared unorthodox treatment by Barbara Hutton, as Elsa Maxwell discovered one day when she asked after it: "'Where are your wonderful pearls, Barbara?" Barbara smiled. "The goose has them," she said. "The goose?" questioned Elsa, astonished. "Mr. Cartier told me," explained Barbara, "that if the goose swallowed my pearls they would come out with a brighter luster.'"[26]

Pearl necklaces such as Barbara Hutton's and the one her aunt, Mrs J. P. Donahue, bought from LaCloche were well known in the trade, and often remained in the possession of one or more dealers, who consigned them to individual jewellers until they were definitively sold. Pearl experts, such as Suzanne Ricaud, who later married Cartier's designer Charles Jacqueau, assembled the best pearls owned by various dealers, turning them into exquisite necklaces, with different coloured threads distinguishing pearls from different sources.

Among the leading pearl dealers in New York at that time were Joseph Frankel (who, as a dealer in diamonds, had acquired the 'Hope' diamond in 1901), and the firms of Adler, Bass and Eisenmann (the latter an associate of the Paris firm of Munroe), while the leading dealers in Paris were Jacques Bienenfeld (who maintained his own flotilla of ships off the coast of Venezuela),[27] Baron Lopez, and Bernard Citroën. Paris was the world's leading market in pearls between 1910 and 1930, employing around four hundred specialists. London, in comparison, represented only about 30 per cent of European trade until after the Second World War, when it became Europe's busiest centre.

The undisputed leader in the pearl trade, however, was the firm of Rosenthal, owned by a family from the Caucasus, where they had originally acted as representatives for Baccarat, the crystal firm. A triumvirate of brothers – Léonard, Victor and Adolphe – brought the business worldwide recognition. For Louis and Jacques Cartier they had nothing but the highest regard, though on a purely professional level: while important trading partners, they were also bitter rivals. The eldest of the Rosenthals, Léonard (b. 1875), settled in the rue Lafayette and later wrote two standard works, *Au Royaume des perles* and *Au Jardin des gemmes*. His brother Victor (1880–1961) moved to the Persian Gulf around 1895 and then to Bombay where, like Jacques Cartier, he counted local dealers and maharajas among his friends. In the case of the Maharaja of Kashmir, the ties extended to their common interest in the country's world-famous sapphire mines.

Around 1910 the rarest white pearls came to Europe from the Persian Gulf, Ceylon (modern Sri Lanka) and Australia, whereas black pearls generally came from Tahiti and Panama. American freshwater pearls from Ohio and Wisconsin were normally confined to the American market. The Persian Gulf had been famous since biblical times for its pearls: Bahrain, with its vast oyster beds, was the Greek Tylos. After its colonization by the Portuguese in the sixteenth century, the Gulf was administered by Arab sheikhs. Bahrain pearls were sent to Bombay, which was the chief trading centre[28] and where, around the year 1910, the lion's share of the market was held by two Arab dealers, Abdul Rahman and Sheikh Jassim, who in consequence of their status were regularly courted by Cartier and Rosenthal. The Bombay market reacted with seismographic sensitivity to disruptive influences in the Gulf and in Europe. If the Gulf's pearl harvest was small, few items of any interest found their way to Bombay. If, on the other hand, it exceeded expectations, there was the danger that the Arab traders would bypass Bombay and deal directly with Paris. But if the European market was endangered, as it was, for example, at the time of the Balkans War of 1912, business in Bombay came to a standstill. At the beginning of the First World War in 1914, Bombay lost 30–35 per cent of its share of the world market, and Abdul

Rahman, the 'Prince of Pearl Traders', went bankrupt, as did nine banks scattered across the Indian subcontinent. In 1917 the Indian market was down a further 30–40 per cent on its previous year's turnover, and only when Rosenthal (together with the bank Bloch Dreyfuss) unexpectedly bought a huge share of the market at between 5 and 7.5 million francs was the situation saved. In 1918 the Indian government placed a temporary ban on the export of pearls.

Cartier's maintained a permanent representative in Bombay, the Parsi Sethna, who sent weekly reports on the state of the market to Paris and London, and frequently arranged for pearls to be forwarded to Europe. Like his father Alfred, Jacques Cartier was the firm's special expert on pearls, and it was he who accompanied the sales assistant Maurice Richard on various journeys to the Persian Gulf and to India. In accordance with Oriental custom he would sit cross-legged in his negotiations with local traders, and he learned the customs, languages and habits of the various nations that he visited. Two of his journeys were recorded in the form of a diary and various other reports.

His ship, the *Tynesider*, left the port of Karachi on 3 March 1911 at the end of his first visit to India (see p. 156). On board were twenty Arabs, including the influential dealer Alibin Ahmed Chiravi from the island of Moharek, Jacques Cartier, his cook, Maurice Richard, the ship's first engineer and the captain. Jacques spent the time practising his Hindustani and considering the idea of a permanent office in Bombay, and frequently sought refuge in the quiet of the captain's private chapel. On 9 March they arrived at Muskat. The Sultan received Cartier in his residence, surrounded by a 'mass of French furniture'. An unexpected caller was the Sheikh of Dubai, accompanied by his servants, 'handsome Arabs with proud expressions, and armed to the teeth'. Was the secret meeting between the two princes an indication that some major sale of pearls was in the offing? The travellers returned to their ship, where they experienced the wonder of phosphorescence in the water: 'The sea was lit with a phosphorescent glow. The bow of the ship ploughed a furrow through the deep-blue waves, which seemed to be shimmering from below. The ship appeared to be surrounded by a girdle of light; fish darted past in dazzling zigzag patterns; a veritable firework display rose up out of the sea.'

They sailed past Musandorn, which 'enjoys the reputation of being the hottest place on earth; neither birds nor insects can remain there in summer, and even the fish leave the waters'; and on to Bander Abbas. On the distant island of Hormuz, the 'Pearl of the Orient', the ruined Portuguese fort beckoned. On 12 March they reached the port of Lingah: 'One would find it difficult to justify the existence of this town: it has neither a proper harbour nor a river, neither woods nor mountains, and not a trace of culture. A few hundred houses, a labyrinth in which a guide is indispensable.' The pearl traders of Lingah received their merchandise from Dubai, reselling the pearls to Bahrain or dispatching agents direct to Bombay. The *Tynesider* arrived at Dubai on 12 March.

It was 285 miles from Dubai to Bahrain, where they dropped anchor on 14 March in the port of Manassa. Jacques Cartier was welcomed by his host, Sheikh Mujbal. The guests were shown to a small house where they spent the night, the servants sleeping on stone benches while raucous birds built their nests in the rafters above them. 'We're never alone for a moment', Cartier confided feelingly to his diary. Sheikh Mujbal placed at Cartier's disposal an old motor car of which he was particularly proud, for there were only two cars on the entire island, everything being transported on the backs of white donkeys, which were as strong as horses. The women wore black veils, which hid them from prying glances and to Jacques they seemed simply 'walking sacks'. At the Europeans' meals with the Sheikh, ginger syrup was drunk and enough food consumed 'to keep the shipwrecked sailors on the raft of the *Medusa* alive for a month'.

The Sheikh suggested a visit to one of the oyster beds and its fisheries, but although the divers opened as many as two hundred oysters, they failed to find a single pearl. Jacques took the opportunity to observe the divers at work. Each diver earned between two hundred and four hundred rupees in the course of the season; he was paid in essential goods and a sum of money which allowed him to pay back what he had been advanced at the beginning of the season. His equipment was simple: nose clip, leather finger protectors, and ear wax for great depths. The diver would stand with one foot in a stirrup, beneath which a stone was attached; he would press the stone with one foot and slide down, with his basket, into the ocean depths. The stone and rope were then immediately pulled back up again, leaving the diver with the basket round his neck free to collect the oysters with both hands, his legs held together pointing upward. As a rule, he would stay down for a minute, after which time he would give the 'puller' a sign by means of the rope, and be pulled up again. The divers were paid so little that they inevitably became enslaved to their masters. In the bazaar, Cartier paid 500 rupees for a pearl weighing 16 grains, intending to have it bleached in Bombay.[29]

Cartier then visited Sheikh Isa on the neighbouring island of Moharek, where his party were shown the hot-water springs, Phoenician tumuli and a German trade settlement which imported rice, coffee and cotton, and in return sent mother-of-pearl to Europe for the manufacture of buttons. Sheikh Isa was

> a handsome old man: I showered him with compliments, for I was slowly coming to understand the Oriental way of expressing oneself. The conversation was very slow: I spoke in English, Sethna translated what I said into Hindustani, and then Sheikh Yusuf Kanon translated it into Arabic for the benefit of Sheikh Isa, so that a sentence of fifty words turned into a conversation lasting half an hour.

Soon, however, the party had to leave Bahrain. It was a solemn occasion: Sheikh Mujbal read from the Quran, while a slave handed round coffee and rosewater. Jacques presented his host with his watch and chain, together with a gold pencil, and to the women of the house he gave costly fabrics. Mujbal returned the compliment with a gift of baroque pearls.

Journeys to India and the Persian Gulf in the footsteps of Tavernier brought Jacques Cartier and his companions into direct contact with the cultures and customs of the Orient. They could judge for themselves, on the spot, what imagination went into the reworking and wearing of pearls. On their return to Paris they presented the designers with

140 Jacques Cartier with two sheikhs on his pearl trip to Bahrain in 1911

141 Brooch. Cartier Paris, special order, 1924. Platinum; two cushion-shaped diamonds, round old- and single-cut diamonds; one drop-shaped 24.62-carat cultured pearl; rock crystal; calibré-cut onyx and onyx beads suggestions and brief sketches. And, just as at the time of the Renaissance strands of pearls had been used as imaginative dress ornaments, in the 1920s fashion designers and jewellers, tired of the traditional pearl necklace, attempted to use pearls in new and unfamiliar ways, in order to incorporate them into the latest fashions. Around 1900, for example, the height of fashion had been the *bayadère*, composed of several strands of seed pearls plaited together and generally decorated with a pendant or tassel.[30] From around 1910 its place was taken by long sautoirs, modelled on the string of pearls of Princess Pless of Germany, which was more than seven metres long, and the pearls of the French actress Cécile Sorel, which reached down to below her waist. At the Metropolitan Opera in New York, Mary Garden caused a furore in the opera *Thaïs* when she appeared wearing a costume embroidered with long pearl sautoirs.

The tendency at the time to exaggerate length was expressed in ear ornaments in the form of large drop pearls, which were all the rage at the time of the *garçonne* style of the 1920s. There were varied ways in which pendant earrings reproduced the form of the eighteenth-century girandole; one was ordered from Cartier's in London by the Rani of Pudukota. But it was New York which at that time already had the greatest turnover in the sale of pearls. 'The salesmen are asking for nothing but pearls, and then more pearls', we read in a report sent to Pierre Cartier at that time. In 1920 Cartier New York launched a novel article of jewelry which was 'neither an ear pendant nor a necklace' but a strand of pearls attached to the ears, with a single drop pearl dangling beneath the wearer's chin. Ideally, it would be complemented by the chic of a bandeau worn low on the forehead and a strand of pearls wound several times around one wrist [**142**].[31]

142 A model wearing Cartier's pearl and diamond ear-pendants-cum-necklace. From American *Vogue*, December 1920

In the 1920s Japanese cultured pearls, full of the charm of novelty, began their successful assault on the markets of Europe and America.[32] Firms such as Cartier's and Chaumet steadfastly ignored the new product: the term 'boules blanches' ('white beads') which was frequently found in insurance valuations treated the new and unpleasant process with the requisite scorn. But it would be wrong to assume that it was the appearance of cultured pearls that precipitated a crisis in the pearl industry. The crisis which really affected the market and which brought about its radical restructuring was the Wall Street Crash. During the 1930s, prices fell to a tenth of those that had been paid up to 1928, and remained at that low level until around 1942, when they climbed back to 15–20 per cent of their former value. But Bahrain, which remained the most sought-after supplier of pearls, had in the meantime lost most of its divers to the new oil refineries, which paid higher wages, offered less unhealthy work conditions, and promised year-round work rather than a mere four months. As a result, numbers fell from 60,000 to under 6,000. The second industry which was involved – the mother-of-pearl market, which was important for the manufacture of buttons – was severely weakened by the spread of synthetic materials. The supplies that reached Bombay from Bahrain became so scarce that after 1942 prices on the Indian market rose to three times their previous level, becoming prohibitively expensive for buyers from Paris and London, and indirectly from America, too.

Between 1920 and 1930 America's annual pearl imports had amounted to around $10 million, but by 1942 this figure had fallen to $200,000, and in the following year it shrank still further. Cultured pearls profited from this weakening of the market. They were already the subject of scientific study and as a result their yields increased. Japan was to produce cultured pearls up to 9.5 mm in diameter, and in the 1950s Burma responded with the world's finest and largest specimens, measuring on average 16–18 mm. Oyster beds continued to be set up in Australia, Tahiti and the Philippines until the 1960s, and since 1968 the descendants of Léonard and Victor Rosenthal have had a leading share in this market. Tahiti is doubly important as one of the few places where black cultured pearls are produced.

CHAPTER NINE

CHARLES JACQUEAU AND THE BALLETS RUSSES

12 - 1 - 12

Writing of the 1925 Exposition Internationale des Arts Décoratifs et Industriels Modernes, Emile Sedeyn in 1934 expressed his regret that Louis Cartier had not published the names of the in-house designers who had been responsible for the firm's magnificent exhibition in the Pavillon de l'Elégance.[1] But Cartier aimed at propagating the firm's name alone as the epitome of exemplary achievement. The contributions of individual designers were consequently viewed as the work of an anonymous collective – an attitude which has important repercussions for the historian, for it has proved extremely difficult to ascribe the surviving sketches and designs to any one designer simply on the basis of stylistic characteristics. As a rule, sketches of ideas and designs left the studios unsigned, the only mark on them being the abbreviation 'A Ex.' (*à exécuter*, to be implemented), added by whoever may have been responsible for the idea in the first place, whether Louis Cartier, Jeanne Toussaint or René Revillon. The chosen design was then forwarded for costing and finally passed on to the workshops.

Because of Cartier's insistence on anonymity, the name of his most brilliant employee, Charles Jacqueau, remained largely unknown outside the firm. But in retrospect Jacqueau appears, alongside Paul Follot and Georges Verger, as one of the pioneers of the Art Deco style.

Charles Jacqueau (1885–1968) was born in Paris, the son of a master butcher from the Morvan. He won first prize for drawing at the Ecole de Neuilly, and in consequence was offered a scholarship to the Ecole des Francs-Bourgeois in Paris. This Jacqueau instinctively turned down, enrolling instead at the Ecole Bernard Palissy, where he studied drawing, pottery and porcelain painting, before transferring in 1902/3 to the Ecole des Arts Décoratifs. To gain further practical experience he then took a job with Raingo Frères, a firm specializing in bronze sculptures, and it was here, in 1909, that the Cartier designer Alexandre Genaille, shortly before moving to New York, noticed Jacqueau almost by chance; and Louis Cartier, sensing the young student's talent, took him on virtually unconditionally.[2]

Cartier's had recently lost Maurice Rauline – one of their most important figures and a leading exponent of the garland style – whose quarrelsome temperament had forced him to resign. His place had been taken by Henri Chenaud, who had joined the previous year and whose work was similarly influenced by the style of the eighteenth century. It was he whom Cartier's entrusted with designing the majority of the tiaras. Emile Thomas (b. 1869), who had entered the studio in 1907, bringing with him a training in architectural design, took over its management on Rauline's departure. His designs were of clear mathematical structure, making up in precision what they lacked in spontaneity of inspiration. Another identifiable designer, Olivier Baloche (1878–1943), who had begun as a tapestry designer, worked at Cartier's in Paris from 1902, then in their London workshop from 1909 to 1911. Also deserving of mention are Gaston Vignal, who was both a designer and an enameller; Edmond Forêt; Finsterwald and Massabieaux, both of whom followed Cartier's to London; and Maurice Duvallet, whose future lay with Cartier's in New York.

The Paris studio, which in the early years of the century already employed eight designers, was housed along with Alfred Cartier's offices at 4 rue de la Paix, where it remained until the First World War. The designers' work was divided into items for stock and special commissions from customers. The majority were naturally intended as stock, but whenever there was an increase in commissions, those designers would be assisted by the other department. Initially Jacqueau was placed in the department producing items for stock, but he soon made himself equally indispensable designing customers' orders.

The garland style which was fashionable at Cartier's in Jacqueau's time was, as we have seen, based on a revival of the Louis XVI style as it was taught at the Ecole des Arts Décoratifs. As an alternative to the revolutionary mode of Art Nouveau, it was an elegant idiom which Jacqueau continued to use occasionally up to the beginning of the First World War. His sketches include examples of all the items produced in this style: tiaras [72], stomachers, necklaces, belt buckles, umbrella handles and boxes. Jacqueau handled the garland style with impressive virtuosity, in command of its every nuance and often inventing new formal combinations. Basically, though, he was too brilliant an innovator ever to feel completely at home in the style's confining world. The greatest service he rendered Cartier's and contemporary design in general was to abandon the garland style,

preceding pages, left

143 A page of designs by Charles Jacqueau for pendants and brooches, inspired by Mughal India and reflecting the palette of the Ballets Russes, as mounted together in the Cartier archives

preceding pages, right

144 Brooch-pendant designed by Charles Jacqueau. Cartier Paris, 1913. Jade, turquoises, sapphires, diamond and a pearl. Pendant made of articulated jade plaques set with sapphires at the intersections, edged with diamonds and turquoises, with a sapphire and diamond drop

opposite

145 Charles Jacqueau (1885–1968), Cartier's most brilliant designer, drawn by his colleague Auguste Lenglen in 1912

146 Brooch designed by Charles Jacqueau. Cartier Paris, 1913. Platinum pin; central bar with two cabochon sapphires and two chains formed of white enamelled links ending in green enamelled pendants, each with three cabochon sapphires

147 Design by Charles Jacqueau for a strawberry-shaped pendant in onyx, coral and diamonds, 1913

148 Design by Charles Jacqueau for a pendant watch in the form of a panther châtelaine in onyx and diamonds, 1914

149 Design by Charles Jacqueau for an onyx and natural pearl tassel pendant, 1922

150 Design by Charles Jacqueau for a shoulder brooch in emeralds, diamonds, onyx and rubies, 1922 espouse bold colours and design, and become the champion of a new aesthetic which, following the First World War, was given official but belated recognition at the 1925 Exposition Internationale des Arts Décoratifs et Industriels Modernes, which gave its name – as 'Art Deco' – to an entire period of early twentieth-century art. Thanks to Jacqueau, it was Cartier's which produced the most convincing examples of the Art Deco style well before the outbreak of the war, giving the firm an artistic advantage that distinguished it from its rivals.

By 1900 it was no longer thought necessary for an artist's training to include a tour of Italy: knowledge of the different historical styles was transmitted by the academies of art. Jacqueau's work lies at the intersection of all these styles. There is evidence of a very early visit to Florence, Rome and Venice (a journey repeated many years later in 1937) and of course of the trip to Russia, accompanying Louis Cartier, in 1911. But the experiences gained on these travels were not such as to affect Jacqueau's style. His later visits to Morocco in 1928 and after were motivated simply by the desire to see his brother who was living there, and were not responsible for the Islamic element in his style, which had been present from as early as 1910. The same is true of his visit to Spain in 1951.

The close cooperation between Louis Cartier and Charles Jacqueau lasted for twenty years, ensuring the highest level of inspiration in all the designs that the firm produced during that period. The first sketches suggesting new motifs were generally the work of Louis Cartier, who would often jot down his ideas, with unpractised hand, on menus from the Ritz or loose scraps of paper. Before Jacqueau's arrival, Louis' influence had prevailed in his work with the designer Maurice Rauline: many new motifs in the garland style were clearly due to Cartier (for example, a rhomb with fluttering ribbons). But from the time of the First World War, when Jacqueau first began to adapt the ideas of the Ballets Russes and of the *Gazette du Bon Ton* for jewelry designs, Louis Cartier's direct influence on the design studios started to wane, a fact which may also have been due to the demands then being made on his time by the firm's international expansion.

In the designs he produced, Jacqueau showed himself to be both a visionary and a realist. His Egyptian, Greek and Chinese fantasies, which were the basis of many of his standard designs beginning in 1910, show his wide-ranging imagination. In the majority of cases it was the Louvre that provided him with his first crucial impression; he visited the museum on countless occasions to sketch objects on the spot. His interests were eclectic: an Assyrian temple relief, an Egyptian stela, a Celtic trumpet-pattern ornament, and a Chinese Famille Noire vase were all recorded in his notebook with precise technical details, to appear at some later date, utterly transformed, in Cartier's products. It is amusing to observe the way in which stylistic motifs noted down in the Louvre emerge in a new and often functional context: an Islamic architectural arch appears as part of an Art Deco comb, and an Egyptian mosque lamp as a stylized pendant, while a Greek column with an Ionic capital turns into a pendant or a letter opener. Conversely, the simple geometric form of an inkwell might be transformed into a pure architectural fantasy in which the sketch was so far removed from reality as to be impractical to execute.

The civilizations that provided Jacqueau with the greatest stimuli were those of Egypt, Islam, India [183], China and Japan. He borrowed from them all. What most interested him in Egyptian art was the stylization of masklike faces, the flat outline of the lotus, and simple architectural cubes. From Indian and Persian miniatures he took stylized plant motifs, and from Persian carpets came the central medallion which reminds the devout Muslim of the garden beyond the grave. His reworking of Chinese motifs is somewhat more superficial. He was fascinated by the writhing forms of the Chinese fire-breathing dragon, as well as by the curving silhouette of Chinese and Japanese temples and the flat outline of the peony, which he adapted in innumerable studies. But since during the 1920s the main emphasis in Cartier's Chinoiseries lay in the use of original Chinese and Japanese lacquerwork, and since such pieces were already perfect, self-contained works of art, the copyist was frequently left merely with the task of designing border ornaments to match the lacquerwork in colour and form.

Among the profusion of designs included in Jacqueau's sketchbooks, or *cahiers d'idées*, are a handful of African motifs inspired by both the 1925 Exposition and the Colonial Exposition of 1931: for instance, they include a Sudanese necklace and bracelet

151 Design by Charles Jacqueau for a belt buckle decorated with satyrs' heads, 1923. Not produced

152 Design by Charles Jacqueau for a sapphire and emerald necklace with engraved sapphire beads and engraved sapphire and emerald plaques, 1924

opposite

153 Page of peacock designs by Charles Jacqueau, in ink on glazed cloth

and a sketch for a necklace with tiger's paw motifs. Greek art, on the other hand, was a relatively minor influence on his work. Admittedly, he used meanders and Vitruvian scrolls as border motifs, and the palmette was incorporated into a Greek tiara, but the canon of Greek forms belonged to that very historicism from which he was striving to liberate himself.

Apart from the Louvre, the other source of inspiration for him was the Jardin des Plantes. Here he observed animals fighting, birds in flight, and plants, and once again he captured every detail with his pen [**276**]. The series of gemstone plants that Jacqueau inspired Cartier's to produce bears witness to his deep affinity with organic nature which resulted in his fellow designers goodnaturedly nicknaming him 'Jacqueau la Fleur'.

Yet all the impressions garnered in museums, churches and in nature itself pale before the shock (no other word can describe it) which the Ballets Russes induced in him overnight.[3] Jacqueau's wife Suzanne recalls him following the Ballets Russes with bated breath, a sketchbook in hand. His obsession with ballet in general was so great that in 1913 his colleagues in the design studio drew playful caricatures of him looking like Isadora Duncan in billowing veils. Diaghilev's dancers – Nijinsky,[4] Karsavina, Ida Rubinstein, Anna Pavlova (who was soon to leave the company) – provoked storms of enthusiasm in the Châtelet Theatre where they first appeared in 1909, pushing the opera performances, which had been intended as the more important part of the programme, very much into the background. In 1910 it was the ballet *Schéhérazade* that fired the imagination of critics, artists and audiences, all of whom reacted as though in a daze to the colour of the costumes and the swirling movement of the production.[5] The colours included an emerald-green curtain which opened to reveal the harem of Shahryar, King of India and China. In the background were orange-coloured pillars and three blue doors, a gold-blue coverlet, and cushions in garishly colourful designs, piled up in indiscriminate profusion. And the sense of movement! Nijinsky, the gold-clad Moor, shot on to the stage, where he joined Zobeida, the favourite wife of Shahryar, at which the frenzied movements turned into a veritable bacchanal, to the accompaniment of Rimsky-Korsakov's music. The choreographer, Michael Fokine,[6] had been inspired by Persian miniatures, while Leon Bakst had designed sets evoking the world of a sultan's harem, flashing with colourful costumes of geometrical design. Overnight Paris fashion designers were persuaded to turn to the Orient in their search for inspiration. The couturier Paul Poiret who, thanks to Ida Rubinstein, had direct access to Diaghilev's world, created turbans topped with aigrettes, and a harem dress with Turkish trousers lifted straight out of *Schéhérazade*.[7]

The impact of the Ballets Russes enabled Louis Cartier and Jacqueau to break free from the confining influence of the somewhat schematic Louis XVI garland style. Although Jacqueau, as we have seen, was to continue to exploit it, the way was now officially open for a much wider choice of unrefracted colours. There could, however, be no clearer proof of Louis Cartier's superb awareness of colour than the fact that, even before the Ballets Russes, the colours used by his designers covered the entire spectrum of complementary combinations.[8] As early as 1903 pendants described as 'Chinese' or 'Japanese' were designed and set either with sapphires and amethysts or with emeralds and sapphires. An entry for 1906 lists tie pins described as 'rainbows' made up of calibré-cut sapphires, emeralds and amethysts.[9] Green was paired with blue, red with black, and purple with bright green, producing brilliant phosphorescent shades which replaced the subtle pastel shades of the fashionable Marie Antoinette style.

A similar revolution had been brought about by the Fauve painters, especially Matisse and Derain, who at the Paris Autumn Exposition of 1905 had first declared their commitment to the use of unrefracted colour. Applied to the manufacture of jewelry, this resulted in contrasting combinations of sapphires and emeralds, amethysts and sapphires, jade and amethysts, with rock crystal being used as the neutral background in a new contrapuntal handling of colour. Colour contrasts were accentuated on enamel surfaces by means of cabochons, while coloured calibré-cut gemstones produced linear border designs which, during the earlier period, had been achieved by means of enamel lines. These bold experiments in the handling of colour were Cartier's unchallenged prerogative, and amounted to nothing less than a revolution in the jewelry trade. Particularly the

Patte gauche
face externe

blue-green match, which Louis Cartier called his 'peacock pattern', was an innovation which, in the light of traditional attitudes towards colour, was bound to be seen at least as risky, if not as simply tasteless. Isolated examples of such colour contrast may be noted in earlier periods, as in the coronation sword of Gustav III of Sweden (1780), where amethysts and emeralds were paired, and in France around 1860 one finds a predilection for green and blue enamelling.[10] Also worth mentioning are a number of peacock feather brooches which were shown at exhibitions and which employed calibré-cut gemstones in blue and green; they included Mellerio's peacock feather brooch of 1867 and Coulon's necklace of 1900.[11] The jeweller Robin produced brooches based on Persian designs, pairing sapphires and emeralds or rubies and emeralds. But the most direct and – in view of Louis Cartier's known predilections – the most likely influence determining his choice of blue and green as a colour combination is probably to be found in enamelled Mughal jewelry of the seventeenth and eighteenth centuries.

The Ballets Russes' use of flat geometrical designs also became generally fashionable around 1910 but found no immediate response in Cartier's designs. In structuring the surface of vanity cases, the immediate inspiration for the *jeux-de-fond* design was Islamic trellis and star motifs, which in the 1920s gave way to Chinese patterns, and only around 1930 to Cubist forms.

Another important collaboration between Louis Cartier and Jacqueau was the setting up of 'Department S' (S for silver), which sold both elegant gifts and everyday consumer goods (see p. 213). Even a cursory glance at Jacqueau's sketchbooks reveals the way in which aesthetic invention and functional design were for him parts of the same creative process. The ornaments that he included are always in their proper place, justified by the functional context of the whole, from which they could not conceivably be divorced. Unlike the earlier garland style, in which ornaments were simply added to one another, though in relation to some central point or axis of symmetry, what the mature Jacqueau now designed was 'structural' ornaments, logical beyond the purely decorative level.

The idea of a functional aesthetic, which tolerated ornamentation only within a meaningful context, had been advocated in England around 1860 by William Morris and his circle, and had had a determinant influence on the Arts and Crafts movement in the later nineteenth century. In turn this had left its mark on Jacqueau's generation of the 1890s. Throughout his life, Jacqueau continued to work on these problems, and developed into a notable innovator. Just as Nijinsky invented a windscreen wiper and a ballpoint pen, so Jacqueau, adhering strictly to the aesthetic rules of Art Deco, invented a pocket chess set in a gold-embossed leather case, a night light, a folding tape measure, a portable toothbrush, and an expensive onyx container for dental floss. He liked to design objects with a twofold function, such as a magnifying glass with a letter opener attached, which were both practical and elegant. There was a direct link between this emphasis upon practicality and the thousand-and-one luxury items that made up the greater part of Cartier's Art Deco range – articles such as vanity cases, cigarette cases and desk sets, which threatened to relegate pure jewelry to a subordinate position. Among the designs for Department S, which Jacqueau provided with his usual extremely precise technical instructions, are sketches for handbags, one with a chequered pattern which anticipates the Op Art designs of Victor Vasarely.

In Jacqueau's choice of materials for his designs, we find an echo of the theory that all materials are equally valid, a belief that artists such as Lalique and Fouquet had propounded around 1900 as a reaction to the overblown, grand style of the Third Republic. Gérard Sandoz had advanced this thesis in 1902: 'Assuming its technique and manufacture to be flawless, a well-designed item of jewelry costing Fr. 200 is just as attractive as one similarly designed and costing Fr. 2 million.' Jacqueau's designs confirm this fundamental tenet: agate, lapis lazuli and coral were used alongside the most expensive gemstones, and priceless diamonds weighing 15 and 20 carats were attached, with great effect, to a simple black silken cord.

What distinguishes Jacqueau's geometric Art Deco forms from those of his rivals is the impression they give of floating on air [143]. Whereas the massive, constructivist forms of Sandoz and Fouquet were often difficult to reconcile with the essential character of jewelry, Jacqueau's geometric forms remained within a framework of dainty lightness. He never tired in later years of encouraging the workshops to produce delicate, lightweight pieces. His instructions repeatedly advised 'surtout très léger' ('above all very light').

In 1947 Jacqueau signed a contract enabling him to spend the following year producing designs for Cartier London. At the same time he introduced Jacques Cartier's son, Jean-Jacques, to the world of jewelry design.

Whereas Jacqueau's artistic vocabulary helped to form the aesthetic language of the 1910s and 1920s, he was completely uninterested in the aesthetic outlook of the 1940s, which did not challenge his imagination, and caused his inventiveness to atrophy. Moreover, his mentor, Louis Cartier, had died in 1942, leaving a gap similar to that suffered by the Ballets Russes following Diaghilev's death in 1929. In view of this, it is not surprising that Jacqueau's style during the late 1930s and 1940s is virtually indistinguishable from the style found in every studio in Paris at the time. What was needed was the artistic enthusiasm of a new generation of designers, which at Cartier's found its ideal expression in Peter Lemarchand, who was to evolve new ideas of jewelry design from the spirit of the post-war years.

154 Sketches by Charles Jacqueau for bracelets and a sleeve clip, *c.* 1925

CHAPTER TEN

PHARAOHS, SPHINXES AND PYRAMIDS

To Howard Carter, the archaeologist, it was 'the day of days, the most wonderful of my life'.[1] On 30 November 1922 *The Times* published a laconic report of the discovery and official opening of the tomb of Tutankhamun, in the remote Valley of the Kings in Egypt. It was the most sensational archaeological find of the twentieth century – comparable with Heinrich Schliemann's excavations at Troy in 1871 – and thanks to astute manipulation of the media it aroused considerable interest outside the academic world. The discovery released a wave of excitement which, overnight, swept the fine arts, literature, fashion and film. An ancient myth had been reborn.

Carter's excavations, undertaken in the service of Lord Carnarvon,[2] are commonly dated to the year 1922, but in fact they were a complicated and long-drawn-out process which took ten years to complete. For eighteen years before the discovery, Carnarvon had poured a fortune into the search for the tomb of Tutankhamun, the pharaoh who married a daughter of Akhenaten and died, aged eighteen, in the year 1352 BC. It was not until 4 November 1922 that Carter came upon a first sealed wooden door, and on 26 November, with the discovery of a second entry bearing the seal of Tutankhamun, he knew that at last he had reached his goal. The antechamber, containing the throne and two life-size statues of the pharaoh, was the first to be inspected. After that came the actual burial chamber: four gold-plated shrines concealed the quartzite sarcophagus, with its one-and-a-half-ton lid. It was not until two years later that the lid was raised; then, to the horror of the academic world, a dispute caused it to be left suspended for a further eleven months. The contents of the coffins within the sarcophagus – the golden mask of the pharaoh, the diadem

embellished with cobra and vulture, the sixteen-row cloisonné pectoral, armlets, rings and much more – were deposited in the Cairo Museum while Carter continued to investigate further treasure chambers until 1932.

Against Carter's wishes, the tomb became a spectacle in which the whole world participated. While Egypt debated bitterly whether or not the treasure should be used to settle the national debt, commerce, industry and public imagination began the systematic exploitation of the find.

Yet there would have been an Egyptian craze during the 1920s even without Tutankhamun. European interest in the ancient Nile civilization dated from at least the eighteenth century: at that time, the newly discovered frescoes at Herculaneum and Pompeii were seen to contain allusions to the cult of Isis which had reached Italy via Alexandria during the Roman period.[3] From the Renaissance onward, the canons of classical Greek and Roman art were taught in every academy, whereas Egyptian art, with its reference to the world of the sacred and mysterious beliefs concerning the afterlife, was considered esoteric and was more sparingly studied.

In 1798 Egypt became the focus of European attention: in that year, aiming to weaken England's colonial position decisively, General Bonaparte launched his Egyptian campaign. It was to end in catastrophe for France, yet it had been planned with considerable foresight as more than a merely military expedition. The leading scientific names of the period – Berthollet, Monge, Denon and Geoffroy de Saint-Hilaire – were associated with the undertaking and brought to an astonished Europe the first topography of Egypt

158 Design for a bandeau decorated with onyx lotus blossoms, 1923

159 Design for a brooch incorporating an antique faience hawk's head, 1925

160 Scarab brooch. Cartier London, 1924.
Egyptian blue-glazed faience scarab with
cabochon emerald, sapphire, ruby and
amethyst. Zigzag border with onyx
and diamonds set in platinum

161 Scarab necklace. Cartier Paris, special
order, 1932. Platinum; oval heart-scarab in
glazed steatite in a diamond and onyx lotus
surround, suspended from a pearl ribbon.
The scarab was formerly in the collection of
the French Egyptologist Gaston Maspero

opposite

162 Winged scarab brooch. Cartier London,
1925. Gold, platinum; round old- and single-cut
diamonds; cabochon ruby, emerald, citrine
and onyx; Egyptian blue-glazed faience

163 Design for a belt buckle with a
winged scarab, 1926

164 Winged scarab brooch. Cartier London,
1924. Scarab carved in smoky quartz with
emerald eyes, wings in Egyptian blue-glazed
faience and pavé-set diamonds with black
enamel outlines and cabochon emeralds

to be based on exact observations, in the *Description de l'Egypte*. This was followed in 1802 by Vivant Denon's *Voyage dans la Basse et la Haute Egypte*, which was to inspire every field of art in the opening years of the new century. At Napoleon's command, Egyptian décor made its appearance in the design of furniture and the art of bronze and porcelain. The Sèvres factory produced Egyptian dinner services and table ornaments in the form of Egyptian statues, temples and obelisks; the emblem of the goddess Isis was incorporated in the Paris coat of arms. The groundwork done under Napoleon eventually enabled Jean-François Champollion to decipher Egyptian hieroglyphs in 1822 and thus to gain a systematic understanding of Egyptian culture and its connections.[4] Of much greater interest to Champollion's contemporaries, Mehemet Ali, vice-regent of Egypt, promised Louis XVIII an obelisk from Alexandria. In 1831 an obelisk, though not the promised one, was shipped to France aboard the *Luxor* and erected in the Place de la Concorde. Its influence on decorative arts and jewelry was immediate. From then on it would be impossible to imagine the repertoire of French and English jewelry without exotic Egyptian motifs alongside themes from the romantic glorification of the Middle Ages.

A second factor in promoting the Egyptian fashion was the long-drawn-out building of the Suez Canal (1859–69), the brilliant accomplishment of the Frenchman Ferdinand de Lesseps. Impressed by such pioneering achievement, the jewellers Mellerio, Boucheron and Baugrand created Egyptian pieces, while Baugrand also decorated his showcase at the Paris Exposition of 1867 with an Egyptian statue and chariot. Two years later, the Empress Eugénie attended the celebrations of the official opening of the Canal by the Khedive Ismail; among the spectators were Théophile Gautier, Henrik Ibsen and Eugène Fromentin. The delayed climax of the festivities came in 1871 with the first performance of Verdi's *Aida* at the inauguration of the Cairo opera house. In the year of the Empress's Egyptian journey Lemonnier, Eugénie's court jeweller, created his aigrette with lotus flower and birds' wings, and in 1873 the Egyptian pieces of the jeweller Emile Philippe, pupil of Jules Wièse the Elder, made their appearance. By this time, the Egyptian fashion was no longer confined to France. In London, the Italian jeweller Carlo Giuliano created a large brooch with two horses' heads, lotus flower and mask.

While Castellani and Fontenay were experimenting with jewelry in the Etruscan style, based on precise and analytical observation, craftsmen working in the Egyptian style contented themselves with a formal repertoire which lacked archaeological authenticity and concentrated on the exotic in pharaonic Egypt. One example is the ancient Egyptian technique of cloisonné enamelling, which was used only sparingly in ancient times, the desired colour contrasts usually being achieved with inlays of stone or glass. In the nineteenth century, however, cloisonné enamel was lavished on jewelry which was called 'Egyptian' but which remained faithful to the Second Empire style of Napoleon III. At the most popular level, souvenirs were produced with sphinxes, lotus flowers, and scarabs in embossed gold, the favourite stones being turquoise, cabochon garnets and lapis lazuli.

At first, the Egyptian creations of Louis-François Cartier, the firm's founder, were much the same as his competitors'. An early entry for an Egyptian piece in Cartier's stock book for 1852 records a scarab bracelet of pearls and enamel; this is followed in 1854 by a scarab brooch, and in 1860 by a scarab ring. In Egyptian mythology, the scarab beetle, sacred to the god of the morning sun, was a symbol of resurrection, and though deprived of its protective character as an amulet, the scarab, in lapis lazuli or garnet, remained a favourite Egyptian motif in the nineteenth century.[5] In 1856 Cartier even sold a scarab brooch in turquoise and diamonds to Princess Mathilde, who also received a pair of Egyptian earrings of unspecified design in 1861.

Cartier's most sophisticated Egyptian piece dates from 1873, when the fashion peaked: it is a châtelaine in the form of an Egyptian head in gold, rose diamonds, rubies and a cameo. From this hangs a watch, its back decorated with an Egyptian figure in traditional headdress, the mount of which is an early example of the use of calibré-cut rubies. The next notable Egyptian pieces come in 1893: a brooch with an Egyptian head and lotus blossoms of matte yellow gold and a lotus brooch with five navette diamonds, a pearl and coloured stones.[6]

It is not surprising that Art Nouveau, supreme in Paris by about 1895, included Egyptian motifs: one example is René Lalique's tiara of 1899 with Isis and lotus motifs. It

is, however, somewhat remarkable to find examples of Egyptian ornament in Cartier's contemporary garland style, essentially eighteenth-century in inspiration. The explanation lies in a stylistic adaptation based on vague formal associations. In 1908, Cartier produced a choker with diamond drops and lotus motifs, and in 1911 a necklace of diamond bars adapted from the ancient Egyptian type known as the 'broad bead-collar'.[7] These pieces were as far removed from true Egyptian forms as the 1906–7 series of obelisk and pyramid clocks in fluorspar, diorite, thulite and porphyry in which Cartier followed late eighteenth-century fashions in interior decoration.

A series of sensational discoveries broadened knowledge of Egyptian history and added considerably to academic literature. After 1850, the French archaeologist Auguste Mariette[8] laid the foundations of the Bulaq Museum in Cairo with a number of important finds, and after Mariette's death in 1881 the French Egyptologist Gaston Maspero continued the work,[9] dividing his time between excavations in Egypt and a professorship in Paris. It was he who investigated the temples of Karnak. In 1908, Edward Ayrton discovered a royal tomb at Thebes and four years later the German Egyptologist Ludwig Borchardt came upon the head of Nefertiti. In 1914 Flinders Petrie excavated the Pyramid of Sesostris II at Lahun. At the same time, large collections of Egyptian art were being assembled, of which the most important in private hands was that of Lord Carnarvon (now in the Metropolitan Museum, New York).

In the wake of these great discoveries, a number of important art dealers specializing in treasures of the ancient Mediterranean world opened businesses in Paris. Among them were the brothers Kalebdjian, from Cairo, and Dikran Kelekian, who was also represented in both Cairo and New York. Young Louis Cartier became a regular visitor to both establishments: neighbourly relations were soon established with Kalebdjian at 12 rue de la Paix, and Kelekian, at 2 Place Vendôme, was not far away. Louis bought rare pieces of antique art from both, which he displayed at his house in the rue Saint-Guillaume: we know of an Egyptian cat in faience from Kelekian, as well as a bas relief portraying the pharaoh Ramesses. That Louis took his business with the two dealers very seriously is indicated by the technical discussion concerning an Egyptian wooden mask; both he and Kalebdjian consulted the curator of the Egyptian department in the Louvre as to its precise identification.

Arising from his study of the art of the Mediterranean peoples, Louis Cartier came up with the idea of a new synthesis in jewelry design which was to enrich the wide-ranging selection at the rue de la Paix with a novel Cartier speciality: fragments of ancient jewelry and *objets d'art* in contemporary settings, presented in a fresh context. The idea was both daring and up to the minute, yet there were interesting precedents in earlier centuries.[10] An exhibition was planned in which jewelry of different periods and cultures would demonstrate the richness of colour and variety of theme of the new design programme. The show opened at rue de la Paix on 2 June 1913 and later at the Copley Plaza Hotel in Boston. The catalogue, embellished with Louis Cartier's favourite motif of a Persian carpet medallion, promised 'a selection of Persian, Indian and Tibetan jewelry to suit the latest fashion'. Although Egyptian jewelry was not mentioned on the title page, an Egyptian lotus pendant and a turquoise amulet featured among the exhibits.

Some of the exhibits were from Kalebdjian's collection; some from the London dealer Imre Schwaiger, a specialist in Indian art. The following year Kalebdjian was to deliver a whole series of Egyptian pieces to Cartier, among them a head from the Saite period in turquoise-blue enamel; a Greek Alexandrian sphinx in gold; two Egyptian capitals with seated cats; a turquoise-blue falcon pendant; a Uraeus snake in cornelian; and a lotus collar in faience and gold. However, Kalebdjian did more than merely supply Cartier. Six months after the latter's exhibition Kalebdjian staged a Christmas show of his own, consisting of a selection of 147 pieces of ancient jewelry. The catalogue observed laconically: 'Today fashion decrees that the elegant Parisienne should wear ancient jewelry; and not merely stale imitations, but the very jewels themselves that once adorned the bosom of an Egyptian queen or a Greek empress.'

The inventive concept of combining ancient and non-European art of earlier epochs in modern settings led Cartier to astonishing syntheses in the fields of Egyptian, Indian and Chinese/Japanese art, which were unique in the Art Deco of the 1920s. In his Egyptian creations Louis Cartier preferred to employ pieces of ancient faience, either figurative

165 Design for a vanity case with a depiction of the god Horus [**167**], 1927

166 'Sarcophagus' vanity case. Cartier Paris, 1925. Enamelled gold, bone, emeralds, onyx and diamonds set in platinum. Curved bone lid carved with female figure and tulip, framed by emerald, onyx, and pavé-set diamond columns with carved emerald palm-leaf capitals. At each end a sphinx with carved emerald face and paws, wearing a sapphire headdress

167 Vanity case. Cartier Paris, 1927. Enamelled gold, coral, lapis lazuli, emeralds and diamonds set in platinum with an engraved Egyptian calcite plaque on each side. On the front, Horus as a youth carries a scorpion and a lion

168 *left* Vanity case. Cartier Paris, 1924.
Gold, mother-of-pearl, coral, lapis lazuli, onyx
and diamonds with an Egyptian blue-glazed
faience figure playing a pipe and surmounted
by a coral, onyx and diamond lotus

169 *above* 'Egyptian' cigarette case. Cartier
Paris, special order, 1929. Gold mount with
lapis lazuli plaques framed by coral, diamond
and enamel; on the narrow sides a turquoise
glazed faience figure of the goddess Bastet
seated on a papyrus column (Late Period,
4th–3rd century BC) against a mother-of-pearl
background; the ends black enamel

or embellished with hieroglyphs, as in the pendants, brooches and buckles produced from 1920.[11] The scarab remained popular: as early as 1907 Louis Cartier had given his first wife a scarab ring, and as late as 1932 he received a commission for a necklace composed of a faience scarab from the Maspero collection, framed in ornamental diamond lotus blossoms [161]. Among the brooches inspired by the Egyptian pantheon we find the goddess Isis, the falcon god Horus, the god Nefertum born from a lotus blossom, and the lion goddess Sekhmet [156].[12] The latter is found in two sketches produced for a customer by the London workshop, with different border designs. Cartier Paris found Sekhmet very popular, and even used her as a motif on hat-pins.

In 1920 Louis Cartier and Charles Jacqueau had created a vanity case in mediaeval style with an ivory plaque from Louis Cartier's collection inlaid on the lid. Later they produced four cases which are the most important examples of work using Egyptian elements. The first is a vanity case with a turquoise-blue faience figure of an Egyptian figure playing the pipes [168], produced during the months in 1924 when Howard Carter was raising the lid of the sarcophagus in Tutankhamun's tomb: a large lotus plant in coral and onyx fans out over a background of lapis lazuli and mother-of-pearl. The following year saw the appearance of perhaps the greatest of these Egyptian-style cases, in the form of a sarcophagus [166]: the arched cover consists of an engraved bone panel depicting a maiden among lotus flowers, framed in archaic Greek motifs and lotus flowers in cloisonné enamel; at its head and foot the sarcophagus is embellished with figures of engraved emerald and calibré-cut sapphires, which recalled the recently excavated mummy of Tutankhamun and the enigmatic Sphinx; on the underside is a gold plaque adorned with a female offering-bearer surrounded by ibises and lotus stems. This case was acquired in the year it was made by Mrs George Blumenthal, wife of the American collector and banker. In 1927 Cartier's produced a powder compact adorned with two bands of lapis lazuli and inlaid with an Egyptian stone relief depicting the god Ched.[13] The last in the series is a 1929 cigarette case of lapis lazuli and coral, decorated on the sides with two antique faience representations of the goddess Bastet shown as a cat on a pillar [169].

170 Lotus flower deity brooch. Cartier Paris for Cartier New York, special order, 1927. Egyptian blue-glazed faience head with enamel, diamonds, emeralds, rubies and onyx set in platinum

171 Design for a brooch depicting the goddess Maat, 1927

While the Egyptian pieces produced by Cartier before 1920 show that there would have been a fashion for things Egyptian after the First World War, it was predictable that the fashion would verge on hysteria – exploited as 'Tutmania' by the film industry and the luxury trade in both Europe and America – from the moment when Elisabeth, Queen of the Belgians, Lloyd George, the French actress Cécile Sorel and the Maharaja of Poona made pilgrimages to the site of the pharaoh's tomb, pursued by the press.[14] To accommodate the streams of tourists from America and Japan, Egyptian railways inaugurated the 'Tutankhamun Special' between Cairo and Luxor. Would not the pharaoh, some asked, punish the desecration of his tomb? According to ancient Egyptian belief, the sun descended to the King of the Dead every evening, where it overcame the powers of Darkness, permitting the Dead to share in the radiance of eternity during the night, and then returned the next morning, rejuvenated, to climb the heavens once more. It seemed that Tutankhamun was taking his revenge when in 1923 Lord Carnarvon died of an insect bite. The legend of the curse of the pharaohs was born, bringing with it fears of impending disaster. Collectors rid themselves of their treasures and rushed to present them to the British Museum. The fashion industry, however, had no such qualms. Tutankhamun umbrellas and cigarettes, Leon Bakst's 'Isis' collection and Madeleine Vionnet's Egyptian models – the curse of the pharaohs became an overnight money-spinner. While the Paris cosmetic firm Ramses promoted their 'Ambre de Nubie' and 'Poudre de Riz au Secret de Sphinx' with sphinxes, pyramids and palms, the jeweller René Boivin, who was in the rue des Pyramides until 1931, decorated his firm's letterhead with appropriate Egyptian symbols.

The silhouettes of sphinxes, obelisks and pyramids came to evoke an entire culture. The fact that imitation hieroglyphs often introduced into Art Deco designs were quite meaningless is hardly to be wondered at. After all, in ancient Rome, the incomprehensible hieroglyphs on late Egyptian monuments had provided decorative models. It is interesting to note, however, that on Cartier's pipe-player vanity case [168] the hieroglyphs are in fact real. During this period Van Cleef & Arpels executed an exquisite series of brooches and bracelets, which conjured up anecdotal Egyptian scenes of pharaohs and priests, lotus plants and soul-birds in designs of coloured tesserae. In 1928 Boucheron, who did not care for the Egyptian style, created a cloisonné enamel tiara with the falcon of the sun for King Fuad, who had opened the 1911 Franco-Egyptian Exposition at the Louvre and who made a further visit to Paris in 1927.

Through Louis Cartier's personal liking for Egyptian art, his designers became more familiar with Egyptian materials and techniques and this led to a new synthesis of colour and form. From then on, the cool Egyptian combinations of cornelian and lapis lazuli, cornelian and turquoise, and turquoise, lapis lazuli and gold enriched the Art Deco palette. Amethyst alone, which had also been known to the Egyptians, was set aside, having played out its dominant role in another fashion context after 1910. But while the ancient Egyptians had preferred gold above all else and used it as the setting for enamels in the cloisonné technique, Cartier's designers preferred platinum. In the common Art Deco combination of black and white – onyx and diamond – platinum had the advantage that it did not introduce another colour.[15]

The low-relief style and hieratic figures of Egyptian sculpture suited the two-dimensional orientation of Art Deco and were transferred without difficulty to the aesthetic of the 1920s. Cartier's designers, above all Jacqueau, despite his unconvincing assertion that the Egyptian style was alien to him, found inspiration in the Louvre, which, since the days of Mariette, could boast the largest Egyptian collection in continental Europe. Moreover, they could encounter remarkable traces of earlier Egyptomania on their sorties into the streets of Paris, for example on the Egyptian house in the Place du Caire or the palm-bedecked fountain in the Place du Châtelet of 1858. Further inspiration was to be found in the study of the technical literature provided by Louis Cartier. Thus the 'torpedo' pendant launched by Cartier's in about 1912 derives from an animal-tail motif on a loincloth of the early XIIth Dynasty,[16] while Jacqueau's lotus blossom tiara of 1923 (later broken up) owed its inspiration to the headdress of the daughters of Djehutihotpe (d. *c*. 1850 BC) in the Cairo Museum.

Next to the pyramid, the most favoured Egyptian architectural form in Cartier's jewelry was the pylon, a structure with sloping sides that served as a gate to a temple. It was first employed in 1913 as a frame ornament on a lotus vase and for the base of a sphinx. Above all, however, the pylon provided the outline for the most splendid of all Cartier's works in the Egyptian style: the 'Temple Gate' clock of 1927 [**155**, **172**]. The case, freely modelled on the Temple of Khonsu at Karnak, was inlaid with mother-of-pearl with blue hieroglyphs. The plinth is adorned with a pharaoh and plants and a Nile river god making an offering, while on top a goddess spreads her wings wide. The coral mount of the clock face is complemented at base and top with a counterpoint of lapis lazuli.

Louis Cartier continued to encourage the production of jewelry in the Egyptian style, but it was Jacques Cartier of London who organized the various exhibitions that were held in Cairo. After his death in 1942 this responsibility passed to Marcel Marson (b. 1900), who had been a sales representative for the firm since 1928. In 1937 he went to Egypt on the occasion of the engagement of King Farouk, and the following year he was sent to Albania for the wedding of King Zog I. Although Cartier's Egyptian style enjoyed a certain vogue up to the outbreak of the Second World War, the symbolic climax of its creative phase was reached in 1929, the year of the Cairo Exhibition, when Jacques Cartier played host to King Fuad, and the company received the royal warrant as suppliers to the Egyptian court.

172 'Egyptian Temple Gate' clock (archive photograph). Cartier Paris, 1927 [cp. **155**]

173 'Egyptian Pylon' pendant with sphinx. Cartier Paris, special order, 1921. Cavetto cornice and frame in onyx, containing stylized lotus flowers in rubies and emeralds on a pavé-set diamond ground, surmounted by a sphinx made of an engraved moonstone and pavé-set diamonds, rubies and emeralds

174 'Egyptian Pylon' pendant. Cartier Paris, 1913. Cavetto cornice and frame in diamonds and onyx containing a vase with a central papyrus bud made from a pear-shaped diamond, and pendant papyrus and Egyptian lilies

CHAPTER ELEVEN

LES INDES GALANTES

In the summer of 1901, during the year of mourning for Queen Victoria, Pierre Cartier was called to Buckingham Palace. He was commissioned to create an Indian necklace from various pieces of royal jewelry for the new Queen, Alexandra, to wear with three Indian gowns sent by Mary Curzon, wife of the Viceroy of India. Pierre Cartier was familiar with the Indian jewelry of the English royal house, which had accumulated as costly presents since the eighteenth century and had become the greatest collection in Europe. However, the jewelry which Queen Alexandra wanted to wear had been mainly designed for men and was therefore too stiff and heavy to harmonize with the fashions of 1900. For this first commission from the palace, the Paris designers created a light and elegant Indian-style necklace, comprising seventy-one pearls, twelve cabochon rubies and ninety-four cabochon emeralds. Alexandra was pleased with the piece and wore it frequently.

For Cartier the commission meant not only the start of a long and profitable period of royal patronage, but also his first contact with the exotic world of the Orient. Thanks to the British imperial experience, Indian influence was much more marked in England than in Paris. It is hardly surprising, therefore, that from 1909 the Paris house assigned all aspects of its Indian business – the purchase of stones in Delhi, customer contacts in Bombay, and contacts with the maharajas during their frequent visits to England – to Jacques Cartier and the London house.

While Europeans harboured grotesque ideas about India ('India the great unknown – most people have a better idea of the moon', Lady Curzon is said to have exclaimed), it became fashionable for the maharajas to make extended tours of the European capitals, frequently undertaken on the pretext of engaging in political discussions in Whitehall or of escorting their sons to Eton or Harrow. The British authorities did not approve of the princes' long absences from their territories; indeed, Lord Curzon twice refused permission for the Gaekwar of Baroda to travel. But the princes relished the freedom and comforts of the great European cities and indulged themselves in luxuries and hotel life. While Curzon thundered against 'this class of uncultured, sporty, womanizing young princes', the Maharaja of Kapurthala dined unconcernedly with Queen Victoria at Balmoral and, later, Ranjitsinhji of Nawanagar attracted all eyes as a cricketer at Cambridge.

The highpoints in the display of European–Indian magnificence were Edward VII's coronation in London and its celebration a little later at the Delhi Durbar, where the King-Emperor was represented by his brother, the Duke of Connaught. The Delhi celebrations were opened by the Nizam of Hyderabad and the Maharaja of Mysore, India's two most powerful princes, and featured the ceremonial elephants of the Maharaja of Benares. At the ball that followed, Lady Curzon created a sensation with a dress by Worth of Paris of peacock feathers adorned with emeralds.[1] Edward VII, while still Prince of Wales, had visited India and Nepal in 1867 but his royal progress of 1906 is more famous. Pictures of Queen Alexandra riding in her howdah, accompanied by the Nawab of Bhopal and Lord Kitchener, stimulated throughout Europe an interest in all things Indian. In the following year Princess Lucien Murat described the gardens of Golconda and the Lake Palace of Udaipur, the 'Venice of India', in *My Journey to India*. Up to the 1920s, India, together with Persia and Egypt, was to provide exotic backdrops for European society life and inspiration to literature, fashion and interior décor. Poiret sketched the Indian turbans in the Victoria and Albert Museum; Diaghilev created his Hindu ballet *Le Dieu bleu*; 'Hindu-brown' became the fashionable colour; and Mrs Payne Whitney decorated her house in Westbury, Connecticut, with Indo-Persian frescoes.

The first contacts with the forms of Indian jewelry and ornament came in the nineteenth century with the world exhibitions.[2] Shortly before the Great Exhibition of 1851 in London the East India Company presented Queen Victoria with examples of Indian jewelry together with the legendary 'Koh-i-Noor' diamond.[3] Further pieces reached Europe following the looting of Delhi after 1857–58. By the 1860s Mughal jades decorated with flowers and birds had become known in England. In addition to its Japanese range, Liberty's began to import Indian designs and jewelry, which were eagerly taken up by the avant-garde, such as the Pre-Raphaelite artist Dante Gabriel Rossetti. In 1876 Victoria was proclaimed Empress of India, and from 1880 Indian jewelry enjoyed a vogue in both England and France. The British jeweller Hamilton set up in Calcutta, while in London the Italian Giuliano enjoyed success with his Indian-inspired enamelled jewelry. In France,

Oscar Massin executed a commission for a belt for a maharaja and his competitor Rouvenat hit upon the idea of the long pin, which he called the 'Kashmirienne', to be worn with the then popular Kashmir shawl. The Paris Exposition of 1867 included engraved and pierced Indian diamonds.[4]

At about this time we find the first mention of jewelry of Indian provenance in the Cartier archives: 1872, Indian earrings of gold and turquoise; 1879, a five-strand pearl necklace with six small enamelled Indian plaques; 1884, two three-rope necklaces with Indian gold coins and Indian enamelled buttons.

It was not until 1900, prompted perhaps by the Paris Exposition of that year, that the firm itself created an 'Indian' ring with two cabochon emeralds. Like the earliest pieces described as 'Egyptian', this ring was formally inspired by the Orient, but its platinum setting was undoubtedly determined by contemporary Parisian trends. Shortly after this Queen Alexandra placed her first order with the firm. But it was not until about 1910 when, under Poiret's influence, fashion began to dictate Persian–Indian aigrettes and pendant motifs, that Indian creations became of any significance. Interestingly, *The Grammar of Ornament* by Owen Jones, a popular pattern book with numerous Indian designs, was frequently used by Cartier's in both Paris and London. In 1910, we find an entry for a pendant in the Persian manner at Cartier New York, and in the same year the *Herald Tribune* was praising the 'Persian and Indian designs of Cartier'.

The first important contacts with maharajas were consolidated during the celebrations of George V's coronation at the Delhi Durbar in 1911, and in the same year Jacques Cartier embarked in the *Polynesia* at Marseilles for his first journey to India. The voyage to Bombay, via Malta, Port Said and Aden, took sixteen days. To his surprise he found that the maharajas, who welcomed him into their palaces, were chiefly interested in pocket-watches, which were then high fashion in Paris and London.

Thanks to the merchants of the East India Company, European watches, clocks and automata had been known in India since the eighteenth century, being among the European wares on sale at their Lal Bazaar in Calcutta. Tipu Sahib, the feared Sultan of Mysore from 1782 to 1799, commissioned, probably from a French clockmaker, a life-size automaton of a tiger which savaged a European to the sound of cries of distress and the roar of a tiger. Jacques Cartier had no man-eating predators on offer, but he did sell a number of harmless watches. The Maharaja of Kapurthala purchased one in blue enamel; the Nizam of Hyderabad one in gold; the Maharaja of Nawanagar one in platinum; and the Aga Khan one ornamented with pavé diamonds. The Nawab of Ranpur was seduced by four chiming carriage clocks, which were to sound the 'charming peal of European cathedral bells'.

Sayaji Rao III, the Gaekwar of Baroda, whom Cartier visited in his five-hundred-room palace of Lakshmi Vilas, proved more fastidious. The founder of India's most modern state, he had proscribed the caste system and introduced free education, and his popularity was demonstrated later at his golden jubilee by the presentation of a cannon made of pure gold, which fired a twenty-one gun salute. But his great passion was jewelry, and he commissioned Jacques Cartier to reset his entire collection in platinum, then more prized than either gold or Indian enamel work in the Westernized courts of India. Shrewdly, Jacques had included some 133 pieces of platinum jewelry in his sample cases for the Indian trip – among them combs, brooches, breast ornaments, an 'Egyptian' necklace, and, of course, numerous watches. The Gaekwar was so taken with the young Cartier that he immediately wanted to entrust him with the maintenance of all his jewelry. However, disturbed by Cartier's growing influence in Baroda, envious Indian jewellers stirred up suspicion among the rival factions at court. After a few days, therefore, Jacques took honoured leave of the 'court circus' and embarked at Karachi for the Persian Gulf (pp. 126ff.).

Jacques Cartier's important Indian journey demonstrated something that was to hold true for the next quarter of a century: Indian rulers were exclusively interested in Parisian jewelry and had no hesitation in handing over their family treasures for reworking in fashionable European styles. Conversely, India's traditional enamel jewelry with its engraved gemstones became something of a craze in Europe, and inspired in the designers of Cartier's Art Deco style a special feeling for the Orient.

It was the colourful quality of Indian enamel work that made the first impression. In contrast to European enamel, which mostly used the cloisonné technique, Indian

opposite

179 Jacques Cartier during his visit to India in 1911 for the Delhi Durbar

180 Cartier's office in New Delhi in the 1930s

181 *Bazu* upper arm bracelet. Cartier Paris, 1922. Diamonds in platinum setting; a central articulated plaque with three detachable pendant leaf-shaped elements on large pavé diamond-set rings champlevé enamel[5] preserved some centuries-old colour patterns. From Benares came the exquisite rose-coloured enamel, with lotus, leaf and bird patterns which in the eighteenth century were influenced by Isfahan. The decorative motifs of Jaipur – birds, elephants and wild boar on a red, green or white ground – were older still. Centuries of consistent manufacture made Jaipur enamel a synonym for enamel itself. Miniature plaques from Jaipur became popular medallions for the lids of Cartier's vanity cases. However, the enamel which had most powerfully fired the imagination of Cartier's designers, even before Jacques' Indian journey, came from Lucknow, the capital of Oudh. Since the eighteenth century this enamel had been fused on silver, with blue and green the dominant colours. Next to the black and pink blend of onyx and coral, it became the colour combination most favoured for Cartier's Art Deco work. Taking his cue from this enamel, Cartier boldly juxtaposed sapphire and Indian engraved emerald, with nothing to soften the startling colour contrast. Even before the Ballets Russes championed this same colour combination, Cartier's produced a necklace with an engraved emerald of 105 carats and a sapphire of 70 carats for J. P. Morgan, which was followed by similar items for Mrs Burns, Eugène de Rothschild and the Aga Khan [301].

Just as Indian enamel influenced Cartier's colour sense, so the towering *sarpech* (*jiqka*) and the drooping *turah*, Indian turban ornaments, influenced the designers in Paris, London and New York, in their choice of motifs. The principal component of the *sarpech* is the Kashmir palm or mango leaf, a cone shape bent over at the point [244], found in Persian Mir and Serabend carpets, Mughal drawings of the seventeenth century and Kashmir shawls of the eighteenth.[6] From 1912 the mango leaf inspired the basic shape of the Cartier version of the fashionable aigrette. In the 1920s, however, it was adapted with a drop stone dangling from its tip [143 *bottom left*] to lapel and hat brooches. The *turah*, on the other hand, was a turban tassel of several strings of pearls fitted to a curved enamel bar; a specially valuable Indian example was the black pearl tassel worn by the Maharaja of Kutch Behar. Cartier derived the rounded tassel indirectly from India via the Ballets Russes and Russian costume and transformed it into by far the most popular pendant motif of the Art Deco period. The Cartier tassel, often made up of hundreds of small pearls or coral or onyx beads, was generally attached, as pendant, to a necklace, to an onyx hoop brooch, or to an embellished jade stirrup bow. When worn as a shoulder ornament, the tassel might be as long as 25 cm.

The Indian *bazu*, an armlet for the upper arm, with its carpet-like central section framed in gold thread, inspired a Cartier bracelet in which a textile-patterned central section of diamonds [181] was secured by a black silk cord. Other designs were derived from the talismanic pendants of crystal or jade[7] with the planetary stones prescribed by Indian astrology. They inspired Art Deco pendants in a variety of colours: jade, amethyst or onyx were inlaid with floral patterns in cabochon gemstones or diamonds recalling the marble friezes of Mughal architecture or the border decorations of Indo-Persian miniatures.

Diamond had many associations with the Hindu pantheon, and was often given a gold setting in the form of a lotus – an allusion to the ancient legend according to which Brahma, the World Principle, had emerged from a lotus blossom. Cartier's designers adapted the idea, assimilating it with the existing lily-of-the-valley setting (see p. 48). Various forms of Indian necklaces, such as the *gulu*, a choker-style wedding ornament, were also influential, while in the 1930s the stiff hoop collar known as *hasli* inspired necklaces and bracelets of massive design.

In India, Jacques Cartier learned to distinguish the age, origin and function of the local jewelry under the guidance of Imre Schwaiger, the Hungarian art expert. Schwaiger, who looked after Cartier's interests in Delhi and negotiated the purchase of Indian *objets d'art* and jewelry, divided his time between Delhi and London (his son later worked for Cartier's in London). It was from Schwaiger that Cartier bought a number of Mughal boxes, an enamelled *turah*, and gold-painted green glass medallions as ornaments for vanity cases, as well as turquoise and crystal figures of the elephant god Ganesha, Krishna the flute player, and Buddha. In addition, precious stones were bought from Hindu, Jain or Parsi merchants.

During the time of Jacques Cartier's Eastern journeys, many stones from princely collections came up for sale. In 1912 and 1913 the Nizam of Hyderabad had both gemstones and antique weapons auctioned while the Gaekwar of Baroda disposed of pearls and jewels.

182 Pair of ear pendants. Cartier Paris, special order, 1935. Platinum, white gold; old- and single-cut diamonds, faceted and calibré-cut rubies, natural pearls

opposite

183 Design by Charles Jacqueau for an
Indian-style headdress ('Coiffe de Maharadjah'),
c. 1926

this page

184 'Elephant' powder compact with lipstick
case. Cartier Paris, 1925. Yellow and pink gold;
cabochon turquoises, mother-of-pearl,
cabochon sapphires; black enamel

185 The Kapurthala turban ornament.
Cartier Paris, commissioned in 1926 by Jagatjit
Singh, Maharaja of Kapurthala. Mounted with
nineteen emeralds of various shapes, round-
and rose-cut diamonds, and pearls. Weight
of central hexagonal emerald: 177.40 carats;
weight of remaining 18 emeralds: 254.84 carats.
From an advertisement in *Spur Magazine*, 1931

opposite

186 Jagatjit Singh, Maharaja of Kapurthala,
wearing the turban ornament, seen in a
photograph signed by him in 1928

FOR THE BROW OF A GREAT PRINCE

*A Cartier creation for the Maharajah
of Kapurthala, who is known for his
excellent taste. One of the most enlight-
ened of Hindu princes, he spends a
part of each year in Paris. He is such
an admirer of French architecture that
he had a French architect go to India
to build him a Louis XVI palace*

*The Maharajah, like most of the other
Indian potentates, has faith in the
increasing value of pearls and precious
stones and regularly devotes a portion
of his annual income to increasing his
collection. The Hindu princes look
upon gems as a permanent investment
to pass from generation to generation*

Jagatjit Singh

Maharaja of Kapurthala

2. 11. 28

opposite

187 Headband. Cartier London, 1930. Mounted with a fringe of cabochon emeralds with diamond tips, the centre of the lyre design set with an engraved emerald of 47.20 carats

above

188 Necklace, Cartier London, 1927. Platinum; the diamond link chain flanked by pierced cabochon emeralds, the pendant mounted with a fancy-shaped cabochon emerald and three cabochon tassels

right

189 Necklace, made jointly by Cartier London and New York, 1928 and 1929, sold to Mrs Edward F. Hutton (formerly Marjorie Merryweather Post). Platinum; the diamond chain mounted with twenty-four cabochon emerald drops and similar beads, the reverse of tapered bead cluster design; pendant with a pentagonal and an oval engraved emerald and five partly fluted emerald drops suspended from a diamond buckle motif

Les Indes galantes 165

190 Fruit bowl brooch. Cartier Paris, 1925. Platinum, gold; pear-, lozenge-shaped and square single- and baguette-cut diamonds; one cabochon emerald and two cabochon rubies; fluted onyx and black enamel

191 Tree brooch. Cartier Paris, special order, 1927. Platinum, gold; round old- and single-cut diamonds; one leaf-shaped carved emerald, one triangular carved emerald; one baguette-cut sapphire, two pear-shaped faceted sapphires, buff-top sapphires and cabochon sapphires; leaf-shaped carved rubies, buff-top rubies and cabochon rubies; black enamel

192 Vase of flowers brooch. Cartier London, 1928. Platinum; round old-cut diamonds; one engraved hexagonal 27.14-carat emerald, one emerald bead studded with a collet-set diamond, one fluted emerald bead, cabochon emeralds; leaf-shaped carved rubies and cabochon rubies; cabochon sapphires; natural pearls studded with collet-set diamonds

At these great auctions the Delhi jewellers were principally interested in emeralds, while those from Gujarat concentrated on pearls. Interestingly, emerald prices remained high, whereas the price of pearls fluctuated.

The emerald[8] is the stone most closely associated with India, even though, paradoxically, the subcontinent has no significant emerald deposits. (By contrast, Ceylon was rich in sapphires and rubies, and in 1881 unexpected finds had revealed the world's most valuable sapphires in Kashmir.) Up to the sixteenth century, the only noteworthy emeralds known in India came from Egypt.[9] From then on Colombian emeralds began to reach India by adventurous routes,[10] through Spain's colonies in the Philippines and the Far East, as the great traveller Jean-Baptiste Tavernier was one of the first to suspect.[11] With these great soft green Colombian crystals the emerald came to be reckoned with the ruby and the pearl among the most valued of stones. This was especially the case in India, where the prismatic form of the beryl crystal, hexagonal in outline, was preserved in the outline of the cut stone [192, 301, 313].

In the early 1910s Cartier's spared no effort in a systematic search for rare Indian stones. In addition to Schwaiger in Delhi they had buying agents, like the Parsi pearl specialist Sethna, in Calcutta and Bombay, and the Bombay Trading Company, an autonomous Cartier subsidiary, developed the import–export trade between India, Europe and America, which would later be used by Cartier's European Watch and Clock Company. In 1912, it is true, the antique 'Roods' red diamond escaped the net, but the wholesale purchase of engraved gemstones and gemstone beads broke all records. Cut and naturalistically engraved with leaf, blossom and berry shapes [242, 245, 301, 313], they recalled the Islamic flower cult of the Mughal emperors and gave rise to some of the airiest creations of Jacqueau in Paris and Alexandre Genaille in New York – flower and fruit bracelets, and brooches in the shape of fruit bowls or flower baskets. The themes were often repeated but never became stereotyped. Of specially inspired design were a fruit bowl for W. K. Vanderbilt; a little Persian tree for Mrs George Blumenthal; and two bracelets and a double clip bought by Mrs Cole Porter [202, 203]. In 1923 an elegant pendant was created from a 136-carat emerald sphere together with an emerald of 42 carats cut to the shape of a bunch of grapes.

Although the terms 'Persian' and 'Indian' were both used in these categories, the reference was always to the art of the Mughal empire which fused Hindu and Persian elements. The nomenclature employed in a special exhibition mounted by Cartier in 1913 was equally variable. In the Indian context the catalogue made special mention of 'a bracelet with eighteen large diamonds, similar to that of the Maharani of Gwalior; a necklace of a cushion-cut and two drop-shaped engraved emeralds, nine large pearls and a ruby bead; an aigrette in Indian princely style, with diamonds and cabochon sapphires; a white jade rose, set with pearls and rubies; a necklace of five emerald flowers on two ropes of pearls; and a turban ornament of white agate with rubies and pearls'. In addition, there were a number of necklaces of sapphire, ruby and emerald beads, from which it emerges that emerald beads cost more than ruby beads of the same quality.

The multi-stranded necklaces of the Indian maharajas, which covered the whole breast [194], started the fashion for casually draped sautoirs of coloured beads [313] which, with hip-length ropes of pearls, dominated the 1920s style in necklaces. Cartier's bead style was plainly Indian though the colour combinations were often outside the Indian colour range: New York, for example, combined rose tourmaline beads with little onyx tubes, amber with engraved sapphire, rose coral with engraved turquoise and Lalique crystal beads. From AD 500 to 1500, India had been the world's principal supplier of beads, with exports to Arabia, Egypt, Persia and Europe;[12] her monopoly was broken only with the advent of the agate industry of Idar-Oberstein in Germany and the glass-bead industry of Venice.

Necklaces made of engraved emerald beads [313], often months, if not years, in the making, were naturally valued more highly than the various types of hardstone bead necklaces in Cartier's range of fantasy jewelry. Thus the London firm was especially proud of an example whose central stone weighed 136 carats; necklaces made for Mrs J. D. Biddle and Mrs J. P. Donahue were surely its equals.

One jewel, destined for an Indian collection, stands out among all these Indian-inspired Art Deco pieces. This was the turban ornament designed for Jagatjit Singh,

193 Handbag. Cartier New York, 1930.
Gold, platinum; one engraved ruby, leaf-shaped
carved emeralds and sapphires, ruby, sapphire
and emerald beads and roundels; cabochon
emeralds; brilliant-, round old- and single-cut
diamonds; seed and natural pearls; ivory-
coloured enamel; fabric covered with
seed pearls

Maharaja of Kapurthala (1872–1949), which breathes the spirit of pure Oriental tradition and seems to owe nothing to European influences [185, 186]. The Maharaja, friend of Theodore Roosevelt and Clemenceau, was a man of sophistication who toured Europe annually from 1900 and whose love of France led him in 1909 to build a palace on the model of Versailles. When Jacques Cartier visited Kapurthala, he found himself waited on by servants in Louis XV-style perukes. In 1926, the year before his golden jubilee, the Maharaja commissioned this pagoda-style tiara from Louis Cartier. An entry in the Maharaja's diary, dated 27 September 1926, reads: 'Lunch at the Ritz, where I was presented to the King of Yugoslavia. Afterwards to the painter Marcel Baschet in full regalia and the finished emerald tiara from Cartier. A piece truly unique of its kind.'

While work was progressing at Cartier Paris on this most elegant piece, the house was also busy with what, in purely quantitative terms, must be the biggest commission of all time: the remodelling of the crown jewels of the Maharaja of Patiala [2, 195]. In 1925 – the coronation year of his neighbour the Maharaja of Kashmir – Sir Bhupindra Singh, Maharajadhiraja, Great King of Kings, the ruler of Patiala (the largest Sikh state in India), opened his treasury and handed over his most valuable pieces to Cartier. The fabulous collection of stones included the 'Victoria' or 'De Beers' diamond of 234.69 carats,[13] which became the centrepiece of the great ceremonial necklace [177, 194].

After years of work, Cartier's had filled casket after casket of jewels for Patiala. The designers had taken the traditional forms of Indian jewelry into account in the resettings, but the new pieces represented elegant reworkings inspired by contemporary Art Deco trends. It was surely the first time that the Paris house had produced an example of the *nath*, a nose ring in diamond, ruby, emerald and sapphire, typical of south India. In addition there was ankle jewelry, armlets, a bracelet of the nine planetary stones, and the exotic *hathpul*, a traditional piece of Rajasthani wedding jewelry worn on the back of the hand, linking bracelet and finger rings. No fewer than 223 pearls were drilled to create a single bracelet. The photographic inventory constituted a 36-page album. In 1928, Cartier exhibited the principal pieces at the rue de la Paix before their delivery to the Moti Bagh palace in Patiala. The show attracted society personalities like J. P. Morgan and his sister Anne, the Duchess of Alba and Mrs Laura Corrigan, and created a sensation in Europe and the United States.

From then on, perhaps influenced by this widely publicized event, maharajas sent increasing numbers of jewels to Cartier's for remodelling. In Paris and London the designers became accustomed to assimilating the mango leaf or the engraved emeralds of Indian jewelry into Art Deco style. The maharajas in return proudly showed off their latest Art Deco acquisitions – labelled as the *dernier cri* at the 1925 Exposition in Paris – once they were back in India. The ruler of Mandi, married to Princess Amrit, daughter of the Maharaja of Kapurthala, had his emeralds, among them an engraved one of 68.81 carats, set into a headdress by Cartier's, while the Maharaja of Patna had his state necklace, with its three antique rose diamonds, remodelled in Paris in 1935.

The commission that stretched the Cartier expertise to its fullest was the resetting and enlargement of the exceptional jewelry collection of the Maharaja of Nawanagar [302, 404]. The Maharaja ruled a small principality on the Katiawar peninsula with its own pearl fishery, though the pearls produced were of only modest value and mostly used in traditional Hindu medicine. He commissioned from Cartier's a necklace of six ropes of pearls, embellished with an engraved emerald of 62.93 carats, for alternative use as a turban ornament. The Maharaja's daughter later recalled that a black servant was specially employed in the palace at Jamnagar to wear the pearls on his velvety skin and so preserve their natural lustre. In Jacques Cartier's opinion, the Prince's emerald collection was 'unequalled in the world, if not in quantity then certainly in quality'. It was further enriched by a state necklace, designed by Cartier's, of seventeen rectangular emeralds [196, 308], including a stone of 70 carats which came from the Turkish sultan. In addition there was a close-fitting collar of thirteen emeralds with two absolutely identical stones at the centre; two turban ornaments, one with a 56-, the other with a 39-carat emerald; and also a two-string bead necklace of rich velvety green. The Maharaja was a frequent visitor to London, notably attending the coronation of George VI, and the settings of these pieces are characterized by the somewhat monotonous, geometrical style of Cartier's London workshops in the 1930s.

opposite

194 Yadavindra Singh, Maharaja of Patiala, wearing the diamond necklace commissioned in 1928 by his father, Sir Bhupindra Singh [177]

195 Emerald and diamond parade necklace and head ornament created for Sir Bhupindra Singh, Maharaja of Patiala, as illustrated in the *New York Herald*, Paris, December 1928

196 Sir Digvijaysinhji, Maharaja Jam Saheb of Nawanagar, wearing the emerald and diamond necklace created by Cartier London in 1926 [308] for his uncle, Maharaja Jam Saheb Ranjitsinhji Vibhaji, *c.* 1935

197 'Baguette' wristwatch. Cartier Paris, 1928. Made by Jaeger. Marked on the dial 'Cartier, France'. Baguette-shaped case of polished platinum and baguette-cut diamonds. Flat, notched winding crown on back. Attachments with baguette-, triangular, and square-cut diamonds forming the letter M. Platinum bracelet with multigem ('Tutti Frutti') motif of carved emeralds, sapphires, and rubies, marquise- and single-cut diamonds, double cord strap, clasp of gold and black enamel, hidden *déployant* buckle of pink gold. Rectangular dial of grained silver with Arabic numerals, inner minute track with indices at 5-minute intervals. Blue steel hands. At the time of its creation in 1925, the 'Baguette' watch was the smallest in the world

198 Bracelet. Cartier New York, special order, 1928. Platinum, brilliant-, round old- and single-cut diamonds; leaf-shaped carved rubies and cabochon rubies; fluted and smooth emerald beads and sapphire beads studded with collet-set diamonds; black enamel

199 Double clip brooch. Cartier New York, 1929. Platinum, 14-carat white gold; brilliant-, round old- and single-cut diamonds; leaf-shaped carved rubies, cabochon rubies and ruby beads; fluted and smooth emerald beads studded with collet-set diamonds; cabochon emeralds; black enamel

200 Pendant. Cartier Paris, created in 1930 for the Aga Khan. Platinum; cushion-shaped emerald (supplied by the Aga Khan) weighing 142.20 carats engraved with an Islamic prayer; onyx and diamond mount

201 Bracelet. Cartier Paris, created in 1930 for the Aga Khan. Platinum; central emerald (supplied by the Aga Khan) weighing 76 carats; band set with engraved sapphire and emerald leaves and onyx. The large emerald is engraved with text from the Quran, which reads, 'Say: God the Almighty gives prosperity to whom He wishes; dispossesses whom He wishes; honours whom He wishes and disgraces whom He wishes; He, the Almighty. He watches over the succession of day and night; out of life he makes death; and out of death, life; He bestows power without reckoning'

202 Strap bracelet. Cartier Paris, 1925, sold to Mrs Cole Porter. Platinum; round old- and single-cut diamonds; leaf-shaped carved sapphires and rubies; emerald beads studded with collet-set diamonds, emerald cabochons; onyx beads (berries); black enamel

203 Double clip brooch. Cartier Paris, sold to Mrs Cole Porter, 1935. Platinum, osmior; brilliant-, round old-, baguette- and single-cut diamonds; leaf-shaped carved sapphires, rubies and emeralds; cabochon emeralds, rubies and sapphires; square carved emeralds; buff-top and calibré-cut rubies and sapphires, faceted sapphires

204 'Hindu' necklace. Cartier Paris,
commissioned in 1936 by Daisy Fellowes
[see **205**, **206**], altered in 1963. Platinum, white
gold; marquise-, baguette- and round old-cut
diamonds; thirteen briolette-cut sapphires
weighing 146.9 carats in total, two leaf-shaped
carved sapphires (50.80 and 42.45 carats),
sapphire beads, one cabochon sapphire; square
carved emeralds, fluted and smooth emerald
beads, cabochon emeralds; leaf-shaped carved
rubies, smooth and carved ruby beads,
cabochon rubies

In the case of a diamond *sarpech*, this manner struck up a strange liaison with traditional Indian forms.[14]

In 1932, Clifford North was sent as Jacques Cartier's representative to the King of Nepal; when he finally reached Kathmandu he found that the European economic crisis of the 1930s had reverberated even in the distant Himalayas. Leaving Delhi, the ten-man party passed through Patna, aiming to cross the Ganges by ferry; from the outset they encountered a number of amusing obstacles. Their Hindu servants resisted setting out at all without favourable omens from the astrologers, while the twenty-one coolies refused to carry European or Muslim baggage through the Nepalese jungle. In Kathmandu, where a cannon sounded the curfew at ten every night, North waited for days for a carriage to take him to the Singha Durbar palace. In the palace itself, a bard recited the praises of the ruler as North spread out his wares in the flickering torchlight. They were valued at a third their true worth by the envious Nepalese jewellers and, in addition, the ruler had read reports of the threatening world crisis in the *Calcutta Statesman*. Business was clearly out of the question, and instead, swaying uncomfortably upon the back of an elephant, North attended the wedding of the ruler's grandson. On the last morning, North was awakened by cackling hens and the bleating of sheep: he was expected to accept a farewell present of livestock, corn, potatoes and oil. He left Kathmandu with an ivory box and signed photographs as gifts from the unpredictable ruler, and with the conviction that 'modern European jewelry with its valuable diamonds and costly settings would appear to be unsuited to Nepal'.

During the 1930s, European interest in India and its culture grew. At the Paris Colonial Exposition of 1931, Cartier's display with an Indian emerald bead tiara won a prize. The exhibition provided a cross-section of the diverse cultures of France's colonies, but once again jewellers and decorators exploited the material shown indiscriminately, combining traditional forms and colours at will. Only this can explain why Cartier's made a hair ornament in the same year for the Maharani of Nawanagar in a traditional Javanese bow shape.

Also by this time travelling conditions and communications had improved enough to encourage visits to India by wealthy if superficial tourists from the United States and Europe. In the opinion of American *Vogue* they were principally intrigued by the bejewelled elephants of Jaipur and the tiger hunts 'set up like a Broadway show', organized by the Maharaja of Kutch Behar and reached by the Darjeeling Express. Though India declined to reveal her secrets to these comfortable 'gentry', they often returned to Paris with 'barbaric' Indian jewelry, as the expensive souvenirs of their trip. Once the pieces had been remade and remounted by Cartier's, *Vogue* and *Harper's Bazaar* considered them the very height of fashion. Elsie de Wolfe's Indian necklace required an almost alchemical transformation by Cartier, and Misia Sert, the recently divorced wife of the painter, wore an eight-strand ruby necklace by Cartier's with, on a red silk cord hanging down her back, a motif sacred to Maya, the Indian goddess of earthly illusions. Trendsetters like Daisy Fellowes [204–206], Mrs Drexel Biddle, Ganna Walska (Mrs Harold McCormick) and Mrs Harrison Williams spread the Indian fashion, which soon even the Duchess of Windsor was to take up.

The Persian Prince Firuz, spoilt favourite of 1920s Paris cocktail parties, was supplanted in the next decade by Princess Karam, wife of the fourth son of the Maharaja of Kapurthala, who wore the sari with as much inimitable chic as Cartier's 'Oriental' jewelry. Who today remembers the 'diamants mystérieux' which she inspired at Cartier's? Apparently applied directly to the skin, they were just as 'mysterious' as the 'invisible setting' which Cartier and Van Cleef patented at about the same time.

The woman on Cartier's staff who proved herself mistress of the entire Indian range was, once again, Jeanne Toussaint.[15] She was in fact already wearing Indian jewelry in the late 1910s when, as an elegant young woman, she entered the firm. Elsie de Wolfe, holding a soirée complete with real elephants at her villa in Versailles, might be feted as an Indian expert, but only Jeanne Toussaint truly understood how a woman of fashion should wear Indian jewelry. Overnight she brought yellow gold, in India sacred to the gods, back into vogue. 'Jewels start a new gold rush', *Vogue* proclaimed in 1933, and the prophecy proved true. For thirty years platinum had determined the style and setting of the best European jewelry. Now these pieces were broken up and remade into exotic, massive gold jewelry, a trend linked to the crisis-laden atmosphere of the pre-war years.

opposite

205 Daisy, the Hon Mrs Reginald Fellowes, wearing her 'Hindu' necklace. Photograph by Cecil Beaton

above

206 Photograph from the Cartier archives showing the initial shape of Daisy Fellowes' necklace in 1936 [cp. **204**]

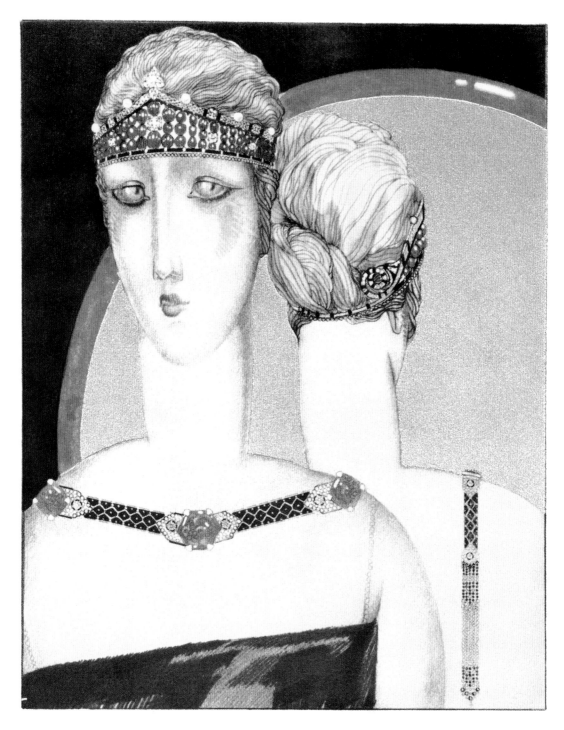

BÉRÉNICE

DIADÈME ET COLLIER, DE CARTIER

Modèle déposé. Reproduction interdite.

CHAPTER TWELVE

'1925':
THE EVOLUTION OF A STYLE

In about 1906, encouraged by Louis Cartier, the main designers of the Paris house – Rauline, Baloche and Thomas – made their earliest ventures into an abstract, geometric style. Simple cubes, polygons and rhombs in calibré-cut coloured stones appeared as the logical reaction against the playful forms of the garland style.[1]

The virtuoso application of the new shapes and cuts of the period gave rise to charming samples of unlimited combinations of forms which first made their appearance on tie-pins.

These were soon followed by geometric diamond pendants.

The new forms were not used for large pieces such as breast ornaments and tiaras, which were still the preserve of the traditional Louis XVI forms. The revolution which was unfolding was a revolution on a small scale, restricted, for the time being, to hat-pins, pendants and brooches.

It has always been tempting to attribute the invention of this repertoire of geometric forms to the influence of the contemporary Cubist painters, but in fact their experiments were of interest only to a small intellectual and artistic elite and had no influence on the decorative arts. Only later were certain decorative and reproducible motifs detached from their painterly context and used in design, in fashion, and finally in industry.

The roots of Cartier's forms in the early twentieth century lie more obviously within the circle of the Vienna Secession. Founded in 1897 by Klimt, Hoffmann and Olbrich, it led to the evolution of a style for architecture, painting and interior decoration based on squares and circles. It is entirely conceivable that in an over-enthusiastic adoption of rigorously geometric forms, Cartier's might eventually have developed aspirations similar to those of the later Bauhaus and to the style of such artist-jewellers as Fouquet and Sandoz. Fortunately, Cartier's geometric idiom was turned in a new direction, because shortly before 1910 the strongest and most up-to-date stylistic influences were flowing from the Orient.

The influence of Islamic forms on late nineteenth-century decorative arts had proved especially fruitful in France: as early as the Paris Exposition of 1878 European manufacturers had shown vases with Arabic decoration. The mosque-style Trocadero was built during this period, and a copy made in 1867 of the Bardo, the palace of the Bey of Tunis, still stands with its cupolas and horseshoe arches in the Park Montsouris.

Obliged to renounce representations of living things, Islamic decorative styles evolved linear–geometric motifs which were used in architecture and the applied arts: lattice and star patterns in rhythmic openwork forms, in various coloured woods, ivory and faience, appear together in mosques.

preceding pages, left

207 The 'Bérénice' bandeau and shoulder ornament, designed by Henri Chenaud (displayed at the Exposition Internationale des Arts Décoratifs et Industriels Modernes held in Paris in 1925 [**209**]). Illustration from *La Gazette du Bon Ton*

preceding pages, right

208 Bandeau. Cartier Paris, 1922. Platinum, gold; round old-, single- and rose-cut diamonds; coral, onyx, tortoiseshell and black enamel

Opposite

209 Cartier display at the 1925 Exposition in Paris. The mannequin wears the emerald, pearl and diamond 'Bérénice' bandeau and the 'Bérénice' shoulder ornament with three engraved emeralds and onyx [**207**], and a brooch in a spiral design of emeralds, pearls and diamonds

210 Brooch-pendant. Cartier Paris, 1912. Platinum; a large lozenge-shaped sapphire weighing 28.70 carats set in a diamond rectangle bordered with calibré-cut sapphires; chain of square-cut diamonds with calibré-cut sapphires and two cabochon sapphires

opposite (from the left, top to bottom)

211 Brooch. Cartier Paris, 1904. Platinum, yellow gold; rubies, diamonds

212 Brooch. Cartier Paris, 1906. Diamonds set in platinum and sapphires set in gold. Interlaced circles with a foliage motif in each, one in diamonds with a central sapphire, the other in sapphires with a central diamond

213 Brooch. Cartier Paris, 1909. Diamonds and rubies in a millegrain platinum setting. Two circular motifs terminating in squares each containing four calibré-cut rubies inlaid with a central diamond

214 Brooch. Cartier Paris, 1914. Platinum; articulated diamond and onyx mount surmounted by engraved rubies and onyx. A pear-shaped pearl weighing 89.09 grains and a pear-shaped red tourmaline weighing 18.45 grams are attached

this page (from the left, top to bottom)

215 Stirrup brooch. Cartier New York, 1920. Onyx, diamonds and sapphires in a millegrain platinum setting; two cabochon sapphires and rigid pendant with a geometrically cut onyx plaque set with three cabochon sapphires

216 Brooch. Cartier Paris, 1922. Platinum; round old- and single-cut diamonds; one pear-shaped emerald weighing 19.45 carats, one drilled emerald bead, cabochon emeralds; coral, onyx

217 Brooch. Cartier New York, special order, 1925. Coral, emerald, enamel and diamonds set in platinum. An inverted stirrup shape in coral encrusted with diamonds at the corners, with a large central cabochon emerald weighing 15.12 carats on a pavé-set diamond ground

218 Temple brooch. Cartier Paris for Cartier New York, 1927. Platinum; one half-moon diamond, baguette-cut and square diamonds

219 Brooch. Cartier Paris, 1928. Platinum; round old-cut diamonds; engraved rock crystal

Louis Cartier's interest in Islamic styles was furthered by the Exposition des Arts Musulmans held in the Musée des Arts Décoratifs in Paris in 1903 and was later deepened by a visit to the Alhambra, the Moorish citadel in Granada.[2]

Indian, Chinese and Japanese motifs also found their place in Cartier's work, enriching the geometric designs with new variations which used the circle and ellipse to conceal the purely constructional elements in the jewelry and create fluent ornamental forms.

Islamic star design, Persian or Chinese medallion, Japanese motif, and 'gong' motif

Parallel to these new forms were unfamiliar colour combinations, red and lilac for example, or blue and green, what Henri Clouzot called 'this mirror of sleeping water, which reflects the heavens and the woods together'. As we saw in Chapter Nine, Cartier's use of the new colour range was partly stimulated by the Ballets Russes, which fused an Oriental fairy-tale world with European eighteenth-century theatre and masquerade – an achievement paralleled in jewelry by Louis Cartier at the same time. The curtain for *Schéhérazade* and Cartier's Persian jewelry derived, ultimately, from the same source.

The designers of the Ballets Russes, above all Benois, integrated French eighteenth-century floral elements in their theatre designs, and Cartier incorporated similar patterns in his new style. This was especially true of the garland, whose curvilinear forms were never wholly renounced by the firm's designers.

The breast ornaments of the garland style yielded under Art Deco to the pendant, which gained in length what had been lost in breadth. Yet the garland extending across the bodice lived on in the geometricized bow shapes of the new pendants [**210**, **215**, **220**, **224**].

With the shift towards verticality favoured by the new dress fashions, the suspended curves of the garland style became falling vertical lines, which might also take the form of a flower vase with cascades of lichen or fountains.[3]

220 Vase brooch-pendant. Cartier Paris, 1913. Emeralds, pearls, onyx and diamonds in a platinum setting. Vase made of a polygonal emerald weighing 11.90 carats. Fruits made from emerald beads and four pear-shaped emerald drops

Even the bar brooch, one of the most popular garland types, was given falling motifs or transformed into a bowl of flowers.

The circle, which with the ellipse was one of Cartier's principal Art Deco forms, was varied and transformed with side motifs derived from nature [236].

Most of Cartier's Art Deco designs derive from the stylization of forms from the vegetable kingdom, as individual plants and fruits were transformed into generalized types [147, 190].

Unlike Boucheron, Cartier's rarely featured naturalistic flowers, complete with petals and calyx. It was only in the 1940s that designers like Peter Lemarchand in Paris and Frederick A. Mew in London began to favour realistic representations of roses, orchids and dahlias. Throughout the 1920s flower ornament was exclusively two-dimensional. The linear treatment of a leaf or a stylized orange tree was of greater interest to the designer than the three-dimensional reality of nature [191].

In this world of forms derived ultimately from nature, it is surprising to find semi-surrealist forms quite uncharacteristic of the Cartier oeuvre, such as a mask suspended on a cord of woven hair, or a winged hourglass.

When considering this period we must not forget the close links between arts, crafts, theatre, literature, and soon film, which were close and yielded undreamt-of inspiration. Louis Cartier, for example, cultivated his connections with Diaghilev, Sert, Foujita and Christian Bérard; he knew the most talented innovators in fashion and décor – Jacques Doucet, Jeanne Lanvin and Coco Chanel; he admired Paul Valéry and Jean Cocteau; and he moved socially with the brilliant Elsie de Wolfe, Misia Sert and Louise de Vilmorin.[4]

At this time a leading figure on the Paris art scene was Paul Iribe (1883–1935).[5] He was at home in theatre, fashion, poster art and film, and the range of his friends and collaborators indicates the extent of his influence: Jean Cocteau represented the world of literature, Misia Sert the Diaghilev circle, and Poiret the world of fashion.[6] Iribe chose as his device a golden rose, and used it in his work for advertising,[7] the theatre and fashion and also to mark his most original creations – eleven jewelry designs made at the prompting of José Maria Sert and executed by the jeweller Linzeler in the rue d'Argenson. The fact that these pieces were presented on silk cushions and turbans was, of course, a tribute to the Ballets Russes. Two years later, *Vogue* carried a report on Madame Poiret's amethyst and emerald pendant, also designed by Iribe and worn by Gloria Swanson in *The Affairs of Anatole* (1921), the first film for which Iribe served as designer. Iribe's most important

221 Pendant. Cartier Paris, 1912, sold to Lady Sackville. Platinum; 99-carat emerald tablet engraved with Indian floral design and set in engraved rock crystal and diamond mount; black silk cord with crystal slides

222 Vase pendant. Cartier Paris, 1920. Platinum; engraved turquoise studded with diamonds; black enamel outline; onyx base with baguette-cut diamond; connected by two onyx and diamond rings to a black silk cord jewel, an emerald aigrette with characteristic sunburst effect, was acquired by Cartier and was still in the vaults of the London branch in 1931.[8]

Writing of the 1925 Exposition des Arts Décoratifs, George Barbier declared: 'The influence of Paul Iribe on contemporary decorative arts, and especially jewelry, is certainly not emphasized as it should be.'[9] Iribe was one of the first to propose large cabochons mounted as rings, and his jewelry was among the earliest made in platinum and iridium. Above all, he influenced contemporary artists in their choice of motifs: a bowl filled with fruit or flowers – a memory of the ballet *Le Spectre de la rose* – was one of his favourites, as it was Jacqueau's [143].[10] Iribe's rose motif inspired carpet designs by André Mare and textiles by André Groult and Bianchini-Férier;[11] it appeared on advertisements for the perfume maker Lubin,[12] and in jewelry with black enamel contours by Boucheron and LaCloche.

Just as in Russia Diaghilev's friends, such as Benois and Bakst and Nouvel, had joined in the Mir Izkusstva (World of Art) movement to promote exhibitions and ballets, so Bernard Boutet de Monvel, Leon Bakst, Georges Lepape, A. E. Marty, Paul Iribe, George Barbier and others formed a group in Paris in the years before the First World War. Their spokesman was Lucien Vogel and his *Gazette du Bon Ton* their platform.[13] The group was in direct contact with the world of theatre and fashion; the rose garland and the Orientalism of the Ballets Russes became their artistic credo.

George Barbier appears today to have been the most prolific of their members.[14] Born in Nantes in 1882, he settled in the Latin Quarter of Paris in 1908 and held his first exhibition in 1911 in the Galerie Boutet de Monvel. His imaginative world was a compound of the carnival and masquerade of eighteenth-century Venice and the bucolic landscapes of ancient Greece, populated by Adonis, Psyche, Bilitis and Ganymede.[15] As a young dandy, Barbier took an interest in jewelry and was deeply impressed by Iribe's designs. He presented himself before Louis Cartier bearing a portfolio of designs, and thus got to know Charles Jacqueau. Louis acquired his watercolour *Nijinsky and Ida Rubinstein in 'Schéhérazade'*[16] and placed a commission for another watercolour, *Lady with a Panther* [274], to be used in the firm's publicity. Barbier's vases, garlands and phosphorescent clusters of fruit were not directly copied but influenced Jacqueau's design of a strawberry pendant [147], an Ionic column, or the network of hanging branches in an onyx tiara. It was Iribe who influenced Barbier in the design of an aigrette of plaited spirals which, in turn,

223 Pendant. Cartier Paris, 1912. Platinum; rock crystal panel with floral engraving, with diamond cluster and border; drop-shaped pearl tassel; plaited silk cord

224 Pendant. Cartier Paris, 1913, sold to the Aga Khan. Platinum; tapered carved rock crystal with cabochon rubies; two pear-shaped emerald drops; bow with rubies and emeralds

225 Pendant. Cartier Paris, commissioned in 1913 by Grand Duchess Vladimir. Platinum; six briolette-cut diamonds of 42.67 carats and a pear-shaped diamond of 4.15 carats suspended from circular-cut diamond arcades

226 Vase pendant. Cartier Paris, 1914. Platinum; carved rock crystal vase with circular-cut diamond handles and central diamond collet; diamond flowerhead and onyx bead garland; pear-shaped diamond tassel

had its effect on a Cartier aigrette of 1913 which looks like a firework showering sparks.[17]

While Cartier's temporary associates, such as Barbier, came from the world of the theatre and journalism, the firm's full-time designers – mostly trained at the Boulle, Germain Pilon or Bernard Palissy design schools – came from the diverse worlds of the decorative arts, though never from the immediate competition:

Henri Chenaud (b. 1876): trained with the decorator Rémond and worked in embroidery and tapestry before joining Cartier's in 1908
Olivier Baloche (b. 1878): a tapestry maker. Joined in 1902

227 Necklace with pendant. Cartier Paris, 1909. Platinum; triangular diamond pendant with drop-shaped diamond fringe, centring on an oval chrysoberyl cat's-eye of 90 carats; black silk cord with diamond motifs

228 Sautoir. Cartier Paris, 1912, sold to Princess Shakovskoy. Platinum; pear-shaped cabochon amethyst with amethyst and diamond calyx suspended from a seed pearl and amethyst bead rope

229 Necklace with pendant. Cartier Paris, 1913. Platinum; twenty-three emerald beads of 252.48 carats flanked by onyx beads on a diamond chain, from which is suspended a vase-shaped pendant tassel

opposite

230 Model displaying Cartier's new 'Trinity' triple bracelet and ring in three-coloured gold, and an onyx and diamond circular brooch. Photograph by Edward Steichen, from American *Vogue*, 1925

Frédéric Beseme (b. 1879): with Lalique from 1919 until 1925, when he joined Cartier's

Charles Jacqueau (b. 1885): in the workshop of Raingo, the bronze sculptor. Joined in 1909

Jean Puchmagre (b. 1890): with Linzeler from 1909 to 1911, at the time when Linzeler was executing Iribe's designs. With Cartier 1913–20

Henri-Louis Lesueur (b. 1891): from 1909 to 1925 with Keller's, 48 avenue Matignon, a gift shop specializing in elegant silver, enamel and leather items. Joined in 1926

Yvonne Cluzel (b. 1895): designed silks for the Maison George. Joined in 1921

Pierre Lardin (b. 1902): chief designer for Edgar Brandt, the wrought-iron artist, until 1925; involved with the creation of the workshop 'La Maitrîse' for the Galeries Lafayette. With Cartier's 1925–26

André Courtillat (b. 1905): in 1920 received first prize for watercolour and ornament in a competition of the Ecoles de la Ville de Paris; in 1924 attended the Ecole des Arts Décoratifs. With Cartier's 1927–31

Peter Lemarchand (b. 1906): from 1924 to 1926 with the jeweller Roger Sandoz in the rue Royale. Joined in 1927

James Gardner (b. 1907): trained at the Chiswick and Westminster Schools of Art and afterwards with E. McKnight Kauffer, the American-born graphic and poster artist who lived most of his life in England. Knew G. B. Shaw and was an enthusiast for the Ballets Russes. Worked with Cartier London from 1924 to 1931, when most of the designs still came from in Paris

With its team of employees experienced in wrought iron, tapestry, textile printing and graphics, Cartier's participation in the great exhibitions of the post-war years presented a creative challenge. In 1921 Cartier exhibited, together with Janesich, Van Cleef and Feuillâtre at the Salon du Goût Français in the Palais de Glace on the Champs-Elysées; in 1924 at the French Exhibition in Grand Central Palace, New York, along with Boucheron, Mauboussin, Van Cleef and Sandoz. In 1925, the Paris Exposition Internationale des Arts Décoratifs et Industriels Modernes, in which industrial design ranked equal with the decorative arts, was a synthesis of all the preceding exhibitions.[18] The idea went back as far as 1912: following the great success of the German stand at the Paris Salon d'Automne of 1910, the competitiveness of the French decorative arts had to be re-established. An exhibition planned for 1916 was tragically overtaken by the outbreak of war; scheduled for 1922, it was postponed to 1924 and finally to 1925.

The exhibition finally opened its doors on 16 May 1925. It covered an area of twenty-three hectares, stretching across the Seine from the Champs Elysées to the Hôtel des Invalides. Every night, the Eiffel Tower gleamed with a Citroën sign in 200,000 coloured electric lights, and Bourdelle's statue of France greeting the nations welcomed visitors who entered the gate on the avenue Nicholas II. Among the 'nations', Austria took part, but neither Germany, whose invitation was issued too late, nor the United States was represented.

The show was organized on the same progressive principles that had governed the Paris Exposition of 1900. Nothing was accepted that imitated earlier styles or lacked stylistic or functional novelty or originality.[19] However, there was a provision that amounted to a charter for the jewellers: 'The fact that a piece derives its inspiration from work in related fields, or from motifs of other times and places, shall not be sufficient grounds for exclusion, on condition that the model has been interpreted, reworked and transposed in a manner that suits the theme.'[20] The exhibits were grouped in five categories:

I   Architecture
II   Furniture
III *Parure*: Class 19 Clothing
               Class 20 Fashion and fashion accessories
               Class 21 Flowers
               Class 22 Gems and jewelry
IV   Arts of the theatre, the street, and gardens
V   Education

The NEW JEWELLERY
from CARTIER

This photograph shows a new Cartier design of bracelet and ring to match, made from three flexible, interlocking, twisted rolls in three tones of gold—red, white, and yellow. They are amazingly chic and very moderate in price. The earrings are cut from one piece of onyx with diamonds coming out like drops of water and pear-shaped diamond pendants. In the hand is held a crystal ring brooch with an unusual Persian design of onyx and diamonds.

THE VERY NEW TRINITY BRACELET AND RING

231 'Yin-Yang' pendant. Cartier Paris, 1919. Platinum, gold; round old-, single- and rose-cut diamonds; two drilled emerald beads; calibré-cut rubies and collet-set cabochon rubies; one emerald, four rubies and four buff-top onyxes on the loop; onyx; black enamel on the clasp

opposite

232 Pair of pendant earrings. Cartier Paris for Cartier New York, 1919. Onyx, diamonds and yellow sapphires set in platinum; flower stems and heads carved out a single piece of onyx, with four diamonds in lily-of-the-valley settings, a central pearl and yellow sapphire drops

233 Pair of pendant earrings. Cartier Paris, 1922. Emeralds, onyx and diamond set in platinum; chain of square-cut diamonds and emerald beads, with pavé-set diamond cylinders studded with onyx; pear-cut emeralds engraved with a chevron pattern

234 Pair of pendant earrings. Cartier London, 1924. Diamonds set in platinum; Persian-style design with stylized palmettes at the top, another palmette at the base, and three marquise-cut diamond drops

Of a total of some four hundred jewelry firms that took part, thirty displayed exhibits with a total value of Fr. 500 million, an impressive figure when compared with the jewelry exports of France for the previous years, which were valued at Fr. 20 million. The jewelry section in the Grand Palais had an exhibition area of five hundred square metres, devised by the architect and jewelry designer Eric Bagge.

Louis Cartier was appointed vice-president of the organizing committee for the *Parure* (Jewelry) category.[21] With twenty-five years' experience of jewelry in the twin contexts of fashion and society, he firmly shared the exhibition's belief in the unity of the decorative arts. His firm's products were to be presented in the fashion context of hats, hairstyles, belts, fabrics and shoes. 'Modern decorative art in all its forms is to be understood as a living reality. A ceramic tile or a wallpaper can only properly be judged *in situ* – a desk lamp only when actually alight on the table.'[22]

Was it Jeanne Lanvin or Louis Cartier himself who had the brilliant idea of being the only jewellers exhibiting not in the Grand Palais but along with the fashion houses in the Pavillon de l'Elégance?[23] Jeanne Lanvin was president of the 'Fashion and fashion accessories' category and like Louis Cartier was interested in the major trends of art history:[24] her 'Décolleté à la Vierge' was inspired by the Madonnas of Raphael; 'Lanvin blue' owed its mystic colour quality to Fra Angelico; and she dreamed of antique jewelry 'on mandarin robes, on Persian silks'. Her private residence had been decorated by Rateau, and it was Rateau, in his workshop at Levallois, who designed the furnishings for the Cartier display.[25]

'Fashion, the mirror of our time, is essentially an art', claimed the official report,[26] and in this survey of fashion and style, sixty-eight years after the publication of Baudelaire's *Les Fleurs du mal*, the fragrance of a perfume was considered comparable to music and the plastic arts. The exhibitors included the couturiers Jenny and Callot; Hermès, who had graduated from saddlers to be the leading fine leather workers; and Cartier's close friend and neighbour, Jean-Philippe Worth.

But how was Cartier's jewelry to be presented as a 'living reality'? The exhibition management advised against the 'paradoxical effect of a cathedral nave providing the setting for jewellers' diamonds just a few cubic centimetres in size'.[27] Like the four couturiers,[28] Cartier presented his pieces on mannequins made by the Canadian Siégel in Saint-Ouen to designs by Vigneau in a style reminiscent of Brancusi and Modigliani [**209**, **238**]. The *Parure* section was promoted with a gala event in which Mistinguett appeared as a 'Diamond Solitaire' followed by the girls from the Casino de Paris in precious stones and velvet ribbons, while Ida Rubinstein in *The Martyrdom of St Sebastian*, with costumes designed by Bakst, drove her admirers into a frenzy.

In the exhibition, the abstract geometric tendencies of Modernism, which were to dominate the 1931 Colonial Exposition, were already asserting themselves alongside the stylized flowers of Art Deco. Georges Fouquet, for example, exhibited a black enamel mask and rings of crystal and ivory; Raymond Templier a tiara of amber and diamonds; and Boucheron a tiara of onyx blossoms as well as a necklace with two great diamond drops. The LaCloche showcase was the one most like Cartier's, with its Chinese forms and clear colours, and with anecdotal motifs from the fables of La Fontaine. The most valuable piece in the entire exhibition was the 136-carat 'Queen of Holland' diamond, which sparkled in the display of the jeweller Friedmann.

Cartier's Art Deco programme, already fully developed by 1920, was represented at the exhibition by 150 pieces, produced in the workshops in the three years since 1922. Some had been created expressly for the exhibition: these were among the jewels, at least thirty-two in number, that were broken up when it was over. Among the specially created jewels were a 38 cm-long brooch for a décolleté made in the Renaud workshop, intended to be viewed from a distance; an emerald shoulder ornament and bandeau, 'Bérénice' [**207**, **209**].[29] The fashion context of the display more or less forbade the inclusion of clocks or vanity cases,[30] but there was an exemplary cross-section of Cartier's work in the categories that were exhibited.

Earrings Pride of place went to the long earrings (up to 8 cm), comprising cascades of blossom shapes with pendant cabochons, mostly of emerald, lapis lazuli or onyx. In 1908 *Vogue* had already commented on long earrings and in 1921 it confirmed that one out of every three women seen in the Bois de Boulogne, lunching at the Ritz or dancing at the Ambassador wore earrings an inch or two in length. Another pattern was based on calyx or bell motifs, Oriental in inspiration, and with hanging bunches of cabochon beads. By contrast, a 'Creole hoop earring' with a diamond and onyx ball recalled a seventh-century Merovingian piece consisting of a 14-faceted polyhedron.[31] The elegant design based on a seventeenth-century girandole, popular from 1906 into the 1930s, was not displayed.

Bracelets Most of the exhibits were geometric link bracelets, of the type that remained popular up to the Second World War and was produced internationally. Their predecessors are to be found in the nineteenth century, or even the Renaissance. The Empress Eugénie, for example, wore a necklace of geometric links.[32] The prevailing colour combination at Cartier's was the black/white contrast of diamond and onyx, while the openwork patterns derived from Persian work. There was only a single bracelet of coloured gemstone leaves, and surprisingly neither a chimaera nor an Egyptian lotus bracelet. Instead there was a spiral snake bracelet of coral and emerald. However, the chimaera motif did appear on a cigarette holder.

Tiaras The Persian style still dominated the world of fashion. At the Paris Opéra Ball of 1922, Persian 'harem pants' were worn and Princess Karam of Kapurthala was escorted by a troop of Persian slaves. But aigrettes and tiaras were exhibits rather than fashion accessories. The exhibition included a traditional bandeau with two black heron plumes; a comb embellished with onyx and diamond orchids [238]; and the 'Bérénice' bandeau by the designer Henri Chenaud [207, 209].

Rings Cabochon gemstones predominated, for example a 35-carat sapphire and a 13-carat emerald. The vogue for emerald-cut diamond solitaires, initiated around 1925, was represented by a 17-carat example. Interestingly, 1924 had seen the birth of the triple gold 'Trinity' wedding-band (*bague trois anneaux*) and the 'Trinity' bracelet that went with it. Both were immediately shown to *Vogue* readers in a photograph by Steichen [230], and Elsie de Wolfe was one of the first to make the ring popular.

Necklaces Here the emphasis was on colour-contrasting pendants – coral beads, clusters of emerald beads, and pearl tassels – on black silk cords or necklaces of onyx cylinders. Large diamond necklaces were not included, being thought out of tune with the artistic trends of 1925. The 'Fuchsia' necklace of carved coral revealed a charmingly playful side to Cartier's programme.

Brooches Here the astonishing fertility of Cartier's imaginative invention appeared at its most convincing, not only in the variety of motifs but also in the endlessly creative adaptation of the brooch as hat, belt, shoulder ornament – or shoe buckle, since the shoe had become a work of art.[33] From about 1915, airy and transparent chiffon and crêpe de chine had been favoured as dress fabrics, and these were clearly not suitable for brooches. But with the advent of O'Rossen's grey flannel suit in 1921 and the immense popularity of furs, sometimes coloured with aniline dyes – caracal for daytime and ermine for evening wear – the brooch could once more be used. The diktat of the great fashion houses such as Chanel still banished the brooch to the fringes of the wardrobe, but Caroline Reboux and Suzanne, the finest milliners in Paris, eagerly took it up. The Parisian hat of the Charles Frederick Worth epoch, bedecked with flowers and fruits, had given way by 1913 to a small unornamented model that snuggled nicely down on the modish Eton crop hairstyles. From 1927 a host of new hat styles – béret, toque, Phrygian cap – provided the justification for an even wider range of hat ornaments.

235 Belt-buckle. Cartier Paris, 1922. Yellow gold and platinum; two onyx rings held together by a matrix turquoise with side-links and centre in onyx surrounded by brilliants

236 Belt-buckle brooch. Cartier Paris, 1923. Platinum; rock crystal ring with onyx and diamonds; strap motifs at the sides decorated with an onyx branch on a pavé-set diamond ground with two emerald beads

237 Brooch. Cartier Paris, 1924. Platinum; rock crystal, diamonds, mother-of-pearl, pearls, black enamel and a cabochon sapphire weighing 57.63 carats

opposite

238 Cartier display at the 1925 Exposition in Paris. Among the mannequin's jewels are an onyx and diamond orchid hair ornament (1923) and a rock crystal and diamond belt with twin onyx tassels

opposite

239 'Egyptian' bracelet. Cartier Paris, commissioned in 1919 by Pierre Cartier. Platinum; bands of calibré-cut onyx alternate with bands of circular-cut diamonds

240 Pendant on chain. Cartier Paris, 1913. Platinum; three pear-shaped diamonds of 39.25, 36.11, and 31.51 carats. The necklace was subsequently altered, and the largest diamond sold to Grand Duchess Vladimir

this page

241 Necklace with pendant. Cartier Paris, 1923, sold to Ganna Walska (Mrs Harold McCormick). Platinum; necklace in sections of emerald beads and cabochon emeralds, with lozenge-, triangular-, half-moon- and baguette-cut diamond links; pendant of seven drop-shaped emeralds of 167.54 carats on half-moon and pear-shaped diamond mount

242 Necklace with pendant. Cartier Paris, 1923, sold to Ganna Walska (Mrs Harold McCormick). Platinum; necklace of sapphire beads with smaller emerald intersections; pendant of one 39.14-carat engraved cabochon sapphire and one 256.60-carat Indian engraved cabochon emerald drop, terminating with a diamond

The brooch as belt-buckle often assumed a symmetrical form derived from bronze Chinese buckles of the nineteenth century [235]. The 'belt-buckle' became one of the basic forms of the Art Deco brooch, in the shape of a double clip. In 1927, Cartier's patented a model with a spring. The central motif of the belt-buckle, a hoop of coral, onyx or crystal, proved from 1919–20 on to be the most popular brooch pattern, embellished with stylized floral elements [236]. One in four of all the brooches exhibited in 1925 was in this hoop style [238], to which were added rectangular and polygonal forms. Floral brooches in the manner of the Ballets Russes were in a minority.

In the case of the brooch, nineteenth-century historicism survived into the 1920s. In addition to Persian, Chinese and Egyptian influences, seventh-century Merovingian forms were reflected in Cartier fibula brooches during the Art Deco period. The fibula as dress clasp was in fact the earliest form of brooch. Cartier's designers were able to study it among the examples of Merovingian art in the museum in the Château of Saint-Germain-en-Laye, and it was to pervade the entire Art Deco programme. As early as 1907 it had become fashionable to secure a kimono or kaftan with a fibula or clasp. A fibula, indeed, had featured as one of the wedding presents of the Queen of Spain. A simple type in the form of a safety-pin (the *broche nourrice*)[34] had featured in the Cartier programme since 1895, first in white gold, later in platinum.

A variant, the crossbow-fibula, caught the attention of designers at Saint-Germain-en-Laye.

A further type, the jabot-pin (*système cliquet* or *à double baïonette*), valued as a lapel or hat ornament, often had chimaera [243] or serpent head terminals, which were indebted to Merovingian models[35] and also recalled Celtic interlace work from Ireland.

Another type of fibula, comprising an open ring with a sliding pin and a bayonet clasp [178], was based on Irish or Scottish models of the eighth century.[36] The first Cartier examples have linear designs in enamel with cabochon gemstones; later they appeared in coral and onyx.

Even these ring brooches in onyx or coral were decorated in the centre with chimaera motifs in a way that recalls the Merovingian 'rouelle' worn as a belt ornament.[37]

opposite

243 'Chimaera' jabot-pin. Cartier Paris, commissioned by Louis Cartier for his wife, 1923. Platinum, gold; round old- and single-cut diamonds; one fluted emerald bead, cabochon emeralds and buff-top emeralds; one natural pearl; carved and fluted coral; cabochon onyx; black enamel

244 'Boteh' jabot-pin. Cartier Paris, 1925. Gold, platinum; round old- and single-cut diamonds; buff-top rubies; carved and pierced jade; black enamel

245 Bracelet. Cartier Paris, 1923. Platinum, gold; round old- and rose-cut diamonds; one engraved emerald weighing 57.80 carats, fluted emerald beads; onyx roundels; black enamel

246 Bracelet. Cartier Paris, 1924. Gold, platinum; round old-, single- and rose-cut diamonds; carved coral; mother-of-pearl; black enamel

In 1917 the large Le Secq des Tournelles collection of ironwork, removed to Rouen, opened to the public as a museum. Before this, parts of the collection had been exhibited in the Musée des Arts Décoratifs. It was recorded in four volumes of *Le Métal*,[38] and Louis Cartier made a number of sketches from this for his design studio. The garland style had derived inspiration from wrought iron, principally of the eighteenth century; now the designers were stimulated to evolve forms based upon hinges and locks designed by Gothic and Renaissance craftsmen. The motif of the doorknocker and the fittings of iron-bound chests occur again and again.

Another important design element, the stalactite or *muqarnas* form, was derived from Islamic architecture, where it occurs at points where support encounters load, as in the transition from the circular base of a dome to the square walls of the supporting space. Louis Cartier was fascinated by this form during his 1922 visit to Granada. As a result we find the stalactite pendant watch making its appearance [**367, 368**] – coincidentally, just at the time when George Barbier was creating his stalactite grotto set for the Folies-Bergère.

The brooches in the 1925 Exposition summed up the endless possibilities of geometric cuts of diamonds and coloured stones: baguette, hexagons and half moons were the ideal 'building stones' with which to construct tiny triumphal arches, pagodas, Taj Mahals, Vendôme columns and skyscrapers. Once again, it was Elsie de Wolfe who, with her 'Temple d'Amour', contributed to the wider application of this delightful miniature art.

opposite

247 Miniature propelling pencil. Cartier Paris, 1929. Pencil in gold and black enamel; square platinum knob and cap set with emeralds and diamonds

this page

248 Brooch-pendant. Cartier Paris, 1922, owned by Madame Louis Cartier. Coral, onyx and diamonds set in platinum. Coral vase suspended from a garland of leaves decorated with coral and onyx berries

249 Seal watch brooch. Cartier Paris, 1929. The brooch a bar of openwork platinum and old-cut diamonds with two buff-top cabochon rubies. Double chain of ruby beads, jade rods, onyx and diamonds. Lugs in old- and baguette-cut diamonds and black enamel. Rectangular polished gold and black enamel case with curved edge, set in a nineteenth-century Chinese jade seal featuring a Buddhist lion, ringed with cabochon rubies, on a base adorned with single- and rose-cut diamonds set in platinum. White enamel bezel with gold dots in reserve. Flat, notched winding crown. Rectangular cream dial with Roman numerals. Blue steel hands

CHAPTER THIRTEEN
VANITY FAIR

preceding pages, left

250 Design for an Art Deco vanity case in onyx with coloured gem-set Chinese vase [**251**], 1927

preceding pages, right

251 Vanity case. Cartier Paris, 1927. Gold, platinum; onyx; cabochon sapphires and emeralds, engraved fluorspar, single- and rose-cut diamonds, carved and engraved coral, cabochon coral. Red, ivory-coloured, black, green and yellow enamel

this page

252 Cigarette case. Cartier Paris, 1912. Hollowed out of agate, with three motifs in calibré- and rose-cut sapphires; catch made of one cabochon sapphire and rose-cut diamonds set in platinum

253 Cigarette case. Cartier Paris, 1913. Gadrooned gold and gold wire, white enamel band, two cabochon sapphires

'Once, Cartier was master of the exquisite *objet d'art*: his miniature plants, destined for the princely boudoir in their delicate glasshouses, recall the Japanese and Chinese art of the *belle époque*, with their jade leaves and quartz blossoms. But today he restricts himself to practical matters – the cigarette case and the vanity case, the familiar necessities of modern life.'[1] Thus wrote a critic in the *Gazette du Bon Ton* in 1925 – referring precisely to items which of necessity had been omitted from that year's exhibition of 'Arts Décoratifs'.

In fact, what the critic saw as a chronological sequence was actually parallel production in Cartier's oeuvre. The Cartier plants [123], representing 'art for art's sake' at its most extreme, may have been somewhat out of place in the post-war period, but the cosmetic articles and desk and smokers' requisites ideally matched the post-war requirements of an aesthetic determined by function. As it happened, these practical articles had been in the Cartier range since 1900, long before Louis Cartier's directive: 'We must make it our business to build up an inventory that responds to the mood of the public by producing articles which have a useful function but which are also decorated in the Cartier style.'

From the beginning such items had formed a part of the firm's repertoire. Among toiletries there were silver shaving brushes (1860), silver mirrors, moustache combs, beard brushes and powder compacts (1890). Desk accessories included pencil cases in jasper (1860) and platinum (from 1874) and gold pen-holders (from 1881). Calendar stands of jasper and agate (1905) were followed by stamp moisteners, paperweights, inkstands and barometers. Even earlier, Cartier's had been producing smokers' requisites – silver lighters (from 1867), matchboxes, and cigarette-holders (1874). A smoker's lamp with ashtray was created in 1906 and bought by the Duke of Alba. But the most varied category was that of men's cigarette cases. From 1900 onwards these were in the Russian style in reeded gold or Russian birch and amaranth, and from 1910 in crystal, agate [252] and jade. Their manufacture was put out to the workshops of Allard et Meyer (Place des Vosges), Kuppenheim (rue Volney), Lavabre, Chailloux (rue Turbigo) and Louis Bock in Colombes as well as to Russian makers such as Ovchinnikov and Yahr. The cases had to be flat, easily slipped into the pocket, scratch-resistant, and, since they were designed for men, restrained in ornamentation. They were therefore less varied in style than that most astonishing of post-war accessories, the *nécessaire de dame* or what the Americans called the 'vanity case', known in France by 1925 as the 'vanity'.[2]

The actual necessities carried by a lady when travelling or at social events changed over time, but how she carried them depended on the extent to which pockets could be accommodated within the silhouette ordained by fashion. Neither the clinging Empire style nor the billowing crinoline of the mid-nineteenth century, which had a steel underframe, allowed pockets. Instead, reticules of various materials such as wool, taffeta or velvet were used, to be superseded for a time in the early 1870s by châtelaine purses, secured by a chain or cord. This period also saw the evolution of the graceful coin purse of silver, enamel, mother-of-pearl or leather, generally carried on a chain attached to a finger ring or châtelaine girdle. Shortly after 1900 a man's model even came into fashion; compartments for coins, stamps and banknotes were contained in a silver case secured with a metal ring to the watch chain.[3]

The vanity case of the twentieth century combined the form and functions of these bags and purses and took over from them the chain and finger ring [168]. The name, however, indicated the contents: powder compact, lipstick, tortoiseshell comb, mirror, and an ivory card reminiscent of the former *carnet de bal*.

The ancestor of the vanity case was the *boîte-à-rouge-et-à-mouches* (patch box) of the age of Louis XV, with mirror, two compartments and a little brush;[4] but the place for that was the dressing table: it could never have been used in public at the theatre or a ball. The first mention of a fabric bag for portable cosmetic articles appears to be in the English *Lady's Magazine* in 1820. Make-up was however frowned upon throughout the nineteenth century, which accounts for the fact that Cartier's toiletries at this period were exclusively for men. *Vogue* does not mention lipstick and eyebrow pencils until 1902–3, and its first references to nail varnish and a vanity case with a powder compartment are in 1907 and 1909 respectively.

Cartier's first simple vanity cases were in yellow gold and often embellished with a monogram. These were followed by models in Fabergé style in *émail pékin* striped in blue or pink and white. Now flat, now cylindrical, they might be up to 12 cm long. They might even contain that 'volupté nouvelle' lauded by the writer Pierre Louÿs – the cigarette. Already in 1893, Eulalia, the Spanish Infanta, had shocked opinion by smoking in public at the Chicago Columbian Exhibition; Baron de Meyer made a portrait photograph of the Marchesa Casati smoking a cigarette. When in 1916 the new fashion was permitted in the Ritz-Carlton Hotel in New York, the taboo was finally broken. The vanity case became increasingly sophisticated, with up to four compartments and sometimes even adorned with a watch. The eccentric Mrs Evalyn Walsh McLean also commissioned a miniature vanity case to be worn with a leather strap on the wrist like a watch [272].

After the war cosmetics became big business. As early as 1914, the singer Lina Cavalieri had had a great success with her book *My Secrets of Beauty*, and in 1921 Helena Rubinstein opened her Paris salons. It was estimated that fifty million American women were using lipstick and, in 1928, Kleenex was invented. Appropriately, after 1930 the vanity case took the form of a box, for which Van Cleef & Arpels patented the name 'minaudière'. Enamel, being easily scratched, was impractical on the broad gold and silver surfaces and was replaced by more resistant lacquer. A resplendent, detachable diamond or gemstone clip provided the clasp, while Madame Larivière went so far as to have the ruby flowers on her Cartier vanity case matched to her bracelet. Later, after the Second World War, the severe rectangular contours softened and the vanity case was made in the form of a gold clutch bag. A total of eight hundred man-hours might be required to make such a piece, divided among a goldsmith, *guillocheur*, engraver and stone-setter, the engraver working by hand, the *guillocheur* with a machine.

In the heyday of vanity cases, the Art Deco period of the 1920s, their exterior decoration demonstrated the designers' fertile imagination: as well as the owner's mono-gram, Indian Jaipur enamel plaques or jade medallions, all-over geometrical patterns – *jeux de fond* – were often used to decorate the sides. Small-scale Arab-style patterns later gave way to Chinese motifs or designs of boldly simplified cubes and bars. If the Cubism of 1910 is to be seen in any of Cartier's production, it is on these cases. Their manufacture was divided between the Renaud workshop in the rue Reaumur and the Bachaumont workshop – both of which were taken over by Cartier – and Boulon et Taragnat.

Less abstract patterns left room for figurative ornament, as in the vanity cases with gazelles where the influence of George Barbier reappears, or a vanity case with a stalking panther under a ruby sun [264].

The greatest variety of ornamentation came in 1924, the year of the Egyptian pipe-player case [168]. The richest, however, came with the use of antique Chinese lacquer plaques,[5] which in the years up to 1929 resulted in a unique series of 'Western/Oriental' vanity cases.

Europe's dialogue with the art of the Far East, which began in the early seventeenth century, is one of the most fascinating chapters in the history of culture. It started with a passion for Chinese silk which later extended to porcelain and lacquer, products which were virtually a monopoly of the Dutch and British East India Companies. The precious cargoes, generally sent by sea, through Dutch Batavia and along the Coromandel coast of India, or from the port of Canton, were marketed in Europe as 'Indian', 'Chinese' or 'Japanese'. By the middle of the eighteenth century, almost every European palace had its 'Chinese' lacquer cabinet – even if the majority were manufactured in European work-shops – to the delight of all those 'tired of the elegance and symmetry of the Greeks'.[6] Essentially, the eighteenth-century interest in Chinese art was a dilettante fascination with the exotic: the architect Sir William Chambers characterized Chinese houses as 'toys in architecture'.[7] By contrast, the nineteenth-century attitude was grounded in the contacts of a pragmatic colonial and commercial policy: France acquired a privileged position through her bases in Indo-China,[8] while Commodore Matthew Perry's expedition in 1853–54 opened up the Japanese empire to enquiring travellers. In England and France the terms 'Japonisme' and 'Japonaiserie' were coined for the influential Japanese fashions in architecture, graphics and the decorative arts.[9] Whistler's decoration of the dining room in the London house of the Liverpool shipping magnate F. R. Leyland is one of many instances of Eastern influence: the artist's painting of the kimono-clad *Princesse du Pays de la Porcelaine* (1876) hung on a wall painted with Japanese golden peacocks. Literary

254 Vanity case. Cartier Paris, 1924. Yellow and pink gold, platinum; cabochon emeralds and engraved emeralds; rose-cut diamonds; mother-of-pearl marquetry; natural pearls; turquoise plaques; black and ivory-coloured enamel

255 Vanity case. Cartier Paris, 1929. Cover decorated with a geometrical pattern in gold, cream-coloured and black enamel; sides decorated with black enamel stripes; button capped with a baguette-cut diamond. The interior is fitted with a mirror, a powder compartment and a lipstick holder

256 Vanity case. Cartier Paris, 1925. Gold, platinum; cabochon sapphires and emeralds; rose-cut diamonds; mother-of-pearl; red and black enamel. The Chinese-style cover is decorated with a crane in cabochon sapphires and emeralds against a ground of 'Chinese' clouds in mother-of-pearl and black enamel. The interior is fitted with a mirror and two compartments with lids. Originally this vanity case was suspended from a chain with a matching lipstick case [see **257**]; it was altered and the two sold separately

257 Design for a vanity case, 1925 [**256**]

Orientalism enjoyed a special vogue in France, represented for example by Judith Gautier's *Le Livre de jade* or Pierre Loti's *Madame Chrysanthème* (1887). After Edmond de Goncourt had completed his studies of Japanese art in the 1890s, it continued in the somewhat precious literary fin-de-siècle genre of Robert de Montesquiou.[10]

The new stimulus from China and Japan also spurred the imagination of contemporary jewelry designers. Shortly after the sack of the Summer Palace near Peking, Eugène Fontenay was using Chinese jades. Lucien Falize, on the other hand, was fascinated by Japonaiserie and sought to employ Japanese craftsmen, as Emile Gallé did in Nancy a few years later. In 1881 Lucien Gaillard began his research into Japanese techniques of lacquer and cloisonné enamel; this found an echo in Cartier's 1885 collection, which included motifs derived from Japanese bronze and lacquer work.

After 1900, the terms 'Chinese' and 'Japanese' are frequently found in the Cartier archives but they are little more than vague formal allusions. Like the terms 'Arabic' or 'Byzantine' they serve only to show the astonishing diversity of the firm's output up to the First World War, which drew upon images and forms indiscriminately. The following examples are enough to indicate the Oriental contribution: in 1898 the firm produced Japanese and Chinese buckles, some with griffin motifs; in 1900, a 'Chinese' nape brooch and a silver belt buckle with 'Dragon and Chimaera fighting'; in 1903, jade pendants engraved with Chinese dragons,[11] and Chinese pendants which were bought by the Duchess of Devonshire and the Duc de Richelieu; in 1906, Japanese brooches and Chinese pendants, and a jade necklace sold to Lady de Grey; in 1907, Chinese gong pendants and 'Japanese' lace pins; in 1912, a lacquered bamboo vase with bronze fittings and openwork jade pendants.

In 1919 Cartier's produced an elegant pendant on a chain in the form of the Chinese Taoist *tai-chi*, symbol of the universal Yin-Yang, with two onyx beads and gemstones [231]. This was a concept ideally suited to the black and white colour scheme of Art Deco.

Apart from these pieces, Chinese and Japanese influence was confined to *objets d'art* – vanity cases, clocks and scent bottles – whereas jewelry design inclined increasingly towards Indian models. In the context of the vanity case, eighteenth- and nineteenth-century lacquer work became extremely important, and, like the Egyptian range, achieved complete integration with the taste of Art Deco.

In fact, Cartier's had handled Chinese lacquer work as early as 1888, when a Chinese lacquer cabinet in the possession of the Vicomtesse de Bonnemain had been sent to them for reconstruction as a jewel case. In 1903, Louis Cartier acquired a Chinese lacquer snuffbox, probably in French eighteenth-century style, from the antique dealers 'Au Vieux Paris'.[12] It was another ten years before the first cigarette cases were produced in Chinese mother-of-pearl mosaic (without lacquer), based on nineteenth-century models. From 1924 Cartier's used true mother-of-pearl-encrusted lacquer, which Louis collected systematically from the leading antique dealers of the time:[13] C. T. Loo in the rue de Courcelles,[14] Michon in the boulevard Haussmann, 'La Pagode', the 'Compagnie de Chine et des Indes' in the rue de Londres, and also Yamanaka, the Japanese dealer in New York. For his own personal collection, Louis Cartier bought a Ming dynasty painting from Kalebdjian, better known as a Middle East specialist.

From ancient times Chinese mother-of-pearl was valued for the rose, lavender-blue and shimmering greens of its innumerable thin layers, obtained from sea- and fresh-water mussels (*Heliotis*). Early mother-of-pearl inlays from the Tang dynasty were too thick to display the iridescence of the full colour range, but the craftsmen of the later Ming and Ching periods used tissue-thin slivers to produce delicately scintillating effects which they heightened still further by the application of artificial colourings.

Mother-of-pearl had a magical authority in the Taoist scheme. Moonbeams and the dust of powdered mother-of-pearl were the food of the immortal He Xiangu,[15] and its insubstantial shimmering colours were, for the Taoists, a token of eternity. Mother-of-pearl was a favourite material in depictions of the Taoist Paradise of the West, which showed the caves of the Eight Immortals, the goddess Djivangmu riding on her phoenix, and the Peaches of Immortality which ripened every three thousand years.

The lacquers used by Cartier's in the 1920s were mostly taken from Chinese bowls, tablets or plaques; the original decorative context thus tended to be lost. Because of their

258 Vanity case. Cartier New York, *c.* 1926. Yellow gold; black and white enamel. At the ends, engraved oval jade set in yellow gold, with brilliant-cut diamonds and a collet-set cabochon onyx. In the centre, white enamel plaque framed by rose-cut diamonds set in platinum; thumb ring in onyx and rose-cut diamonds

opposite

259 Vanity case. Cartier Paris, 1927. Yellow and pink gold, platinum; cabochon sapphires and emeralds; single-, old- and rose-cut diamonds; coral; moonstone; facet-cut topazes; black enamel. The interior is fitted with a mirror, two powder compartments with lids, two powder puffs with gold tabs, and a lipstick holder

260 'Day and Night' vanity case. Cartier Paris, 1927. Gold, platinum; baguette-and rose-cut diamonds; cabochon sapphires and rubies; mother-of-pearl; cornelian, nephrite, various hardstones; black enamel. The interior is fitted with a mirror, two compartments with lids, a lipstick holder and space for a comb. Cover and base are decorated with mother-of-pearl marquetry attributed to Vladimir Makowsky (see p. 212). On the cover is a coastal scene in Chinese style; a ruby representing the setting sun creates the illusion of a distant horizon where the two mother-of-pearl panels meet

261 Vanity case. Cartier Paris, 1928. Gold, platinum; rose-cut diamonds; cabochon sapphires; fluorspar, jade; mother-of-pearl; coral; onyx; black enamel. The interior is fitted with a mirror, two powder compartments and a lipstick holder in the centre. The inlaid plaque was produced in Cartier's workshops, copying a Chinese Famille Verte plate (Kangxi period, 1662–1722) from Louis Cartier's private collection

262 Vanity case. Cartier Paris, 1924. Gold, platinum; rose-cut diamonds; two wooden plaques inlaid with mother-of-pearl; agate, malachite, azurmalachite, turquoise and coral; coral, mother-of-pearl, turquoise, onyx; black enamel. The nineteenth-century Chinese wooden plaques on the cover came from Louis Cartier; seen here are two of the three Han heroes accompanied by the stork of long life and sheep. The turquoise plaques at top and bottom and the talisman below the onyx ring came from the stock known as the 'apprêts Louis Cartier'. At the top of the case is a small dragon made from pavé-set rose-cut diamonds; the 'Shou' (long life) motif is repeated in rose-cut diamonds on the turquoise plaques. Interior fitted with a mirror and a cigarette compartment with a gold bar pierced with the 'Shou' motif small format the motifs that came to hand were not concerned with the great themes of Taoist mythology. Even so, they conjure up the poetic and allegorical feeling for nature at the heart of Taoism. On one of these Cartier lacquers two of the Immortals are strolling under the summer moon, deep in conversation; on another a maid lights her mistress's way with a lantern; on another we observe a sage with his disciple in a pine grove. These little panels, which sit well with the Art Deco ensemble of coral, lapis lazuli and onyx, are often further embellished with cabochon gemstones: rubies may serve to pick out cherry blossoms or trace the line of a bridge, a sapphire lights up a distant boat, the moon shimmers through the facets of a rose-cut diamond.

Their preoccupation with China led designers to find ideas in various branches of the Chinese decorative arts. A plate in Louis Cartier's own collection provided the model for the court lady who graces a mother-of-pearl box of 1928 [**261**]; an eighteenth-century fluorite seal in the Musée Guimet suggested the outline for a vanity case; while the trellis work patterns of Chinese furniture inspired brooches and also an important tiara. In his delightful reminiscences, *Elephants in the Attic*, James Gardner, a designer with the London firm from 1924, describes an instructive lesson he learned as a young man from Jacques Cartier: 'He would often open the bookcase, take out a leather-bound volume on Chinese furniture and turn to the illustration of a black lacquered table. I was to observe how the legs terminated.'[16]

Motifs drawn on time and time again were the seated Buddha and the Japanese Hotei, the fat-bellied god of happiness, who appears from 1901 onward on ashtrays and table bells, sometimes in jade, sometimes in rose quartz or turquoise, alternating as ornament with the similar Billiken [**347**]. Similar to Fabergé's two jadeite Buddhas for King Chulalongkorn Rama VI of Siam is Cartier's large Buddha in rose quartz and lapis lazuli made by the Fourrier workshop in 1928. Small jade Buddhas became brooch ornaments, and Mrs Harrison Williams wore a hand of the Buddha in jade on her Cartier flower bracelet made of engraved gemstones.

In addition to using Chinese lacquer, Cartier's designers covered the surface of their boxes with Chinese geometrical patterns. After all, even the mother-of-pearl inlays of Chinese lacquers were built up from standardized geometric elements. By the early seventeenth century more than fifty-five basic forms had been in use, which might serve, for example, to represent the foliage of a tree or the outline of a temple, while crushed fragments of mother-of-pearl provided the earth. The artists of the Ch'ing period (1644–1911), who created the lacquers used by Cartier, had, like their contemporaries working in porcelain, bronze or carpets, a deep *horror vacui* and covered every surface in repeating patterns built up of rhombs, hexagons, scales or circles. Landscape features were indicated by standardized decorative symbols, which were used by Cartier for the *jeux de fonds* of his vanity cases.

The basic elements of Chinese geometrical patterns, representing sky, water, and earth

These and other Chinese symbols were taken over in Cartier's Art Deco, either directly or in modified form. Various Chinese signs, for example, depict the clouds as 'cloud eddies', 'turbulent clouds', 'cloud ribbons' and 'cloud peaks' – the latter taken over by Cartier as a pendant motif in 1907. Found already on Sassanian silver, though without its cloud connotation, the ornament further appears in the Indo-Islamic cultural area and, travelling backwards and forwards along the Silk Route, was adopted in China also with the meaning of 'sceptre' or 'sword pommel'; in Japan, on the other hand, it signified 'temple gong'. The term used by Cartier is simply 'gong' [**101**, *ill. p. 182*].

The swastika is another motif frequently encountered in the decoration of Cartier's 1920s vanity cases. In origin an ancient Aryan or Vedic symbol associated with the cult of the sun, it has been traced as far afield as Scandinavia and Peru. In China, where it was regarded either as one of the sixty-five auspicious footprints of the Buddha or as the seal of his heart, it was much prized as 'the good luck symbol of thousand-fold efficacy'.

Adaptation of the meander was a simple matter; in many cases it developed from the swastika, occurred already on archaic bronzes, and was frequently given a dragon's head termination. In the garland style of the pre-war years, Cartier had made frequent use of the Greek meander; by contrast the Chinese variant made an ideal border pattern for vanity cases, and reappeared in 1934 as a dragon-head brooch.

Compared with that of China, Japanese art played a comparatively minor role in Cartier's output. Whereas Boucheron, for example, made use of Japanese lacquer work in both the *hiramakie* and *takamakie* techniques of raised gold work, Cartier's ignored it almost entirely. However, the Japanese *inro* did influence the form of Cartier's finger-ring vanity case. A little drug and medicine case comprising a number of horizontal compartments fitting one above the other and held together by a silk cord, the *inro* was worn by Japanese gentlemen at the waist under the kimono sash (*obi*). The cord was tightened by a sliding toggle (*ojime*) of, for instance, coral or metal, and fixed to a carved *netsuke* of wood, ivory or lacquer which was tucked into the sash. Cartier's ring vanity cases originally made use of a Japanese-style silk cord, but this gave way to the more practical enamel chain, ending in an onyx finger ring or a lipstick [**257, 262**].

If Chinese lacquer panels and mother-of-pearl inlays were taken over from miniature artworks of earlier centuries, they were also produced in Europe in the 1920s from Oriental models. An artist who specialized in the re-creation of Chinese lacquer and gemstone work was the Paris-based Russian Vladimir Makowsky (1884–1966); his works can often be identified as he sometimes signed them with a small black M. A coastal scene by him uses traditional Chinese vertical perspective in which a ruby as the setting sun creates the illusion of a distant horizon along the join of the little panels [**260**]. Sometimes, engraved mother-of-pearl rhombs of European workmanship were even used to frame genuine Chinese lacquers.[17]

Enamel plays a comparatively subordinate role in the Chinoiserie vanity cases of the period. Instead we find monochrome lacquer, similar in colour to tortoiseshell in its natural state. Chinese lacquer of the Ming period was built up from as many as two hundred separately dried layers: the French Art Deco lacquer artists contented themselves with about twenty layers.

During the First World War, aircraft manufacturers had employed Indochinese and Annamite workers to lacquer propellers, as their skin was apparently less affected by the fumes than a European's.[18] A number of workshops were established in the Boulogne-sur-Seine region and after the war they were able to take on commissions from Paris jewellers. The firm of Phung Dinh Van, which worked for Cartier's, had a workforce of fifteen Indochinese and had been established around 1915. From the salon of the couturier Madeleine Vionnet to the liners *Atlantique* and *Normandie*, lacquer was all the rage in interior decoration during the 1920s and 1930s.[19]

Cartier's used lacquer on scent bottles and table clocks with pink mirror panels, which, with their strictly cubic structure, are the firm's purest contribution to 1930s modernism. Ever since Mrs Harrison Williams had decorated her Paris residence with mirrors painted by Drian, the mirror had enjoyed a considerable vogue. In addition to large bottles in mirror glass, there were dainty snuff bottles of agate or quartz, presented as sets of two on elegant lacquer stands. A piece made for Mrs Blumenthal integrated the design of stand and bottles into a stylish unity, whose stepped contours echoed contemporary skyscraper architecture. But the impact of Chinoiserie was also felt in the field of toiletries. The Maharani of Nawanagar acquired a complete toilet set, comprising brushes, mirror, boxes, scent bottles, glove stretchers and mantel clock, done in Chinese lacquer set in obsidian. The Paris perfume houses were equally ready to embrace Chinese influence. Poiret had introduced his little 'Nuit de Chine' bottle in the pre-war years; in 1925 came Elizabeth Arden's perfume, 'Ming', in its lacquer bottle; and in 1929 *Vogue* wrote of Guerlain's 'Liu' that 'the bottle sits in its package like a Buddha in its shrine'. Perfume makers and couturiers often pursued common ends (Chanel's 'No. 5' dates from 1921 and Lanvin's 'Arpège' from 1927). After their competitor LaCloche had created the perfume 'No. 1', Cartier's had to launch their own scent. The inspiration once again came from Jeanne Toussaint. Her personal favourites were Poiret's 'Aladin' and 'Coupe d'Or', and it was with these in mind that she contacted the perfume maker Pinaud. Unfortunately, their plans were interrupted by the Second World War. The names of famous precious stones, such as 'Nassak' and 'Cumberland', were registered, and the 'Jubilee' diamond, sold by Cartier's around this time, provided the outline for a faceted perfume bottle, which sadly was never made.[20]

Chinese motifs began to set the style in haute couture at least as early as 1923, the year of the Paris Opéra Chinese Ball. Egyptian modes found themselves challenged by 'coolie' coats and 'mandarin' hats. Molyneux and later Mainbocher declared themselves for China and in 1927–28 Lucien Lelong created his 'Confucius' model.[21] Cartier's evening bags of Oriental brocade provided the ideal matching accessories for the new styles which transformed elegant Parisiennes into *princesses lointaines*.[22]

These evening bags, together with a range of gift items, were the creations of 'Department S' in the rue de la Paix, also under the creative direction of Jeanne Toussaint. The Department, like the boutique established by the couturier Jean Patou, was a forerunner of the fashion and jewelry boutiques of the 1950s. The trendsetters of the 1910s, such as Princess Zenaida Yusupov or Nancy Leeds, had favoured evening bags in gold weave (*maille d'or*) or embroidered in seed pearls. But Jeanne Toussaint established new forms and colours which suited both the clothes and the mood of the fashionable world: simple elegance now began to give way to 'chic', with its characteristic blend of erotic daring and stylish vitality. Wherever Madame Letellier (wife of the mayor of Deauville), Elsie de Wolfe or the Cole Porters were to be found – visiting the races at Auteuil, discovering a new jazz band at the Boeuf-sur-le-toit, or pro-claiming the dawn of the cocktail age in the Ritz Bar – their fashionable *tout ensemble* was sure to match the occasion. (In 1922 couturiers like Patou even began presenting sport collections.)

The essential accessory was the bag [268–270]. As a rule, Cartier's models were more refined than those by Poiret, Ruzé & Babani in the boulevard Haussmann, or Duvelleroy. The firm bought costly materials from Wagner (in the Place des Victoires), Worth, Worms and Johny. These were often valuable embroidered brocades from Renaissance Europe, China or Persia, which permitted only very sparing adornment. On the other hand, with ribbed taffeta or reindeer leather, the full Art Deco colour range could be brought into play and the results could compare with the most expensive vanity cases of the period. The bag with pharaoh clasp made for Mrs Clarence Mackay, and other models for Madame Martinez de Hoz, Mrs Blumenthal and Mrs Harrison Williams, were quite simply the most elegant of their time. The rectangular clutch bag [270], carried casually under the arm, was a simpler variant, and the models in crocodile or red calf leather that Hermès produced for Cartier's from 1922 were adorned only with the owner's monogram. In 1926 Cartier's patented a special handbag clasp.

The international financial crisis of 1929–30 brought about a restructuring of the market which was reflected in the development of Department S: Cartier's 'democratic' department adapted itself to the new social conditions and the changes in pricing (reduced wages for the craftsmen and reduced profits for the firm). Its practical and functional range – smokers' requisites and desk accessories, watches, bags and vanity cases – suited a newly price-conscious clientele.

Between 1928 – the year before the Wall Street Crash – and the end of 1930, a shift occurred in the turnover of stock in the department. Sales at the lower end of the range – gold and silver cigarette lighters, for example, retailing at about Fr. 890 – rose by some 50 per cent, but sales of really expensive and exclusive items such as cigarette cases made of jade, lacquer and precious metals fell by the same amount. The more sophisticated vanity cases gave place to powder compacts in black lacquer embellished with the Chinese character for 'long life', selling at about Fr. 1,500.

Around 1930 no object was too insignificant to be enriched by the Cartier treatment: Louis Cartier used a Yale key decorated in the finest available Peking enamel, while the New York branch launched writing paper in ocean blue for Palm Beach fanatics. At this time Department S in Cartier New York had an especially enthusiastic clientele and after the Second World War, when the Paris Department S was only a memory, Louis Devaux, president of the New York firm between 1946 and 1949, set up similar boutiques in the department stores of Saks Fifth Avenue, Neiman Marcus, and I. Magnin in New York, Dallas and Los Angeles.

267 Miniature powder compact and lipstick case. Cartier Paris, 1931 and 1933. Gold, platinum; rubies, diamonds, black enamel

268 Handbag. Cartier Paris for Cartier New York, 1924. Black satin; platinum, diamonds, onyx (80% actual size)

269 Handbag. Cartier Paris (Department S), 1929. Black reindeer hide; gold, platinum, engraved oval ruby weighing 11.52 carats, eight leaf-shaped carved rubies, seven leaf-shaped carved emeralds, single-, baguette-, square- and fancy-cut diamonds; black enamel. Engraved on the frame inside: 'MRS. CONDE NAST 1040 PARK AVENUE NEW YORK CITY' (80% actual size)

this page

270 Evening clutch bag, 'Aladdin' model.
Cartier Paris, 1927. Silk, mother-of-pearl frame
engraved with geometric motifs on a silver
ground, bordered with coral rods, black
enamelled links on yellow gold; clasp with the
'Dog of Fo' or Buddhist lion in jade on an onyx
base, rose-cut diamonds (80% actual size)

opposite

271 Motorist's travel set with clock. Cartier
New York, *c.* 1917. Gold, black and white
enamelled 'LV' monogram and decoration,
glass, wood, leather, brass (90% actual size)

After 1930 there was an increasing trend towards justifying the luxury article by its function. The multipurpose gadget had a novelty value which might be thought to make the expense worthwhile. A magnifying glass was adapted for use also as a letter opener and might even incorporate a watch; a fountain pen that would write at both ends might contain a calendar. A complicated desk set of jade, lapis lazuli and agate combined inkwell, penholder, vase and table clock. In the 1930s it was nevertheless rare to find a functional item decked out in the formal repertoire of Chinoiserie: the age favoured the pragmatic Modern style, and a desk set of 1931 in the form of a Japanese temple garden was the last great example of the type and uncharacteristic of its time.

'Our age is one of invention, machinery, industry, science and commerce', wrote Paul I. Frankl in *New Dimensions* in 1928. It was a creed that glorified the machine and made no attempt to consider the social problems caused by unemployment in the depression that followed the Wall Street Crash. Among a privileged upper class for whom the automobile and the aeroplane were the fashionable means of transport, 'beauty is speed' achieved the status of an aesthetic canon. With Pierre Frondaie's bestseller, *L'Homme à l'Hispano*, the automobile even became the hero of a novel. Derain and Paul Morand with their Bugattis seemed to be celebrating the dictum of the Futurist Marinetti, that a racing

car was more beautiful than the Winged Victory of Samothrace. As early as 1914, Cartier's had created a 'cantine d'automobile' in royal blue enamel for Elsie de Wolfe [cf. **273**] and in 1930 they produced a cigarette box in the form of a miniature car. André Citroën commissioned a brooch in the shape of a car with the firm's trademark in coloured stones.

Still more lavish were the fittings of the great yachts of the period, such as the Duke of Westminster's *Flying Cloud* or the Vanderbilts' *Alva*. Yachting was so popular that the rue de la Paix shop exhibited special yachting gifts in the Green Salon. The 1930s were not only the age of fashionable picnics and cocktails [**273**] – Cartier's produced shakers engraved with recipes and also ivory champagne swizzle sticks – but the age of the sporting trophy. Cartier's made countless trophy designs in silver – for the fastest boat, the tennis champion, or the polo champion – which were executed by the Linzeler workshop in the rue d'Argenson.

In 1933 Cartier exhibited a trophy made from platinum and crystal at the 'Century of Progress' Exhibition in Chicago which was thought to be the largest piece of platinum ever wrought by a jeweller. It was a time when symbolic trophies and official commemorative presents went hand in hand. When the Atlantic liner *Normandie* sailed on her maiden voyage in 1935, her passenger list included Ganna Walska (Mrs Harold McCormick), Walt Disney, Mrs Jay Gould, and Pierre Cartier. To commemorate the event, the wife of the French President was presented with a Cartier cigarette box, incorporating a clock, with the ship's route engraved on the lid.

opposite

272 Miniature vanity case with two compartments. Cartier Paris, commissioned in 1930 by Mrs Evalyn Walsh McLean. Gold; leather strap (actual size)

this page

273 Travelling cocktail set. Cartier New York, *c.* 1930. Silver shaker, two flasks with caps, a fruit-squeezer and six tumblers. Each element is stamped with the monogram 'JCC', and together they fit into a black leather case with the same monogram (50% actual size)

1914 GEORGE BARBIER

CARTIER Copyright

CHAPTER FOURTEEN

CHIMAERAS, DRAGONS AND GREAT CATS

Cartier's jewelry designers did not pay much attention to the theories of the Bauhaus, the German design school directed from 1919 by Walter Gropius. This was partly a matter of personal inclination and partly because they realized that the formal principles of architecture and industrial design, no doubt adaptable to table clocks, boxes or desk sets, could not so readily be applied to the realm of jewelry. Two competitors, Gérard Sandoz and, to a degree, Raymond Templier, did indeed make the attempt. Both liked to create jewels in cube, triangle or disc shapes, with surfaces broken up by colourful and dynamic patterns of linear perspective. The geometrical forms, ideally suited to cigarette cases and other utilitarian objects, were strictly sculptural in effect, and it is significant that Sandoz later turned to abstract painting and Templier to jewelry with strongly sculptural tendencies. In fact their jewelry derived from an aesthetic diametrically opposed to that of Cartier's, being unrelated to the female form and having a character and weight completely incompatible with the diaphanous textiles of the mid-1920s.

At Cartier's, by contrast, Louis Cartier and Charles Jacqueau, an ideal partnership of creative imagination and technical expertise, transformed the contemporary geometrical style with understanding. Their decoration was 'modern' but never 'mechanistic', as they restricted geometry to the settings of brooches, the borders of cigarette cases or the supports of pendants. The focus of a Cartier *objet d'art* was the often figurative ornamental motif; the focus of a jewel was the precious stone. The principle was practical as well as aesthetic, since the Cartier *objet d'art* was often of considerable size. The firm's 'mystery clocks', among its largest creations, might reach a height of 40 cm; to cover such a surface with a network of geometric patterns would not only have made severe technical demands but would also have produced an unacceptably monotonous effect. By contrast, a valuable jade statuette [351] or an inlaid piece of Chinese lacquer provided a central coordinating element.

The Orient – the world of myth and fairy tale – provided the themes for Cartier's vanity cases, table clocks, scent bottles and other decorative objects. For the three young Cartier brothers, Persia, India and above all the limitless steppes of China seemed to be landscapes pregnant with myth and domains between heaven and earth where the imagination sought in vain for certainties. Yet the legends and sagas were also fascinating, and their symbolism, deriving from secret and ancient origins, could, at least, be understood in decorative terms.

Cartier's achievements in integrating the fairy-tale world of myth and saga into the context of contemporary decorative arts marked a clear break with the course taken by his competitor René Lalique. Through the early 1900s Lalique's work had seemed to breathe the pine-laden air of the ancient world of Germanic saga; however, after he opened a glass factory at Combe-la-Ville near Paris in 1909 and put on his last jewelry show in 1912, he banished all narrative symbolism from his work. His ideas turned to a demythologized art whose key lay in the imitation of rock crystal in glass. The symbolism that survived into this new creative dimension achieved its effect not in narrative but in starkly hieratic terms. Cartier, on the other hand, did not regard rock crystal as a perfectly translucent material in the service of a new factual reality. Apart from a few mystery clocks it was seldom used alone, but usually for contrast in combination with onyx and coral.[1]

The chimaera, a fabulous and gruesome monster of Eastern legend, inspired one of the most important motifs in Cartier's design vocabulary. Its importance lies not so much in the iconography of the monster itself as in Cartier's inspired use of it for the bracelets in antique style, terminating in animal heads, which are the most original arm ornaments of the Art Deco period [278–280].

Animal bracelets dating from the eighth–seventh centuries BC were discovered in the Elburz mountains in Iran; they appear with lion heads on Assyrian reliefs depicting King Assurbanipal; they were popular in Lydia and Cyprus from the sixth century and in Greece from the fourth century BC. The principal types were bull-, ram-, deer-, and snake-heads, which were taken up by Roman and Etruscan jewellers who also used them on earrings and necklaces.[2] In the modern world, animal-head bracelets came back into

preceding pages, left

274 *Lady with a Panther* by George Barbier, commissioned by Cartier in 1914 as a display card (see p. 229)

preceding pages, right

275 Evening bag. Cartier Paris, 1961. Satin; gold, emeralds, diamonds, black enamel. Ordered by Barbara Hutton as a gift for her former sister-in-law, Princess Nina Mdivani

opposite

276 Studies of panthers by Charles Jacqueau, *c.* 1913

277 Powder compact. Cartier Paris, 1927. Yellow and pink gold, platinum, rose-cut diamonds, mother-of-pearl, malachite, lapis lazuli, red and black enamel, millegrain setting. The cover, inlaid with mother-of-pearl, gold, malachite and lapis lazuli, is by Vladimir Makowsky (see p. 212). Inside are a mirror, a powder compartment and a powder puff fashion in the 1870s thanks to the work of the Italian jeweller Fortunato Pio Castellani (1793–1865) and the Frenchman Eugène Fontenay (1823–87), both of whom used themes and techniques from antiquity within the Napoleon III style.

The chimaera of Greek mythology is a fire-breathing monster, with the forequarters of a lion, the body of a goat, and the hindquarters of a dragon, which was slain by the hero Bellerophon on the winged horse Pegasus. Even in antiquity, however, there was no agreement as to the exact form of the beast and over the centuries it became simply a synonym for 'monster', like the terrifying Gorgon or the enigmatic sphinx. We encounter the chimaera on nineteenth-century jewelry in the work, for example, of Joseph Fannière (1820–97) and Alphonse Fouquet (1828–1911), with his chimaera tiara of 1878. The motif became so popular that by the end of the century the Paris jewellers Plisson & Hartz were producing little series of chimaera brooches made of gold. It was in this late Romantic tradition that Cartier produced a chimaera pendant in 1883: it depicts the monster, complete with wings and a scaly comb, within a crescent moon of diamonds [17]. In a sequence of smaller and less fearsome chimaera brooches produced up to the year 1904, the attributes of the chimaera are combined with those of the equally mythical griffin.

In the 1920s the chimaera enjoyed a renewed vogue, and Cartier's, breaking free of ancient Greek iconography, turned to a type derived from various Oriental prototypes. One influence was undoubtedly provided by the Indian sea-monster or *makara*, used in a bracelet design that remained virtually unchanged from the sixteenth to the nineteenth centuries. The two animal heads that meet with open jaws are based on the Indian crocodile (*Gavialis gangeticus*), depicted in art since the third century BC as either fish or reptile.[3] With time, the monster's jaws became extended into snouts or trunks so that the original resemblance to the crocodile was lost. Cartier's did not use the *makara*-head ending in their chimaera jewelry, although it was much discussed in the studio, and pure *makara* bracelets were later produced [280]. They did, however, take up the Indian enamelling on the inner surface of the bracelet, while replacing the original flower design with abstract scale patterns.

The animal heads as such became streamlined stylizations of the Chinese chimaera, the *kilin*. Only the dragon head remained of the scaly cloven-hoofed monster. In China the dragon itself (*lung*, standing for positive protective forces and the male principle) was venerated as a natural force and early on became the personal symbol of the emperor, protecting him with its depiction, staring out, on the front and back of his imperial robe. According to legend, the dragon was originally a wingless sea creature which had soared up to heaven and, far from being punished for its presumption, had been received into the heavenly regions. Thus the Chinese dragon, despite its double nature, is not, like the chimaera or dragon in the Western Christian tradition, a symbol of evil which has to be defeated, but rather a power of nature to be honoured. The five-clawed dragon adorned the imperial standard. From the seventeenth century onward the dragon was carved on jade bracelets and buckles, mostly depicted in pairs, together with the heavenly pearl, the legendary object of the dragon's quest.

Cartier's chimaera bracelets thus combined the tradition of animal-head bracelets of the ancient Mediterranean, the Indian *makara*, the Chinese dragon, and even African variants (in the firm's records this bracelet form is described as Sudanese).

The firm's production for 1922 started with a bracelet ordered by Louis Cartier, which was to prove decisive for future examples of 1927, 1928 [278, 279] and 1929. Two chimaera heads of carved coral with bejewelled combs are shown playing with two carved spherical emeralds, an apparent allusion to the legend recorded by the Indian poet Bhartrhari of the pearl or precious stone which the monster *makara* carried in its jaws, and which is possibly related to the Taoist legend of the dragon being fed pearls by Guanyin.

This bracelet, followed by a chimaera jabot-pin in 1923 also ordered by Louis Cartier for his wife [243], is one of the most convincing ventures into sculpted jewelry of the 1920s. LaCloche produced a little series of dolphin bracelets of unpolished rock crystal, enamel and precious stones, but they do not bear comparison with Cartier's chimaeras. The chimaera bracelet, with its sculptural surface, exploded the framework of traditional jewelry design. As a precious small piece of sculpture it belonged to that borderline

278 Design for a 'Chimaera' bracelet [279], 1928

279 'Chimaera' bracelet. Cartier Paris, 1928, sold to Ganna Walska (Mrs Harold McCormick). Gold, platinum; cushion-shaped, single-, pear- and baguette-cut diamonds; two fluted emerald beads, one carved emerald, buff-top emeralds and cabochon emeralds; two leaf-shaped carved sapphires, cabochon sapphires and buff-top sapphires; carved coral; green, blue and black enamel

280 '*Makara*' bracelet. Cartier Paris, special order, 1929. Platinum; pear-shaped diamonds, round old-, single- and French-cut diamonds; cabochon sapphires, buff-top sapphires and emeralds; gadrooned rock crystal (throat)

281 'Chimaera' bracelet. Cartier Paris, special order, 1954. Platinum, white gold; marquise- and brilliant-cut diamonds; fluted coral beads, buff-top cabochon coral category of *objets d'art* which Cartier's cultivated on a level with jewelry during the Art Deco period. So it is not surprising that this motif was built into a special standing clock design in which the dial was framed by a chimaera bracelet in the closed form of the Indian *makara* model. The workshops produced clocks of this type in 1925 and from 1928 to 1931. For the first time the entire hoop of the bracelet, and not merely the figurative upper section, was of carved stone, generally bright green or white jade, or even crystal.

Nineteenth-century travellers mistakenly applied the term 'chimaera' or 'Dog of Fo' to the Buddhist lion, the symbolic animal of the Buddha Sakyamuni (*Fo* being Chinese for Buddha). This creature stood guard over houses and temples throughout China as the protector of the Buddhist faith. However, since lions were unknown in China, the carvings took on the contorted features of a fabulous monster, part dog part lion. Cartier's used the Buddhist lion in another clock type, with a frame of two crystal pillars which suggest an Oriental temple gate with two lions crouching as guardians [348]. The chapter ring in black Tonkin enamel emphasizes the black–white contrast of the overall design.

The chimaera motif was developed much more freely in the complex structures of the mystery clocks than in the bracelet. It appeared on two clocks of 1924 and 1926 as a creature in a giant carapace, with beard and ringed tail [349]. In 1929 it lay in wait for its prey on the rim of a jade bowl [334] or, belching fire, coiled itself round a coral tree stump.

Clock designs using the motifs of the *makara* bracelet and the Buddhist lion [348]

In 1954 the chimaera style enjoyed a renewed vogue under the inspired direction of Jeanne Toussaint, but now its terrifying aspect was banished and it was transformed into a comical, amiable pet. The bracelet was made either of coral or of lapis lazuli, and Toussaint preferred the bright salmon pink coral to the intense red 'moro' coral of earlier days. Chimaeras entirely set with precious stones – generally rubies, emeralds and yellow and white diamonds – were produced as novelties. In 1959 a yellow and white dolphin bracelet was introduced; it is a curious fact that in ancient mythology the dolphin played a symbolic role similar to that of the Indian *makara*. From the distribution of the few examples of the chimaera bracelet it appears that the style appealed to women of self-assurance as well as refinement; in 1928, for example, the Polish singer Ganna Walska, wife of the wealthy Harold McCormick, selected the bracelet with the two largest emerald beads of 48 carats [279]. In the 1960s Daisy Fellowes and Baroness d'Erlanger became devotees of the chimaera, associating themselves with a tradition which continues down to the present day.

The chimaera bracelet was the product of collaboration among a number of Cartier workshops. The lapidaries had the most time-consuming job. The large coral stalks from which the bracelet bands were cut came only from Japan; they were imported to Europe via Italy, and were available in Paris from the Italian specialist coral dealer Borelli. Lapis lazuli, on the other hand, still known in the early years of the century as 'matière russe', was obtained by Cartier's from the Russian dealer Isaharoff, who had branches in both London and Paris. But in later years the Paris market was principally supplied by travelling Afghan merchants.

Louis Bozzacchi's workshop in the rue de Turenne was entrusted with carving the chimaera forms. Bozzacchi (1860–1922) was a native of Milan, a city whose lapidaries, such as the Miseroni, were already famous in the sixteenth century. About 1900, Bozzacchi trained for a time with the well-known cameo cutter Lemaire, and his facility with cigarette cases, small animals and statuettes brought him commissions from as far afield as Russia and from Fabergé. His workshop, employing between fifteen and twenty craftsmen, including some Vietnamese, was already doing work for Cartier's at the turn of the century. The workshop was taken over on his death by his daughter Josephine, one of the few women lapidaries in Paris, and her husband Henri Durand; in 1941 her fourteen-year-old son Claude began his initiation into the secrets of the family business. Cartier's designers supplied precise working drawings for the chimaeras and often wooden models for the bracelet bands, from which Durand created plaster models of the required design for Cartier's approval. Between 250 and 300 man-hours of painstaking craftsmanship went into the production of a single finished coral or lapis lazuli chimaera bracelet. Once the chimaera heads were ready, the job was taken over by the Lavabre workshop and ended only when the assembly was complete.

Whereas the chimaera had its imagined lair in the jaws of hell, the panther or leopard roamed the bush of Africa, the jungles of India, the steppes of Central Asia and China, and Asia Minor. The panther, unlike the lion, was a great rarity in mediaeval and Renaissance Europe. *Panthera*, the panther, was differentiated at this time from *pardus*, the leopard, and was considered a gentle beast loved by the entire animal kingdom save the dragon ('all animals love panthera', wrote Spenser in one of his sonnets). But it was first actually seen at the spiritual and temporal courts of Renaissance Europe: in 1479 Louis XI of France expressed his thanks to the Duke of Ferrara for the present of a splendid panther, and his successor Louis XII returned from victory at the Battle of Milan with Lodovico Sforza's cheetah, with which he hunted in the forest of Amboise. The panther was presented in art as a valuable hunting animal, a famous example being the frescoes in the Medici Chapel at Florence by Benozzo Gozzoli; and two gambol delightfully in the foreground of Titian's *Bacchus and Ariadne*. Painters who had not had the opportunity to study the animal's anatomy contented themselves with its pelt: leopard skins, like crocodile skins, were lovingly preserved in the cabinets of curiosities of the sixteenth century. In the seventeenth century, the panther skin formed part of the triumphal standards carried in victory processions. In the eighteenth century, as attitudes towards nature and life in the wild changed under the influence of Rousseauism, the pelt of the great cat prompted thoughts of the paradisal innocence of a Robinson Crusoe life untouched by civilization: idealized paintings of Europe's distant colonies depicted the 'noble savage' clothed only in his leopard skin. The French painter Jean-Baptiste Nattier (1685–1766), when he depicted the beauties of Versailles as the goddesses of antiquity, included the panther skin among the attributes of their boudoirs.

282 Jeanne Toussaint in the 1960s

The panther motif was much in vogue at the time of the First World War. In Paris, Princess Elsa de La Tour d'Auvergne and Cécile Sorel, actress at the Comédie-Française, introduced the leopard skin into interior décor. Above all, however, the motif was established by Elsie de Wolfe (1865–1950), who had made her debut as an amateur actress in her native New York and, after her brilliant décor for the Colony Club in 1907, became the preferred interior decorator of the fashionable world. As Lady Mendl, this talented woman was a famous hostess in the post-war years and one of the great supporters of the Cartier image, both in Europe and in America; as early as 1919 the gallery at her Villa Trianon in Versailles was decorated with leopard-spotted velvet and zebra skins. The style was maintained by Paul-Louis Weiller in the staircase of his residence, 'Le Noviciat', in tiger-chintz curtains for Condé Nast, publishers of *Vogue*, and a good deal later, but still under Elsie's influence, in the leopard skins and zebra upholstery in the Paris salon of the couturier Mainbocher. In the meantime, the panther motif became universally accepted and entered the vocabulary of many interior decorators: the Pavillon de l'Elégance, where Cartier's exhibited in the 1925 Exposition des Arts Décoratifs, was decked out with panther skins (by the fashion house Jenny) and zebra skins (by the Callot sisters), while the wrought-iron balustrades of the pavilion glorified the prowling panther.

As early as during the First World War Cartier's designers found the modish panther skin a fruitful source of inspiration for abstract designs in onyx and diamond. The first panther pattern appeared in 1914 on a wristwatch [361] and in 1915 Cartier's offered a pendant watch whose leopard-spot pattern was wrongly described as 'tiger skin' [362]. Two years later another wristwatch, called 'Tortue' because of its bellied shape, was decorated with spots.

But in this early phase Cartier's did not yet depict the panther as such. As in interior decoration, the fashion was still only for small surfaces flecked in black and white [361, 362]. Once again, the elaboration of the idea is traceable to Charles Jacqueau, as shown by a design in his sketchbook for a pendant watch of 1914 [148].

Abstract dot patterns appeared again between 1922 and 1927, this time in a floral context with an orchid hair ornament for the 1925 Exhibition [238], as well as on a little tree brooch with the novel feature of a diamond mounted with the point upwards. Later still, flecked patterns in the form of onyx thorns on a diamond ground had no conceivable association with the panther. How far this dissociation from the great cat could go is clearly illustrated in the Egyptian 'Sarcophagus' vanity case of 1925 [166], where the two engraved emerald sphinxes at the ends have flecked black-and-white decoration.

As the years went by, however, the panther was to become one of Cartier's favourite motifs. About the year 1900 the bold image of the 'Lady with a Panther', reminiscent of the mediaeval image of the Lady and the Unicorn, had emerged as a new subject in European art. But whereas her forerunner represented an allegory of chastity and courtly and heavenly love, the Lady with a Panther enters the subtly charged field of demonic eroticism. The ambivalent character of the Lady–Panther combination was expressed by the Belgian artist Walter Sauer in his *Femme devenue panthère* of 1919 and the Belgian symbolist Khnopff in his picture *La Caresse*.

Reality mimicked art: after her triumph as Napoleon's son in *L'Aiglon*, Sarah Bernhardt received her admirers holding a panther on a leash, the Marchesa Casati appeared at the Longhi ball in Venice as an animal tamer, with Negro slave and panther, and Boni de Castellane fantasized about Indian slave girls strolling with panthers in the gardens of his château, Le Marais, near Rambouillet. American *Vogue* presented Ida Rubinstein with a leopard in 1913. The sequence continues in the arts, with statuettes by Chiparus and of *Diana the Huntress with Deer* by the Swedish porcelain factory Orrefors, down to Erté's *Lady with a Leopard*.

In 1914 Louis Cartier commissioned a *Lady with a Panther* from George Barbier as a display card [274].[4] The picture, later used in the firm's advertising, shows a lady in a fashionable Poiret gown with a black panther crouching at her feet.

Jeanne Toussaint, involved in a discreet friendship with Louis Cartier, had the pet name 'Panther', and her apartment was adorned not only with panther carpets but also with an onyx panther vanity case (probably made about 1917) from Cartier's – the firm's first depiction of the entire animal. It was the first vanity case in a series with decorations in miniature (probably the smallest zoomorphic motifs of the entire Art Deco period) based on designs by Barbier, presented in balanced symmetry between two emerald cypress trees: a stalking panther [285], dogs at play, or a leaping gazelle. Jeanne Toussaint also had a vanity case in black and gold stripes with an applied panther in onyx and diamond, and a matching cigarette case.[5] Later examples of the panther motif show the animal in all positions – lying down, at play and fighting.

The most significant of these panther vanity cases, a miniature masterpiece of colour, appeared in the year of the Exposition des Arts Décoratifs. Its style is again related to George Barbier but also to Paul Jouve (1880–1973), whose fascination with elephants and big cats had produced the illustrations for Kipling's *Jungle Book*. The vanity case depicts a black enamel panther prowling in a fairy-tale garden beneath a ruby sun [264].

In 1931 the great Colonial Exposition was held in the grounds of Vincennes. Frescoes by Ducos de la Haille and lacquer panels by Jean Dunand depicted the jungles of the French colonies filled with tigers and elephants, and the exhibition's reading room was dominated by a picture of a panther stepping into water. There was a display of French jewelry featuring the claws and teeth of the great cats, to which Cartier's contributed Jacqueau's necklace with tiger-paw motif.

283 Panther clip brooch. Cartier Paris, 1949, sold to the Duchess of Windsor. Platinum, white gold; single-cut diamonds; two pear-shaped yellow diamonds (eyes); one Kashmir cabochon sapphire weighing 152.35 carats; cabochon sapphires (spots)

Many years went by before, in 1948, the Duke of Windsor placed an order for a panther brooch as a present for the Duchess. It consisted of a cabochon emerald of 116.74 carats on which there was an outstretched golden panther flecked with black. This was the firm's first fully three-dimensional treatment of the motif. Two years earlier the Duchess had lost jewelry valued at £20,000 in a robbery at Ednam Lodge in England. The replacement pieces were of artistic rather than obvious material value, and the panther brooch fitted excellently into the new range. The following year the Windsors took delivery of a cabochon sapphire of 152.35 carats with a crouching diamond panther flecked with sapphire spots [283], and three years after that they completed this suite of panther jewelry with an articulated bracelet in the form of an outstretched panther.[6]

284 Tiger brooch. Cartier Paris, 1929. Platinum; single-cut diamonds and fancy-shaped onyx (stripes)

285 Vanity case. Cartier Paris, 1928. Gold, pink gold, platinum; diamonds, emeralds, rubies; black enamel

286 Panther jabot-pin. Cartier Paris, commissioned in 1957 by Princess Nina Aga Khan. Platinum, white gold; brilliant- and single-cut diamonds; cabochon sapphires (spots); two green garnets (eyes)

287 Panther bracelet. Cartier Paris, commissioned in 1958 by Princess Nina Aga Khan. Platinum, white gold; brilliant- and single-cut diamonds; cabochon sapphires (spots); marquise-shaped emeralds (eyes); onyx (nose)

288 Articulated panther pendant. Cartier Paris, commissioned in 1958 by Princess Nina Aga Khan. Platinum, white gold; brilliant- and single-cut diamonds; cabochon sapphires (spots); marquise-cut emeralds (eyes); onyx (nose)

289 Kingfisher clip brooch. Cartier Paris, 1941. Platinum, gold; brilliant- and single-cut diamonds; two leaf-shaped carved emeralds, weighing 17.66 carats in total; faceted and calibré-cut sapphires; two cabochon rubies

290 Bird clip brooch. Cartier Paris, 1944. Gold, platinum; brilliant- and single-cut diamonds; four cabochon emeralds, weighing 14.42 carats in total; oval faceted sapphires; two navette-shaped cabochon rubies

Daisy, the Hon. Mrs Reginald Fellowes [205], daughter of the fourth Duc Decazes, who often entertained the Windsors on her truly royal yacht, the *Sister Anne*, and shared with the Duchess of Windsor the title of the world's best-dressed woman, is known to have commissioned a panther brooch of sapphire and diamond. This jewel was clearly modelled on the pendant emblem of the Order of the Golden Fleece, founded in 1430 by Philip the Good, Duke of Burgundy. Jeanne Toussaint replaced the hanging ram's fleece of the order with the drooping form of a leopard entwined with an ornamental band of baguette diamonds which recalls the pendant form of the original ornament.

In 1957, a new panther enthusiast appeared at Cartier's: Princess Nina Aga Khan, the beautiful consort of Prince Sadruddin Aga Khan, who was to acquire within a few years the most extensive *parure* of panther jewelry. First came a jabot-pin with outstretched panther [286], similar to the Duchess of Windsor's [283]; the lower clasp was formed by a 30-carat sapphire, but that was replaced with a round cabochon coral. The next year the Princess added an articulated panther pendant [288], another variant on the Golden Fleece emblem, which could also be worn as the frontal clasp of a multi-strand pearl necklace, and an exceptional open panther-head bracelet [287], reminiscent of ancient Mediterranean animal-head models. In 1960 she acquired a second bracelet of fluted gold; the panther-head terminals also served as earclips, while the gold bracelet became the handle of one of Cartier's most original evening bags. A ring with crouching panther completed the series.[7]

By contrast with the Princess Aga Khan, Barbara Hutton, then the world's richest heiress, settled for the tiger variations in Jeanne Toussaint's menagerie. The striped pelt was represented by canary-yellow diamonds and onyx in a pair of earclips on the Golden Fleece theme, and these were followed by a spectacular tiger bracelet and an evening bag with enamelled tiger ornament [275].

Jeanne Toussaint kept a close eye on the whole panther range and was fortunate to find congenial collaborators like Peter Lemarchand, the designer who established the panther silhouette of the 1940s. Like many of Cartier's designers, Lemarchand (1906–70) studied at the Ecole Boulle in Paris, from 1919 to 1924. He worked with Roger Sandoz, the jeweller in the rue Royale, before joining Cartier's in 1927. In 1935 he began a five-year stint in the London firm, which led him in 1939 to the Indian courts of Jodhpur and Bahawalpur. From there he returned to Paris and worked freelance at the rue de la Paix. He was so quick at putting his ideas down on paper that only a few hours a week at the drawing board were required; but even this brilliant designer was not allowed to miss Jeanne Toussaint's Tuesday conferences. He spent most of his time painting in his Montparnasse studio, where he gave lessons to Pierre Cartier's daughter, Marion.

Lemarchand was divided from Jacqueau not just by a generation, but also by a new design awareness of nature and wildlife, free of the stylization of Art Deco. Whereas, in the last analysis, Jacqueau's animal figures worked in terms of symbolism and myth, Lemarchand maintained an anecdotal approach. In a tribute to him in 1948, Jeanne Toussaint spoke of 'our common love for animals and birds'. From their shared dream-world emerged fairy-tale forms of great cats and shimmering Oriental birds [289, 290] – endearing toys to match the mood of Europe and the United States after years of austerity. Lemarchand's animal figures have vigour, plasticity, and an inimitable sense of movement – thanks, it must be said, to the virtuoso technique of the Cartier craftsmen who executed the designs and who could capture the articulate litheness of a great cat or emphasize the tail of a bird of paradise with a flexible platinum setting. According to his colleagues, Lemarchand spent hours in the zoo at Vincennes registering every nuance and reflex in the movements of the cats. In the Louvre he was fascinated by the Egyptian bronze cats of the goddess Bastet, and their playful poses were to be revived in his panthers.

In keeping with the austerity of the war years, Lemarchand created a delightful image whose symbolism was clear to friend and foe alike – a caged, silent songbird. In a second version made in 1945, after the signing of the German surrender at Rheims, the little bird is chirruping blithely at the open door of its cage [393].

291 Coral necklace. Cartier Paris, 1934, sold to Maria Félix. Platinum; string of coral beads with black enamel and diamonds from which are suspended carved coral bells with onyx, coral, diamond and emerald clusters

292 Palm-tree necklace. Cartier Paris, special order, 1949. Woven, polished gold, platinum; single-cut diamonds; ruby beads studded with collet-set single-cut diamonds

293 Blackamoor head clip brooch. Cartier London, 1958. Gold wire, platinum; brilliant-cut diamonds; one pear-shaped sapphire; cabochon turquoises; carved black tortoiseshell

294 Blackamoor head clip brooch. Cartier Paris, 1955. Gold wire and twisted gold, platinum; brilliant-cut diamonds; cabochon turquoises; carved black tortoiseshell

295 Palm-tree clip brooch. Cartier Paris, special order, 1957. Platinum, white gold; brilliant- and baguette-cut diamonds; seven cushion-shaped Burmese rubies, weighing 23.10 carats in total

296 Flower clip brooch. Cartier Paris, special order, 1962. Platinum, white gold; brilliant- and baguette-cut diamonds; one octagonal emerald-cut yellow sapphire weighing 12.49 carats

CHAPTER FIFTEEN

THE GREAT NECKLACES
THE LONDON WORKSHOPS
GEM DEALERS

The great necklaces

The yellowing photograph albums of the years around 1900, with their princely wedding groups, court balls and diplomatic receptions, reveal an astonishing uniformity among the types of jewelry allowed by both fashion and protocol. The close-fitting choker, extended by giant ropes of pearls, provides a stylistic complement to the breast ornament; the two together dominate the fashion silhouette so completely as to leave no room for large necklaces as such. Apart from the ever popular lavallières, the few necklaces designed as overall ornaments for the bosom consisted of radiating gemstone motifs in the eighteenth-century style or, like the necklace of Mrs Cornelius Vanderbilt [27, 37], were in a form adapted from the breast ornament – half corsage, half neck ornament.

As the Oriental taste in fashion and jewelry took over from about 1910, the choker was considered dated, and the long diamond chain, harbinger of the heavy sautoir of the late 1920s, began its triumphal progress. Lina Cavalieri, the most beautiful opera singer of her day, made a sensation at the Metropolitan Opera in New York with a frivolous chain of this kind which fastened at the shoulder seam of her dress. Those who could afford it flaunted a handsome diamond drop on the sautoir. Cartier's set 40-carat stones as pendants of this type for Baroness Henri de Rothschild in Paris and Mrs Rita Lydig in New York, while Grand Duchess Cyril was conspicuous with a cabochon sapphire of more than 300 carats.

During the austerity years of the First World War, the ostentatious parade of high society gave way, for a time, to the socially more acceptable ideal of charitable works and care for the suffering, exemplified by the Duchess of Marlborough and Countess Greffulhe. But in 1916, when the Paris Bourse reopened, the Assembly resumed its sittings and the Opéra took up its repertory again after a lapse of one and a half years, the curtain rose once more on the round of pleasures which the Parisians reckoned they had too long denied themselves. Lord Derby's reception for the King and Queen of England at the British Embassy heralded the spring awakening impatiently awaited by the jewellers and fashion houses.

There were conflicting fashion trends in the immediate post-war years. While Chéruit sketched out his elongated line in gowns for Madame Errazuriz, Lanvin launched the 'period'-inspired *robes de style* that so enchanted Cécile Sorel. The jewellers enlisted followers from both camps. The vertical hipless line, which reminded Poiret of an undernourished switchboard operator, finally won the day, and the long pearl sautoir was seen as its logical accompaniment in the field of jewelry. Anything that looked like pearls was permitted: even the wealthy Mrs Stotesbury extended Cartier's great emerald necklace with artificial pearls with the result that, one Paris fashion writer commented, an observer could never be sure 'where Cartier stopped and Técla [a cheap general store] began'.

After 1925 the diamond sautoir again took over from the pearl. At the Théâtre Daunou in Paris, the actress-director Jane Renouardt nightly dazzled her worshipping critics and admirers with hers. In fact, the diamond sautoir completely usurped the role of the classic necklace, while Eastern-inspired bead necklaces or Cartier's coral and onyx 'Fuchsia' necklace for Ganna Walska belonged generally to the realm of fashion or costume jewelry. In this field the couturiers gradually ceased to be dependent on the jewellers; indeed, as the 1920s advanced, they became competitors. Coco Chanel took the young jewelry designer Fulco Verdura under her wing and in 1932, encouraged by Paul Iribe, launched her own jewelry collection.[1] A necklace terminating in a comet was the Iribe–Chanel reply to the 'traditional' style of the rue de la Paix, which was not felt to be sufficiently 'barbaric'.[2]

Yet the large necklace remained the province of the jewellers. It was Cartier's sensational creations that provided the focus of the Autumn Show at San Sebastian in 1919, when the firm's most valuable piece was exhibited at the Hotel Maria Cristina, occupied by wealthy Cubans and Argentinians. The jewel comprised a long diamond chain from which hung the world's largest cut sapphire, a drop of 478 carats.[3] The previous history of the stone is shown in the following sketches.

preceding pages, left

297 The Duke and Duchess of Windsor, 1957. The Duchess is wearing her amethyst necklace which was created in 1947 [298]

preceding pages, right

298 Bib necklace. Cartier Paris, commissioned by the Duchess of Windsor, 1947. Twisted 18-carat and 20-carat gold, platinum; brilliant- and baguette-cut diamonds; one heart-shaped faceted amethyst, twenty-seven emerald-cut amethysts, and one oval faceted amethyst; cabochon turquoises

opposite

299 Necklace. Cartier London, commissioned in 1937 by Sir Digvijaysinhji, Maharaja Jam Saheb of Nawanagar [196]. Platinum, yellow gold; designed as a succession of pavé-set and baguette-cut diamond sections, supporting a fringe of claw-set cushion-cut rubies interspaced with circular old-European and baguette-cut diamonds, the latter also forming channel-set frames around the fifteen larger single rubies, the back with rectangular step-cut rubies and further diamonds, the clasp set with two pentagonal rubies, another ruby of similar shape at the front

A   The original diamond necklace of 1912, which Cartier Paris fitted with six cushion-shaped sapphires and a sapphire drop of a total of 224.10 carats.
      The sapphires were then unmounted and sent to New York, where an identical diamond necklace was made to receive them.
      (In the Paris necklace they were replaced with onyx; that was broken up in 1914.)

B   In 1913 the New York necklace was reworked in Paris and a great 478-carat drop sapphire added to the seven original stones.

C   Still in 1913, the seven sapphires were removed and the great sapphire was attached by a ring of calibré-cut sapphires.

D   In 1919 the sapphire drop was transferred to a diamond necklace, and the ensemble bought in 1921 for Queen Marie of Romania [300]. (The necklace, sold to Nancy Leeds in 1911, had been bought back by Cartier in 1919 without its two central stones; the diamond drop was transferred to a new diamond necklace that Mrs Leeds – by then Princess Anastasia of Greece – wore in 1921 on the occasion of the marriage of her son, William B. Leeds, to Princess Xenia of Russia.)

opposite

300 Queen Marie of Romania wearing her pearl and diamond tiara and her 478-carat sapphire drop sautoir, 1921

A   **B**   **C**   **D**

The Cartier display in San Sebastian became the talk of the town: the Queen of Spain, Victoria Eugenia [74], the Queen Mother, Maria Cristina, and the Princess of Bourbon arrived from the nearby Miramar Palace. The Queen tried on the sapphire jewel and remembered it the following year. It was King Alfonso's custom to buy two new diamonds every year for his wife's antique diamond sautoir; but he was not tempted to purchase the Cartier piece. 'Only the nouveaux riches can afford such luxuries', he observed: 'we kings are the nouveaux pauvres of today!'

At about the same time, as Louis Cartier was to recall later, the giant stone was to clear the name of a Parisian dealer in precious stones. The case concerned the theft of a sapphire from the Polish Count Branicki. The stone had been stolen from its hiding place, the Count's tobacco jar in his Warsaw residence, and all the evidence suggested that it had found its way to Paris. There it had been acquired in all innocence by a dealer who had it cut down because of its great size. He was hauled before the courts and accused of having cut the stone, knowing it to be the largest of its kind, so as to destroy all trace of it. But Louis Cartier, whose grandfather had once handled Count Branicki's stone, was convinced of the dealer's honesty. Called as an expert witness, he astonished the court when he unwrapped the firm's own giant sapphire. It was obvious that the stolen stone had not been unique, and Louis went on to prove the dealer's innocence.

Two years after the exhibition in Spain the sapphire drop was to be bought by King Ferdinand of Romania. But he too appears to have approached the purchase with caution. First Cartier's had to pledge to cancel the sale should 'serious and unforeseen events' intervene. (Was the King, perhaps, thinking of his bleak exile in Iasi during the First World War?) The purchase price of Fr. 1,375,000 was to be paid in four instalments up to 1924. Ferdinand's beautiful consort, Queen Marie [300], was at that time forty-six, at the height of her fame, and the ideal ambassador for Romania's interests. When in Paris she lived at the Ritz, which flew the Romanian flag, and the public followed her every move. But large jewelry had not yet excited her interest; there was nothing in her collection to match the

overleaf, left

301 Necklace. Cartier Paris, commissioned in 1927 by the Aga Khan, enlarged in 1928. Platinum; alternate sapphire and emerald beads, and diamond roundels; in the centre, an engraved emerald weighing 24.62 carats is set above a cabochon sapphire weighing 25.60 carats; the engraved emerald pendant weighs 70.46 carats

overleaf, right

302 Begum Andrée, wife of the Aga Khan, wearing her emerald tiara (which could be worn as a necklace) and a necklace also by Cartier, 1930

Russian ruby pieces of her recently dead mother, the Duchess of Saxe-Coburg-Gotha. Marie preferred to wear a Greek cross or, when she visited the Paris Opéra, her pearls. At about the time she received the sapphire drop she also acquired a Cartier pearl tiara which she liked to wear in the 'Byzantine' manner with a band of pearls framing her face. However, the great sapphire sautoir was the perfect companion-piece for the magnificent sapphire tiara the Queen had bought from Grand Duchess Vladimir when she fled from Russia [85]. Marie wore them both at her coronation receptions and when she sat for her portrait to Philip de László.[4]

In the year of her coronation in Bucharest, the marriage of her daughter Marie (Mignon) to Alexander I of Serbia also took place. The King, who had recently ordered 350 pairs of cufflinks from a jeweller, entrusted the major commissions to Cartier's, and Farinès, the firm's star salesman, hurried to Belgrade with designs for tiaras and emerald bracelets. Queen Marie of Serbia, as obsessed with emeralds as her mother was with sapphires, had bought a Russian tiara of cabochon emeralds from Princess Putyatin (who when she was Grand Duchess Marie had done Russian embroidery for Coco Chanel). Following the strict Empire style of the tiara, Cartier created a sautoir out of eighteen magnificent emeralds from the Serbian crown jewels which, for sheer splendour, bore comparison with the Romanian sapphire jewels. It was realized six months before the birth of Queen Marie's son Peter (1923); his wife Alexandra was to wear it at their wedding. Later, unfortunately, it had to be sold.

The newspaper reports of Cartier's monumental display of the redesigned Patiala jewels (see p. 169) – 'Paris Amazed By Oriental Gems' – gave the Aga Khan the idea of selling unwanted stones from his collection through an exhibition at Cartier's. Revered by twelve million Ismaili Shi'a Muslims as the forty-eighth Imam,[5] the Aga Khan had been born in Karachi in 1877 and had followed the development of Cartier's, both in the Orient and in Europe, from his youth. His first purchase, in 1902, had been a breast ornament with a heart-shaped diamond, shortly followed by a wheat-ear and a laurel-leaf tiara. Later, like Cornelius Vanderbilt and J. P. Morgan, he was an admirer of Cartier's Art Deco productions, brilliant and colourful masterpieces that appealed to his own pronounced colour sense.

The diamonds which the Aga Khan was proposing to sell comprised thirty-eight round stones, and three drops of 40, 38 and 35 carats respectively. Pierre Cartier set them as a gigantic necklace which was first displayed at the French Exhibition in Cairo in 1929. At the official opening it was admired by King Fuad who, however, bought his Queen Nasli a diamond tiara. Another exhibition followed immediately at Alexandria, and two months after that the piece went on display at the International Exhibition in Barcelona's Montjuich Park. The Aga Khan's necklace, displayed on a mannequin from the fashion house of Callot [303], proved a sensation – but failed to change hands. Part of Cartier's Barcelona exhibit also featured at the Ibero-American Exhibition in Seville, where the Colombian government had erected a 'Temple of Emeralds'.

The necklace went on its travels once again, this time by the Orient Express to Belgrade, for inspection by Queen Marie. But the city was on the verge of war: tensions between Serbs and Croats were smouldering in the provinces and the constitution had been suspended. That autumn the country was renamed Yugoslavia and a new constitution was promulgated by the far-sighted King. It was hardly a propitious moment for the sale of a major piece of jewelry. Thus, on the eve of the Wall Street Crash, the great necklace was broken up again into its constituent parts. Cartier's bought the 35-carat elongated drop and attached it to a necklace destined for the New York firm. The 38-carat drop was returned to the Aga Khan,[6] and the 40-carat one provided the centrepiece of a necklace for his son, Prince Ali Khan. In the meantime, Cartier London sold the remaining round stones to the King of Nepal.

The dispersal of what had perhaps been the largest private jewel collection before the First World War – that of Grand Duchess Vladimir (p. 107) – took place in the early 1920s. The Duchess had fled Russia late in 1919 and died in France the following year. According to the chroniclers of high society, she used to put everyone else in the shade when she appeared, glittering with emeralds, at Boni de Castellane's balls in the Palais Rose. After her death, the jewels were divided among her four children, with whom both Pierre and Louis Cartier had personal connections. From her son Boris, Louis acquired a 107-carat emerald[7] and a magnificent emerald necklace of nineteenth-century Russian work [*p. 248*, A].

Two years after the Grand Duchess's death, Louis Cartier showed the legendary emeralds to King Alfonso of Spain, who may have recalled his ironic outburst over the San Sebastian sapphire drop, when he thought that the time for buying such treasures was past. In one sense, Alfonso was right: from now on the world's great jewels were destined to find their home not in Europe but in the United States.

Cartier's American jewelry parade had begun with a necklace of nine large emeralds ordered in Paris by Eva Stotesbury, the spoilt wife of 'Morgan's man in Philadelphia'. With its hexagonal centrepiece, the necklace could almost stand comparison with Grand Duchess Vladimir's. Thanks to the swelling fortune of her banker husband, Eva could realize her dream of a 1920s Versailles. At their mansion, Whitemarsh Hall, crammed by the dealer Duveen with his most expensive furniture and works of art, the word 'excess' required redefinition. A radical remodelling was prescribed for the emerald necklace; the work was done in New York, in 1923, by Pierre Cartier. The number of emeralds was increased to nineteen and a matching tiara was added. In a similar manner, two years before, Pierre had created a giant emerald *parure* for Nancy Leeds by combining an epaulette with a necklace. When it was completed, the widow of America's tin king sat to the Hungarian portrait painter Philip de László [77], just as Queen Marie had done in distant Romania.

No wonder that in due course the Vladimir emeralds also found their way to America, mounted in the severe form of an Art Deco necklace for Edith Rockefeller McCormick. The daughter of John D. Rockefeller Senior, founder of the family fortune, she had married Harold Fowler McCormick, son of the Chicago Reaper King, in 1895; but the marriage ended melodramatically in divorce in 1922. Edith sought refuge with Carl Jung in Switzerland and spent the rest of her life absorbed in a fantasy project to build the futuristic town of Edithton – a project prematurely terminated by the 1929 Crash. In 1935, three years after her death, the emerald necklace was once more broken up in Chicago and the stones handed over to Cartier by the executors for the asking price of $480,000.

By this time Barbara Hutton, the Woolworth heiress, had inherited her $42 million and become Countess Haugwitz-Reventlow. It was apparently her former sister-in-law, Roussy Mdivani, the new Madame Sert, who drew Barbara's attention to the Rockefeller emeralds.[8] 'There is an emerald necklace at Cartier's that came from the Romanovs, and

I can get you a special price.' But the 'special price' did not long remain a secret: 'Countess Buys Emerald Collection For Over A Million Dollars', ran the headlines, without making a notable contribution to Barbara's popularity. The emeralds were sent across the Atlantic in two shipments, the first liner carrying a consignment of ten packets, the second just the precious 100-carat stone. From her neo-Palladian mansion in London, Wingfield House, Barbara had Cartier's in Bond Street make up the emeralds as a pair of earrings,

A The emerald necklace of Grand Duchess Vladimir
B The emeralds set in a new necklace by Cartier London for Barbara Hutton, 1930s
C The emeralds reset by Cartier London for Barbara Hutton after the war
D The emeralds reset by Cartier Paris for Barbara Hutton, 1947

A   B   C   D

a necklace and a ring. The necklace consisted of a heavy chain with the 100-carat stone at the centre in the massive style of the 1930s [**B**].[9] After the Second World War its design was obsolete, and it was remodelled [**C**]. Barbara, who had in the meantime become Princess Troubetzkoy, was now a devotee of India (which had often provided a refuge) and of yellow gold. Her enthusiasm, together with that of the Duchess of Windsor, Daisy Fellowes and Countess Surmont, did much to promote the popularity of the metal. Once more the emeralds were returned to Cartier's, where André Denet, the principal salesman, and Lucien Lachassagne, the designer, supervised the creation of a jewel in the Oriental style which Barbara could use either as a necklace or as a tiara [**D**, **407**], and which she wore latterly in Morocco.

Another relic of the days of the tsars, spirited out of Russia by an unexplained route, was a 197.75-carat briolette-cut sapphire which brought Cartier's together again with the McCormicks. Harold McCormick had barely been divorced from his first wife, Edith, before he married the Polish opera singer Ganna Walska. She had already extracted from her former husband, Alexander Smith Cochran, known as 'the richest bachelor in the world', a wedding present very much to her taste – the choice of whatever pleased her best at Cartier's. Ganna Walska was driven by her ambition, not only to be marvelled at for the splendour of her jewelry, but to be famous for the pure gold (so-called) of her voice. McCormick, who had already brought the singer Mary Garden to the Chicago Opera, advanced his wife's ambitions out of conjugal infatuation and by the expenditure of considerable funds. For Ganna McCormick, who resided in her château near Versailles and was later to buy the Théâtre des Champs-Elysées, Cartier's created a necklace, combining the Russian sapphire with a 256.60-carat engraved Indian emerald, whose step-by-step transformations [**A**–**F**] were even more chameleon-like than the Queen of Romania's sapphire necklace [*p. 243*, **A**–**D**].

A (1923) A 256.60-carat engraved emerald, with a sapphire of 39.14 carats

B (1927) The engraved emerald, the sapphire mounted crosswise above it, and an emerald of 33.58 carats

C The engraved emerald, sapphire and emerald, plus a Russian sapphire of 197.75 carats

D The Russian sapphire, suspended from two emeralds of 22.10 and 16.48 carats

E The two smaller emeralds, with a different pendant

F The Russian sapphire and the engraved emerald: the necklace of Ganna Walska, Mrs Harold McCormick

304 *left* Necklace. Cartier London, 1929. Mounted with thirty-one briolette-cut diamonds of 101.60 carats, baguette-cut diamonds, and 280 rubies of 199.06 carats (including the 27.32-carat central stone)

305 *below* Sea-monster necklace. Cartier London, 1930. The heads in circular- and baguette-cut diamonds holding a tubular engraved emerald, the necklace mounted with two strings of tubular engraved emeralds and circular- and baguette-cut diamonds

306 Sautoir. Cartier London, special order, 1930. Platinum; square brilliant-, round old-, single- and rose-cut diamonds; leaf-shaped carved rubies, cabochon rubies and ruby beads; pearls

307 Necklace. Cartier London, commissioned in 1932 by Lady Granard. Platinum; round old- and rose-cut diamonds; one cushion-shaped polished emerald weighing 143.23 carats

308 *right* Necklace. Cartier London, 1926, sold to the Maharaja of Nawanagar [cf. **196**]. The six lower emeralds weighing 224.08 carats (including the 70.24-carat bottom stone) on circular-, half-moon- and baguette-cut diamond mount

309 *below* Necklace. Cartier London, 1937. Mounted with fifteen square, rectangular and hexagonal emeralds weighing 134.45 carats and circular-cut diamonds, from which a 45.02-carat emerald cross is suspended

During the 1930s Cartier London quite overshadowed the Paris firm in the production of large necklaces [e.g. **299**]. Most of them were diamond or coloured stone sautoirs, of which an astonishing number were sold in England. Between 1933 and 1938 London produced approximately 280 necklaces, including forty-five examples of coloured bead sautoirs.

One of the most original designs was a magnificent necklace of 1937, which consisted of fifteen emeralds with a cross pendant cut from a single 45-carat emerald [**309**]. The 4-cm-long gem belonged originally to Queen Isabella II of Spain (1830–1904), who gave it to the Empress Eugénie. From her it passed via Queen Victoria and Princess Beatrice to Queen Victoria Eugenia of Spain, from whom Cartier bought it and sold it to Madame Patiño.

The London workshops

The stocks of the Bond Street shop were never so extensive, nor its designers and workshops so busy, as during the later years of the reign of King George V and Queen Mary. The king died in 1936, but the epoch really came to an end only with the outbreak of the Second World War in 1939. Cartier London had become independent of Paris in 1919, and set up its own workshops two years later. At first, while the goldsmiths and stone-setters were all British, the designers were predominantly French. Up to 1929 there was a daily traffic in gemstones between the Paris and London firms; the then London director, Arthur Fraser, recalled later how he frequently carried cases full of precious stones between the two companies, without any customs formalities. The practice came to an end in 1929 when the Chancellor of the Exchequer imposed a duty. Jeanne Toussaint, who never went to London, later had photographs of the Paris creations sent to Bond Street so that the current styles of the rue de la Paix should not be forgotten.

310 'Dinner Hour in the Grand Restaurant of the "Queen Mary"': advertisement for Cartier London, *c*. 1935

Cartier London distributed the making of jewels and clocks among their three subsidiaries: Sutton and Straker, a goldsmiths' workshop in Clarendon House, Bond Street, under the direction of George Straker; Wright and Davies, directed by Sam Mayo, in Ormond House, Rosebery Avenue, which produced cigarette cases, vanity cases and clock cases; and English Art Works. English Art Works, directed by Felix Bertrand and specializing in large necklaces, was one of London's largest workshops in platinum jewelry, and had begun in Cartier's premises before moving to 105 New Bond Street. The company's name itself made it absolutely clear that there was no question of foreign labour competing with native craftsmen. Even before the First World War, Cartier's New York branch had had to defend itself against criticism on these grounds, and in the English crisis of the 1930s, when 60 per cent of the goldsmiths were unemployed, Cartier London seemed especially vulnerable to the same accusation. It was only when Queen Mary, during the Depression years, visited English Art Works, where sixty skilled English craftsmen earned their living, that the critics fell silent. With regard to designers too, Jacques Cartier was careful to give preference to native designers over French. Peter Lemarchand was the great exception. He came over from Paris in 1935 and up to the outbreak of war was working in London: his naturalistic style, his tropical birds and flowers, exerted a lasting influence in England. Later visits by French designers, such as Jacqueau's in 1947, were shorter and usually for specific jobs. Like the Bernard Palissy, Boulle and Germain Pilon design schools in Paris, the Chiswick School of Arts and Hampstead's Central School of Arts and Crafts taught jewelry design and other branches of the trade. George Charity, who joined Cartier's in 1925, was trained at Chiswick, as was Rupert Emmerson, the designer of seventeen snuffboxes for the collector Peter Wilding (now in the British Museum).

311 A craftsman jeweller in English Art Works, London

312 English Art Works, London, 1922

On the other hand, the rigid geometric style, which appears so often in London's output during the 1930s, and which is so different from the contemporary style in Paris, was mostly the work of Frederick A. Mew, who occupied a position almost comparable to that of Jacqueau in Paris. Just as in Paris the most imaginative creations generally sprang from the joint inspiration of Louis Cartier and Jacqueau or Lemarchand and Toussaint, so in London Jacques Cartier regularly discussed things with Mew and the Frenchman Massabieaux who, though no designer himself, skilfully directed the design studio. Mew designed charming bird brooches like his friend Peter Lemarchand, dahlias and other flowers made of citrine, and in 1953 the diamond tiara for Queen Elizabeth the Queen

313 Sautoir. Cartier New York, special order, 1925. Platinum; single-cut diamonds; one carved hexagonal 85.60-carat emerald, fifty fluted emerald beads weighing an estimated total of 517 carats; natural pearls

this page

314 Necklace. Cartier London, 1938, sold to Mrs Horace Dodge and subsequently remodelled to the form shown here. Platinum; twenty-four emeralds; baguette- and square-cut diamonds. Total weight of the emeralds 123.72 carats (including the 15.29-carat pendant stone). The original necklace had thirty-three emeralds – eight more in the circle, and one more at the back of the neck – and did not have the bar at the bottom, presumably added for a further pendant

Mother [76]. A fellow designer with Mew in the commissions department was Ernest C. Frowde, though his work tended to be somewhat dry and academic and lacked Mew's rich imagination. In 1933 the two worked on designs for a crown for the Gaekwar of Baroda, which, however, was never made.

Protocol and etiquette at the Court of St James had changed little since the First World War. Tiaras were still obligatory at receptions and balls; sautoirs of geometric pattern took the place of the breast ornament which, with the changing dress line, had become dated. Generally the sautoir had two strands at the front, with a pendant hanging down the low-cut back. Bandeaux, sautoirs and bracelets were interchangeable in form and structure and multi-purpose: thus sautoirs and bandeaux might be worn as brooches and bracelets, and Lily Damita and Gertrude Lawrence demonstrated on stage and screen how five or six might be worn to chic effect on black silk evening gloves.[10]

Rubies and emeralds were favoured among coloured gems, but if they proved too expensive the acceptable substitutes were amethyst, topaz or aquamarine, the last being a special favourite with Englishwomen for sautoirs and tiaras. Amethyst, from which large crystals were easy to cut, provided massive purple sautoirs. One of these was ordered in 1926 by the Duchess of Marlborough (the former Gladys Deacon), and another, a little later, by Lady Cunard, the feared and famous Emerald. Both of these American-born ladies had their sautoirs admired and copied from Palm Beach to the Riviera.

By contrast, aquamarine was most often used in chokers, from which earclips and double clip brooches could be detached. In England double clips in characteristic buckle shape were made popular by the Rani of Pudukota and Lady Cunningham-Reid, and represented the 'find' of 1930s jewelry. But aquamarine was also cut in five-pointed, six-pointed and rhomb shapes, unusual forms which livened up the monotonous sequence of stones in a sautoir. Moreover, aquamarine seemed to hold distant memories of that strange, azure-blue stone, the eerie blue diamond.

Fancy-coloured diamonds cropped up now and then at Cartier's from old Indian collections. On the European–American market they were completely unrelated to the course of the stock exchange. One of the earliest fancy-coloured diamond sautoirs found its way from Cartier Paris to Kiev in 1914. Surely the shimmering palette of the ballet *Schéhérezade* inspired the names of its pastel graded stones – narcissus yellow, lemon yellow, aquamarine blue, sultan green, topaz, gold, shrimp pink and lilac. In 1930 Madame Gaston Fournier, the daughter of the last of the Tiffanys (who had died in 1902), was presented with a necklace of seventy-one fancy-coloured diamonds, and the following year Cartier London created a necklace from six pink diamonds, of which two came from the collection of the Maharaja of Nawanagar, and the clasp from the Gaekwar of Baroda. The jewel was later broken up again.

One of the two Nawanagar stones, however, of 9.50 carats, found its place in that most precious cascade of coloured diamonds known to history, the ceremonial necklace of the Maharaja himself [404]. Jacques Cartier, who assembled the piece, called it 'a really superb realization of a connoisseur's dream' and confessed that in no other epoch could a comparable jewel have been created. The necklace consisted of two strands of round diamonds linked on both sides by a fancy-pink stone. The 9.50-carat pink diamond formed the first stone of the pendant. Below it hung an azure-blue stone of 26.26 carats,[11] and below that 'the world's most beautiful pink stone' of 22.97 carats, which, according to Jacques Cartier, came from a world-famous jewel. The centrepiece of the pendant was the 'Queen of Holland', the blue-white diamond of 136.32 carats which came from the same mine as the 'Cullinan' and was cut in Amsterdam in 1913 (it had been exhibited at the 1925 Exposition des Arts Décoratifs in Paris by the Dutch diamond dealer F. Friedmann, who had branches in Paris and New York).[12] The pendant terminated in a green diamond – 'a rare stone indeed', exclaimed Jacques Cartier admiringly – and a pink rhomboid stone of 15.62 carats.

Before this extraordinary piece was sent to India the London branch, as a playful improvisation, combined the blue and pink stones with the 'Polar Star' diamond into a temporary necklace which was put on display [400]. It was only when Cartier's acquired the 'Queen of Holland' that the idea of the definitive, spectacular colour combination, now known to history as the 'Nawanagar Necklace', was born.

315 Necklace. Cartier London, commissioned in 1938 by Merle Oberon. Platinum; flexible chain in round-cut diamonds, from which twenty-nine graduated cabochon emeralds, tipped with diamonds, are suspended

316 Crocodile necklace. Cartier Paris, commissioned in 1975 by Maria Félix, after a design by Gabriel Raton. The articulated gold bodies set with 1,023 brilliant-cut fancy intense yellow diamonds weighing 60.02 carats in total; two navette-shaped cabochon emeralds (eyes), 1,060 emeralds weighing 66.86 carats in total; two cabochon rubies (eyes) (50% actual size)

317 Snake necklace. Cartier Paris, commissioned in 1968 by Maria Félix, after a design by Gabriel Raton. The articulated platinum, white gold and yellow gold body set with 2,473 brilliant- and baguette-cut diamonds, weighing 178.21 carats in total; two pear-shaped emeralds (eyes); green, red and black enamel (50% actual size)

Gem dealers

Cartier's discovered the world's most remarkable stones not only in old collections, but also in the stocks of the leading diamond and precious stone dealers all over the world. The latter entrusted their remarkable treasures to Cartier's the more willingly since, as dealers and lapidaries, they were interested in bulk sales of new cuts. With Cartier's they were guaranteed that daring cuts, represented since 1900 by the trapezoid, the *obus* or shell case, the unstepped square and later the baguette, would find optimum application in the wide spectrum of their international production.[13]

It is hard to say whether technical or aesthetic considerations came first in determining the new cuts of the period. But it is certain that the new geometric cuts stimulated jewelry designers to the bold formal combinations of Art Deco. In 1902 the American David C. Townsend evolved a cut which, in the ebullience of the dawning era, was called 'the twentieth-century cut' or the 'jubilee cut'; the upper and lower sides of the stone each had forty facets. But this cut was expensive, and furthermore 'round' diamonds were less in demand than the new geometrical forms which matched the contemporary feeling for the cube.

The great pioneer among the diamond dealers around 1900 was Atamik Eknayan (1847–1925). When he was young, the important dealers were located at the Bosphorus, Aden and Cairo, where they brought their wares from India on the way to Venice, Frankfurt and Lithuania. The discoveries in Africa, exhibited in Paris from 1867, disturbed this network. Napoleon III had already made every effort to establish Paris as the centre of the diamond-working industry;[14] and in 1872 the young Armenian Eknayan moved there. He opened his first cutting house on the boulevard de la Villette in 1893; it moved to Neuilly, where experimental cuts were to be developed. But Eknayan was as influential as a dealer in Paris and New York as he was as a lapidary. It was from him, in 1909, that Cartier acquired the historic 90.38-carat 'Indian Briolette' diamond [**401**], as well as the 'Blue Heart' diamond of 30.82 carats (also known as the 'Unzue Heart') [**402**].

When the sons of Isaac Joseph Asscher of Amsterdam, Joseph and Louis, set up a diamond-cutting business in Paris in 1899, it supplied Cartier's from the start. In 1908 the Amsterdam head office was commissioned by Edward VII with the cutting of the 'Cullinan', at that time the largest diamond ever mined. In 1919 the Asschers moved their cutting house to Versailles, where they philanthropically provided work for war wounded and war orphans. Relations between Cartier's and the Asschers remained friendly well into the modern era. Thanks to Cartier's, Asscher's were spared harassment by the Vichy regime during the Second World War and by 1948 150 cutters and 50 apprentices were back at work at Versailles; Louis Cartier's son Claude received his first instruction in diamond expertise from Asscher's of Amsterdam.

The Armenian Carlo Sirakian (1885–1976) was another Cartier supplier. After the Turkish massacres, he left Constantinople through Bulgaria and began business as a diamond dealer in Romania. About 1913 he settled in Paris and went into partnership with = Manouk Mezbourian, who worked for Eknayan. Sirakian's speciality was the cutting of diamonds as hexagon, shell, kite, pentagon and rhomb, almost exclusively for Cartier's.[15]

But Cartier's most personal association was with Raphael Esmerian (1903–76). His father Paul (Bobros) began life as a lapidary in Constantinople before he set out on the trail for the 'Golden West', settling as a twenty-year-old in Paris in 1890. Unlike Eknayan, he specialized in coloured stones, a field in which the small Armenian colony in Paris, with Esmerian's uncle Margossian at its head, held the lead. In 1919 Paul introduced his son Raphael into the secrets of his profession. During the 1920s the Esmerians were the leading gem dealers in Europe, and for fifteen years they maintained a branch in London, which brought them into close contact with Jacques, the youngest of the three Cartier brothers. Later, at the invitation of the jeweller Raymond C. Yard, Raphael Esmerian, as much aesthete as dealer, went to New York, where, as friend and near-neighbour, he was to supply Pierre Cartier with often spectacular coloured stones over a period of some thirty years.[16]

'THE JEWELLED FLIGHT OF TIME'

318 One of the workshops where Cartier's elegant timepieces were created, *c.* 1927

319 Mystery clock with central axle, one of the very first produced. Cartier Paris, 1920. Made by Coüet. Base-plate of gold; base (containing movement) of ebonite with a fleurette of rose-cut diamonds set in platinum; rounded support of gold with black enamel decoration; 'Japanese' screen of ebonite, rimmed with gold; in the corners fleurettes of rose-cut diamonds set in platinum; below 6 o'clock a motif of gold, turquoise, and black-and-white enamel edged with white gold. In the centre a chamfered rectangle of transparent citrine; chapter ring of gold and turquoise-blue enamel with gold Roman numerals and dots in reserve; inner row of rose-cut diamonds set in platinum; hands of platinum and rose-cut diamonds. 8-day movement

this page

320 Clock with two annular dials. Cartier Paris, 1904. Octagonal chased silver-gilt base; Louis XVI-style vase in slate-blue marble with movement inside; silver-gilt Louis XVI garlands, handles, and laurel-leaf moulding. Time displayed on two annular dials: hours a green enamel band with white Roman numerals set in blue enamel cartouches separated by yellow dots at the half-hour, edged with interlacing white enamel fillets; minutes a white enamel band with black indices plus Arabic numerals and gilt screws at 5-minute intervals; time indicator a fixed pointer in the middle of the garland motif. 8-day movement

During the nineteenth century, Cartier's stock comprised not only jewelry and goldsmiths' work but the entire range of *objets d'art* of a specialist antique dealer. The first watches are mentioned in 1853. These were not timepieces from Cartier's own workshops but bought-in pocket-watches of gold, silver, copper and steel, often ornamented in Second Empire style with onyx, pearl and enamel inlay. The principal work of this period was the 'Egyptian' pendant watch of 1873, decorated with rubies and rose-cut diamonds (see p. 144).

To meet the demand of connoisseurs for collectors' pieces in the great tradition of French horology, Cartier bought at auction and from specialist dealers. These acquisitions included a Louis XIV silver pocket-watch; a watch by Lépine decorated in painted enamel; two pieces by the greatest of the French watchmaking dynasties, Bréguet (see p. 292); and a watch in the form of a seal, fitted with a musical box, made in Geneva about 1820. The most interesting models were sold on richly ornate châtelaines of different colours of gold and enamel in Louis XVI style. These traditional-style pendants were decorated with conventional late eighteenth-century motifs such as quivers and arrows, turtledoves and flower garlands [13]. A châtelaine watch of 1874 was ornamented with urns and a little temple of love. Besides watches, seals and charms were also hung on the châtelaines, which were sometimes called *breloquets* (from the French *breloque*, 'charm'). In 1875 we find an entry for a châtelaine watch in peacock-eye enamel, an eighteenth-century technique revived by Boucheron; fitted with seals and charms, it was sold to the Prince de Wagram.

In the 1890s, Cartier's were supplied by the greatest watchmakers of the period, chief among them Vacheron Constantin of Geneva (founded in 1755).[1] They delivered a number of pieces between 1893 and 1899, when Cartier's moved to the rue de la Paix. Among them was a simple steel bicycle watch, a model with neo-Gothic designs, and a valuable pocket-watch decorated with *scènes galantes* in the manner of Watteau. In 1896, Cartier bought a watch decorated with enamel birds and flowers from Ferdinand Verger of Paris, father of the brilliant Georges Verger, who was to work for Cartier's in the 1930s.[2] Barely three years later Cartier's produced their first platinum pocket-watches. One of the earliest, a heart-shaped model embellished with pavé diamonds, was bought by J. P. Morgan.

Between 1872 and 1892, Cartier's inventory records no fewer than 408 watches and châtelaines. The range of stock increased still more dramatically after the firm moved to the rue de la Paix in 1899 and Louis Cartier, associated with his father since the previous year, contributed his expertise.[3] His involvement in the watchmaking department had three objectives: to add table clocks to the range of pocket-watches; to build up in-house production; and to explore the market possibilities of the wristwatch, of whose future he was convinced.

Table clocks

The firms of Brédillard, in the rue Jean-Jacques-Rousseau, and Dagonneau, rue des Petits-Champs, with their factories in Geneva, were among the first suppliers of movements for Cartier's table clocks (*pendules* or *pendulettes*). From 1904 Cartier's were using movements made by Prévost in the boulevard Sébastopol, and this workshop was soon undertaking the bulk of Cartier's commissions. In 1911 they supplied a table clock with an electrically illuminated dial, bought by the Aga Khan. The enamelled cases for these Prévost movements were provided by the Dubret workshop in the rue d'Hauteville. In a few instances Cartier's bought cases from Yahr, the Moscow enameller, who worked from detailed designs. A single table clock might require the skills of many different workshops: for a pyramid clock of 1906, for instance, the marble-like thulite was furnished by the lapidary Varangoz to Cartier designs, Dubret's provided its enamel settings, Brédillard the movement, and Prévost made the accompanying barometer, thermometer and compass as well as the three dials with their hands. The glasses were fitted by a small workshop called Charbonnier. In other instances the jewellers Lavabre enamelled the casing, the Bako workshop was co-opted for crystal cases, and Haas in the boulevard Sébastopol decorated the dial.

Just as the firm's contemporary garland-style jewelry was inspired by eighteenth-century décor, so from 1901 onward table clocks took the form of garlanded urns in pure Louis XVI style [320]. With bodies of marble, hardstone or porcelain, they were clearly related to the *pendules à cercle tournant* as illustrated in Jean-François Forty's copper engravings of 1771. The clock movement, set horizontally in the body of the urn, drove an

321, 322 Watch brooch. Cartier, *c.* 1880. Brooch in gold depicting a bird between two dolphins. Round gold case with floral patterns. Flat winding crown on pendant; gold trefoil pendant bow. White enamel dial, with Arabic numerals ringed by a minute track in gold dots with lozenge-shaped indices at 5-minute intervals; gilt Louis XV-style hands

323 Clock with strut in the form of a Louis XVI cartel. Cartier Paris, 1904. Made by Cesard, Brédillard, and Prévost. Cut-out ivory plaque with gold feet and edges. Bezel, frame and tapered column in gold guilloché and blue and green enamel. Volutes, fluting, and fillets in white enamel; decoration (urn, etc.) in gold with motifs in millegrain-set rose-cut diamonds and platinum. Round silver-gilt case and strut. Round white enamel dial, chapter ring with Roman numerals inside a minute track with dots and Arabic numerals at 5-minute intervals. Gold hands. 8-day movement

opposite

324 *above left* Desk clock with full strike and quarter repeater. Cartier Paris, 1910. Made by Prévost and Bako. Agate base. Silver case with guilloché blue enamel, white enamel fillets, rose-cut diamond studs on the sides, gold beading along the bottom. Handle fastened with polished agate. Cabochon moonstone repeater button. Bezel ringed in white enamel beads. White enamel dial with Arabic numerals ringed by a minute track of gilt indices and black Arabic numerals at the quarter hours. Hands in rose-cut diamonds and platinum. 8-day movement

325 *above right* Desk clock with minute repeater. Cartier Paris, 1910. Made by Prévost and Bako. Ivory base and case, friezes in gold bearing the words 'L'amitié vous l'offre' (A gift of friendship). Moonstone cylindrical repeater button. Gold and turquoise enamel bezel with gold laurel leaves in reserve. White enamel dial with Arabic numerals ringed by a minute track of gilt indices and black Arabic numerals at the quarter hours. Hands in rose-cut diamonds and platinum. 8-day movement

326 Desk clock with strut. Cartier Paris, 1914. Made by Coüet. Bevelled rock crystal surround, silver case and strut. Carved crystal dial with ebonite ground. White enamel chapter ring with gold Roman numerals and fleurettes in reserve around an inner minute track of gold dots in reserve, outer ring of rose-cut diamonds and platinum. Hands in platinum and rose-cut diamonds. 8-day movement. The strut was originally of rock crystal

annular dial. Fabergé had created similar clocks – an egg decorated with a snake in 1889 and a 'Madonna Lily Egg' in 1899, while his 'Vase Egg' of 1902 for the Duchess of Marlborough was contemporary with Cartier's urn clocks. In 1907 Cartier returned to the form with a miniature egg-shaped version in which a diamond star pointed to the time on the revolving band.

A further model, a silver-gilt pillar clock incorporating a barometer, referred back to a design by the Louis XVI *ornemaniste* Jean-Charles Delafosse. Cartier also employed the Neoclassical motif of a fluted half-column in a table clock with horizontal dial; when pressed, it rang a little bell to summon a dilatory servant.

At this time, the application of enamel to these eighteenth-century forms was the preserve of Fabergé. Cartier now lavished the riches of Fabergé's enamel palette on his own table clocks, using lavender blues, violets, pinks, Empire greens or stripes [**110**, **111**, **113**]. Bold colours were enamelled on silver; delicate pastel colours, by contrast, on gold. The patterns, guilloché on the metal ground and visible through the transparent enamel, were variously described as 'Russian' (with radiating rays), 'moiré', with 'scales', 'barleycorn', or 'Louis XVI'. At first these table clocks, among the most favoured gifts of the Edwardian period, were square, then from 1908 circular, and from 1909 arched. Mottoes traced in diamonds, such as 'Le temps passe, les pensées restent' (Time passes, thoughts remain) or 'L'amitié vous l'offre', were designed to express for all eternity the feelings of the donors despite the remorseless advance of time. Edward VII, Lady de Grey, Constantin Radziwill and Zenaida Yusupov were among the enthusiastic devotees of these early Cartier timepieces.

A

B   **C**

327 Chronoscope. Cartier Paris, 1920. Black and white enamel on gold, the reverse in ebonite. The photograph is of Queen Mary

D

Around this time Maurice Coüet (1885–1963), a young man in the Prévost workshop, was developing a talent which was later to raise Cartier's table clocks to the highest levels of inspired craftsmanship. Coüet's grandfather was a regulator of table clocks for Bréguet and may be the same as the Coüet who was working around 1850 in the Place Dauphine, and who exhibited ring watches at the 1867 Paris Exposition. Even earlier, in 1806 and 1820, there is evidence of yet another clockmaker called Coüet. Maurice learned the basics of his craft in his father's small workshop in the cathedral city of Evreux, then moved to Prévost's in Paris and subsequently set up in business with five assistants in the rue Saint-Martin. From 1911, the little workshop was supplying table clocks exclusively to Cartier's. Coüet was a clockmaker of inventive genius in the great tradition of the craft established in the Renaissance. Since the sixteenth and seventeenth centuries, clockmaking had evolved, along with its sister disciplines of mathematics, physics and optics, to the status of an art. Armed with the expertise inherited from the Bréguet tradition, Coüet began to modify the Cartier range with a series of delightfully conceived designs firmly grounded in mathematics.

His first inventions on commission from Cartier's were a series begun in 1912 of 'planet' or 'comet' clocks in round, square or arched cases [**A**, **330**]. Their star decoration was remarkably similar to the Islamic-style jewelry that Cartier's were producing at the same time. The first model consisted of two superimposed dials. The lower one, of sky blue enamel, rotated to give the illusion of a diamond star gliding across the heavens. A crescent moon in diamonds indicated the ensuing hours of night. On a second model the central 'sky zone' carried a comet tail along the dial while the minute pointer, set under the circle of the hours, circled the outer ring.

In 1919 a third 'abstract' variant appeared, which harked back to the chronoscope of the seventeenth century. Three hidden arms each bore four roundels with numbers for the hours [**B**] which, revolving on their axis, appeared in turn on the left-hand side of the dial. As the indicator glided across the scale it simultaneously marked the minutes [**C**], and then disappeared off the right-hand side. This series of clocks also served as photograph frames, and as truly regal gifts adorned the most famous salons of the period; the donor's portrait was often that of one of the monarchs of Europe [**327**, **329**].

The fan-shaped dial of the jade 'Carp' clock of 1925 operated on a different principle [**D**, **328**]. The minutes were marked on a rotating disc and the hours on an outer semicircle of crystal across which the hour hand moved from VI to VI, and was then brought back to its starting position by a spring mechanism (hence the term 'retrograde hand').

It is a matter of personal judgment whether these early 'illusion' mechanisms count as true mystery clocks. Coüet loved baffling mechanical illusions and must have studied their imaginative application by the Lyonnais clockmaker Nicolas Grollier de Servières

328 'Carp' clock with retrograde hand. Cartier Paris, 1925. Made by Coüet. Gold base-plate, obsidian base with Japanese-style corners ringed by coral beads (containing movement). Two Chinese eighteenth- or nineteenth-century carps carved from grey jade, coral eyes in black enamel, rose-cut diamond motifs, frosted rock crystal 'water', mother-of-pearl 'waves' studded with cabochon emeralds, edged with blue enamel. Fan-shaped rock crystal dial, platinum Roman numerals (from VI to XII and back to VI) set with rose-cut diamonds, 'shaded' by mauve lacquer. Hour hand a dragon of platinum set with rose-cut diamonds, edged in mauve lacquer. Below, a rotating crystal disk with a 'railway' minute track and Arabic numerals at 5-minute intervals, ringed by pearls, and mother-of-pearl waves edged in red enamel. Minute hand a fixed pointer of mother-of-pearl and diamonds. 8-day movement (75% actual size)

329 Clock with rotating hours and photograph frame. Cartier Paris, 1922. Made by Coüet. In the shape of a milestone, decorated in blue enamel with gold dots in reserve, white enamel rim with gold decoration in reserve, ebonite edge and back ringed in gold. Gilt case, Bakelite back, gilt strut. Photograph frame ringed in white enamel with a row of gold circles in reserve. Minute track on upper rim with gold Arabic numerals in reserve. Hours indicated by twelve pear-shaped white enamel cartouches with gold Roman numerals in reserve, which successively rotate and point to the minutes [see p. 266, **B**, **C**]. 8-day movement. The photograph is of Prince Nicolae of Romania

330 Day and night 'comet' clock. Cartier Paris, 1920. The sun (day) and star (night, seen here) are fixed to a disk that rotates once every twenty-four hours. Made by Coüet. Surround an agate ring, back an agate plaque. Gilt case and strut. Centre and lower part of dial in gold and dark blue enamel in a 'starry firmament' pattern. Chapter ring in gold and white enamel with Roman numerals separated by gold fleurettes in reserve (from VI to XII and back to VI), inner minute track in gold and white enamel with Arabic numerals at 5-minute intervals separated by gold crosses in reserve, rimmed with gold beads. Hours indicated by two platinum and rose-cut diamond pointers, a sun and a star. Minute hand in rose-cut diamonds and platinum. 8-day movement

331 Pillar clock. Cartier Paris, 1927, sold to Sir Bhupindra Singh, Maharaja of Patiala. The clock case slowly descends the pillar; when it reaches bottom, after eight days, it must be moved back to the top by hand. Made by Coüet. Gold base-plate, lapis lazuli base, two mother-of-pearl plaques inlaid with coral stars, surround in malachite rods and gold and blue enamel motifs. Lapis lazuli pillar with cornelian bands ringed in gold and cabochon turquoises. Flaring top with a concave malachite disk. Gold case edged with lapis lazuli plaques (malachite plaques on back). Mother-of-pearl dial, chapter ring with inlaid coral Roman numerals. Gold and blue enamel hands, with three cabochon emeralds and a rose-cut diamond.
8-day movement

332, 333 'Turtle' clock, seen from the side and from above. Cartier Paris, 1928. Platinum; the nephrite turtle on onyx and gem-set base supporting on its back a desk clock with mother-of-pearl, turquoise and lapis lazuli face, and lapis lazuli numerals. Hinged enamelled lid, set with a ruby and rose-cut diamonds. (This is different from the clock with a 'swimming' turtle.)

(1593–1685/86), whose inventions, later called *horloges mystérieuses*, were hailed in his own lifetime as miniature wonders of the world.[4] The mechanism of Coüet's jade 'Carp' clock [**328**] was ultimately derived from Servières' 'Fan' clock – as, indeed, was the 'Turtle' clock of around 1927, whose main feature was a turtle swimming in a hardstone bowl filled with water. In place of hands, the mechanism operated a magnet under the bowl which moved the turtle around the bowl to mark the hours. The most sophisticated variation on the 'Turtle' clock was a jade version of 1929 which had a chimaera crouching on the rim [**334**]. Another original creation, the jade 'Drum' clock of 1938, can also be traced to the inspiration of Grollier de Servières. Within the mechanism, an appropriately balanced weight revolved to counterbalance the drum carrying the 'dial'.

Three large table or mantel clocks were made between 1926 and 1928 with Chinese carved jade panels on front and back [**344**]. An onyx pedestal concealed the lever movement, which drove the hands by a shaft through a hollow stone ball, and along a Chinese dragon climbing up the back panel. The restricted colour range of black, red and green, the dragon pointer, and the jade panels engraved with Chinese landscapes give these clocks the fashionable Chinoiserie appearance already discussed in connection with Cartier's vanity cases (see pp. 205–9). Tardy, in his book on French table clocks, classifies these three jade clocks as *semi-mystérieuses*, a term which can be suitably applied to the comet clocks and the models inspired by Grollier de Servières.

The pillar clock [**331**], called by Tardy 'pendule à gravité', also belongs to the *semi-mystérieuses* group; its slender shaft of lapis, cornelian and turquoise rests on a mother-of-pearl and coral base.[5] As time passes, the clock slides down the pillar, controlled by a system of cogwheels; at the bottom of the run, it is moved to the top again by hand, and the process is repeated. Coüet's application of gravity has a certain similarity to a model by Grollier de Servières, in which a drum clock rolls down an inclined track. Cartier's made two pillar clocks with Egyptian finials, one of which was bought by the Maharaja of Patiala. The idea was taken up again in 1927 in the shape of a slender jade portico.

Made of stones of strongly contrasting colours, these clocks gradually displaced the table clocks enamelled in the Russian style. Coral, onyx, jade, rock crystal and ivory expressed the new aesthetic of Art Deco, and incorporated in their design elements from the arts of China, Japan and India.

A technique known in ancient China was the application of kingfisher feathers on paper or metal for use as hair ornaments or as the backgrounds for pictures. From 1920, Cartier's used kingfisher feathers for clock dials [**340**], the shimmering turquoise-violet mosaic gently contrasting with the colours of jade, coral and onyx. Particularly elegant examples were designed for the clock department by Jacques Andrey (b. 1896).

An addition to the Art Deco programme, prompted by Louis Cartier, was the production of a tall mantel clock fitted with a handle. It was in the tradition of the nineteenth-century officer's clock and was often reduced in size to a miniature carriage clock. Another new production was the simple globe clock of 1925, made of lapis lazuli, enamel or gold, which could be turned on its base. It remains an open question whether Coüet knew the sphere clocks of Jacques de La Garde, the sixteenth-century French clockmaker.[6]

In 1919 Maurice Coüet set up a Cartier workshop at 53 rue Lafayette [**337**], which employed thirty specialists, as well as freelances like the lapidary Fourrier.[7] Clockmakers

334 'Chimaera' clock. Cartier Paris, 1929. The carved animal lurks on the edge of a bowl filled with water, in which a leaf-shaped motif driven by a magnet indicates the hours. Materials and colours unknown

335 Desk clock. Cartier New York, 1928, made in France for the European Watch and Clock Company. Nephrite base and top, coral supports ringed by black enamel. Gold case with black enamel decoration. Silver dial with guilloché sunray decoration, chapter ring with Roman numerals ringed by a 'railway' minute track. Cathedral-type hands in blue steel. 8-day movement

336 Desk clock with strut. Cartier Paris, 1929; the case, originally of ivory, was reworked in ebonite in 1930, prior to sale. Made by Coüet. Ebonite case, strut a gilt Y set into the back. Dial in lacquer depicting a Chinese landscape with a cabochon moonstone for the moon. Chapter ring in mother-of-pearl mosaic with gold and black enamel Roman numerals, framed by two rows of coral rods separated by gold and black enamel motifs, a ring of rose-cut diamonds and platinum at each corner. Dragon-shaped hands in rose-cut diamonds and platinum. 8-day movement

opposite

337 Cartier's clock workshop in the rue Lafayette, Paris, headed by Maurice Coüet, 1927. On the top shelf in the distance is the 'Egyptian Temple Gate' clock [**155**]. A crystal 'Chimaera' clock is in the process of being made on the bench at the left

made movements, and cases were decorated by enamellers, *orfèvres-boîtiers*, stone-setters and *guillocheurs*. The workshop also produced other Art Deco masterpieces, such as vanity cases, which spread the fame of Cartier's throughout the world. Although Coüet worked exclusively on the clocks, the whole workshop bore his name. His colleagues included his brother René; from 1922 to 1926 René Bourdon, who had been trained by Verger and Bréguet; and Félix Laumonier, who had patented an electric regulator. The clock workshop had its own designers, such as Alexandre Diringer, who had joined Cartier's as a seventeen-year-old in 1910 and was attached to the clock division in 1922. Three years later Coüet was joined by Alfred Loquet (b. 1884). Important designs for clocks, notably mystery clocks, were supplied by Charles Jacqueau and Georges Rémy, though their major work was in jewelry.

London and New York manufactured simpler types of clock in their own workshops. From 1919 the export of the Paris models was handled by the European Watch and Clock Company, a Cartier subsidiary with offices in Paris and New York. The initials 'E W C' will often be found with the workshop and stock numbers on Cartier's export pieces [**335**, **346**].

A model patented in 1937 had claims to be a mystery clock in the wider sense: the 'Prism' clock by Gaston Cusin. Born in 1897, Cusin had made his first clock when he was fourteen and had been working with Maurice Coüet since the move to the rue Lafayette. It was the underwater periscope that gave him the idea for a clock with a dial reflected through prisms, and the principle was also applied to a few wristwatches. In 1984 Cusin's invention enjoyed a renewed popularity.[8]

Less significant for the future were the expensive electric watches experimented with at the same time. Although some four hundred left the workshop in the rue d'Argenson between 1935 and 1938, and a special company, 'Delvicar', was founded, the models were unwieldy and too expensive. The electric watch which Louis Cartier took to Budapest, which had stopped working before he left the Gare de Lyon in Paris, may have convinced Cartier's of the unprofitability of the project, which the Second World War soon brought to an end.

Jeanne Toussaint, at the urging of Louis Cartier, had presided over the *haute joaillerie* since 1933; from 1937, however, she increasingly devoted herself to the creation of clocks. She was a woman of taste and was in direct contact with a buying public who, under the impact of the Front Populaire, economic crises, devaluation and unemployment, were less interested in large commissions than in objects made of gold and imaginative gifts.[9] Convinced of this, Toussaint took over the charming ivory and black enamel 'Domino' pocket-watch from the London workshop and promoted it as the gift idea for 1939. The elegant Madame Martinez de Hoz ordered four of them straightaway at Cartier's exhibition in Deauville.

Jeanne Toussaint was also the inspiration behind an inclined table clock in mother-of-pearl mosaic, embellished either with an ancient Egyptian motif or with her favourite animal, the panther. Her other symbolic animal, the turtle, gave rise in 1962 to a table clock of three turtles, one above the other, in lapis lazuli and gold. The fact that Gaston Guillemart, the craftsman entrusted with the work, wrestled with its technical problems for two years was of little concern to Jeanne, who was prepared to impose her ideas on the workshop. In the same way, she must be credited with the successful completion of the 1960 'Bottle' clock: Jeanne had come across the bottle, fitted with a gold Russian stopper, in an antique shop; it was Maurice Coüet who achieved the *tour de force* of getting a clock through its narrow neck.

Cartier's clock department had long been at the service of eccentric customers whose quirks found their way into literature. Among them was the idiosyncratic Prince Constantin Radziwill, who, obliged to give a Christmas present to a hated relation, commissioned Cartier to produce the ugliest object in the world. To his entire satisfaction, Cartier made him a clock in the shape of a Swiss chalet in gold and diamonds, with a cuckoo to sound the hours.[10]

The clocks that ultimately satisfied the most eccentric customers also incorporated Cartier's most famous invention, a perfect balance of the technical and aesthetic – the famous mystery clocks.

Mystery clocks (Pendules mystérieuses)
'Marvels of the clockmaker's art,' the *Gazette du Bon Ton* called them in 1925, 'unreal and seemingly woven from moonbeams, they veil the mystery of time in the shadow of an ancient divinity of jade, between two pillars of rose quartz, enamelled with black dragons.'[11]

The 'mystery clock' depended on a secret which was supposed never to be revealed. Over-inquisitive salesmen in the rue de la Paix, who tried to force explanations from the craftsmen, were rebuffed. The wonder clocks guarded their secret like the Sphinx, and Cartier's protected them from the eyes of prying admirers. At a virtually private exhibition in Biarritz in 1922 the Queen of Spain was able to admire three examples (later sold to New York), but not a single one was shown at the great 1925 Art Deco Exhibition.

Maurice Coüet was twenty-eight when he presented the first of his 'mystery clocks' to Cartier. It is not known how many years of theoretical preparation lay behind the project. Coüet knew the *pendules mystérieuses* of earlier periods, such as those by Jean-Eugène Robert-Houdin (1805–71), the Blois clockmaker, who settled about 1835 in the Marais in Paris and later, like Mathieu Planchon, devised mystery clocks and automata, or the clock by Guilmet displayed in Paris in the Musée National des Techniques.[12] The fascination of Coüet's invention is based on the principle of an adroit optical illusion. The hands seem to float in space apparently without any connection to the movement [339–342, 345–347, 349–351]. In fact each is fixed to a crystal disc with a toothed metal rim which is driven by worm gears concealed in the frame of the case. Coüet's first mystery clocks relied on a lateral double-axle system. In 1920 he devised another model using a single central axle, and subsequently both principles were applied. The movement was sometimes housed in a massive base of onyx or jade, above the saddle of some fabulous monster (as in the 'Turtle' clock), or, as in the 'Portico' model, in the entablature or lintel above the clock [347].

Since every part was hand-made, production of a mystery clock took between three and twelve months, and even in the 1980s their manufacture required up to seven months. In 1925 each clock passed successively through the hands of six or seven specialists; besides the watchmakers, there were the designer, the *orfèvre-boitier*, the enameller, the lapidary, the stone-setter, the engraver, and the polisher. As we have seen, the designs for the cases were often by Charles Jacqueau or Georges Rémy. But since many of the mystery clocks fitted into established categories, the designer's job was often merely a matter of integrating the valuable animal sculptures bought by Louis Cartier into the overall design of the base, and consulting the clockmaker in order to establish the ideal position for the dial of the clock in relation to the movement. The great rock crystals for the pillars of the 'Portico' model, the onyx, and the little figures and Buddhist lions for the 'roof' were cut and polished by the Fourrier workshop [347]. Rock crystal was also used for dials [339–342, 345–347, 350, 351]; sometimes it was replaced by citrine [319, 349], and, once only (in 1931), by aquamarine – always materials whose transparency did not detract from the illusion of the hands being trapped inside. These hands were works of art in their own right, created by enamellers and stone-setters together, and gave the appearance of a writhing dragon as they revolved, which contributed to the Chinoiserie effect. Diamonds were used only sparingly in the ensemble of the clock; most common were cabochons and eight-cut diamonds, less sparkling than brilliant cuts.

It is not certain how many mystery clocks, which were exclusive to the Paris firm, were made during the peak production period between 1912 and 1930, though the number may have exceeded ninety. Production after the Second World War continued up to 1970, and was resumed in 1977 with designs from the 1920s. A number of different types can be distinguished.

The first is Model A, rectangular in form, with which production commenced in 1912 [339, 340]. The movement operated on a double-axle system, housed in a vertical frame often embellished with laurel leaves or mother-of-pearl. The base was of onyx, pale agate, obsidian or nephrite; later, of ribbed gold (1949) with a cabochon ruby on the axle pin of the hands. A version dating from 1944 has a domed base and an arched crystal case. According to the firm's archives, one of the first examples was sold in 1913 to J. P. Morgan, Jr. Cartier's records show that there was a gap in the production of Model A clocks between 1914 and 1918, which is inexplicable except in terms of the disruption caused by wartime conditions. A model went to Queen Mary in 1924 and in 1940 Goering bought one with an onyx base. Five years later General de Gaulle, by then head of the French Provisional Government, together with Gaston Palewski, presented a model with a lapis lazuli base to Stalin.

A second model was created in 1920 and went through nineteen variations up to 1931 [319, 341, 342]. For the first time a single central axle was used, which ran through the

Mystery clock of Model A type

339 Mystery clock of Model A type. Cartier Paris, 1914, sold to Count Greffulhe. Made by Coüet. Base of agate (containing movement); four cabochon sapphires at the corners. Main body of rock crystal. Gold beading along the bottom. Transparent centre framed by laurel-leaf motif in gold and white enamel; chapter ring of white enamel with gold Roman numerals and fleurettes in reserve; inner ring of platinum and rose-cut diamonds. Hands of platinum and rose-cut diamonds. 8-day movement

340 Mystery clock of Model A type. Cartier Paris, 1929. Made by Coüet. Gold base-plate. Onyx base (containing movement). Rock crystal case with gold beading along the bottom. Transparent rock crystal centre, frame of gold and kingfisher feathers; garland motifs of rose-cut diamonds set in platinum; four square, collet-set rose-cut diamonds at the corners. Chapter ring of gold and kingfisher feathers with Roman numerals and inner rim of rose-cut diamonds set in platinum; a rose-cut diamond at each hour. Hands of platinum and rose-cut diamonds. 8-day movement

341 Mystery clock with central axle. Cartier Paris, 1922. Made by Coüet. Gold base-plate. Onyx base (containing movement). Chinese-style pillar in onyx with gold and black enamel motifs at top and bottom, turquoise-blue enamel rib at the base. Transparent rock crystal centre. Chapter ring in gold and turquoise enamel with appliquéd Roman numerals in rose-cut diamonds and platinum alternating with gold fleurettes in reserve. Hands in platinum and rose-cut diamonds. Polished gold back with black enamel, polished gold edge. 8-day movement

342 Mystery clock with central axle. Cartier Paris, *c.* 1926; the platinum-and-diamond F and motifs on the base were added at a later date (the clock entered the collection of King Farouk of Egypt). Made by Coüet. Chinese-style base-plate in onyx with gold and coral motifs. Onyx base (containing movement), with a gold fillet at the foot and two stylized gold dragons on the sides; the letter F and flanking motifs in rose-cut diamonds and platinum. Gold and black enamel shaft, four cabochon corals. Transparent rock crystal centre. Chapter ring in gold and black enamel with appliquéd Roman numerals in rose-cut diamonds and platinum, gold Chinese decoration in reserve. Dragon-shaped hands in rose-cut diamonds and platinum. Gold back with decoration in black enamel and gold in reserve. Edge in gold, black enamel, and coral rods. 8-day movement

343 'Screen' clock of *semi-mystérieuse* type. Cartier Paris, 1922. Made by Coüet. Gold base-plate, onyx base (containing movement). Two onyx half-rings decorated with gold and black enamel motifs hold a gold and black screen adorned with coral rods. White jade dial without glass, carved with a Chinese scene and a Chinese text on the back. In the corners coral collet-set in gold. Chapter ring with appliquéd Roman numerals in rose diamonds and platinum. Hands in rose diamonds and platinum. 8-day movement shaft or, in later versions, through a hollow coral sphere. The bases were mostly of onyx and the hexagonal dial framed in coral, turquoise, lapis lazuli and enamel. This second model was subject to three variations from 1920–21: an octagonal model with an 8-cm 'Chinese' pillar; a model with a dial of circular citrine, on an enamelled pillar with lateral struts; and a model in the form of a rectangular cartouche with Japanese corners of ebonite (a hard vulcanized rubber), with a dial of cushion-shaped citrine, and a similar rectangular model with bevelled corners.

A third model, the 'Ecran' or 'Screen', in form a rectangular panel, appeared in 1923; seven variants had appeared by 1928 and the model continued up to 1954 [345, 346]. The motive power was carried by a central axle system through a hollow sphere on the base. Stylistically, this type is characterized by coral rods (one example has jade rods [345]) which frame the circular dial, and struts connecting the clock with the base. The same casing had already appeared in 1922, though not in connection with a 'mystery' movement: there the dial was not transparent, but was decorated with mother-of-pearl marquetry, Chinese lacquer, engraved jade [343, 344], or kingfisher feathers.

Mystery clock of central axle type

A further category of mystery clocks comprised those using the central axle system with a pendant dial. However, at its first appearance (1920), in the form of a Chinese gong in a white enamelled frame, the idea was simply a matter of optical illusion, as the mechanism still consisted of a movement fixed in the base and a double-axle drive.

Subsequently, the six famous 'Portico' models were characterized by suspended dials and transmission to the hands via a central axle. They were designed as a freestanding Oriental-style portico or gateway, its pillars resting on a massive onyx base and crowned with a simple entablature or lintel that contained the movement.

Mystery clock of screen type

1923	Model in crystal with twelve-sided dial, crowned with a Billiken [347]
1924	Model in crystal with octagonal dial, square pillars and vase motifs
	Model in pink quartz with twelve-sided dial with mother-of-pearl, square pillars and two Buddhist lions
	Model in crystal with twelve-sided dial, crowned with a Buddhist lion (head to the right)
	Model in crystal with twelve-sided dial, crowned with a Buddha
1925	Model in crystal with twelve-sided dial, crowned with a Buddhist lion (head to the left)

Contemporary with the 'Portico' models was a series of twelve animal or figure clocks, in which the dial either rested on supports or was suspended from above. Stylistically these derived from the Louis XV and Louis XVI *pendules à sujet* in which the clock movement rested on the back of an animal. The bull, horse and rhinoceros, generally of bronze, were then the most popular supporting beasts. Cartier's produced an 'Elephant' clock inspired by a silver-gilt example of 1620 by Tobias Kramer and the Louis XV elephant clocks occasioned by the visit of Siamese envoys to Paris.

Although they lacked the symbolism of dynastic commissions and the ceremonies of present-giving associated with Fabergé's Easter eggs for the tsars, these figurative mystery clocks enjoyed comparable prestige in Cartier's production and are today considered the most valuable of all collectors' items with the Cartier signature. They appeared as follows:

1922	'Mandarin Duck' clock of Chinese jade, with vertically mounted twelve-sided dial and blue enamel frame. On an onyx base. The duck *c.* 1800
1924	First Chinese agate 'Chimaera' clock, vertically mounted with hexagonal crystal dial. On a gold base with enamel motifs. Chimaera nineteenth-century
1925	Chinese jade 'Carp' clock, with vertically mounted fan-shaped crystal dial [328]. On an obsidian base. The two jade fish eighteenth- or nineteenth-century. (As said above, the 'Carp' clock is based on an idea of Grollier de Servières and is not one of Coüet's transparent mystery clocks. However, insofar as it is a figurative model, it belongs here.)
	Chinese jade 'Vase' clock with jade bird and rose quartz and sapphire flowers. On an obsidian base. The Chinese carving nineteenth-century

Chinese crystal 'Turtle' clock, with vertically mounted twelve-sided crystal dial. On an onyx base. The turtle nineteenth-century

1926   Second Chinese agate 'Chimaera' clock, with vertically mounted round citrine dial [349]. On a nephrite base. The chimaera similar to the one on the 1924 model

Clock with the Chinese goddess Kuan Yin holding a branch of flowering *ling-shi*. The twelve-sided clock next to her on an onyx base. The goddess early nineteenth-century

1927   Chinese crystal 'Chimaera' clock, its twelve-sided dial hanging in the jaws of the chimaera. On a rose quartz and lapis lazuli base. Chimaera nineteenth-century. In 1937 the clock was exhibited in Egypt, where Princess Chivekiar, Prince Fuad's former wife, showed an interest in it. Dismantled in 1953

1928   Chinese jade 'Elephant' clock, the dial in the form of an onyx howdah on the back of the animal [350]. On an onyx base. The elephant *c*. 1800, presumably acquired from the London dealer and Indian expert Imre Schwaiger. The saddlecloth of mother-of-pearl marquetry and coral beads, the work of the stone-setter Bouillet, was allegedly the most time-consuming ornamental detail on any of the mystery clocks

1929   Clock with Chinese jade Buddhist lions, with vertically mounted, round citrine dial and coral tree. On an onyx base. The two animals nineteenth-century

1930   Chinese coral 'Chimaera' clock with vertically mounted octagonal dial in mother-of-pearl frame. On black lacquered silver base. Chimaera nineteenth-century

1931   Clock with the Chinese goddess Kuan Yin in jade, with jade chimaera, jade vase and coral tree [351]. Movement with striking chimes. The hardstones nineteenth-century

345 'Screen' mystery clock. Cartier Paris, 1923. Made by Coüet. Gold and onyx base-plate. Jade base (containing movement). Two onyx half-rings with gold and black enamel motifs hold a rectangular screen in gold, black enamel, crystal, jade rods at top and bottom, and jade on the sides. Gold back with black and white enamel. Transparent rock crystal centre. Chapter ring in white enamel with gold Roman numerals and fleurettes in reserve, around a ring of rose-cut diamonds and platinum; corners decorated with rose-cut diamonds and black enamel. Platinum hands with rose-cut diamonds. 8-day movement

346 'Screen' mystery clock. Cartier
New York, 1926. Made by Coüet for the
European Watch and Clock Company.
Polished gold base-plate, rectangular
polished onyx base (containing movement).
Two onyx half-rings with gold and black
enamel motifs hold a rectangular screen in
gold, black enamel, rows of moonstone rods
along top and bottom, and moonstones on the
sides. Gold back with white and black enamel
decoration. Transparent rock crystal centre.
Chapter ring in white enamel with gold Roman
numerals and fleurettes in reserve, an inner
row of rose-cut diamonds and platinum,
corner motifs in rose-cut diamonds
and black enamel. Hands in platinum,
rose-cut diamonds, and black enamel.
8-day movement

opposite

347 Large 'Portico' mystery clock (the first in a series of six in the form of a Shinto shrine gate). Cartier Paris, 1923, owned by Ganna Walska (Mrs Harold McCormick). Made by Coüet. Gold base-plate; two columns in rock crystal, decorated at top and bottom in gold and black enamel, set on cubic bases of onyx and rock crystal. Gold and black enamel lintel (containing movement), topped by two cabochon corals and a rock crystal Billiken. Transparent rock crystal centre hanging from a rock crystal crossbar via two yellow-gold fixtures. Chapter ring in gold and black enamel with Roman numerals in platinum and rose-cut diamonds. Platinum hands with rose-cut diamonds. Gold back with black enamel, gold edges decorated with black enamel fillets. 8-day movement (65% actual size)

348 Clock with Buddhist lions. Cartier Paris, 1926. Made by Coüet. Ebony base-plate (added later to support a protective glass display case), rock crystal platform and pillars carved at the top into two Buddhist lions leaning on gold, black and red enamel motifs, diamonds, and collet-set cabochon coral. Three-stepped bases in lapis lazuli with potted flower motifs in coral, black enamel, platinum, rose-cut diamonds, emeralds, and leaf-shaped carved sapphires, cabochon rubies, pearls and onyx beads. Between the pillars, a gold and black enamel motif with carved coral studded with cabochon emeralds and sapphires, diamonds, and four diamond motifs at the corners. Hexagonal gold case that pivots horizontally, edged with coral gadrooning and corner links in platinum, diamonds and black enamel. Back in mother-of-pearl marquetry edged with lapis lazuli plaques. Hexagonal dial in mother-of-pearl mosaic, chapter ring with stylized gold and black enamel Roman numerals alternating with gold, black enamel, and diamond palmettes. Snake-shaped hands in gold and black-and-white enamel. 8-day movement (90% actual size)

349 'Chimaera' mystery clock. Cartier New York, 1926. Made by Coüet for the European Watch and Clock Company. Gold base-plate and base (containing movement); lower black enamel border, median row of calibré-cut onyx, and at the corners four motifs in gold with black enamel and pearls. A block of nephrite, decorated with two coral frogs, supports the agate chimaera (Chinese, nineteenth-century) crested with gold and black enamel, eyes in cabochon emeralds, gold claws, gold and black and red enamel saddle fringed with natural pearls. Centre a transparent, faceted citrine. Chapter ring in gold and black enamel with eleven stylized Arabic numerals in rose-cut diamonds and platinum. A rose-cut diamond at 6 o'clock, gold lozenges in reserve at the half hours, an inner ring of rose-cut diamonds and platinum. Dragon-shaped hands in rose-cut diamonds and platinum. Gold and black enamel back decorated with gold clouds in reserve. Red and black enamel edge, eleven pearls aligned with the hours. 8-day movement

350 'Elephant' mystery clock. Cartier Paris, 1928, sold to the Maharaja of Nawanagar. Made by Coüet. Onyx base with Japanese-style corners, coral feet. Jade elephant with saddle blanket and harness (Chinese, *c.* 1800), eyes of rose-cut diamonds rimmed with black enamel, on the forehead a rose-cut diamond set in a carved coral disk ringed by black enamel; at the end of each tusk a pearl rimmed by black enamel. Harness studded with cabochon corals, saddlecloth in mother-of-pearl marquetry with black enamel, ringed with coral beads. On the elephant's back, a small mystery clock in the shape of a pagoda (containing movement). Base in gold and black enamel with a row of jade balls, coral uprights, sides and back in faceted mirrors edged in black enamel, onyx roof with four bell-clusters in corals and pearls. Transparent centre in rock crystal, framed by small faceted mirrors, edged with black enamel, corner motifs in rose-cut diamonds and platinum. Chapter ring with Arabic numerals in rose-cut diamonds and platinum. Dragon-shaped hands in rose-cut diamonds and platinum. 8-day movement

351 Striking mystery clock with the goddess Kuan Yin. Cartier Paris, 1931. Made by Coüet. Onyx base with Japanese-style corners (containing movement); a row of pearls along the top and gold and dark-blue and turquoise-blue enamel border along the bottom. Two carved nephrite plinths: one supports a white jade figurine of Kuan Yin standing on a base of gold, black enamel, and coral rods; the other supports a single-axle mystery clock on a gold, turquoise and black enamel base decorated with pearls and red enamel. At the sides are a white jade chimaera and a white jade vase with cabochon turquoises, holding a branch of coral studded with baroque pearls. Transparent octagonal centre in bevelled rock crystal. Chapter ring in gold and turquoise enamel with appliquéd Roman numerals in rose-cut diamonds and platinum alternating with gold dots in reserve. Inner blue enamel rim. Gold back with black enamel, gold edge. Dragon-shaped hands in platinum, rose-cut diamonds and black enamel. 8-day movement. The jades are Chinese, nineteenth-century. The chimaera originally carried a branch of coral, now lost. When the clock was being moved, the figurine could be detached and placed in a special drawer in the base of the original case (65% actual size)

352 'Turtle Chimaera' clock. Cartier Paris, 1943. Made by the Cartier workshops. Silver base-plate edged with black enamel. Rectangular white onyx base (containing movement). Turtle chimaera carved in coral (Chinese, nineteenth-century) with emerald eyes. Base and neck of baluster-shaped vase highlighted by bezel-set and channel-set old-cut diamonds. Dial a gold ring. Chapter ring of white onyx plaques, separated by coral rods 'shaded' by a line of black enamel and topped by a collet-set old-cut diamond. Hour hand a pointed flower in platinum and old-cut diamonds. 8-day movement. The hour pointer is driven by a disc that turns within the ring, pointing to the coral rods as hour markers. Made during the shortages of the Second World War, this re-used the coral figurine from a dismantled clock of 1928

Pocket-, pendant and wristwatches

Dagonneau, Brédillard and Prévost, who from 1900 provided movements for table clocks, were also Cartier's first suppliers of movements for pocket- and pendant watches, including the then fashionable *remontoirs de dames*, ladies' flat pocket-watches. Up to the First World War ball-shaped watches of guilloché enamel, recorded at Cartier's from 1889, were popular. Worn on a chain from the Duparc-Lenfant workshop, they won admirers as far away as Russia and the United States. Princess Lobanov Rostovsky had one in rare, orange-coloured enamel (1902), while the Queen of Portugal sported a model in blue and white banded enamel (1904). Expensive models might be pear- or egg-shaped and set with diamonds; hexagonal pendant watches with calibré-cut ruby frames; or the charming flower-basket watch in diamonds (1909) that Nellie Melba selected.

Among the watchmakers employed by Cartier's, Joseph Vergely [**366**], though forgotten today, proved indispensable with his talent for gold-coin watches.[13] Born in the Auvergne in 1872, he completed three years in the watchmaking school in Cluses, joined Cartier's old firm in the boulevard des Italiens as watch salesman and repairer in 1896, and mastered the technique there. Twenty-dollar, hundred-franc and five-pound gold coins were sawn in two and inset with an ultra-flat movement 1.5 mm thick, with a Bréguet overcoil balance spring. The coin was opened by pressing a little button, and when closed revealed nothing of its contents. Queen Alexandra presented Edward VII with one made from a coin issued to mark his coronation. Vergely, whose patriarchal mien earned him the soubriquet of 'Père Vergely' at Cartier's, subsequently headed the Paris office of the European Watch and Clock Company mentioned above, where he furthered the experiments with electric watches. Yet his first and most important service was to introduce into the firm the man who, like Maurice Coüet in the clock department, was to revolutionize the manufacture of small watches: Edmond Jaeger.

Born in Andlau in Lower Alsace, Jaeger (1858–1922) learned his trade with Lebert in Epernay and with the chronometer manufacturer Gabriel. But he gained his most important experience with Bréguet in the rue de la Paix in Paris. Back in 1775, Abraham-Louis Bréguet (1747–1823) of Neuchâtel had settled on the Quai des Morfondus, where he made the most refined watches of his time: watches with perpetual calendars, chronometers and automata, with which he supplied the French navy, Marie Antoinette and the tsars. The company, which employed up to a hundred watchmakers during the Napoleonic period, remained in the Bréguet family, but frequently moved premises in Paris, and in 1855 engaged the services of the Englishman Edward Brown, whose family was to continue the Bréguet workshops. It was Brown who took on Jaeger.

By 1905, however, Jaeger had his own business, employing five workmen, in the rue Saint-Sauveur north of the Marais, for centuries the clockmakers' district. In 1907 he moved to the rue Réaumur and signed a fifteen-year contract with Cartier's, giving the firm exclusive rights to his output.[14] This included Jaeger's chronometers, his anchor watches with flat Jaeger calibres, and every new Jaeger invention. For their part, Cartier's guaranteed regular annual orders of at least Fr. 250,000.

Although Jaeger had been one of Cartier's suppliers before the 1907 contract, Louis Cartier did not relinquish his connections with Brédillard, Dagonneau and Prévost. In 1907 Prévost delivered four watches set into parasol handles, all bought by the Russian Countess Uvarov. One of them may have been intended as a wedding present for Mademoiselle Messéna d'Essling, who was married that year to the Marquis de Montesquiou-Fesenzac. *Vogue* mentioned it on this occasion without naming the maker. In 1907 Jaeger collaborated on the egg-shaped clock mentioned above (p. 266). Otherwise he concentrated on small flat watches, produced Vergely's coin movements, and about 1910 supplied pocket-watches in fashionable rock crystal cases that found an eager audience as far away as New York.

Cartier New York were supplied exclusively with Jaeger watches through Cartier Paris. Initially, the New York watchmaker Braun merely undertook repairs, at a salary of about Fr. 150 per week – compared with the 300 paid to a master *bijoutier* or the 500–600 to a stone-setter. In 1910, however, he achieved the creation of an extra-thin rock crystal watch, with invisible diamond setting and winder, which was so much talked about that it was followed by further models in geometric shapes from 1912 on.[15] Among them, Pierre Cartier's own model with a single hand was considered far and away the most stylish.

353, 354 Pendant watch. Cartier Paris, 1908. Made by Jaeger and Lavabre. Gold case with guilloché decoration and iron-grey enamel. Central rose ruby ringed by little spikes of rose-cut diamonds; outer ring a row of rose-cut diamonds and platinum on front and back; edge set with calibré-cut rubies. Bezel a ring in rose-cut diamonds and platinum. Fluted winding crown capped with a cabochon ruby below 6 o'clock. Oval pendant loop in rose-cut diamonds and platinum. Silver guilloché dial, with Arabic numerals ringed by a minute track. Bréguet hands in blue steel

355, 356 Watch brooch. Cartier Paris, 1908; watch and brooch sold on the same day to King Edward VII. Made by Jaeger, Lavabre, and Picq. Brooch of gold with guilloché decoration and iron-grey enamel; six collet-set, old- and rose-cut diamonds, rimmed by white enamel, surrounded by platinum and rose-cut diamonds in laurel-leaf motif. Pendant chain (*régence*) of pearls and platinum links; an 'M' motif in rose-cut diamonds at each end; millegrain setting for all diamonds. Suspension rings of platinum and rose-cut diamonds. Gold case with guilloché decoration and grey-blue enamel; faceted emerald

in the centre surrounded by rose-cut diamonds and white enamel, rimmed with rose-cut diamonds on front and back, extending into a twist that serves as pendant bow; edged with calibré-cut emeralds. Bezel of gold with radial guilloché decoration and translucent grey-blue enamel. Winding crown capped with rose-cut diamond

357 Watch on pearl 'ribbon' necklace. Cartier Paris, 1910. Made by Jaeger, necklace by Lavabre. Platinum case. Central monogram ('C H E') in rose-cut diamonds, outer ring in rose-cut diamonds on front and back. Bezel a ring of rose-cut diamonds. Winding crown capped with rose-cut diamond. Triangular suspension ring in rose-cut diamonds and platinum. Necklace a ribbon of millegrain-set pearls and platinum; sprung ring in rose-cut diamonds and platinum, two collet-set old-cut diamonds. Silver dial with guilloché sunray pattern, with Roman numerals around a minute track. Bréguet hands in blue steel

358 Pocket watch with chain and matchbox. Cartier Paris, *c.* 1910. Made by Jaeger, chain by Lenfant. Chain of gold and white enamel and pearls. Matchbox with gold and white enamel decoration, white enamel monogram in a gold ring, with catch in gold and rose-cut diamond; striking surface on the edge. Watch case with decoration identical to matchbox. Winding crown on horseshoe-shaped gold pendant. Gold bezel with white enamel fillets. Gold-plated guilloché dial with eleven Arabic numerals ringed by a minute track. Seconds subdial at 6 o'clock. Bréguet hands in blue steel

359 *top right* Pocket watch. Cartier Paris, 1914. Made by Jaeger. Platinum case, raised platinum bezel with eight screws. Fluted winding crown on pendant capped with a cabochon onyx. Triangular suspension ring in platinum. Silver dial, with Roman numerals around a 'railway' minute track. Blue steel hands

360 *right* Pendant watch. Cartier Paris, 1918. Made by Jaeger. Fibula brooch (*romaine*) of platinum and rose-cut diamonds, two plaques of onyx. Moiré pendant ribbon (*régence*) fringed at the bottom with rose-cut diamonds. Fibula ring of onyx and rose-cut diamonds. A slide of platinum and rose-cut diamonds allows the watch to be positioned along the ribbon. Oval case of platinum, bezel of rose-cut diamonds. Winding crown at 12 o'clock capped by a rose-cut diamond. Silver dial, with Roman numerals around a 'railway' minute track. Hands of blue steel

361 *far right* Panther-pattern wristwatch. Cartier Paris, 1914. Made by Jaeger. This watch marks Cartier's first use of the 'panther-skin' motif. Platinum case with pavé-set rose-cut diamonds studded with onyx. Winding crown capped with a cabochon onyx. Nautical-ring attachments, rose-cut diamonds, eight onyx bars. Moiré strap, onyx and diamond clasp, *déployant* buckle of pink gold. Millegrain setting for all diamonds. Dial with guilloché decoration, with Roman numerals around a 'railway' minute track. Bréguet hands of blue steel

362, 363 'Panther' pendant watch. Cartier
Paris, 1915, sold to Pierre Cartier. Made by Jaeger.
Platinum and onyx bar brooch with old-cut
diamonds holding a cord knotted to a diamond-
studded T-bar. Onyx and diamond slide, ring in
old-cut diamonds and onyx. Platinum case, pavé-set
with old-cut diamonds and onyx, framed by old-cut
diamonds. Three pear-shaped collet-set pendant
diamonds. Winding crown behind double-hoop
pendant bow set with diamonds. Millegrain setting
for all diamonds. Silver dial, with Roman numerals
outside a 'railway' minute track. Blue steel hands

364 Watch brooch. Cartier Paris, 1925. Brooch in onyx, platinum, coral, single- and rose-cut diamonds. Pendant ribbon, slide with rose-cut diamonds and two black circles; rings in rose-cut diamonds and platinum, gold and black enamel triangular fastener. Case in gold, platinum, single-cut diamonds, and black enamel. Green enamel bezel with white dots. Winding crown capped with rose-cut diamond. Stirrup link in single-cut diamonds edged with calibré-cut onyx, around a second, movable stirrup in gold and black enamel. Linked to an enamel plaque with multicoloured 'Persian'-style decoration on both sides, edged with single-cut diamonds. Silver dial, with Roman numerals. Blue steel hands. Originally on a braid necklace, the watch was mounted as a ribbon brooch in 1926, prior to sale

365 *right, below* Mystery pocket watch. Cartier Paris, 1931. Made by Jaeger. Platinum case edged with fillets. Winding crown on back at 12 o'clock. Off-centre crystal dial, with Roman numerals in black enamel

opposite

366 Design for the 'Pompom', a stalactite watch [**367**], by Joseph Vergely, 1925

367 'Pompom' stalactite watch. Cartier Paris, 1925. Made by Thibault. Gold and blue enamel case, with rose-cut diamonds and gold squares in reserve along the base; on the sides platinum, lapis lazuli batons and single-cut diamonds; pendant pearl drop, platinum motif, lapis lazuli and single-cut diamonds. Attached to a cord by a gold stirrup over which slides a platinum cover with old-cut diamonds topped by an emerald bead; the winding crown serves as clasp. A cylindrical slide in rose-cut diamonds ringed by black enamel adjusts the length of the cord. White dial, with Arabic numerals in white enamel cartouches. Blue steel hands. To make it easier to tell the time when the stirrup is flat against the bezel, the numerals 6 and 12 appear on both sides of the stirrup

Yet the bulk of New York's stock still continued to come from Paris;[16] and Edmond Jaeger maintained a small agency in New York in his own name.

Like Louis Cartier, however, Jaeger was convinced that the future lay not with the pocket-watch but with the much more practical wristwatch. This presented no technical difficulties; but it was a matter of convincing Cartier's exclusive clientele of the 'modernity' of an article which only a short time before had been tried out by soldiers in the trenches.[17]

As early as 1888 Cartier's had offered three ladies' wristwatches with rose-cut diamonds, and gold link bracelets. These must have been ahead of their time, since other models did not appear until 1892 and 1894, the latter having to wait until 1901 for a buyer. Like the jewelled bracelet, the wristwatch only began to come into its own when, after 1901–2, fashion ceased to dictate long sleeves, and long gloves were no longer required for evening wear. Cartier's saw this as a remarkable opportunity to establish a new form of wrist jewelry.

In 1906, Cartier's produced a series of wristwatches with Brédillard movements, finished in platinum, and already fitted with a jewelled winding crown – of cabochon ruby, cabochon sapphire or pearl – for which Cartier's later became famous. The series that followed was based on collaboration with Jaeger: fitted with a white leather strap, the watches were framed with diamonds, and their attachments embellished with cabochon emeralds. The new element of colour was enchanting, and the model was chosen for gifts by Edouard de Rothschild and the Vanderbilts as well as by Pierre Cartier himself. Sapphire, ruby and amethyst lug embellishments soon followed. A series of technical and aesthetic innovations continued far into the 1920s. Besides the still fairly small number of wristwatches, it also embraced the pendant watch known as 'régence'.

A

B

1906	The 'Tonneau' model, in the shape of a little cask (*tonneau*) [**368, 377, 378**]
	Ladies' models equipped with a pearl bracelet threaded on metal wire; the process, patented by the Godefroy workshop, was later taken up by the Duparc-Lenfant workshop
1908	Ladies' models with moiré straps of ribbed black silk and sliding rose-cut diamond buckles
	Long moiré sautoirs carry diamond-set pendant watches
	Onyx is the rage. Onyx ball-shaped watches are prized as mourning jewelry
1910	The gold *boucle déployante* (literally 'unfurled' or 'spread out' buckle) appears. The visible part of the fastener consists of a rectangle set with rose-cut diamonds, ornamented with an acanthus tendril, the initial of the owner, or the buckle pin. In 1913 Joseph Vergely was to give it its distinctive 'D' shape. One model of 1910 has a double buckle
	Bracelet lugs in the form of buckles
	Creation of a square wristwatch with rounded corners
	Production of a hexagonal watch with 'double-Z' lugs [**A**]
	A round case is devised for the 'Tonneau' model
	A wristwatch made with a strap of calibré-cut sapphires
	Creation of a diamond watch with bezel, lugs and strap of square-cut diamonds; the model is still made with stones of various cuts
1911	The 'Santos Dumont' model [**B, 372, 385**] goes on sale to the public. It is named after the Brazilian pioneer aviator Alberto Santos Dumont (1873–1932), who from 1897 amazed Parisians with flights in his own balloons and flying machines, and in 1901 received the Deutsch Prize for the return flight between Saint-Cloud and the Eiffel Tower. Louis Cartier knew Santos Dumont at the time both socially and as a client. Starting in 1906, Santos Dumont made brief flights in a heavier-than-air machine and appreciated a watch which was easier to use than a pocket-watch and which also matched his elegant style. (There is a photograph of him in his balloon basket, sporting a carnation in his buttonhole!) Long afterwards, in 1911, Santos Dumont agreed to have the watch put into production. When we recall the numerous clocks, snuffboxes, fans and so on *à la montgolfière* which followed the balloon ascent by the

Montgolfier brothers in 1783, it is no surprise that Santos Dumont's name should have been given to a watch[18]

A small egg-shaped watch with stirrup outline fixed on the watch bracelet

Pendant watches influenced by the Oriental forms of contemporary jewelry

Production of ring watches with rose-cut diamonds. A ring watch appears in the Cartier archives as early as 1878; the style regained popularity *c.* 1933

1912   Crystal pendant watches in invisible *serti illusion* diamond setting

Appearance of an oval wristwatch as the starting point for the 'Baignoire' model

Creation of an octagonal pendant watch

Creation of a pendant watch hidden in a pearl tassel, sold to the Maharaja of Indore

Creation of a square pendant watch in onyx and diamond, framed in an open circle

Completion of a pocket-watch showing local times in Paris, London and New York; sold to Mrs Stotesbury

1913   Creation of a watch with a moiré strap and central lug attachment [C]

The 'Tortue' model [D, 373, 384] appears, a development of the 'Tonneau' model [368]

Creation of a wristwatch with engraved crystal case [E, 369, 383]

Pendant watches in the form of tasselled lanterns and Islamic star shapes [F, 374]

Gold chronograph with hour hand and date

Production of a 'mystery' pendant watch with a round crystal case, on a moiré ribbon

1914   Development of the 'Santos Dumont' model, with straight outline [G]

Wristwatch with onyx and diamond 'panther' decoration on the bezel; lateral lugs in the form of nautical rings [361]

Further models with panther decoration appeared up to 1917

1915   The 'Tortue' and 'Santos Dumont' [385] are the most popular models, followed by the 'Baignoire' type

Pendant watches in onyx, crystal and diamond enjoy great popularity

1919   Following the First World War the 'Tank' model, designed two years earlier by Louis Cartier, goes on public sale, with gold bars evoking the tanks used by the Allies [H, 386]

1920   Completion of a 'Tank' watch with scrolled lugs [I]

Following a suggestion by Louis Cartier, a diamond watch is set into a pearl, worn on a platinum chain

1921   Creation of a bell-shaped wristwatch ('Cloche'), vertical or horizontal [J]

Horizontal disc pendant watches (*montres cachet*) and, a little later, stalactite watches [366, 367] make their appearance. According to *Vogue* the pendant watch was all the rage. By 1925 it was the latest fashion, and the wristwatch retreated into the background

1922   Creation of a wristwatch with a royal blue enamel bezel and gold numerals

Wristwatch with buckle-shaped gold lugs [K]

Creation of a 'Snake' watch of calibré-cut onyx

Chinese 'Tank' model, framed on all sides in gold bars [L]

1923   Creation of a wristwatch with gold lugs in the shape of shell cases [M]

Large 'Tank' watches with curved cases (*modèles cintrés*). One of the first is sold to the Maharaja of Kapurthala[19]

1925   A pendant watch is built into a hollowed engraved emerald of 136 carats;[20] sold to one of the Dolly Sisters

Platinum watch with second hand, calendar and the phases of the moon

Creation of the ladies' 'Baguette' wristwatch, at the time the smallest in the world.[21] A case width of 6 mm was made possible by setting the escapement and movement on different planes. Subsequently the model had a golden sliding cover with diamond *baguettes* [197]

C   D

E   F

G   H

I   J

K   L

M   N

368 'Tonneau' wristwatch. Cartier Paris, 1913. Platinum; the curved dial with circular-cut diamonds, on black silk moiré strap with *déployant* buckle (actual size)

369 Rock crystal wristwatch. Cartier Paris, 1913. Platinum; the engraved rock crystal mount in a diamond surround, on black silk moiré strap with *déployant* buckle (actual size)

370 Hexagonal wristwatch. Cartier Paris, 1913. Platinum; the case within rose-cut diamonds, surround with central strap attachments, black silk moiré strap (actual size)

371 Pearl and diamond wristwatch. Cartier Paris, 1913. Platinum; the case within circular-cut diamond surround, with diamond shoulder motifs connected to pearl strung bracelet; *déployant* buckle (actual size)

372 The 'Santos Dumont' wristwatch. Cartier Paris, 1911. Platinum. (actual size)

373 'Tortue' wristwatch. Cartier Paris, 1913. Platinum; set with circular-cut diamonds, with cabochon sapphire winder, on black silk moiré strap with *déployant* buckle (actual size)

1926	Creation of a wristwatch with leather strap and dial facing inward, to protect it (for sports, etc.)
1927	The 'Ceinture' model appears, with chamfered or 'Japanese' corners [N]
	Production of a watch to wear while playing golf, with a decorated cover and gold pencil
1928	Cigarette lighter with built-in watch
	Patent for a wristwatch clasp that slides over the hinged, rectangular case
	'Tank' watch with hour and minute windows (*à guichet*)
1929[22]	Appearance of a gold wristwatch with cover
	Creation of a watch bracelet of engraved coloured stones, the dial hidden under an emerald cover
	Production of a crystal skeleton watch
	Watches on cigarette cases, lipsticks, letter openers, money clips, etc.
	Pocket-watch *à éclipse*: the square enamelled case with covered dial opened by pressure on the side
1931	A waterproof 'Tank' watch appears
	Creation of an octagonal platinum 'mystery' pocket-watch
1932	Creation of a man's wristwatch with reversible case (*montre reversible*)
1933	Patent for a wristwatch with central lug attachment (*modèle Vendôme*)
	Patent for a wristwatch clasp, one of whose ends lay across the bezel
	Patent for cufflinks-watch, a model later sold to King Farouk
1934	Prospectus of Cartier New York describes the models then in fashion: clip watches and diamond wristwatches for ladies; for men, belt-buckle watches, sports watches with covers, electric watches and travellers' alarms
1936	Creation of a ladies' wristwatch with leather-covered spring bracelet
1938	Creation of an egg-shaped gold pocket-watch with compass and sundial
	Patent for a wristwatch without hands by Gaston Cusin
1939	Patent for a 'mystery' movement suitable for wristwatches, the transparent dial vertically divided in the middle by the axle carrying the hands
1965	Creation of an egg-shaped wristwatch
1978	Creation of the 'Santos' sports watch with screw motifs on both gold bezel and steel bracelet. As Cartier's best-selling contemporary watch it is exhibited for its exemplary design in the Musée de l'Air in Paris

374 Hexagonal 'Islamic' pendant watch. Cartier Paris, 1913. Gold and white enamel, with pearl winder; the reverse with diamond in 'illusion setting'; on black silk cord (actual size)

375 Pendant watch. Cartier Paris, 1913. Reverse. Platinum; two interlacing letters 'C' in diamonds; pearl and diamond surround; on silk moiré strap with diamond motif (actual size)

376 Oval pendant watch. Cartier Paris, 1913. Platinum; rose-cut diamond surround; on black silk cord with twin diamond motifs (actual size)

377 'Tonneau' wristwatch. Cartier Paris, 1907. Made by Jaeger, Lavabre, and Duparc. Gold case, bezel a row of half-pearls. Winding crown capped with a half-pearl. Bracelet of platinum and pearls, square clasp of platinum, pearls, and single-cut diamonds. Silver dial with radial guilloché decoration, with Roman numerals around a 'railway' minute track. Blue steel hands

378 'Tonneau' wristwatch. Cartier Paris, 1908. Made by Jaeger. Gold case (with a monogram on the back). Winding crown capped with cabochon sapphire. Leather strap, tongue buckle. Silver dial with guilloché sunray pattern, with Roman numerals around a minute track. Bréguet hands in blue steel

379 Wristwatch. Cartier Paris, 1908. Made by Jaeger. Gold case and bezel, six lozenge-shaped rubies alternating with six rose-cut diamonds at each hour. Winding crown with cabochon ruby. Lugs with four cabochon rubies, white leather strap, gold tongue buckle. Silver dial with guilloché sunray decoration, with Arabic numerals ringed by a minute track. Bréguet hands in blue steel

380 Wristwatch. Cartier Paris, 1911. Made by Jaeger and Lavabre. Gold case decorated with a ring of white enamel dots; bezel a row of rose-cut diamonds. Winding crown capped with a half-pearl. Screw lugs capped with four natural pearls; satin strap, rectangular tongue buckle in platinum and millegrain-set, rose-cut diamonds. Silver dial with guilloché sunray decoration, with Arabic numerals ringed by a 'railway' minute track. Bréguet hands in blue steel

381 Acanthus-pattern wristwatch. Cartier Paris, 1912. Made by Jaeger. Case with gold back. Winding crown capped with rose-cut diamond. Bezel, hinges, and acanthus-pattern lugs in platinum and rose-cut diamonds. Bracelet made of alternating rows of pearls and onyx beads, rectangular clasp in platinum and rose-cut diamonds, onyx plaque, pink gold folding buckle. Millegrain setting for all diamonds. Silver dial with guilloché sunray decoration, with Roman numerals around a 'railway' minute track. Bréguet hands in blue steel

382 Wristwatch. Cartier Paris, 1912. Made by Jaeger. Platinum case. Winding crown at 12 o'clock capped with a rose-cut diamond. Bezel and lugs in platinum and rose-cut diamonds. Moiré strap, rectangular clasp in platinum and rose-cut diamonds, pink gold folding buckle. Millegrain setting for all diamonds. Silver dial, rotated 90 degrees, with Roman numerals around a 'railway' minute track. Blue steel hands

383 Wristwatch. Cartier Paris, 1913. Made by Jaeger, crystal engraved by Petremont. Platinum case, engraved rock crystal surround bordered by platinum and single- and old-cut diamonds. Bezel in single-cut, four collet-set, single- and old-cut diamonds at quarter hours. Winding crown capped with a rose-cut diamond. Lugs in rose-cut diamonds and calibré-cut onyx bars. Moiré strap, clasp in platinum and rose-cut diamonds, onyx plaque, gold folding buckle. Millegrain setting for all diamonds. Silver dial, with Roman numerals ringed by a 'railway' minute track. Bréguet hands in blue steel

384 'Turtle' wristwatch. Cartier Paris, 1913. Made by Jaeger. Platinum case, bezel a row of millegrain-set single-cut diamonds. Winding crown capped with rose-cut diamond. Rigid lugs in onyx and single-cut diamonds. Moiré strap, rectangular clasp frame in platinum and millegrain-set rose-cut diamonds, onyx plaque and pink gold folding buckle. Silver dial, with Roman numerals ringed by a 'railway' minute track. Bréguet hands in blue steel

385 'Santos Dumont' wristwatch. Cartier Paris, 1915. Made by Jaeger. Gold case, gold raised bezel with eight screws. Winding crown capped with a cabochon sapphire. Leather strap, yellow and pink gold folding buckle. Silver dial, with Roman numerals around a 'railway' minute track. Bréguet hands in blue steel

386 'Tank' wristwatch. Cartier Paris, 1920. Made by Jaeger. Gold case, platinum lugs. Winding crown capped with a cabochon sapphire. Leather strap, tongue buckle. Silver dial, with Roman numerals around a 'railway' minute track. Bréguet hands in blue steel

387 Wristwatch. Cartier Paris, 1925. Made by Jaeger. Gold and red enamel case, bezel set with cabochon sapphires and emeralds, a baguette-cut diamond at 9 and 3 o'clock, platinum back. Winding crown capped with rose-cut diamond. Platinum lugs set with old- and single-cut diamonds, two leaf-shaped carved emeralds, cabochon sapphires, gold and red enamel. Double-cord strap, two slides in platinum with cabochon rubies, gold and black enamel clasp, platinum and single-cut diamond hoops, concealed pink gold folding buckle. Silver dial, with Arabic numerals. Blue steel hands

CHAPTER SEVENTEEN

SWORDS FOR ACADEMICIANS
CARTIER'S PATENTS
THE SECOND WORLD WAR

Swords for Academicians

Jacques-Louis David (1748–1825), Napoleon's favourite artist, was responsible not only for the astonishing canvas depicting the Emperor's coronation, but also, apparently, for the design of the black ceremonial dress decorated with green olive branches worn by members of the Académie Française. Later it came to be supplemented with a sword presented to the new Academician at a private ceremony by friends, admirers, or a committee from his home town.

Between 1931 and 1974 Cartier's received twenty-three commissions for these sumptuous ornaments – twenty-three historic commissions, recorded with great solemnity in the annals of the firm. They brought Cartier's into contact not only with artists and scholars, hardly familiar figures in the rue de la Paix, but also with the history of the Academy, one of the most prestigious institutions in the Western world. The Academy originated in an association of scholars, formalized by Richelieu in 1634 to foster the French language. The great dictionary was the sole fruit of its labours, but that was sufficient to spread its renown throughout France. Dissolved at the Revolution, it was reconstituted in Year III (1794) as a part of the Institut de France, whose five sections survive to this day: the Académie Française, the Académie des Inscriptions et Belles Lettres, the Académie des Beaux-Arts, the Académie des Sciences, and the Académie des Sciences Morales et Politiques.[1] Since 1806 it has convened in the Collège des Quatre-Nations, whose semicircular structure, designed on Roman models by the architect Louis Le Vau, dominates the Quai de Conti. The solemn protocols and ceremonies of the academies were definitively established under the First Empire. Each year six public sessions are held under the famous dome, one devoted to each academy and a final joint assembly. The closed sessions are held on Thursday afternoons.

At least since the time of the painter Horace Vernet (1789–1863), whose sword as a member of the Académie des Beaux-Arts carried the emblems of his profession and of his favourite pastimes – the palette and the hunting horn – the swords of the Academicians have reflected their work and significance.

Cartier comes into the story because the moment a candidate for the Academy learned of the intended presentation he visited the firm to discuss the decorative scheme with the designers. The resulting discussions and correspondence offered the designers a rare opportunity to emerge from their imposed anonymity and, like Louis and Pierre Cartier, to make themselves known: the speeches at the presentation ceremonies were among the few occasions when the names of the designers were mentioned in public. Thus Daniel Rops, elected to the Académie in 1956, congratulated Georges Rémy in his speech on 'the magic and the charm of an ornament which, in consequence, spreads Cartier's fame around the globe'.

In this context it is interesting to hear what Rémy himself had to say about his preparation for the work. 'I had many serious talks, imaginary and real, over a period of weeks with the future Academician, immersing myself in his personality and his world, and we had many a chat, too, before I embarked on the job.' Such conversations ranged from childhood impressions to the world of nature, from the candidate's home life to art and religion. Throughout, the designer was alert for easily intelligible yet artistically significant symbols that could be crystallized and transferred to the sword. The themes had to be kept distinct. 'The most difficult thing', said Rémy, 'is to incorporate the dominant elements into the design and yet remain selective. After all, one has to have a harmonious design and not merely a collection of obvious symbols.' Pierre-Henri Simon, a writer elected to the Académie Française in 1966, expressed it admirably: 'I wanted simplicity of line, moderation of symbol and restraint of ornament. If there had to be luxury, then I wanted it in the quality of the material, rather than in any kind of ornamentation.'

Over the years, Cartier's developed a special formal vocabulary in the design of these Academicians' swords to meet both the official regulations and the individual wishes of the candidates. The designers had to be familiar with ancient symbols: for example, the owl as the bird of wisdom, Mercury's staff as the symbol of peace, and two-headed Janus as the tutelary god of gates and doors. But they also had to be able to create new symbols, explicable purely in terms of the Academician's work. Sometimes the juxtaposition of familiar and less familiar images could create formal problems: the 1954 sword of

preceding pages, left

388 Jean Cocteau's design for his own sword, on his election to the Académie Française, 1955

preceding pages, right

389 The hilt of the sword of Jean Cocteau [see **393**]

opposite

390 Design for the sword of the Duc de Lévis Mirepoix, 1954. The sword was presented to him on his reception as a member of the Académie Française on 18 March 1954 the Duc de Lévis Mirepoix [390] displayed both the Order of the Holy Ghost and an aeroplane!

Of the twenty-three swords produced between 1931 and 1974, the first was for the Duc de Gramont, admitted to the Académie des Sciences for his services to optics and astronomy [391], and the last for Professor Hamburger, elected for services to medicine. Cartier's trusted only a few of its designers with the work. Among them were Charles Jacqueau, who designed the sword for André Maurois in 1939; Peter Lemarchand; and, in the case of Hamburger, Pierre Ludwig, who was on the design staff from 1963 to 1977. But the greatest number of swords, fifteen in all, were designed by Georges Rémy (1907–75), who after four years at the Ecole Boulle worked with Cartier's from 1925 to 1973. Although inducted into the spirit of Cartier's ethos by Chenaud and Jacqueau, he was far closer in mood to his contemporary colleagues Lemarchand and Lachassagne. Rémy was not outstanding as a creator of original motifs and, though he continued with Lemarchand's panther and bird of paradise designs after the latter's death, he lacked a true, sympathetic understanding of Lemarchand's dream world. Yet Rémy was second to none in his feeling for proportion and the architectonics of a work of art. With his brilliant analytical sense, he could easily have made a career as an art critic. He tackled the complex problems of outline and function presented by his beloved table clocks and desk accessories like an architect. Even his numerous designs for rings breathed the true spirit of the geometer, and it was not by chance that Jeanne Toussaint dubbed him 'the ring king'. It was therefore to be expected that most of the sword designs would fall to him. A typical example of his work, not executed, is the design for a sword for the architect Guillaume Gillet: the instruments of the surveyor are integrated into the ornamental weapon with an impressive logic, while not a single unnecessary detail breaks the dynamic flow of the design.

In 1966 the historian and novelist Maurice Druon was elected to the Académie Française; the following year Rémy produced his design for the sword. The monogrammed hilt rested, as on an architectural support, on a bull, Druon's birth sign. In a veritable tour de force, the hammered pure gold setting was inset with chrysolite, the author's bright green birthstone, while the figure '4', sacred to the god Zeus, referred to Druon's work *Les Mémoires de Zeus*. In 1963 Rémy had produced similarly symbolic designs for the sword of the novelist Joseph Kessel: the lion's head on the pommel, for which the head of the workshop, André Gagniand, made the terracotta model, had originally been designed as an all-too-heraldic lion rampant.

Rémy's sword design for the Professor of Medicine Cordier came from the world of Renaissance anatomy. Since the sixteenth century, wax, bronze or wooden models of a flayed man, with sinews and muscles exposed, had served as demonstration figures. In the masterly drawings of Michelangelo, Leonardo and later Houdon, they evolved into an artistic genre in their own right. In his original design Rémy first envisaged a freestanding bronze of a flayed man, which would have expressed his artistic vision more clearly than did the final flat silhouette relief. Unhappily, but perhaps not surprisingly, there was often a certain discrepancy between preparation and execution in these sword designs.

The most original design for these swords unquestionably came from a 'poet laureate', Jean Cocteau (1889–1963), who became a member of the Académie Française in 1955 [388, 389, 393]. The Cocteau commission provided a late encounter with one of Diaghilev's original collaborators.[2] Leon Bakst had stumbled on a folio of Cocteau's drawings when he was drawing-master to the children of Grand Duchess Vladimir. As a result, the twenty-two-year-old received a commission for two posters for the ballet *Le Spectre de la rose*, followed by work on the unsuccessful ballet *Le Dieu bleu* and in 1917 *Parade*. In constant orbit round the Ballets Russes, Cocteau had come to know Louis Cartier and the style of the house. Moreover, at the time when the choice of the sword was being made, he was acting jointly with Jeanne Toussaint as artistic adviser to the banker's wife Francine Weisweiller in her choice of Cartier jewels. She was to contribute the rubies and diamonds for Cocteau's sword, while Coco Chanel parted with an emerald of 2.84 carats. Cocteau himself designed the outline of the sword. Over the years he had worked under the aegis of Orpheus, the mythological poet and musician:

opposite

391 Designs for the sword of the Duc de
Gramont, 1931. The sword was presented to
him on his reception as a member of the
Académie des Sciences on 20 June 1931

392 Design for the sword of Jacques de
Lacretelle, 1938. The sword was presented
to him on his reception as a member of the
Académie Française on 27 January 1938

this page

393 The sword of Jean Cocteau. Cartier Paris,
1955. Gold, silver; one step-cut emerald; eight
cabochon rubies; one old-cut brilliant; ivory,
onyx; steel blade

in 1927 there was his poem *Orphée*, in 1950 the film of the same name, and still later, in 1960, his film *Le Testament d'Orphée*. The hilt of the sword [**389**] depicts the poet's flowing profile surmounted by his lyre; the pillar entwined with a ribbon alludes to the theatre (especially tragedy), and the horizontal *porte-crayon* or pastel-holder to Cocteau's graphic art. Other symbols were more concrete: the ivory ball grasped by a hand at the point of the sword refers to his play *Les Enfants terribles*, and the lances allude to the grille of the Palais-Royal where Cocteau lived as a neighbour of Colette. Like his writings, the sword was signed with a six-pointed star in diamonds and rubies.

Cocteau's sword remains unique in the Cartier oeuvre; in many other cases the swords are bound by tradition and convention. But it should not be forgotten that official commissions were happy to rely on the symbols and allegories that had been appearing on coins, memorials and charters since the nineteenth century, and Cartier's designers often had no option but to follow suit. Furthermore, most of the designs date from after the Second World War, when the art of the goldsmith was seeking new sources of inspiration.

Cartier's patents

More than any other historical event, the Second World War placed the whole Cartier enterprise in a critical situation. The fact that platinum was virtually unobtainable mattered little, since it had been displaced in public favour as early as the 1930s by the fashion for yellow gold. But in 1940 the wholesale trade in gold was expressly forbidden by the Banque de France. If a customer commissioned a piece in gold, he had to supply the full weight of metal required himself: in the case of platinum it was 135 per cent. If gold and platinum were melted, the State had the right to 20 per cent of the fine content.

Even before the war Cartier's had been experimenting with new precious metal alloys at their workshops in the rue Bachaumont, with the collaboration of Professor Cotton of the Sorbonne, among others. The new alloys were to be both lighter and better value than the traditional precious metals. One of the alloys favoured at the time by Cartier consisted of gold with small quantities of cobalt and chromium. Two gold alloys were patented in 1930 and 1934, the latter containing beryllium, which yielded a particularly hard metal. Another, much prized by the public as 'l'or Cartier', was no less than the classic yellow gold, launched at a time when rose-tinted gold, achieved through increased copper alloy, had lost its noble appeal. In London, the Worshipful Company of Goldsmiths decided in 1932 that 14-carat gold should replace the 12- and 15-carat varieties, while in New York Pierre Cartier suggested that the local Battelle Institute should experiment with palladium – not even recognized in France as a noble metal.[3]

At this time, the most important man in Cartier's technical department was Georges Bezault, born in 1888, who had joined the firm at the age of twenty-three. In 1937 he began some interesting experiments with a new alloy, platinix, almost as pliable as platinum but easier to obtain. Like the watchmaker Gaston Cusin, Bezault embodied the inventive spirit of the firm in the 1930s. Basic to the Cartier repertoire are his necklace clasps, stone settings (*châtons*) and hinges.

Although a committee comprising Louis Cartier, Edmond Forêt, Charles Jacqueau and Gérard Desouches considered the latest proposals from the design studio, the question whether an aesthetically satisfying jewel also met technical requirements could only be answered after tests conducted by Georges Bezault. In 1935 the committee was joined by Jeanne Toussaint, who two years earlier had begun to preside over the *haute joaillerie* and whose first job was to launch crystal jewelry in the massive style of the 1930s.

No period was so rich in Cartier patents as the decade preceding the Second World War. In 1927 and 1934 the firm patented its clip system for brooches. The idea was, it seems, conceived by Louis Cartier while examining a clothes peg; its technical realization was achieved by Georges Bezault. In 1933 Cartier registered a patent for the *serti mystérieux*, a technique for invisibly setting calibré-cut stones in a mosaic pattern by securing the undersides of the stones by parallel metal rails. Louis Cartier considered that the method damaged the calibré-cut stones, however, and it was not much used. Cartier's

Paris patents were supplemented by numerous inventions in the New York branch. Here Jules Glaenzer and Edmond Forêt were especially inventive, the latter conceiving a flower brooch of quivering blooms *en tremblant*. For many years a narcissus brooch with reversible petals enjoyed popularity; set with yellow gold on one side and gemstones on the other, it was designed for both afternoon and evening wear.

The Second World War

On 10 May 1940 the German armed forces occupied Paris. By the following August eleven leading members of Cartier's staff were in prison. They included Louis Devaux, who was to be nominated chairman of the firm on his release, Pierre Claudel, and the designers Lachassagne and Rémy. Jeanne Toussaint was in Ciboure at the time and the Jacques Cartiers were in Saint Jean-de-Luz, while Louis Cartier was in Lisbon waiting in vain for a visa to the United States. The rue d'Argenson workshop was temporarily closed, and the shop in the rue de la Paix carried on with a much reduced stock of valuable pieces. The principal concern was not to fall foul of Reichsmarshall Goering, quartered with the German general staff in the neighbouring Ritz Hotel. The essence of the problem was that the firm, which had already had to open its books to German inspection, might be saddled with a German commissar, and its stock, which included 50 million francs' worth of jewelry deposited by customers, might be taken off to Berlin. So the most valuable pieces were secretly transferred in boxes and cases to Biarritz, where a provisional Cartier operation opened in the summer of 1940 with fifty-four employees. Nevertheless, that same summer the firm, together with the Bourse and the banks, returned to Paris.

394 'Oiseau libéré' brooch. Cartier Paris, 1944. Gold, platinum; rose-cut diamonds; one cabochon sapphire; lapis lazuli; coral

In England at the same time, the bombing of Southampton highlighted the danger which threatened Cartier London. Shortly before he died in 1942, Louis Cartier instructed Etienne Bellenger, the London sales director, to shift the London stock to safety on the Kintyre peninsula in the Scottish Highlands. Bellenger had already placed offices in New Bond Street, his home, and the firm's Rolls Royce at the disposal of General de Gaulle, leader of the London-based Free French Government. De Gaulle used the opportunity to inspect Cartier's English Art Works, which, under the war emergency, was producing aeroplane parts. The designers Rupert Emmerson and George Charity were honoured with commissions to design the insignia and medals for de Gaulle's enterprises, which were to end triumphantly in 1944 with a victory parade through the streets of Paris.

CHAPTER EIGHTEEN

THE GREAT TRANSACTIONS

In 1908 Cartier's had at their disposal the two most spectacular historic diamonds then on the market: the 'Star of the East' [**397, 398**] and the 'Hope' [**397, 399**]. Even today it is still not clear exactly where the former, a drop-shaped diamond of 94.80 carats, originally came from. Legend attributed it, like so many others, to the treasures of the Turkish Sultan Abdul Hamid II, deposed in 1909; but the stone was already in the possession of Cartier Paris in 1908, the year of the Turkish military revolution, where it was seen by Evalyn Walsh McLean, daughter of the gold prospector Thomas F. Walsh. Spoilt since childhood, when she had been driven to her Washington school in a coach, she had just married Edward Beale McLean, heir to the dollar millions of the *Washington Post*. Furnished with $100,000 each, the pair were on their honeymoon in Paris when Evalyn suddenly remembered that she had still not chosen her father's wedding present to her. She betook herself to the rue de la Paix. 'We have just the thing for you', said the salesman at Cartier's, as Evalyn recalled later. 'Then', she went on,

> he hypnotized me by showing me an ornament that made bright spots before my eyes [**398**]. . . . A line of diamond fire in square links of platinum where it would touch my throat became a triple loop and from the bottom circle was depended an entrancing pearl. It was the size of my little finger-end and weighed 32¼ grains. The pearl was but the supporting slave of another thing I craved at sight – an emerald. Some lapidary had shaped it with six sides so as to amplify, or to find at least, every trace of colour. It weighed 34½ carats. This green jewel, in turn, was just the object supporting the Star of the East. This stone, a pear-shaped brilliant, was one of the most famous in the world – 92½ carats. All lapidaries know it. With fingers that fumbled from excitement I put that gorgeous piece around my throat.
>
> 'Ned,' I said in mock despair, 'It's got me! I'll never get away from the spell of this.'
>
> 'A shock might break the spell,' said Ned, 'Suppose you ask the price of this magnificence'.
>
> 'Well,' I said to the man at Cartier's as I put my index finger in my ears, 'how much?'
>
> He whispered, 'Six hundred thousand francs, madam.'
>
> 'You mean a hundred and twenty thousand dollars?'
>
> He cocked his head to one side so that his nod was made obliquely.
>
> 'After all,' I said to Ned, 'this is really an investment. Besides, this is 15 December and I can tell my father it's a double gift to cover both my wedding and Christmas present.' So we signed the bill and Cartier's sent us kids out into the world with the Star of the East.[1]

Was it merely coincidence that the McLeans turned up in Paris again just two years later when the 'Hope' diamond [**397, 399**] was awaiting a buyer at Cartier's? 'Pierre Cartier', Evalyn McLean continues,

> came to call on us at the Hotel Bristol in Paris. He carried, tenderly, a package tightly closed with wax seals. I suppose a Parisian jewel merchant who seeks trade among the ultra-rich has to be more or less a stage manager or an actor. . . .
>
> 'You told me' [he said] 'when you bought from me your wedding present, the Star of the East . . . that you had seen a jewel in the [Sultan's] harem [in Constantinople], a great blue stone that rested against the throat of the Sultan's favourite' . . .
>
> 'I guess I did.' . . . It was too early to argue and, after all, I had seen jewels on Turkish ladies that made my fingers itch.

'Of course you did', Cartier replied, and after this masterly introduction history did the rest. Originally, Evalyn was told, the stone had been part of a blue diamond of 112³⁄₁₆ carats, which Tavernier had sold to Louis XIV in 1669. In 1673 it was recut to 67⅛ carats and was known thereafter as the 'Blue Diamond of the Crown'. In 1749 the French court jeweller Jacquemin set it, together with the dragon-shaped spinel known as the 'Côte de Bretagne' and a hexagonal diamond of 31¾ carats, to form the emblem of the Order of the Golden Fleece; in 1792 this, and a number of other pieces from the French crown jewels, were stolen from the Garde-Meubles in what is now the Place de la Concorde. It seems that the 'Golden Fleece' was broken up in England, and in all probability the stone of just 45½

preceding pages, left

395 The 'Louis Cartier' diamond is one of the very few gems of more than 100 carats to have received a D certificate (Flawless) from the Gemological Institute of America

preceding pages, right

396 The 'Burton-Taylor' diamond, of 69.42 carats, set as a ring. It was later mounted in a necklace [**411, 412**]

opposite

397 Mrs Evalyn Walsh McLean wearing the 'Star of the East' diamond [**399**] as an aigrette and the 'Hope' diamond [**400**] on a pearl necklace

398 The 94.80-carat 'Star of the East' diamond below a hexagonal emerald of 34 carats and a pearl of 32 grains, mounted on a diamond chain. Piece of unknown manufacture sold by Cartier in 1908 (actual size).

carats which turned up in London again was the 'Blue Diamond of the Crown'. It is recorded as being in the possession of the gem dealer Daniel Eliason in 1812, and in 1830 he sold it to Henry Philip Hope of the famous banking family. Hope died in 1839. The stone went to his nephew Henry Thomas, who exhibited it in the Crystal Palace in 1851, and it remained in the family down to Lord Francis Hope, who in 1894 married the American actress May Yohe and the following year went bankrupt. In 1901 the 'Hope' was auctioned in London and went to the New York diamond dealer Joseph Frankel's Son.[2] Here it was, it seems, offered to W. K. Vanderbilt at a price of $500,000. In 1909 it appeared unexpectedly in the sale of just eight diamonds by the collector Salomon Habib in Paris,[3] and was knocked down for Fr. 400,000 ($80,000) to Rosenau, the dealers from whom Cartier's acquired it.

Yet for all Pierre Cartier's salesmanship, Mrs McLean was not at first attracted by the stone. After she returned to America on the *Rotterdam*, he let her have it on approval for a weekend. 'For hours', she recalled, 'that jewel stared at me. The setting had been changed completely to a frame of diamonds [**399**] and there was a splendid chain of diamonds to go about my neck. At some time during the night I began to want the thing.' But the initial negotiations spanned several months and involved a lawsuit which took until 1912. The selling price was $180,000, which included $10,000 for another setting in the form of a diamond bandeau.[4] There was to be an initial payment of $40,000 and Cartier's agreed to discount $26,000 against the return of the emerald and pearl necklace that had incorporated the 'Star of the East' [**398**]. The balance of $114,000 was to be settled within three years.[5]

And the legendary curse? Evalyn McLean received warnings from May Yohe, from her mother-in-law, and even from Mrs Goelet, who was later to wear Prince Yusupov's black pearls without a care. Cartier had wisely inserted a clause in the contract – 'customer's privilege to exchange goods in case of fatality' – and when Mr McLean, fearful of the curse, refused a medical examination, his wife returned the 'Hope' forthwith. But Cartier's sent it back promptly. Now, Evalyn had another idea.

399 The 'Hope' diamond (45.52 carats) mounted by Cartier in 1910 as a pendant surrounded by diamonds

We set out in my electric victoria for the church of Monsignor Russell.

'Look, Father,' I said to him, 'this thing has got me nervous. Would you bless it for me?'

We were in a small side room of the church and Monsignor Russell donned his robes and put my bauble on a velvet cushion.

As he continued his preparations the storm broke. Lightning flashed. Thunder shook the church . . . [but] Monsignor Russell's Latin words gave me strange comfort.

Ever since that day, I've worn my diamond as a charm.

Any troubles the 'Hope' brought were generally of a financial nature. Mrs McLean wore it on the same necklace as the 'Star of the East', but insurance on the stone cost $24,000 a year and it was frequently pawned. Yet she never thought of selling. 'At the moment it is impossible to put a value on the stone', she wrote in 1944 to Pierre Cartier, who had just spent New Year's Eve in the McLeans' circle. 'These ignorant fools [the Internal Revenue] think you can walk in with the Hope diamond or the big white diamond and get a million dollar loan overnight.'

No doubt the most eccentric figure ever to feature in Cartier's records, Mrs McLean died in 1947. Her seventy-four-piece collection, including the 15.46-carat 'Star of the South' (another historic diamond bought from Cartier's), was acquired by the jeweller Harry Winston in 1949.[6] In 1958 the 'Hope' found its final home in the Smithsonian Institution, Washington.

The dealer Salomon Habib, however, remains an enigma to this day. Was it true that his diamonds, which included the 70.20-carat 'Idol's Eye', had fleetingly been in the possession of Sultan Abdul Hamid? Did Habib know the Sultan, and what sort of relationship did he have with him? It appears that Alfred Cartier was summoned to Constantinople in 1909, the year of the Habib auction, to make a valuation of the Sultan's treasure.[7] At a further auction held in Paris in 1933, Habib's unsold diamonds from 1909 were again put up for sale, together with 'Le Golconde Doré', a 95.40 carat diamond also said to have belonged to the Sultan, which remained unsold. In 1938, however, Habib approached Cartier's for assistance in redeeming the stones pawned in Paris and London.

Over the years Cartier acquired many historic jewels at auction in Paris, the most famous being the 'Thiers pearls' (see p. 118). Another unique acquisition was a rose brooch, 15 cm wide and set all over with diamonds, which came from the 1904 auction of the property of the late Princess Mathilde. That same year, Louis Cartier sold the great flower to one of the company's firmest supporters, Mrs Cornelius Vanderbilt of New York [27]. For the thirtieth birthday of the Prince of Wales (later King Edward VIII), Mrs Vanderbilt held a ball at Spencer House, London, at which a giant cake was carried in. When cut, it was revealed to be packed with 'surprises' which she had selected at Cartier's. The Prince, however, arrived late and in a bad mood, and merely greeted the spectacle with a sullen 'How vulgar!' The next day Mrs Vanderbilt returned the whole lot.[8]

In 1920, a six-day auction was held in Lausanne to dispose of the jewels of Princess Vera Lobanov-Rostovsky (née Princess Dolgorouky), who had died at Vevey. She had been a customer of Cartier's since 1900 and had named Louis Cartier in her will as one of three jewelry experts. The auction drew all the major buyers and experts to the shores of Lake Geneva. The prize items were a three-rope necklace of pink pearls, originally in the possession of Tsar Nicholas I, and a 118-carat diamond.[9] Louis Cartier bought the Tsar's necklace for Fr. 553,000 and received congratulations on such a valuable acquisition from Queen Olga of Greece and Princess Dolly Radziwill. In Cartier's opinion the auction, which realized a grand total of Fr. 3,470,000, initiated the steep upward trend in jewelry prices which set in with the 1920s, despite massive sales by ruined Russian aristocrats.

In addition, news of the discovery in 1925 of the jewelry cache in Prince Yusupov's Moscow palace haunted the international press. Allegedly the hiding place had been betrayed by the son of the mason who devised it in 1917. Secret passages from the picture gallery led to two underground dungeons, from which were recovered 255 brooches, 13 tiaras (among them the Cartier tiara bought in 1914 [84]), 42 bracelets and 210 kilos of assorted *objets d'art*. By this time, however, Princess Zenaida and her son Felix had already got the historic pearls and diamonds out of the country (see p. 124). After an unsuccessful American journey, in which he had planned to raise money by selling his precious stones, Felix approached Pierre Cartier in 1922 and offered him the following diamonds:

> The 'Ram's Head', a 17.47-carat stone, light rose in colour and cut in the shape of a flattened octahedron. This diamond had seemingly been given by Catherine the Great to her favourite, Potemkin. Cartier's bought it in 1927 and sold it to Daisy Fellowes. It was stolen from her in 1939 and has not been seen since.
>
> The 'Sultan of Morocco', a steel-coloured diamond of 35.67 carats, said to have been in the possession of the Yusupov family since 1840. In 1924 Cartier's debated whether to display the stone at the great 1925 Art Deco exhibition. In 1926 or 1929 (the records are not clear) the diamond was sold to America. As late as 1969 Cartier's arranged to display it in the World of Gems Exhibition held in the New York State Museum. In 1972 it passed into the possession of the jeweller F. J. Cooper of Philadelphia.
>
> The 'Diamond Earrings of Marie Antoinette', with two drop diamonds of 34.59 carats, which had allegedly belonged to the Yusupov family since 1802. When and to whom Cartier's sold them is unclear.[10]
>
> The 'Polar Star' [400], a cushion-shaped diamond of 41.28 carats, originally the property of Joseph Bonaparte, Napoleon's elder brother. Its second owner was Princess Tatiana Yusupov (1769–1841). The name comes from its cut as an eight-pointed star. From 1924 the stone was lodged, with interruptions, with Cartier London, and it was then pledged along with other Yusupov jewels with the London firm of T. M. Sutton until Cartier's redeemed it. In Paris in 1928 they sold it for £48,000 to Lydia, Lady Deterding, the wife of the Dutch oil magnate.[11]

400 The 'Polar Star' diamond, of 41.28 carats, suspended from a necklace of 33 collet-set diamonds, with a cushion-shaped fancy-blue diamond weighing 26.26 carats and a cushion-shaped pink diamond weighing 22.97 carats. The piece was made up by Cartier London for temporary display (see p. 256): the blue and pink diamonds were soon incorporated in the 'Nawanagar Necklace' of 1931 [404]

Other Yusupov treasures included the 'Blue Venus', carved from a single light blue 11-cm-long sapphire, on a base set with a ruby with Medusa-head intaglio; a Buddha carved out of ruby from the Summer Palace near Peking; and a statuette of Jupiter ascribed to Benvenuto Cellini.

Another Russian treasure to find its way to Cartier's was the marriage crown of the princesses of the imperial house. It was a delicate piece with six diamond arches

surmounted by a simple diamond cross, and both Grand Duchess Helen, daughter of Grand Duchess Vladimir, and Grand Duchess Marie, daughter of Grand Duke Paul, who both owned magnificent Cartier tiaras, had worn it at their weddings. In 1927 it was auctioned by Christie's in London on the instructions of a Soviet syndicate, and shortly afterwards Pierre Cartier ran it to earth in a Paris antique shop. Like the Lobanov and Thiers pearls before it, the crown was sent to New York, where the demand for historic jewels was greater than in Europe. Later, Prince Christopher of Greece gave a melancholy account of an unexpected encounter with the crown:

> At the time I was in New York, visiting Pierre Cartier in his office. Suddenly he said: 'I would like to show you something.' He took a velvet case from his private safe, laid it on the table and opened it. Within lay a diamond crown with six arches rising from the circlet and surmounted by a cross. 'Do you recognize it?' he asked me. I nodded wordlessly, seized by a sense of melancholy that rose from the depths of my memory. It was the crown of the Romanovs. My mother had worn it and her mother before her; it had adorned all the princesses of the imperial house on their wedding days. All at once, it seemed to me the room was filled with shades of long-dead brides.'[12]

The silver service ordered by Napoleon from Biennais and Cahier on his return from Elba also found its way to New York. Its 919 pieces were laid out as if for a banquet for all the world's crowned heads, in Cartier's Louis XVI rooms on Fifth Avenue. After Napoleon's fall, Louis XVIII (1815–24) had had the service decorated with his own arms. Evidence of royal etiquette is provided by the engraved *bouche du roi* casserole, used to serve food reserved for the king. The service passed via the Comte de Chambord, the last of the senior Bourbon line, to Don Jaime de Bourbon, who disposed of it to Cartier's.[13] It was exhibited in 1923, not only in New York, but also in Boston and Pittsburgh museums.

Apart from isolated historic *objets d'art*, Cartier's main concern, ever since it had first established itself in the rue de la Paix, was with the valuation, resetting, display and sale of precious stones. In this area Louis Cartier had an art collector's eye, and his father and brothers deferred to his unerring instinct. Louis was later to recount how he held the last remnants of Marie Antoinette's necklace in his hand, that string of twenty-two diamonds owned by the Duke of Sutherland which Louis described as 'the largest antique chain of diamonds I have ever seen'. In addition, Louis bought a cross pendant and a ring in the possession of Pope Benedict XV (1854–1922), pieces whose fascination went far beyond their value as stones.

In New York, by contrast, Pierre Cartier often had the task of incorporating a historic stone in a Cartier jewel. Examples include the drop-shaped diamond known as the 'Star of South Africa' of 47.69 carats [403], whose discovery in 1869 had unleashed diamond fever in South Africa,[14] and the drop-shaped 'Morgan' diamond of 35 carats, which J. P. Morgan had given as a wedding present to Mrs Stotesbury, and which she had set in one of her Cartier tiaras.[15]

The series of historic stones handled by Cartier's as brokers offers a glimpse into a realm of cultural history which tells of private destinies, shattered hopes, ambition and tragedy and, sometimes, fleeting happiness. The series begins with a drop-shaped cabochon emerald of 75 carats belonging to an Indian maharaja, which Cartier began negotiating for in 1901. In the same year we read of a 15–16-carat fancy-pink Golconda diamond which came from a famous necklace – possibly what Cartier referred to in a letter to W. K. Vanderbilt as 'a splendid stone of antique cut from a necklace of the Portuguese royal house'.

Two stones recalled the generous legacy of eighteen diamonds bequeathed by Cardinal Mazarin (1602–61) to the French crown. Two Mazarin diamonds, one of $18^{11}/_{16}$ carats, the other of $16^{9}/_{16}$ carats, were shown at the Paris Exposition of 1900 and set the following year by Cartier's for Madame Hériot.[16]

In 1909 Cartier's received the 90.38-carat drop diamond later known as the 'Indian Briolette' from the great dealer Eknayan, who had cut it shortly before. Initially set as a pendant with a 126-grain pearl [401], the splendid stone was combined the following year with two 22-carat emeralds and the same pearl to form a brooch, which was sent to the New York branch. In 1911 the diamond returned once more to Eknayan, before Cartier's sold it to George Blumenthal.[17]

opposite

401 The 'Indian Briolette' diamond of 90.38 carats, mounted below a square-cut diamond and a pearl of 126 grains. Cartier Paris, 1909 (actual size)

402 The 'Blue Heart' or 'Unzue Heart' diamond of 30.82 carats and a blue triangular diamond mounted on a circular, navette and pear-shaped diamond breast ornament in lily-of-the-valley design. Cartier Paris, 1910 (actual size)

403 The 'Star of South Africa' diamond. Pear-cut diamond weighing 47.69 carats, mounted as a pendant brooch, decorated with old-cut diamonds in lily-of-the-valley setting, made by Cartier New York at the end of the 1910s

Among the largest of all the stones set by Cartier was the 1910 cushion-shaped 'La Tour d'Auvergne', owned by the Princess of the same name. Four years later she led the 'Diamond Ballet' at the 'Gemstones Ball' adorned with her historic diamonds, among which not the least eye-catching was the 116³/₃₄-carat diamond.[18]

In 1910 Cartier's bought the 'Dudley' emerald of 6⅞¹/₆₄ carats from the New York dealer Joseph Frankel's Son, and at almost the same time sold the valuable 30.82-carat 'Blue Heart' diamond, also cut by Eknayan, in a lily-of-the-valley breast ornament to Mrs Unzue of Argentina [402].[19] If the blue of the 'Hope' diamond was described as 'indignant indigo' or steel blue, the heart diamond glows a deep sea blue and is still among the most remarkable blue diamonds in the world.

The sensation over the 'Hope' diamond had barely died down, and the final instalment had still to be paid by the McLean family, when Cartier's got hold of another piece from the former Hope collection – the 52.17-carat 'Hope' spinel. Bought from the London dealer Peake's, the rectangular red stone adorned a simple brooch by the Picq workshop before being set by Cartier's in a necklace.

These great transactions were interrupted by the First World War, though it was during the war years that Pierre Cartier achieved his spectacular coup of exchanging his two-rope pearl necklace for the Morton Plant palace on Fifth Avenue (see p. 121).

In 1921 we find an important pair of earrings – part of the historic Leuchtenberg emeralds – at Cartier New York. They comprised two emerald drops, each framed in ten diamonds and each fitted to a hexagonal emerald and thirteen diamonds. The complete set of jewels had originally belonged to the Beauharnais family before it passed to the Russian ducal family of Leuchtenberg; from them it was bought by a Paris syndicate to which Cartier's belonged.[20] Except for the earrings, the jewels were broken up in Paris, despite a subscription organized by the Louvre to prevent this. The following year Cartier's took the emeralds to Spain to show to the Queen and Queen Mother. However, this did not lead to a sale at the time because, as the salesman Farinès reported back to Paris, the Queen Mother merely 'pouted significantly'.

In 1924 Cartier's acquired another historic pair of earrings, this time going back to the Empress Maria Theresa and until 1918 preserved in the Treasury in the Hofburg in Vienna. In 1921, together with other Habsburg treasures, they were offered for sale in Lucerne. The earrings themselves, through mysterious circumstances, reached the dealer Bienenfeld, who passed them on directly to Cartier's. Set with diamond drops and described as of the 'very finest quality, of unheard-of beauty and absolutely white', they allegedly found a buyer in India.

In 1933, as the waves of the economic crisis spread ever wider, Cartier's transactions began to extend to particularly famous stones, many of which had been in private collections for centuries. Some negotiations foundered on the unreasonableness of the owners, who refused to accept offers which were in keeping with the new economic realities. Thus Cartier's turned down the offer of the blue 35.32-carat Wittelsbach diamond, even though the firm already had plans to show the stone to the King of Nepal. In 1928 negotiations were in hand for the historic diamond briolette necklace presented by Napoleon to his consort Marie Louise on the birth of the King of Rome. Even in 1937 there was still talk of its being taken over by Cartier London with a view to the approaching coronation of King George VI. But here too the negotiations foundered on the owner's indecision.

Up to the Second World War the London branch was the arena for many important transactions. It was here, in the 1920s, that the 20-carat 'Cambridge' diamond, called after Lady Mary Cambridge, was set into a necklace, and in 1930 a 69.67-carat diamond drop, the 'Excelsior', spent some time in the London shop.[21] The stone was procured, like the Maria Theresa diamond drops, by the dealer Bienenfeld. Used by Cartier's to embellish a three-strand diamond necklace, the 'Excelsior' was the largest of twenty-one stones produced by the cutting of the original rough stone in 1903.

In 1931, Cartier London received one of the most remarkable diamonds ever, a sparkling olive-green brilliant of 12.86 carats. Other green stones known to exist by this time were the apple-green drop diamond of Augustus the Strong in Dresden, and a 6.40-carat stone owned by the King of England. Jacques Cartier had been offered the olive-green diamond by the wife of the Cairo jeweller Buchinger. Originally an oval stone of

opposite
404 Design for the most precious cascade of coloured diamonds known to history, the ceremonial necklace of the Maharaja of Nawanagar, devised by Jacques Cartier, 1931 (see p. 256). It consists of two strands of round diamonds linked by fancy-pink stones. The first stone of the pendant is a 9.50-carat pink diamond; below that is an azure-blue stone of 26.26 carats; below that 'the world's most beautiful pink stone', of 22.97 carats; the centrepiece of the pendant is the 'Queen of Holland', a blue white diamond of 136.32 carats; the pendant terminates in a very rare olive-green diamond of 12.86 carats and a pink stone of 15.62 carats

Projet N°3

FINAL PROJET ACCEPTED

ROUND DIA
NAVETTES
STOCK.

3.10   2.04   1.94   3.69   4.61

4.35   5.15

5.35

3.74   3.23

Jam Saheb's
necklace

5.44   2.96   2.47   6.34
6.26   2.35   2.80   5.13
7.40   3.18   2.64   6.47
8.31   3.65   3.02   6.65
9.00   4.17   3.36   7.33
       5.50   3.51   8.63
9.15   5.56   4.83
11.50   6.17   9.60
14.43 5.71   7.97   13.40
              6.65 JAM'S PINK 9.50
                              6.91
                              8.20
13.89 JAM'S   12.23   13.58
LOOSE STONE   JAM'S LOOSE STONE

16.25   13.85   12.95
17.43   14.44   20.00   15.95
                              JAM SAHEB'S
Jam Saheb's   necklace
necklace

JAM'S OWN STONES The late
                   pink sapphire
                   been

GREEN DIA SUPPLIED 12.84

TREFOIL STOCK RING

PINK DIA 15.62 STOCK R

17.5 carats, it was said to come from the collection of the Nizam of Hyderabad. Through one of his friends it was sold to Princess Natalia Narishkin; after the war it came back onto the market and was recut in Antwerp to 12.86 carats. In 1931 Jacques Cartier attached it to the great necklace for the Maharaja of Nawanagar [404], where, together with the pink diamond, it formed the lowermost tip of the cascade of coloured diamonds which remains unique in the history of jewelry to this day (see p. 256).

In 1933 the talk was of three other legendary diamonds – the 'Pasha', the 'Nassak' and the 'Porter Rhodes'. It seems that Ibrahim Pasha of Egypt had bought the diamond that was to bear his title for £28,000 in 1848. How and when it left Egypt is unknown, but in 1933 the London company of T. M. Sutton offered it to Cartier's. The trail then vanishes until the 'Pasha' turned up in Egypt again, and was later bought from King Farouk by the Italian jewellers Bulgari and sold to Barbara Hutton. The slightly octagonal form of the stone did not appeal to this capricious customer: she had it recut at Cartier's to 38.19 carats and set in a ring, which sparkled on her finger in India, Palm Beach and Monte Carlo [407].[22]

The 'Nassak' (still called the 'Nassuck' in the nineteenth century) was, like the 'Idol's Eye', supposed to have been taken from the eye of a temple god. The stone belonged to the family of the Duke of Westminster for nearly a century before he sold it to the jeweller Georges Mauboussin, who exhibited it in America in 1926. In 1933 Cartier's were preparing various designs for a crown and a turban at the request of the Gaekwar of Baroda. Jacques Cartier suggested that the prince should buy the 'Nassak', which had come onto the market, so that it could be introduced as the central stone in the turban ornament. The Gaekwar let the crown project lapse, but all the same the 'Nassak' found its way to Cartier London, where the designer Frederick A. Mew used it to embellish a five-string pearl and diamond necklace. In 1936 Cartier's exhibited the 'Nassak' at their Monte Carlo branch, opened the year before, and in 1937 the 80.60-carat triangular stone was recut as a rectangular stone of 47.41 carats.[23]

'The most precious square diamond in the world', Cartier's called the 'Porter Rhodes' while it was on their premises in 1933. The original 73-carat diamond, seemingly sold by the Duke of Westminster, was recut to 56.60 carats by the London firm of Jerwood & Ward. Cartier's acquired it from the estate of Solly B. Joel, the diamond mine owner, with the King of Nepal in mind.[24] In the event, however, it was sold to Sir Ernest Oppenheimer, passed later to the Maharaja of Indore, and was bought from him by Harry Winston in 1946.

405, 406 The 'Jubilee' diamond made into a brooch. Cartier Paris, 1937. Platinum; the 245.35-carat stone, cut with 88 facets, gave its name to a new cut, a combination of rose- and brilliant-cut (actual size)

In December 1935 Cartier Paris mounted a great display of historic diamonds, among them the 'Jubilee'. This stone had been cut to 245.35 carats in 1897, the year of Queen Victoria's jubilee. It was displayed at the Paris Exposition of 1900, at which time it was already valued at Fr. 7,000,000 ($1,400,000). In 1935 this diamond, the world's fourth-largest cut, was sent for sale to Cartier London by the heirs of Sir Dorab Tata, a rich Parsi of Bombay. Again, the firm looked first to the Gaekwar of Baroda, who in 1928 had appointed Cartier's as 'the only adviser for purchases of precious stones in the whole world'. The firm's representatives were prepared to hand over the 'Jubilee' to the Indian ruler in a Wiesbaden hotel at an asking price of £75,000. But the Gaekwar, who wanted the diamond for the State treasury, sought authorization for the purchase from the treasury department in Baroda. Although in 1937 he was still receiving the department's vigorous encouragement, he decided he was too old and declined to buy, as in 1933 he had declined the crown. So in 1937 Cartier's sold the 'Jubilee' to Paul-Louis Weiller. The original dramatic setting as a turban aigrette, conspicuous against a background of white heron feathers, was transformed by Jeanne Toussaint into a brooch with baguette diamonds, suggestive of either a six-pointed star or a stylized turtle [405, 406].

In 1935 there was talk of a 50½-carat pink diamond which was to be recut at Cartier's as a 30-carat drop. A far more important talking point, however, was the historic 32.82-carat 'Cumberland' diamond. Although in the end Cartier's decided not to buy it because of its 'banal colour and shape', this diamond was the subject of an episode in the firm's history both dramatic and comic. It was given its name because it had been presented, in 1746, to the Duke of Cumberland by the City of London. Cartier's first exhibited it, together with the 'Nassak', in Monte Carlo in 1936. In 1938 Jacques Cartier and the salesman Marcel Marson made a business trip to Albania, where the marriage of King Zog I and his Hungarian Queen, née Geraldine Apponyi, was being celebrated. They were startled by the contrast between the brilliant receptions in the Durazzo palace and the 'unimaginable poverty in Tirana'. The bride selected a few pieces of jewelry, while the King appraised the 'Cumberland' and waved a diamond magnifying-glass about, but bought nothing. The trip would have ended in tragedy had Cartier and Marson flown back with the five carefully packed jewel chests, for the plane crashed between Tirana and Brindisi. A large part of the jewels were burnt; the remainder turned up later on the black market in Rome and Naples. The accident, however, did not deter Cartier's from returning to Albania in the autumn of the same year for the jubilee celebrations of the tenth year of the King's reign. Marson took more than a hundred pieces, including the 'Cumberland' again and a pair of diamond drops of 35.57 carats, on this new expedition. The temperature in Tirana was 38 ºC, it was unthinkable to telephone Paris, and the telegraphic connection was constantly interrupted, with the result that the code devised expressly for this journey was quite useless: ANTELOPE = King Zog; EAGLE = the King wants; BEE = the king is favourably inclined; WEASEL = the king's sister; PLUM = tiara; BANANA = gold; DATE = diamond ring; FIG = emerald ring. The King, who was urgently awaiting credits from Rome, changed his mind every day and finally made such a risible offer for the important stones that Marson turned his back on Albania with the philosophical comment: 'Cartier does not go a-begging.'

In 1938, the salesman Fernand Teneau asked for the 'Cumberland' for the St Moritz branch, founded in 1930.[25] In the Engadine mountain village Lady Deterding, Countess Haugwitz-Reventlow (Barbara Hutton), the von Opels and the Harrison Williamses ruled as uncrowned monarchs, and their presence justified the inclusion in Cartier's display of not only the 'Cumberland' but also a magnificent 49.64-carat navette diamond and a rectangular diamond weighing 33.68 carats. Furthermore, the director of the Afghan National Bank was also staying in St Moritz and held significant credits from the King of Afghanistan for the purchase of jewels.

In the Cartier archive for 1937, there is mention of a 38.85-carat diamond in the shape of a spearhead, reminiscent in outline of Prince Yusupov's 'Ram's Head' diamond. In the same year Annie, Viscountess Cowdray, deposited her black pearls with Cartier London, and Mrs Horace Dodge (then Mrs Dillman) paid $115,000 dollars for the most sensational ruby of the time from Cartier New York; the stone, named after King Thibaw of Burma (r. 1878–85), weighed 26.13 carats and had previously belonged to J. P. Morgan, from whose daughter Pierre Cartier had acquired it.[26]

During the Second World War the Canadian geologist John T. Williamson became famous for his discovery in Tanganyika (now Tanzania) of what was then the world's largest diamond mine. In 1947, after tough negotiations, he sold it to Sir Ernest Oppenheimer. That same year the mine yielded a rose diamond weighing 54 carats in the rough, which Williamson gave as a wedding present to Princess Elizabeth. The remarkable stone was recut in London to a rose-coloured brilliant of 23.60 carats and inspired Frederick A. Mew of Cartier's to design an edelweiss brooch with the diamond set in its heart [408, 409].[27]

In 1961 Cartier's bought the emerald jewelry of the Empress Eugénie at Stuker's auction house in Berne. The collection comprised a necklace, ring and brooch in a clumsy twentieth-century Madrid setting, with nine emeralds which may have come from the tiara made for the Empress by the jeweller Lemonnier. Eugénie had bequeathed the emeralds, hidden in a fan case, to her goddaughter the Queen of Spain, who did not at first realize its value and casually put it aside. Cartier's set the emeralds as the pendant motifs of a large diamond necklace.[28]

Four years later Cartier New York sold the 'Vega' navette diamond, a 14-carat stone named after the star. In 1971 Rosemarie Kenmore, wife of the then president of the firm, discovered a 38.71-carat cushion-shaped, canary-coloured diamond in India. Named after her, it was to feature in many subsequent exhibitions.

The interest in these stones, however, paled before the publicity surrounding the 69.42-carat diamond drop associated with Elizabeth Taylor [396, 410, 411]. In 1967 the stone was sold by Harry Winston to Mrs Harriet Annenberg Ames, and it turned up in 1969 as the centrepiece of an auction at Parke-Bernet, New York. Then the 56th largest cut diamond in the world, it challenged its admirers to find a fanciful name for it after Parke-Bernet promoted it as the 'No Name Diamond' and flew it out to the film star in

407 Barbara Hutton wearing the emeralds of Grand Duchess Vladimir in a tiara [p. 248, D] and the 38.19-carat 'Pasha' diamond set in a ring, 1947. Photograph by Cecil Beaton

overleaf, left

408 Portrait of Queen Elizabeth II with her daughter, Princess Anne. She is wearing the edelweiss diamond brooch made by Cartier in 1953 [410]. Photograph by Marcus Adams

overleaf, right

409 Brooch in the form of an edelweiss, with a stem of baguette-cut diamonds, two leaves in marquise-cut diamonds, and petals in brilliant-cut diamonds, 1953. In the centre is the 'Williamson' pink diamond, weighing 23.60 carats

opposite

410 The 'Burton-Taylor' diamond weighing
69.42 carats [**397**], set as a pendant, given to
Elizabeth Taylor by Richard Burton in 1969
(reduced: cp. **396**)

below

411 Elizabeth Taylor during the 42nd
Academy Awards ceremony in 1970. She
is wearing the 'Burton-Taylor' diamond
in a necklace

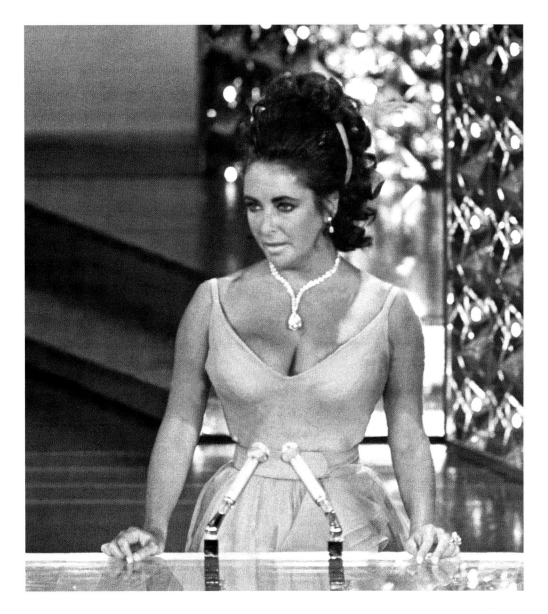

Switzerland. However, at the auction on that memorable 23 October, the stone was bought not by Miss Taylor but by Cartier's, for $1,050,000. Four days later they sold it on, at a nominal profit, to Richard Burton for $1,100,000.

Before it was handed over to Burton's representative, however, Cartier's exhibited the million-dollar stone in New York and Chicago – one of the biggest publicity successes of the 1960s, which provoked the *New York Times* to make the malicious comment that peasants were forming lines to gape at 'a diamond as big as the Ritz'. It has been known ever since as the 'Cartier' or 'Burton-Taylor' diamond.[29]

For the time being, the last in the long line of illustrious gems which have passed through Cartier's over the past eight decades is the 107.07-carat flawless drop-shaped diamond cut in 1976 and subsequently sold to a European collector [**395**]. Symbolically, it was christened with the name of the man who had instilled in the firm its standard of perfection: 'Louis Cartier'.

NOTES

INTRODUCTION (pp. 7–9)

[1] This incident, which took place in Paris, is retold here in Glaenzer's own words. In 1908–9 he travelled with the pearl expert Maurice Richard to Singapore, Saigon, Hong Kong, Canton, Shanghai and Bombay. In Bangkok he was granted an audience with the King, to whom Fabergé also showed his wares at the time.

[2] The Duke of Windsor, *A King's Story*, London 1951, p. 51.

1. FROM APPRENTICE TO COURT JEWELLER (pp. 12–19)

[1] The witnesses to the marriage were the seed-merchant J.-F. Benard and the carpenter Jean Tandonnet. Also present were Pierre Cartier's paternal uncle and Jean-Pierre and Jacques-Noël Cartier, both coach-painters by profession.

[2] According to the *Almanach du Commerce*, Picard is known to have worked in the rue Montorgueil since 1834. He should not be confused with the goldsmith and *bijoutier* of the same name who was Jouquoy's successor and who produced silver snuff-boxes, lighters, etc.

[3] Princess Mathilde's purchases began in 1856. In 1861/62 Cartier sold her a bracelet decorated with the imperial bees. Interestingly, that may have been included in the auction of her jewels, held after her death in 1904 (lot 141).

[4] Princess Cristina Belgiojoso (1808–71) had settled in Paris in 1831, where her salon was the meeting-place for many exiled politicians. In 1848 she hurried back to Milan to help in the uprising against Austria, contributing a battalion of volunteers. In 1855–56 she embarked on a Grand Tour of the Orient.

[5] See Henri Vever, *La Bijouterie française au XIXème siècle*, Paris 1906, p. 108.

[6] One of Léonide Leblanc's most valuable jewels was a blue diamond ring, which was sold after her death, ostensibly as an item of historic interest. Her collection of jewels was auctioned between 29 July and 4 August 1891, while the actress was still alive. Her famous four-strand necklace of 212 pearls weighing 3,300 grains fetched Fr. 181,000. Since Cartier did not sign his jewels, it is impossible to tell which of the pieces may have been his. The only signed items were by Rouvenat.

[7] Not to be confused with Duc Charles de Brunswick (1804–73), a connoisseur of jewelry, who lived in a magnificent mansion in the rue de Beaujon in Paris. He moved to Geneva in 1870 and left his vast fortune to the town; it was there, too, that his collection of jewels was auctioned.

[8] See Vever, cit. at n. 5, p. 252.

[9] In a letter dated 25 August 1873 to his son Alfred, Louis-François Cartier wrote: 'Prosper is drawing in the sales ledger . . . , just as you would do.'

[10] The term 'galvanoplasty' derives from the name of the Italian physiologist Luigi Galvani (1737–98), who in 1791 developed his theory of animal electricity on the basis of an experiment on frogs' legs. The galvanoplastic process is a technique by which a layer of silver is dissolved in a chemical solution and then fused on to a metal base by means of an electric charge.

[11] See Geoffrey Munn, *Castellani and Giuliano, Revivalist Jewellers of the Nineteenth Century*, London 1984.

[12] The French sculptor Jean-Baptiste Carpeaux (1827–75) created *Dance* for the front of the Paris Opéra in 1869. The building itself was the work of Charles Garnier (1825–98).

[13] The jeweller Robin was one of Cartier's suppliers and was the first to popularize matt gold in France, a fashion that was already known in England at the time. The gold was dipped in an acid bath, which caused a thin layer of chemically pure gold to form on the surface, thus producing the desired matt effect.

[14] Girandoles were originally candelabra with several arms, but during the seventeenth and eighteenth centuries they became a popular motif for brooches and ear jewelry in the form of three pendant drop-shaped stones.

[15] One of the jewellers who took up the fashion for animal jewelry was Hubert Obry (1808–53), who specialized chiefly in animals of the hunt.

[16] The firm of Plisson et Hartz produced chimaeras, lizards, crabs and turtles, while Charles Marie, Jr, produced dragonflies, frogs and crabs.

[17] See Marie-Noël de Gary, *Les Fouquet: bijoutiers et joailliers à Paris, 1860–1960*, Paris *c*. 1983.

[18] See Vever, cit. at n. 5, p. 706.

2. RUE DE LA PAIX (pp. 22–29)

[1] The planned marriage between Princess Victoria, who was a daughter of Edward VII, and Prince George of Greece came to nothing, as did subsequent plans for her to marry the Earl of Rosebery. Prince George married Marie Bonaparte in 1907; Rosebery did not remarry, and Princess Victoria remained a spinster. In 1902 she bought a tiara from Cartier's.

[2] Described by the novelist and travel-writer Louis Enault (1824–1900), who was also the author of *Les Diamants de la Couronne*, 1884.

[3] Following Boucheron's move to the Place Vendôme in 1893, the square became Paris's second most important centre for jewelry. Lalique established himself there in 1905 (no. 24), the same year as Chaumet (first at no. 15 and, from 1907, at no. 12). They were joined in 1906 by Van Cleef & Arpels (no. 22) and by Cardeilhac (no. 24) and in 1945 by Mauboussin (no. 20).

[4] In 1190 King Philippe Auguste granted statutes to perfume makers together with glovemakers, which is why the guilds' coats-of-arms contained three gloves. The two guilds remained associated until the end of the eighteenth century, and as late as 1815, on the eve of the Battle of Waterloo, Napoleon received a pair of perfumed gloves from Houbigant.

[5] Jacques Doucet, the 'poet of the cravat', famous as a patron of the fine and decorative arts, entered his father's firm in 1875, the year of Louis Cartier's birth. He later added a fashion department.

[6] Most of the buildings in the rue de la Paix have a central main entrance leading to an inner courtyard, with shops to the left and right of the entrance. This explains the otherwise rather confusing fact that two shops regularly have the same number.

[7] While the salerooms were decorated in Louis XVI style, various changes were made between 1926 and 1937 to bring them more into line with contemporary taste. One such alteration was the introduction of display cabinets in the Cubist spirit of Art Deco. They were supplied by the firm of Fred Sage, which had branches in both London and Paris.

[8] See Anita Lesley, *Edwardians in Love*, 1974, p. 18.

[9] In 1924 Cartier New York bought Dreicer's stock for $2.5 million. Dreicer's collection of paintings went to the Metropolitan Museum of Art.

[10] Cartier New York's stock was valued at Fr. 6,325,183 in 1911, a figure made up as follows: jewels Fr. 4,152,477; precious stones Fr. 1,472,272; gold and silverware Fr. 700,434.

[11] During the 1920s the New York workshops became known as the 'American Art Works'. Housed in Cartier's premises in Fifth Avenue, they employed up to seventy jewellers and goldsmiths working under the supervision of Paul Duru (1871–1971). The chief stone-setter was Paul Maîtrejean (1883–1975), who set the 'Hope' diamond. At a later date, his son Philippe Maîtrejean (b. 1914) designed a golden handbell set with a 970-carat aquamarine. The jeweller Dominik Sala was regarded as New York's leading expert in his chosen field. The number of employees was reduced to around twenty-five following the outbreak of the Second World War, and in 1941 the workshop was shut down completely. After the war, Cartier signed an exclusive contract with the independent firm of Wors & Pujol, which was housed under the same roof as the jewellers. They were taken over in 1974 by Henry Larrieu, who had been Pierre Cartier's last apprentice between 1938 and 1941. In turn, Larrieu's father had been the American Art Works' *donneur d'or*, responsible for distributing the amounts of precious metal required by the various goldsmiths.

A second workshop, known as the 'Marel Works', housed on the opposite side of the road in 52nd Street, specialized in gold objects such as picture frames, trophies and vanity cases. It was taken over by Cartier's in the 1950s.

[12] Maurice Duvallet left Cartier New York in 1920, and Alexandre Genaille remained behind as their principal designer. Duvallet then worked for Charlton (1933–39) and for Van Cleef & Arpels (1943–63). He was responsible for the ballerina brooches that Van Cleef & Arpels launched in the 1940s.

The most talented of Cartier's designers in New York during the 1940s and 1950s was Maurice Daudier. He had previously worked for Cartier in Paris and London, and designed jewelry for Mrs Merriweather Post and Mrs Donahue, among others, before his retirement in 1963.

Alfred Duranti (b. 1940) was engaged as a designer by Claude Cartier in 1956, at a time when the workshop employed six designers. He designed the pearl and ruby necklace for the 'La Peregrina' pearl as well as a diamond necklace for the engraved 'Mogol' diamond, both of which were bought by Richard Burton for his then wife, Elizabeth Taylor.

[13] In 1935 Paul Iribe published *Rue de la Paix, Place Vendôme, vitrine de la France*. Cartier's neighbours in the 1930s were the antique dealer Jacques Seligmann et Fils to the left, and the fashion house Martial et Armand to the right. Of the jewellers there in the nineteenth century Mellerio, Chocarne, Aucoc, Fontana and Vever remained. At no. 2 was the jeweller Rozanès. No. 4, the building that housed Alfred Cartier's office, was also the address of René Linzeler, the gold- and silversmith. Cartier sold his silverware, cutlery and candlesticks, some of which were designed by Paul Iribe with his characteristic rose motif. In the rue de la Paix, Linzeler went into partnership with Marchak from Kiev, while his second workshop, at 9 rue d'Argenson, was taken over by Cartier at the outbreak of the Second World War. LaCloche, at 15 rue de la Paix (founded in 1897 and until 1901 at 28 Place Vendôme), had by then gone into liquidation. At no. 17 were the jeweller Morgan and Berlioz Leroy, successor to Paul Hamelin. At no. 18 was Polak, and at no. 19 Albert Janesich, who closed down in 1932. Marzo, who had been associated with Eugène Laillet in 1911, was at no. 20. Tiffany remained at no. 25, but the New York branches of Spaulding and Charlton had closed down.

3. THE GARLAND STYLE (pp. 33–57)

[1] See Henri Clouzot, *Le Style Renaissance en France au XIXème siècle*, Paris 1936.

[2] See Rudolf Berliner and Gerhart Egger, *Ornamentale Vorlageblätter des 15 bis 19. Jahrhunderts*, Munich 1981.

[3] Cartier had bought an ornamental fibula as early as 1873. Louis Cartier's library, which contained one of the foremost collections of eighteenth-century illustrated books, was looked after from 1929 by Louis Devaux, Fernand Teneau and François de Bolvary. Devaux (b. 1907) was the president of Cartier Paris from 1942 to 1946 and of Cartier New York from 1946 to 1949, when he became president of Shell in France.

[4] Between 1900 and 1910 a number of designers engaged by Cartier had been trained in wrought ironwork, for instance Henri Chenaud, who had previously worked for Baguès. Olivier Baloche had worked on tapestry design, which, like lacemaking, was one of Louis Cartier's particular interests.

[5] In New York, pearl lace was still a great novelty for jewels as late as 1910.

[6] Eve Lavallière made her debut in 1891 at the Théâtre des Variétés. She had previously worked in a hat factory, tying ribbons or cravats known as *lavallières*, from which she derived her stage-name (her real name was Eve Ferroglio). She died in a convent in 1929.

[7] The lovebirds motif is found in Cartier's designs as early as 1881. In 1900 he produced a pendant with an altar and doves. In the eighteenth century there had been a fashion for engagement rings with doves, which were symbols of love and fidelity.

[8] Shoulder knots were known in the eighteenth century. An important example dating from 1768 is in the Grünes Gewölbe in Dresden.

[9] Nancy Leeds' emerald epaulette was reset in 1921, when it was combined with the emeralds from a lavallière dating from 1911 to produce the large emerald necklace worn by Mrs Leeds in László's portrait of her [77]. In 1926, after her death, Cartier was commissioned by her executors to sell her jewelry, and a number of her emeralds were bought by Lady Deterding.

[10] Gilles Légaré (b. c. 1610) was a Paris goldsmith and enameller whose clients included Louis XIV. His book *Livre des ouvrages d'orfèvrerie* became the most important seventeenth-century work on ornamental design for jewellers and goldsmiths.

[11] Sévignés are also referred to as *dauphines* and *cravates dauphine* in Cartier's records.

[12] See A. E. Fersman, *Les Joyaux du trésor de Russie,* 1926, pls LIII, LVIII, LXI.

[13] Curved, three-dimensional bows were a speciality of French workshops. As late as 1910 Cartier had difficulty introducing the techniques involved in making them to New York.

[14] See Fersman, cit. at n. 12, pls XLV, LVII.

[15] By around 1830, lace from Flanders, Venice, England and France had begun to suffer the effects of competition from the new machine-made variety. As a result, the numbers entering the profession fell to the point where it was feared in Normandy that the famous *point d'Alençon* would disappear altogether. The situation was saved by Queen Margherita of Italy, who established a workshop on the island of Burano; both the Empress of Austria and the last Tsarina of Russia lent their support to the ailing craft.

[16] Platinum is one of a group of six metals, with iridium, osmium, palladium, rhodium and ruthenium. Small additions of iridium produce an alloy of the required hardness.

[17] The backing of silver with gold in the eighteenth and nineteenth centuries was intended to strengthen the soft silver setting and to prevent the oxidizing metal from coming into direct contact with the skin or with clothes.

[18] See D. MacDonald, *A History of Platinum*, London 1960.

[19] In 1782 Antoine Laurent Lavoisier oxidized platinum, an experiment observed by Benjamin Franklin; but the commercial production of platinum still lay some way ahead.

[20] It was not until 1804 that the English scientist William Hyde Wollaston successfully produced a practicable form of malleable platinum. It was also Wollaston who discovered palladium and rhodium.

[21] Jean-Baptiste Fossin was the head of François Nitot's workshop. He later took over the business and established himself in the rue de Richelieu. In 1845 he handed over the firm to his son Jules, who in turn sold it to Prosper Morel in 1854. Joseph Chaumet (1854–1928) married Morel's daughter.

[22] As against an annual production of only 5,900 kilograms. The difference was due to melting down old pieces. Ninety per cent came from Russia, the rest from Colombia and the United States. The price per kilogram in 1895 was Fr. 3,000, compared with Fr. 10,000 in 1822, the year platinum was discovered in the Urals. In 1870 it was as low as Fr. 1,560, following the failure of the Russian experiment. At the end of 1900 a gramme of platinum cost between Fr. 2.95 and Fr. 3.00 in New York. Every month Cartier New York workshops required two kilograms of platinum 3mm thick, in addition to 300 grammes of 20 per cent platinum wire and 300 grammes of 15 per cent platinum wire. Although America had its own deposits, Cartier's imported the platinum they required, duty-free, from the Paris-based firms of Lyon Allemand and Caplain Saint-André. New platinum deposits were discovered between the two world wars: in the early 1980s South Africa produced 75 per cent of the world market, while the remaining 25 per cent came from Canada, the Soviet Union, Zimbabwe, Colombia and the United States.

[23] In Paris a new, far cheaper alloy, magnalium, was first used in 1902. It was produced by mixing aluminium with 10–25 per cent magnesium, the resultant alloy weighing less than the somewhat lustreless aluminium on its own.

[24] Oscar Massin had made aigrettes with lily-of-the-valley settings around 1860–70. The Rosenborg Collection in Copenhagen contains a number of eighteenth-century jewels with this type of setting.

[25] A letter dated 3 December 1900 indicates that it was through Worth that Cartier first heard of the Grand Duchess Vladimir's charity bazaars in St Petersburg. The Grand Duchess was later to make it possible for Cartier to set up in Russia (see Chapter 7).

[26] The Directoire style came back into fashion in 1888 as a result of Sarah Bernhardt's appearances in Sardou's *Tosca*.

[27] The 'Récamier' hairstyle was popularized by the actress Marguerite Brésil.

[28] According to the 1903 edition of the *Revue de la bijouterie, joaillerie et orfèvrerie*, there was considerable demand for turquoise jewelry at the time, especially in London. Lady Londonderry, the arch rival of Cartier's regular patron, Lady de Grey, owned a magnificent turquoise tiara, as did Baroness Leopold de Rothschild and Mrs Cavendish-Bentinck.

[29] Cravats were a special kind of lavallière, a velvet ribbon overlapping at the front, with diamond tips.

[30] Among Marie Bonaparte's acquaintants at an earlier period had been Alexander Graham Bell and Pierre Curie. In 1925 she moved to Vienna, where she became a colleague and supporter of Sigmund Freud. She was fond of rubies: the engagement ring which Cartier designed for her was set with a ruby of 2.37 carats. She was given a ruby and diamond brooch by the King of Greece, and from her fiancé she received a ruby cross and, on the first anniversary of their engagement, a ruby and pearl sautoir.

[31] Cartier had used onyx in items of mourning jewelry as early as 1910, in pieces made for the Widener and McLean families.

[32] Four of Cartier's leading customers went down with the *Titanic*: J. J. Astor, George and Henry Widener, and Edgar J. Meyer.

[33] Caroline Otéro (1868–1964) enjoyed the patronage of Leopold II of Belgium, and was often to be seen literally 'covered with jewels' that had been bestowed on her by Albert of Monaco, the Shah of Persia, Muzaffar-ed-Din, the Khedive of Egypt and Baron Ollestreder of Berlin. She once appeared at the Paris Opéra triply decorated with a necklace of the Empress Eugénie's, a necklace

that had belonged to the Empress of Austria, and the famous pearl necklace of Léonide Leblanc. In her hair she wore a glittering diamond tiara, and as ear studs two diamonds each weighing 50 carats.

Cartier also had dealings with the actress Wanda de Boncza of the Comédie-Française. Her collection of jewels, auctioned in 1902, included twelve 'bodice or hair ornaments' of unspecified origin, together with a black drop pearl from Cartier's weighing 29¼ grains, which was sold for Fr. 21,700. Cartier's customers included other celebrated actresses, such as Eleonora Duse, Geneviève Lantelme, Gabrielle Dorziat, Gaby Deslys, Gabrielle Réjane, Cécile Sorel, Lillie Langtry, Forzane and Mistinguett. Emilienne d'Alençon, who for many years was a rival of 'la belle Otéro', appears in Cartier's archives between 1903 and 1922. Polaire ordered a diamond belt 42 cm long.

[34] In 1901 Cartier's dismantled a number of items of Olga de Meyer's jewelry, including twelve brooches, seven bracelets and three necklaces, which were reset as new pieces. That same year, they sent a cabochon ruby and diamond brooch to Olga de Meyer in Bayreuth.

[35] The album contained texts by Rodin, Jacques-Emile Blanche and Jean Cocteau, and was dedicated to Cartier's customer, the Marchioness of Ripon, formerly Lady de Grey. It was she who brought the Ballets Russes to England and received Nijinsky at her family home, Coombe Court.

[36] See American *Vogue*, December 1917.

4. TIARAS (pp. 61–83)

[1] Gabriel-Louis Pringué, *Trente ans de dîners en ville*, Paris 1948, pp. 122, 104.

[2] Stephen Birmingham, *The Grandes Dames*, New York 1982, p. 32.

[3] Joseph J. Thorndike, *The Very Rich*, New York 1981, p. 53.

[4] Consuelo Vanderbilt Balsan, *The Glitter and the Gold*, New York 1952, p. 152.

[5] Andrew Barrow, *Gossip*, London 1978, p. 174.

[6] What is probably the earliest pictorial representation of a diadem in the form of a helmet band survives in a battle scene depicting Tuthmosis III (1504–1450 BC). The pharaoh can be seen wearing a kind of crown/helmet; around it, as a sign of his rank as military leader, a diadem is wound, the loose ends of which are tied together to form a knot. On the later mummy of Tutankhamun (1371–1352 BC), the fabric ribbon and its two loose ends are reproduced in gold for the first time. In spite of its importance in Egyptian culture, the diadem was not an Egyptian invention. It appears contemporaneously in Median cultures, from which it passed to Persia in the sixth century BC, and was regarded as a sign of royal dignity from the time of Alexander the Great onward.

One of the jewels to survive from the Twelfth Dynasty of Egypt's Middle Kingdom (1929–1717 BC) is Princess Khumet's floral wreath of gold, lapis lazuli, cornelian, turquoise and enamel. Garlands such as this, which were a second source of inspiration for the modern tiara, were further adapted during the Mycenaean period as well as by the Etruscans.

The diadem reappeared as a fillet in 325 during the reign of Constantine the Great, and from then on only the emperor had the right to wear it. At the same time, the diadem developed into a closed circlet which no longer needed fastening. Geometrical uprights were first added in 438 by the Byzantine Princess Licinia – a design which was to result centuries later in the medieval open crown decorated with plaques. In the reign of the Emperor Justinian (483–565), the golden circlet was adorned with arches crossing at the apex, an idea derived from the military commander's strap helmet. This design culminated in the arched crown familiar in the West, a form reserved for emperors and kings. In addition to its function as a symbol of sovereignty, the diadem was also a symbol of any high office in Byzantine and early medieval art. The Ravenna mosaics, for example, show angels wearing white diadems.

[7] A painting long attributed to Leonardo da Vinci depicting Lucrezia Crivelli, known as *La Belle Ferronnière* (the beautiful wife of the blacksmith), sparked off the fashion for *ferronnières* in France.

5. ART NOUVEAU · RELIGIOUS THEMES · THE FIRST WORLD WAR (pp. 87–89)

[1] On the occasion of the 1900 Paris Exposition, the *Revue de la bijouterie, joaillerie et orfèvrerie*, lending its support to the Art Nouveau movement, complained that 'Messrs Falize Frères have remained all too loyal to the ornaments, bows and aigrettes of Gilles Légaré and Maria & Babel'. It was a criticism aimed at all those firms producing garland-style jewelry.

[2] The term 'Art Nouveau' comes from the name of a gallery opened in Paris by the Hamburg art dealer Samuel Bing (d. 1905) at 22 rue de Provence. It was later run by his son Marcel (d. 1920). Its main rival was the 'Maison Moderne' of the German art critic Julius Meier-Graefe.

[3] Goethe's *Faust* was translated by Gérard de Nerval and illustrated by Eugène Delacroix in 1827. Gounod's version dates from 1859. In his *La Bijouterie française au XIXème siècle*, Paris 1906, Henri Vever mentions the year 1895 in connection with Le Turcq's 'Faust' bracelet, whereas Cartier's records list it under 1894.

[4] Another Art Nouveau portrayal of a woman's head was produced at the Plisson workshop, which was particularly famous around 1900 for its miniature animal brooches.

[5] *Plique-à-jour* is a form of transparent enamelling in which enamel surfaces of varying colours are outlined in metal. Eugène Fontenay had made a fan using this technique in 1852, following its rediscovery by the enameller Briet. Around 1864 the patent for the *plique à jour* process was held by Boucheron.

[6] The superstition regarding opals dates from the nineteenth century, when, fearing competition from the newly discovered Australian opals, Hungarian and Slovak mine owners are said to have issued dire warnings about the dangers of opals. Sir Walter Scott's 1829 novel *Anne of Geierstein*, whose heroine is killed by an opal, also influenced popular feeling.

[7] The collection is now in the Musée des Arts Décoratifs, Paris.

[8] Tiffany & Co. did something similar during the nineteenth century, when they bought up the pieces that were left over from the laying of the Transatlantic Cable and sold them in four-inch lengths.

[9] During the war, Louis Cartier served in the air corps, Jacques was a lieutenant in the dragoons, and Pierre served in the 23rd Territorial Regiment in Cherbourg.

[10] Inside were inscribed the words, 'ceinture authentique, faite d'obus de 75: Arts Union' ('authentic belt, made from a shell from the 75: Arts Union'). In 1918 Nellie Melba gave a charity recital at the Ritz in New York for the benefit of the Arts Union. She also auctioned, at $250 each, a number of Baron de Meyer's photographs, one of which was bought by Pierre Cartier. Cartier's contribution to the auction was a flag brooch set with gemstones, which sold for $1,000. The total sum raised was $5,000.

[11] Marshal Foch was elected to the Académie Française shortly after the Armistice, following in the footsteps of his illustrious predecessor, the Duc de Villars (1653–1734), who, as Marshal of France, had negotiated the Peace of Rastatt and subsequently been elected to the Academy.

6. UNDER THE SPELL OF FABERGÉ (pp. 93–101)

[1] Wooden boxes made of amaranth, ebony and Cape wood, on the other hand, came from Alexander's.

[2] Among Cartier's other suppliers in Russia were Lagoutiev of Ekaterinburg (amethyst necklaces, ashtrays and parasol handles), and a lapidary called Sourovi who specialized in carving animals.

[3] Svietchnikov, for example, demanded 50 roubles for a nephrite ashtray, whereas Woerffel wanted only 30; he also asked 20 roubles for an umbrella handle, as against Woerffel's 17. One of Svietchnikov's Orletz vases cost 450 roubles.

[4] In 1904 Pierre Cartier bought the following items from Woerffel: 8 umbrella handles made of jade, etc., 2 letter openers, 2 ashtrays, a seal in the shape of a mushroom, 2 tomatoes, 2 pears and an apple.

[5] Japanese *netsukes* were carved of wood or ivory, or made of metal, etc. They were attached to a silk cord and used for suspending various objects of everyday use from the wearer's belt.

[6] In 1907 Cartier's inventories listed over two hundred different types of animal.

[7] *Vogue* is describing the collection of Duchess Guido Sforza (née Anna Autokolsky), the daughter of the Russian sculptor whose collection of Egyptian, Chinese, Indian and Persian art was housed in Passy near Paris. See *Vogue*, 1 August 1916.

[8] Early examples of these gold and gemstone flowers can be found in Central Europe from the Renaissance onward. Since the fifteenth century the papal 'Golden Rose' had been awarded to distinguished individuals by the pope on the fourth Sunday of Lent. The Kunsthistorisches Museum in Vienna has a series of gemstone bouquets dating from the seventeenth century, and the Grünes Gewölbe in Dresden has an ornamental altar by Johann Heinrich Köhler, dating from around 1730, surmounted by three coral vases containing enamelled gemstone flowers. The Viennese jeweller Grosser was commissioned by the Empress Maria Theresa to

produce a jewelled bouquet, which she gave as a present to her husband; it is now in the Schatzkammer in the Vienna Hofburg.

9 Even before 1910 Russian goldsmiths were already looking for places to settle in Europe and America. In 1906, for example, the brothers Oscar and Nathan Heyman from Goldingen (modern Kuldiga) in north-west Russia settled in New York. They had been brought up in the tradition of Fabergé, and soon began working for Cartier, being among the first workshops in New York to use platinum.

10 It seems that Berquin-Varangoz's workshop may have provided Fabergé with flowers. Writing to Cartier from St Petersburg in 1914, Sarda describes a marguerite in a crystal vase which he had seen in Russia: it was inset with cairngorm and had a silver mount; the stem and leaves were of nephrite, and the flower and vase were housed in a glass case. He comments, 'The plant appears to me not to have been made in Russia. It looks like those from the rue de la Paix, except that it is less fussy, simpler and more lifelike.'

11 In 1906 Cartier lent Henri Lavabre Fr. 50,000. The workshop thereafter worked exclusively for Cartier's, executing their models and designs until 1921.

12 Just as Fabergé was commissioned by Grand Duke Nicholas to design a jadeite statuette of Queen Victoria, so in 1911 Cartier ordered the figurine of a Russian Grand Duke from Denisov-Uralski. It was later bought by Mrs Cavendish-Bentinck.

13 It seems that the fantastic Billiken was invented and patented by Florence Pretz in 1908.

7. IN ST PETERSBURG (pp. 104–13)

1 Gatchina is situated some 80 km to the west of St Petersburg. The palace dates from the time of Prince Orlov but was extensively rebuilt under Paul I.

2 Ian Vorres, *The Last Grand Duchess*, London 1964, p. 43.

3 Grand Duke Paul (1860–1919) was the son of Alexander II. He was married twice, first to Princess Alexandra, the daughter of King George and Queen Olga of Greece, and then in 1902 to Olga von Pistohlkors, who was first created Countess Hohenfelsen and later Princess Paley [61].

4 Following the Revolution, Grand Duchess Xenia (1875–1960) settled in England, where she disposed of her jewelry in a series of somewhat unfortunate transactions. A pearl pendant which she sold to Lady Deterding turned up at a Christie's auction in Geneva in November 1980 (lot 647).

5 The extent of the retinue which Russian princes took with them on their travels to Europe is indicated by an account of the household that accompanied the wife of Grand Duke Konstantin, sister-in-law of Alexander II, to Montreux. It consisted of four ladies-in-waiting, a French masseuse, a gentleman-in-waiting, hairdresser, jeweller-in-waiting, servants and Cossack officers.

6 Most of the French crown jewels were sold at auction in 1887 in the Pavillon de Flore at the Louvre. The bidders included the firms of Tiffany, Boucheron, Aucoc, Bapst, Garrard, Rosenau and Vever. Some of the items continued to circulate within the trade for years afterwards, while others were broken up. In the case of the present item, it is not clear whether it was taken over by Cartier in its original form, or whether it had already been reset.

7 The latter received Cheyrouze at Tsarskoe Selo shortly after Christmas, and complained about a letter he had received from Cartier: 'I am their customer: my tradesmen do not use that tone when addressing me.' In fact, Louis Cartier was anxious that protocol be strictly preserved. He wrote from Paris, rebuking Farinès for not having gone in person to present Grand Duchess Vladimir with a bouquet of flowers. Fabergé went in person to the palace to deliver his Easter eggs to the Tsarina, while those for the dowager Empress were delivered by his closest assistant and, at a later date, by his children.

8 According to a decree of Paul I dating from 1796, the crown jewels of the dynasty, as well as further inherited items, belonged to the dowager empress and not to the empress, who on state occasions was required to walk behind her mother-in-law on the arm of the emperor.

9 Boucheron had opened a branch in Moscow in 1899, furnishing it with the original wooden panelling from his first shop in the Palais-Royal.

10 Consuelo Vanderbilt recalled her visit to St Petersburg in 1902, when she bought a pink enamel snake's egg from Fabergé: 'After dinner the Grand Duchess showed me her jewels, set out in glass cases in her dressing room. There were endless parures of diamonds, emeralds, rubies and pearls, to say nothing of semiprecious stones such as turquoises, tourmalines, cat's-eyes and aquamarines.' Consuelo Vanderbilt Balsan, *The Glitter and the Gold*, New York 1952, p. 160.

11 The ruby tiara incorporating the 'Beauharnais' ruby weighing 5.22 carats was bought back by Cartier's following the Revolution. In 1921 it was bought by Nancy Leeds (by then Princess Anastasia of Greece) as a wedding present on the occasion of the marriage of her son William to Princess Xenia of Greece.

12 In February 1912 newspapers in St Petersburg carried the following announcement: 'The business community of St Petersburg intends to file an official complaint about foreign competitors with the Ministry of Trade and Industry. The individuals concerned have been involved in illegal private transactions (in hotel rooms), have not paid taxes or patent annuities, and their merchandise has not been cleared through customs.' This announcement, it must be said, was directed at traders in general, not simply at jewellers.

Cartier tried to remain in contact with his customers in Russia even when he himself no longer went there regularly. Farinès, for example, was sent off to Kiev in midsummer, travelling via Vienna, where he made an abortive attempt to call on the actress Katharina Schratt, an intimate friend of the Emperor Franz Joseph. Unfortunately, the wealthy Kiev sugar manufacturer Teretschenko proved to be less interested in large pearls than rumour had reported. He had already ordered items from Cartier's while in Cannes, and had found a pearl necklace at LaCloche's.

13 Also in 1910 the Tsarina organized a bazaar in the Kleinmichel Palace, when the Grand Duchess was also in charge of one of the stands. Among those who took part was Sarah Bernhardt, who, the next day, was led in triumph to Tsarskoe Selo.

14 Dr Emanuel Nobel, the Stockholm oil tycoon, was one of Fabergé's leading customers, ordering presents and luxury items for himself and his staff. The following spring he bought a pearl necklace and a pair of fir-cone pendants from Cartier's.

15 Now such lorgnettes are popular collectors' items with no practical function, but Cartier had to obtain the Grand Duchess's prescription from her eye specialist in St Petersburg and forward it to Paris.

16 The jewel subsequently passed into the possession of Queen Frederike of Greece, who sold it in New York after the Second World War, the proceeds going to the Hellenic Red Cross. It was bought by the Swiss collector Maurice Yves Sandoz.

17 The egg later found its way from Russia to America in somewhat mysterious circumstances, though it may have been included among paintings and furniture from some of the finest private Russian collections which were being sold to America at that time. In 1930–31 Andrew Mellon and Samuel Henry Kress began building up the National Gallery's collection in Washington and acquired a number of Russian works in this way. The Cartier egg was acquired by the Metropolitan Museum in New York in 1951, as part of the estate of Laird Shield Goldsborough. The stand, which was originally 2 cm in height, was replaced by a wooden base which is too narrow and which foreshortens the base of the egg.

18 Felix Elston, the son of Friedrich Wilhelm IV of Prussia and Countess Tiefenhausen, married Elena Sumarokov. He was the maternal grandfather of Felix Yusupov, and his own family's last male descendant.

19 See Léonard Rosenthal, *Au Jardin des gemmes*, Paris 1922, p. 274.

8. PEARLS (pp. 117–29)

1 *Le Pavillon de l'Elégance*, 1925, no. 10.

2 Marriages between Europeans and Americans which made the headlines at this time were those of Miss Goelet and the Duke of Roxburghe; Consuelo Vanderbilt and the Duke of Marlborough; Miss Grant and the Earl of Essex; Miss Jerome and George Cornwallis West; Miss King and the Marquis of Anglesey; Miss Longworth and the Comte de Chambrun; Miss Field and Prince Brancaccio; and Miss Coudert and the Marquis de Choiseul.

3 See Stephen Birmingham, *The Grandes Dames*, New York 1982, p. 41.

4 Eva Stotesbury's pearl necklace, which prompted the purchase of the Dodge pearls, consisted of 77 pearls weighing 2,225.52 grains. She had previously bought a smaller necklace from Cartier's, made up of 49 pearls weighing 656 grains.

5 The price of the Dodge pearls was exaggerated by newspapers at the time and a figure as high as $1.5 million was quoted, whereas the actual price was $825,000. Horace Dodge bought them in 1920 following the successful outcome of a $40 million lawsuit involving the Ford Motor Company.

6 According to Vever, the Empress Eugénie that same year sold a three-strand necklace of 121 pearls weighing 4,260 grains, which was bought by Loew, a former colleague of Baugrand's, for La Païva. On her death it was sold to Kraemer and then to Boucheron, who made several necklaces from it.

7 See Alphonse de Sondheimer, *Vitrine XIII*, Hamburg

1966, p. 41. Caroline Otéro, who owned a strand of these pearls, no doubt acquired them through Cartier.

8 By 1924 the necklace, which also incorporated pearls belonging to Madame Thiers' sister, Mademoiselle Dosne, had come to comprise three strands of 145 pearls weighing 2,140 grains. Also in the collection were an Indian necklace, a cross pendant, and a diamond, ruby and sapphire châtelaine. Works of art included a *Pietà* attributed to Michelangelo, two angels by Verrocchio, bronzes, ivories, etc.

9 The clasp was later acquired by Pierre Cartier for his wife Elma, who wore it as a brooch.

10 See Paul Claudel, *La Perle*, Paris 1965, p. 351.

11 Morton F. Plant (1852–1918) has been described as an industrialist, philanthropist and yachtsman. He inherited the Plant Investment Company, concerned with railways and shipping.

12 In 1970 the Landmarks Preservation Commission placed a preservation order on both this building and the one by Charles P. H. Gilbert at 4 East 52nd Street.

13 Following the death of her first husband, Mrs Mae C. Plant married William Hayward and then John E. Rovensky. She died in 1956, and on 23 January 1957 the two pearl necklaces and their accompanying case were auctioned by Parke-Bernet Galleries (lots 114–116) for $151,000, a price which reflects the market's slump in the 1950s as a result of the increased popularity of cultured pearls. Whereas at the turn of the century pearls had commanded the same prices as Old Masters, a major work by Rembrandt could now fetch at auction $2,300,000 – the price paid in 1961 for his *Aristotle Contemplating the Bust of Homer*.

Mrs Rovensky had also bought from Cartier's a spectacular pearl and diamond pendant with a 15-carat triangular diamond and five Oriental pearls weighing 472 grains, in addition to the legendary Rovensky diamond necklace. The latter had a 46.5-carat pear-shaped diamond from Tiffany & Co. as a pendant. Necklace and diamond together were sold for $385,000 at the same auction.

14 'The world's most expensive pearl necklace' was for a time owned by Cartier and offered to Edward VII, the German Emperor and the King of Portugal, among others. It may possibly be the same as a necklace recorded in Cartier's archives in 1910, made up of thirty-seven pearls weighing 947 grains. Was it perhaps offered by Mrs Leeds in part payment of the much more expensive necklace she bought from Cartier's that same year?

15 Every Easter Mrs Alice Keppel, close friend of Edward VII, would spend three weeks in Biarritz, at the Villa Eugénie, as guest of Sir Ernest Cassel. Her regular visitors included the King.

16 She subsequently became a member of the Greek royal family, through her marriage in 1921 to Prince Christopher.

17 'La Régente' was an egg-shaped drop pearl weighing 337 grains which Nitot set as part of a tiara for the Empress Marie Louise in 1811. In 1853 it was reset by Lemonnier as a breast ornament for the Empress Eugénie and was sold in 1887 under the name 'Rossel'. According to G. F. Kunz in *The Book of the Pearl*, Fabergé bought the pearl for the Yusupovs, and a surviving photograph confirms their ownership of it.

18 According to Lord Twining in his *History of the Crown Jewels of Europe*, the 'Azra' pearl was part of the Russian crown jewels until 1783. Following the Russian Revolution, it was acquired by Lydia, Lady Deterding, presumably through Cartier. Cartier's dismantled the original necklace of 110 pearls, of which the 'Azra' had been the centrepiece, resetting it as a diamond band. Lady Deterding lost the pearl in Paris. The remainder of the necklace, together with an exceptional black button pearl and a triangular diamond, formed part of the Deterding sale held by Christie's in Geneva in November 1980 (lot 648).

19 The necklace consisted of thirty black pearls weighing 937.84 grains, the largest being 73.28 grains. Catherine the Great had three children by her liaison with Prince Potemkin, known as the Demoiselles d'Engelgardt. One married a Yusupov prince, and another Count Branicki. The necklace, handed down to Count Branicki, subsequently passed into the hands of Princess Radziwill, formerly Countess Bichette Branicka, who bequeathed it to Felix Yusupov's mother.

20 Black pearls are found on the islands of Touamotu, Gambier, Fiji and the Marquesas, as well as off the coast of Panama and Mexico. Certain mineral salts present in sea-water, together with the type of plankton on which the oyster feeds, apparently combine to produce the black coloration of the pearls.

Among the most famous black pearls are a necklace made up of thirty pearls weighing 1,040 grains in the Austrian crown jewels; a necklace with seven additional drop pearls belonging to Princess Mathilde and sold in her auction in 1904 (lots 16–22); and the necklace of Annie, Viscountess Cowdray, made up of forty-three pearls weighing 882 grains, together with a spherical pearl weighing 105.6 grains. The German house of Anhalt-Dessau owned some of Europe's finest black pearls. Equally famous were the black pearls of the Empress Eugénie, who kept them to the end of her life, when they passed into the hands of Princess Clotilde, the daughter of Prince Napoléon Victor.

Nina Dyer, wife of Baron Heinrich Thyssen and later of Prince Sadruddin Aga Khan, owned a black pearl necklace made up of three strands, one of forty-nine pearls weighing 787.44 grains, one of forty-nine at 644.72 grains, and one of fifty-three at 979.52 grains. It was auctioned by Christie's in Geneva in May 1969, together with the black pearl earclips which she had also bought from Cartier's (lots 101 and 102).

21 See Alex Ceslas Rzewuski, *A travers l'invisible cristal*, Paris 1976, p. 189.

22 'La Pelegrina' is the name given to a perfectly spherical pearl of silvery lustre weighing 111½ grains. In 1818 the vice-president of the Imperial Russian Academy of Medicine, G. Fischer de Waldheim, said it was in the possession of the Zosima Brothers, Greek antique dealers in Moscow. It was presumably identical with the 27½-carat 'Reine des Perles', which had been stolen from the Garde Meubles in Paris in 1792. It was in turn stolen from the Zosima Brothers, and may have reappeared briefly in a Moscow convent shortly before 1840. It is now missing, presumed lost.

The Yusupov pearl, on the other hand, is slightly oval in shape and weighs 133.20 grains. The family is said to have acquired it in 1826. There is no truth

in Felix Yusupov's claim that it was 'La Peregrina' rather than 'La Pelegrina'. The former was handed down through the Spanish royal family from the time of Philip II until it was taken out of the country by Joseph Bonaparte in 1813. Hortense de Beauharnais gave it to her son, who later became Napoleon III, and he sold it to the Marquis of Abercorn. In 1969 it was sold at auction at Parke-Bernet Galleries, New York, to Elizabeth Taylor. The catalogue weight of 203.84 grains exactly matches that given by Lord Twining in his *History of the Crown Jewels of Europe*. Twining also puts forward the view that 'La Pelegrina' rather than 'La Peregrina' was the sister of the pearl belonging to Karl II, last heard of in 1734, and that 'La Peregrina' was the pearl given by Philip IV of Spain to his daughter Maria Teresa on the occasion of her marriage to Louis XIV, and later bought by Tatiana Yusupov. Since 'La Pelegrina' and 'La Peregrina' have frequently been confused throughout history (even the son of the Marquis of Abercorn erroneously speaks of 'La Pelegrina'), the puzzle will probably never be solved. However, since Fischer de Waldheim applies the name 'La Pelegrina' to a spherical pearl, it can only have been at a much later date that the same name was applied to the Yusupovs' oval pearl. According to G. F. Kunz in *The Book of the Pearl*, London 1908, Mr Henry Hiller of New York made enquiries about 'La Pelegrina' in St Petersburg and was shown two magnificent drop-shaped pearls.

23 Paul Claudel, *La Perle*, Paris 1965, p. 352. Claudel's son Pierre, who was a diplomat, married Pierre Cartier's daughter Marion.

24 Clarence Mackay was the son of John William Mackay, born in Dublin in 1831, who emigrated to America in 1840, and became one of the four silver barons of the Comstock Lode in Nevada, the richest ore deposit ever discovered (1859). In 1883 he founded the Commercial Cable Company in order to break Gould's monopoly both in that area and in telegraphy. Clarence's wife, Katherine Alexander Duer, was, along with Mrs Rita Lydig, one of the wealthiest of Cartier's patrons in New York.

25 Having divorced Misia in 1927, José Maria Sert married Roussy Mdivani, Alex Mdivani's sister. *The Boulevardier* said of him in 1932: 'He adores parties, the spectacle of life, but never entertains formally by way of reciprocity. Instead he sends to his hostess some exquisite bibelot chosen at Cartier's.'

26 Philip Van Rensselaer, *Million Dollar Baby*, London 1979, p. 177. In 1935 Cartier valued the pearl necklace at $500,400.

27 Following the First World War, the Austrian dealer Jacques Bienenfeld established himself in the rue Lafayette in Paris, at the same time opening branches in Bahrain, New York and London. His Paris office employed a staff of eighty. Bienenfeld invented a machine for drilling pearls and from 1924 to 1932 edited the journal *La Perle*.

28 Pearls had been revered in India for many thousands of years as holy beings associated with the gods of the Hindu pantheon, and are mentioned as such in the *Ramayana* and *Mahabharata*. According to the *Atharva-Veda*, IV, 10, the pearl is the offspring of the moon. 'There is not a single Indian who does not regard it as his sacred duty to drill at least one pearl on his wedding day' (Caire and Dufie, *La Science des pierres précieuses*, 1833).

[29] 1 grain = ¼ carat. In order to calculate the price of a pearl on the basis of its weight, the grain weight is multiplied by itself. The resultant figure is then multiplied by a factor of x according to the beauty of the individual pearl. For example, a pearl weighing 5 grains at a value of 3 x: 5 x 5 = 25 x 3 = 75. Kunz traces this formula back to Anselmus Boethius de Boodt's *Gemmarun et Lapidum Historia* of 1609, though he suspects it to have been Oriental in origin.

Just as the seeds of the carob tree (*Ceratonia siliqua*) determined the carat as a unit of weight, so the reddish-black seeds of the *Abrus precatorius* fixed the Indian *rati* as a measurement for pearls. The *rati* = ⅞ carats = 3½ grains. The pearls were weighed in *rati*, which was then converted into *chows*: 60 *chows* = 36 grains. To make the situation even more complicated, one Bahrain *chow* equalled 4 Basra *chows*, which were the same as 5 Poonah *chows*, the only measurement valid in Bombay. In contrast to natural pearls, cultured pearls are weighed in carats.

Prices were calculated in Indian rupees (70,000 rupees = Fr. 116,000). In the course of the voyage, a great deal was heard about one particular pearl, an exceptional specimen weighing 10 grains and selling at 1,200 rupees per *chow*. Because of its rarity, it fetched ninety times its weight.

[30] For an eighteenth-century *bayadère* see Kunz, *The Book of the Pearl*, ill. facing p. 346. *Bayadères* are mentioned in Cartier's records from 1891 onward.

[31] A possible model may have been the strands of pearls found in Byzantine-inspired Russian costumes, where they hang down from a hair ornament or headdress and frame the wearer's chin. See Kunz, *The Book of the Pearl*, ill. facing p. 174. In addition, Oscar Massin produced head jewelry with feathers and pendant chains 'en esclavage' in the second half of the nineteenth century.

[32] An early form of the modern cultured pearl was produced in China in the thirteenth century, and the same process was again attempted by the Swedish naturalist Carl Linnaeus (1707–78) but abandoned as being unprofitable. The method used today was invented by the Japanese researchers Tatsuhei Mise and Nishikawa, who created their first cultured pearls independently of each other in 1904. The much more famous Kokichi Mikimoto (1858–1954) acquired his patent for cultured pearls in 1916, having previously dealt in natural pearls. His technique was the same as had been used in China, but it is no longer employed today. However, Mikimoto played a more important part in the commercialization and spread of cultured pearls than any of his competitors.

9. CHARLES JACQUEAU (p. 133–39)

[1] Emile Sedeyn, *La Bijouterie, la joaillerie, la bijouterie de fantaisie au XXème siècle*, Paris 1934.

[2] At the same time Alfred Cartier took on Suzanne Ricaud as a pearl-threader. In 1914–15 she worked for a time as Louis Cartier's secretary, but then left the firm. She was one of the most sought-after pearl specialists in Paris, joining the firm of LaCloche in 1921. She married Charles Jacqueau in 1942.

[3] The earliest contact with the Ballets Russes may well have come about through Louis Cartier, who knew Diaghilev and thought highly of Leon Bakst, the company's leading set and costume designer. It was Bakst, more than anyone else, who was responsible for a style which is still generally thought of as typical of the Ballets Russes. Cartier's chief contact, however, was with the designer George Barbier, who was both a chronicler and a spectator of the Ballets Russes in Paris.

[4] In 1909 Nijinsky wore a choker in *Le Pavillon d'Armide*. According to his wife Romola, 'Nijinsky laid aside the choker, which Benois had designed for him; he failed to notice that in doing so he had launched a new fashion. At first the jewel-studded ribbon was worn low around the neckline of his costume, but he did not like it that way and so he wrapped the jewel more tightly round his neck. Cartier quickly took note of this novel idea, and socially ladies in Paris and London were soon wearing close-fitting chokers of black moiré silk, diamonds and pearls *à l'Armide*.' 'Nijinsky developed a genuine passion for sapphires, and each time they were in Paris, Sergei Pavlovitch [Diaghilev] bought him a sapphire ring from Cartier's. Vaslav claimed that he owned the finest sapphires, and he soon came to be known as the "King of Sapphires".' See Romola Nijinsky, *Nijinsky*, London 1970, pp. 73, 151.

[5] According to Harold Acton, 'for many a young artist "Schéhérazade" was an inspiration equivalent to Gothic architecture for the Romantics or Quattrocento frescoes for the Pre-Raphaelites.'

[6] Fokine's relationship with Diaghilev was similar to that of Jacqueau with Louis Cartier. In both cases there was a lively exchange of creative ideas, Diaghilev and Cartier both playing the more active roles.

[7] The greatest influence here, for Fokine and for Poiret, came from the Persian miniatures in Victor Gouloubev's collection. In 1911 the painter Valentin Serov designed the stage curtain for *Schéhérazade* to look like a Persian miniature. Louis Cartier owned a valuable collection of Persian miniatures which were exhibited in 1931 in London, and in 1933 at the exhibition of Islamic art in the Metropolitan Museum in New York.

[8] Writing in 1930 in his autobiography, *En habillant l'époque*, the fashion designer Paul Poiret, like Louis Cartier, asserted the precedence of his own unrefracted colours before those of the Ballets Russes. The influence of the Ballet Russes did not, in any case, date merely from 1909–10. The Russian artists Valentin Serov and Mikhail Vrubel had been awarded gold medals at the 1900 Paris Exposition, where their Oriental use of colour had caught the imagination of all who saw their work. In 1906 Diaghilev organized an exhibition of Russian art at the Grand Palais which came as a revelation to many people; and his 1908 production of *Boris Godunov* caused a sensation, thanks to the designs of Alexander Golovin and Alexander Benois.

[9] Calibré-cut gemstones had existed in the eighteenth and nineteenth centuries (see, for example, Cartier's Egyptian watch of 1873), but they became the height of fashion in Paris around 1902. Lapidaries who specialized in this technique were Dubois and Gouspeyre. Picq's workshop used calibré-cut gemstones from 1899 in many of the smaller items of jewelry, such as tie-pins, which they produced for Cartier.

[10] In the 1870s Boucheron made a green and blue iridescent enamel bracelet which he called 'Roue de paon' ('Peacock Fan').

[11] See Peter Hinks, *Nineteenth-Century Jewellery*, London 1975, ill. facing p. 81.

10. PHARAOHS, SPHINXES AND PYRAMIDS (pp. 142–50)

[1] Howard Carter (1873–1939), British Egyptologist. In 1899 he was appointed Inspector General of Monuments of Upper Egypt by the Egyptian government. From 1902 he supervised the excavations in the Valley of the Kings by Theodore M. Davis and afterwards worked for Lord Carnarvon.

[2] The family of George Edward Stanhope Molyneux, 5th Earl of Carnarvon, effected small purchases through Cartier from 1898, at first only at the boulevard des Italiens, among them a round brooch, a trinket pendant, a pink enamelled cane handle, a cigarette box and a large stomacher.

[3] Isis, consort of the god Osiris, whom she restored to life after his death. In pictorial representations she appears as a woman with a throne on her head. Her cult spread to Greece and Rome after Egypt came under Roman domination.

[4] Jean-François Champollion (1790–1832), French Egyptologist. Appointed to a teaching post at Grenoble as early as 1809. In 1824 he became Conservator of the Egyptian Collections at the Louvre. In 1828–29 he made an expedition to Egypt and in 1831 was appointed to the Chair of Egyptian history and archaeology at the Collège de France.

[5] The scarab is a kind of dung beetle. The comparison of the sun with it was based on the observation of the little ball of dung which the scarab pushed along the ground. It was posited, by analogy, that a similar force moved the sun across the sky day after day.

[6] The Egyptian lotus, a white waterlily (*Nymphaea lotus*), was a symbol of both fertility and the sun. In the latter aspect it was sacred to Horus, Lord of the Heavens, and to Nefertum, God of the Morning Sun, who arose each morning from a lotus blossom.

[7] A similar necklace, consisting of seven strings of flat, disc-shaped beads of blue faïence and gold, was later found in Tutankhamun's tomb.

[8] Auguste Mariette (1821–81), French Egyptologist. In 1850 he discovered the ruins of the Serapeum at Memphis, in the course of an expedition supported by the French government. In 1858 he was called to Cairo by Ismail Pasha to be Director of Ancient Monuments. He inspired the foundation of the Bulaq Museum in Cairo. Other excavations include the temple at Edfu.

[9] Gaston Maspero (1846–1916), French archaeologist, appointed Director of the Bulaq Museum and of the Antiquities Service in Egypt after Mariette's death in 1881. He continued Mariette's excavations at the Pyramid of Saqqara. He published numerous basic works in Egyptology, among them *Egyptian Archaeology* (1887).

[10] Ancient gems were being reset as early as the twelfth and thirteenth centuries, often to reinterpret their theme when it no longer had religious meaning. Later, a thirteenth-century Hohenstaufen eagle cameo was given a new context in a Viennese onyx and gold casket of about 1720 (Residenz Museum, Munich). Some time before 1722

Melchior Dinglinger mounted a Roman cameo of the Emperor Claudius in a Baroque setting for the Saxon court (Grünes Gewölbe, Dresden). More daring still, in the manner of Louis Cartier's syntheses, a Mexican Olmec mask of green pyroxenite and onyx was enlarged to a half-length figure with robe and diadem in German Baroque style and set in a bronze niche (Residenz Museum, Munich).

11 In a special Tutankhamun number of 26 January 1924, the *Illustrated London News* assembled a series of 'archaeological' jewelry pieces from Cartier London.

12 Sekhmet had a double role as the tutelary divinity of warriors and the protectress of temples.

13 As the protector of wild animals, Ched rode on a crocodile and held snakes in his hand.

14 In 1917 Hollywood produced the film *Cleopatra*; in 1923 came *The Ten Commandments* with décor by Paul Iribe, in which twenty-four sphinxes adorned the city of Ramesses II.

15 Black and white colour contrasts are found only rarely in Egyptian jewelry, mostly involving silver. Queen Nefertari, *c.* 1280 BC, owned two silver bracelets with black inlay.

16 See the apron of Senebtisi (Metropolitan Museum, New York, No. 08.200.29): Cyril Aldred, *Jewels of the Pharaohs*, London 1971, ill. 9.

11. LES INDES GALANTES (pp. 155–75)

1 It is interesting that though Lady Curzon ordered her state trousseau from Worth of Paris, she had it embroidered in India according to local patterns, which were not without their influence on design before the First World War.

2 Further contacts, still not fully explained, can be traced as early as the sixteenth century. Besides stylistic traits that point to Flanders and even Italy, the late-sixteenth-century 'Canning Jewel' includes Indian details such as a lotus-engraved ruby and an Indian pendant motif (Victoria and Albert Museum, London). It is equally unclear whether the Indian *sarpech* was influenced by gifts from Europe (see Chapter 4).

3 In 1852 the 'Koh-i-Noor' was reduced from 186.06 carats to 106 1/16 carats in a rose-cut by the Dutchman Voorsanger. Queen Victoria wore it in a brooch, in a bracelet or in a hair circlet. Queen Alexandra wore it in her crown. In 1911 it adorned the crown of Queen Mary and it is now in the crown made for Queen Elizabeth (the Queen Mother) for her coronation in 1937.

4 Boucheron displayed pierced diamonds, the work of the cutter Bordinckx, in the 1867 Exhibition. In 1880 he created a ring from a block-shaped diamond, and in 1889 he (and Legrand) produced diamond roundels. Boucheron showed diamonds engraved with flowers in the 1900 Exhibition.

5 *Champlevé*, literally 'raised field'. An enamelling technique in which cells are cut to a design in the metal base (copper), then filled with powdered enamel of various colours and fired to fuse the enamel. In Europe the technique flourished principally in the twelfth and thirteenth centuries. Later, *basse taille* enamel was used in India; in this the engraved motif was covered with transparent enamel of various colours.

6 The mango tree was revered in India and its fruit known as the king of fruits. The palm-frond motif on Persian Mir and Serabend carpets is called *mir-i-bota*. Today the mango or Kashmir palm motif is known in Bengal as *kalka* or *kolka*, which probably derives from the Turkish *kalga* (leaf). See *La Mode des chales cachemire en France*, exhibition catalogue, Palais Galliéra, Paris 1982; also Emma Pressmar, *Indische Ringe*, Frankfurt am Main 1982.

7 Jade was used under the Timurids, ancestors of the Mughal rulers of India; a great jade monolith, for example, adorns the tomb of Timur (d. 1405) in Samarkand. It is now assumed that jade-working in eighteenth-century India was done by Chinese craftsmen. The jadeite used in India came from north Burma.

8 Emerald is a beryllium-aluminium-silicate, deriving its green colour from traces of chromium oxide. It belongs to the beryl group, together with aquamarine, Morganite (pink beryl), heliodor (golden beryl), etc. In ancient times emerald and beryl were regarded as two distinct minerals. Pliny the Elder distinguished twelve subspecies of 'emerald' which were distinct from 'beryllus'.

9 Egyptian emerald mines were systematically worked from 330 BC to AD 1237. Forgotten after 1740, they were rediscovered in 1816 by the French explorer Cailliaud. In 1899 Edwin Streeter, author of *The Great Diamonds of the World*, attempted to exploit the mines again, but without any great success: Egyptian emeralds were small and of low quality.

10 Colombian emeralds first became known in the West when Hernando Cortés, who had received magnificent emeralds from Montezuma in Mexico City and in Tenochtitlan as early as 1519, returned to Spain with cut stones. In 1537 Jiménez de Quesada conquered New Granada (Colombia) and so discovered Chivor. The mines of Muzo were first discovered in 1567 and rediscovered in 1895. In 1920 the mine of Chivor was reopened. Chivor emeralds, with their characteristic pyrite inclusions, are basically yellower than the Muzo stones.

11 Jean-Baptiste Tavernier (1605–89), a French jeweller and gem dealer who undertook six Indian journeys between 1638 and 1668. He returned with large stones, among them one later to be cut to 45.52 carats, the 'Hope' diamond. Cardinal Mazarin and Louis XIV were among his customers. In 1676 his famous travel journal, *Les Six Voyages de Jean-Baptiste Tavernier*, appeared. By the time he died, this had been translated many times. A further English translation of 1889 contributed to a deepening interest in India and her precious stones.

12 Indian manufacture of beads dates back to the fourth millennium BC; turquoise, lapis lazuli and cornelian were the stones most commonly used. In Roman times the city of Ujjain was the principal exporting centre. India was also known for the production of glass beads, the industry being centred on Arikamedu (Pondicherry). See Peter Francis, 'When India was Beadmaker to the World', *Ornament*, vol. 6, no. 2 (1982).

13 The 'De Beers' diamond was found as a stone of 428 carats in South Africa in 1888. It was exhibited in Paris in 1889; afterwards it probably went directly into the possession of Patiala. The stone, a light yellow colour, follows the 245.35-carat 'Jubilee' as the world's fifth largest cut diamond.

14 In 1933 the Maharaja of Nawanagar was succeeded by his nephew, Jam Saheb Digvijaysinhji [**196**], who

in 1938 bought from Cartier's a red diamond of 2.32 carats, a brick-coloured diamond of about 3 carats and a golden diamond of about 3.75 carats.

15 Jeanne Toussaint loved to wear bunches of pearls or gemstones, hanging in glittering cascades of colour from brooches or pendants. The idea derived from the Indian *turah* and found an echo in Cartier's supple gold-bead jewelry of the post-war years, which also took up the motif of the butter beads of Krishna. The latter symbolized the essentials of life and are generally represented on rings by four pierced beads and a pale Ceylon ruby. Indian and Surrealist sources were combined in the popular 1938 brooch of a black lacquered hand holding a coral flower, which recalled the gesture of the flower-holding emperors in the finest Mughal miniatures of the seventeenth century. Toussaint and Louis Cartier both collected such miniatures.

12. '1925': THE EVOLUTION OF A STYLE (pp. 179–97)

1 Technical innovation in the 1920s was represented by the new baguette cut known for a time as the *diamant bâton*. A contrast to the fashionable triangles and rhombs, this cut, which involved a comparatively large wastage, first appeared about 1909. As late as 1912–13 the early baguettes still had rounded corners and had to be firmly integrated into the geometry of the jewel.

2 During the second half of the nineteenth century artists and designers had been stimulated by impressions from the French North African colonies. Chassériau, Delacroix and the so-called Orientalists had depicted the desert, markets, and other scenes. Charles-Edmond Duponchel (1795–1868), among others, produced Arab-style jewelry. The Moorish bathroom of La Païva in her house in the Champs-Elysées and the Arab Hall in the London house of the painter Lord Leighton (1830–96), inspired by the palace of La Zisa in Palermo, are further instances of Moorish influence.

3 In the 1925 Exhibition the motif of the fountain was to assume almost the character of a leitmotif. It featured in plaster at the main entrance, in wrought iron, and in Lalique's glass waterfall in the *Parfumerie* section. Mauboussin's fountain tiara, which permitted an exemplary use of baguette diamonds, was well known.

4 Misia Godebska (1872–1950) married Thadée Nathanson in 1893. Between 1905 and 1909 she was married to Alfred Edwards and from 1920 to 1927 to José Maria Sert. Since in the Cartier context she features most interestingly as Madame Sert, this fourth name is retained throughout for simplicity. The case is similar with Elsie de Wolfe, who is referred to by her maiden name though she became Lady Mendl when she married Sir Charles Mendl in 1926.

5 Iribe worked on *Le Témoin* and also on *Schéhérazade*, the review founded in 1909 by François Bernouard and Cocteau. On one of the title pages he set a sultana wearing an aigrette within the décor of the Diaghilev ballet of the same name. See, for Iribe, the outstanding work *Paul Iribe* (1982) by Raymond Bachollet, Daniel Bordet and Anne Claude Lelieur.

6 See *Les Robes de Paul Poiret racontées par Paul Iribe* (1908). In 1911 *Les Choses de Paul Poiret vues par George Lepape* appeared, which Iribe answered with *L'Eventail et la fourrure chez Paquin*, with drawings by Barbier and Lepape.

7 As early as 1909 Iribe had designed advertising for the jeweller 'Maxima', for 'Novelty' pearls, and also for the pearl specialist Juclier.

8 The emerald aigrette formed part of the jewelry designed by Iribe for the play *Comoedia Illustrée*, in which in 1911 his wife, the actress Jeanne Dirys, appeared, wearing a hat by Chanel.

9 *Vogue*, September 1925.

10 In 1910 *Le Témoin* devoted a special issue to the Ballets Russes in which Iribe illustrated *Schéhérazade*. It was followed by a number featuring Nijinsky, with graphics by Iribe and verses by Cocteau. In 1914 Iribe published the album on *L'Après-midi d'un faune* compiled by Baron de Meyer.

11 In 1912 Louis Süe, the interior decorator, had opened 'L'Atelier Français'. After the war, with André Mare, he renamed it 'La Belle France'; that led in 1919 to the 'Compagnie des Arts Français' in the Faubourg Saint-Honoré. Flower garlands and baskets of fruit were virtual leitmotifs in its products. In 1912, one year before his American tour, Poiret opened his 'Ecole Martine', followed by the 'Atelier Martine', where for a time Dufy was a collaborator.

Paul Follot (1877–1941) followed a similar path. Coming from Meier-Graefe's 'Maison Moderne', he had already been designing jewelry in new forms between 1910 and 1914. From 1923 he headed the 'Pomone' workshops in the department store Au Bon Marché, designing as its symbol a fruit-laden tree. His furnishings designed in 1913 for Germain Lubin used the cornucopia as motif. In 1928, Follot and Serge Chermayev were put in charge of the department of decorative arts at Waring and Gillow in London. In England they popularized motifs such as the bowl of fruit, cornucopia and garland. In 1928 René Prou, the representative of rational modernism, took over from Follot at the Bon Marché in Paris.

12 Apart from Lubin, Iribe also worked for Jeanne Lanvin. He designed the firm's golden trademark of Jeanne Lanvin with child for the 1927 'Arpège' scent bottle (the bottle itself was by Rateau).

13 Lucien Vogel, whose importance is still not properly recognized, was the publisher of *Femina* in 1906 and later of *L'Illustration des modes*, which became *Le Jardin des modes*. From 1912 to 1925 he published *La Gazette du Bon Ton* and from 1928 *Vu*, a weekly photo-magazine from which *Life* developed in 1936.

14 George Barbier published the albums *Nijinsky* (1913) and *Karsavina* (1914) with poems by Vaudoyer and also *Modes et manières* (1914). He designed the sets for *Casanova* (1919), for *Lysistrata* by Maurice Donnay, *La dernière nuit de Don Juan* by Rostand, and *Manon* by Henri Bataille. Barbier's depictions of Harlequin recall Nijinsky in *Le Carnaval*, in which he first appeared in 1910 with Karsavina and which influenced many *Vogue* titlepages, among them the crinoline ladies by Helen Dryden (American *Vogue*).

15 Barbier is described in Jean-Louis Vaudoyer's *George Barbier* (1929) as 'un peintre vraiment grec'.

16 The watercolour comes from the 1913 Nijinsky album and is now in a private collection in London. See *La Renaissance de l'art français et des industries de luxe*, 1918, no. 5, p. 162.

17 For Iribe's tiara see *Art et décoration*, 1908, no. 4, p. 105, and *Femina*, July 1912.

18 In 1864 the Union Centrale des Beaux-Arts appliqués à l'Industrie was founded, under English influence. It was involved in the organization of exhibitions in Paris (1867), London (1871 and 1874), Vienna (1873) and Philadelphia (1876). In 1882 the Union merged with another association which in 1877 had independently founded the Musée des Arts Décoratifs on the model of the South Kensington (now Victoria and Albert) Museum in London. Renamed the Union Centrale des Arts Décoratifs, it staged exhibitions in the Palais de l'Industrie. In 1890 the Société d'Encou-ragement à l'Art et à l'Industrie was founded. The review *Art et décoration* was launched in 1896 and *L'Art décoratif* two years later (it continued to appear up to 1914). The Société des Artistes Décorateurs was founded by Grasset, Guimard, Follot and others in 1901 following the success of the Paris Exposition of 1900. The major exhibitions held at the Palais Galliéra include one on book binding (1902) and 'La Parure précieuse de la femme' (1908). See *La Bijouterie, la joaillerie, la bijouterie de fantaisie au XXème siècle*, Paris 1934.

19 See *L'Exposition internationale des arts décoratifs et industriels modernes*, Paris 1923: 'Admitted to the exhibition are works of new inspiration and genuine originality, by artists, craftsmen, industrial and fashion designers and publishers, as long as they are in tune with the decorative and industrial arts of today.'

20 Ibid.

21 The Committee for the *Parure* section comprised M. Dausset as president, Fouquet-Lapar as president of the chamber of trade, Georges Fouquet as additional president, Louis Aucoc, Louis Boucheron and Louis Cartier as vice-presidents (which explains why Cartier's could exhibit without competition). The committee members were Paul Brandt, Hugues Citroën, Dusausoy, Linzeler, Raymond Templier and Van Cleef. The jury included, among others, Georges Fouquet and J.-L. Vaudoyer (later to write on George Barbier: see n. 15).

22 See op. cit. at n. 19.

23 See *La Renaissance de l'art français* for 1925; the magazine referred to the participants as 'four incomparable couturiers, the leading jeweller in Paris and doubtless in the whole world, a great ironworker and a fine leather worker'.

24 Jeanne Lanvin became one of Cartier's customers about 1922 when she ordered a necklace of pearls, diamonds and crystal roundels.

25 The Cartier display cost Fr. 178,000. Cartier's contribution amounted to Fr. 125,000. After the exhibition, Rateau made a buy-back proposal to Louis Cartier.

26 Paul Léon, *L'Exposition des arts décoratifs et industriels modernes – rapport général* (1927).

27 François Carnot, *Rapport de l'exposition internationale* (1921).

28 The great couturiers regularly bought from Cartier's, both on their own account and for their customers. Callot features in the sales records from 1908; others included Chanel, Doucet, Doeuillet and Madame Paquin.

29 The shoulder ornament, composed of pearls, diamonds, emeralds and onyx, was adorned with three engraved emeralds of 153, 88 and 141 carats. It yielded three brooches, one of which was bought by the Glaoui from Morocco.

30 Only fifteen watches and clocks, of little interest, were exhibited. Both mystery clocks and the richly decorated vanity cases in Chinese and Egyptian styles were absent.

31 See Eugène Fontenay, *Les Bijoux anciens et modernes*, Paris 1887, p. 120.

32 The Empress Eugénie's link necklace featured in the auction of 1887 as lot 28. For a Renaissance necklace of the same type, see Yvonne Hackenbroch, *Renaissance Jewellery*, London 1979, p. 222.

33 See op. cit. at n. 23.

34 See Fontenay, cit. at n. 31, pp. 338, 339.

35 Saint Germain-en-Laye museum, I–17, 716.

36 Major fibulas were discovered in 1854, including Scottish examples. A revival of Celtic forms was observable between 1840 and 1860, and later in the productions of the English firm of Liberty's.

37 See Fontenay, cit. at n. 31, p. 439.

38 *Le Métal*, published by E. Longuet (n.d.), comprised four volumes: I: *Le Fer*; II and III: *Le Bronze, le cuivre, l'étain et le plomb*; IV: *Les Métaux précieux*.

13. VANITY FAIR (pp. 201–19)

1 *Le Pavillon de l'Elégance*, special number of *La Gazette du Bon Ton*, no. 10, 1925.

2 The word occurs, for instance, in Paul Léon, *L'Exposition des arts décoratifs et industriel modernes – rapport général* (1927).

3 See Vanda Forster, *Bags and Purses*, London 1982.

4 These held the patches of black taffeta which were gummed to the face as artificial beauty spots.

5 The word 'lacquer' derives from the Portuguese *lacca*; in the eighteenth century it was called 'shellack'. The terms refer to the sap of the lacquer tree, the most important species of which, *Rhus vernicilflua*, is found throughout China south of the Yellow River. See Sir Harry Garner, *Chinese Lacquer*, London 1979.

6 A letter of 1749 by Mrs Montagu.

7 Sir William Chambers published his *Designs of Chinese Buildings* in 1757 and his *Dissertation on Oriental Gardening* in 1772.

8 The dealer Jean Dupuis began his voyages of discovery up the Red River in 1860, the year in which French and British troops stormed the Summer Palace near Peking. The French expedition to Indo-China under Doudart de Lagrée and Francis Garnier took place in 1868; in 1883 France asserted a protectorate over Annam and Tonkin; in 1886 Tonkin became a French colony. Siam (now Thailand) became a French protectorate in 1867. In 1876, Korea opened her ports to European trade.

9 The London International Exhibition of 1862 included a display of Japanese bronzes, lacquers and porcelain, and the Paris Exposition of 1867 showed French faïence following Japanese patterns (the 'Rousseau service'). At the Paris Exposition of 1878, the dealer Samuel Bing showed Japanese bronzes and lacquer work, while the ethnographical exhibition in the Trocadéro presented the Far-Eastern finds of Emile Guimet and Félix Régamey. (The Musée Guimet opened in Lyon in 1878, but moved to Paris the following

year.) The Japanese Exhibition followed in 1883, with loan exhibits from Bing, Camondo and Sarah Bernhardt. Whistler had already stumbled on woodcuts by Hokusai in Paris in 1856 and by 1880 the department store Au Bon Marché was selling albums of Japanese woodcuts. The London firm of Liberty's, founded in 1875, introduced such artists as Morris, Ruskin and Rossetti to Japanese wares, while the architect E. W. Godwin designed houses for himself and Whistler showing Japanese influence.

The Milanese politician Henri Cernuschi, who, like Guimet, travelled to Japan in 1871, bequeathed his collection to the city of Paris in 1896. Two years earlier, the Louvre had received the great Grandidier Collection (now in the Musée Guimet).

[10] Edmond de Goncourt published *Outamaro* in 1891, *L'Art japonais* in 1893 and *Hokusai* in 1896.

[11] Jade jewelry became popular with the rising fashion for things Chinese. In the 1920s Cartier's jade jewelry for Mrs Wellington Koo, wife of the former Chinese ambassador to London, became renowned.

[12] Far-Eastern lacquer, mostly Japanese, had proved a stimulus to a number of eighteenth-century box designers – Adrien-Jean-Maximilien Vachette, Pierre-François Drais and the German Heinrici, to name but a few.

[13] According to Sir Harry Garner the term *laque burgauté* (from 'Burgau', mother-of-pearl mussel), first used in 1862 for porcelain with mother-of-pearl lacquer, should be avoided.

[14] C. T. Loo (1880–1957), the greatest dealer in Chinese art of his time. Some time after 1902 he opened a business in the Place de la Madeleine and had branches in Shanghai and Peking. In 1926 he built the Chinese pagoda in the rue de Courcelles as his business premises.

[15] He Xiangu was one of the Eight Immortals. Her emblem is a lotus stalk, often surmounted by a peach.

[16] James Gardner, *Elephants in the Attic*, London 1983.

[17] Mother-of-pearl – popularized in the cheaper synthetic forms of nacrit and nacrolack – was part of an industry that included ivory, horn, etc., and their derivatives, such as xylonite. Other synthetics were galalith, celluloid and Bakelite, invented in 1917. Cartier used ebonite, a black vulcanized rubber, for his fine cigarette boxes.

[18] Lucien Gaillard was employing Chinese craftsmen as early as 1900, and they introduced their French colleagues to the art of lacquering. However, they left France before they had established their own school.

[19] Jean Dunand (1877–1942), creator of these examples, had been initiated into the technique of lacquer by the Japanese Sugawara; he himself made lacquer with forty layers. At the same time he supplied Madeleine Vionnet and Madame Agnès with belt-buckles and handbags, which were shown at the 1925 Exhibition. During the artist's lifetime, Cartier's assembled the first show of his work in the United States, on the sales floor of their Fifth Avenue branch.

[20] The 1930s saw further contacts between Cartier's and cosmetic firms: in 1931 two vanity cases were fitted with Patou's new lipstick. In 1935 Cartier patented a new lipstick cartridge that could be opened with one hand, which was taken over by

Elizabeth Arden for a popular model. There were, too, relations with the firms of Coty and Houbigant, whose lipsticks and powder compacts were incorporated in the vanity cases. In 1948 Louis Devaux granted the firm of Lenthéric a further lipstick licence.

After the Second World War, since the major impetus for the cosmetic industry came from Hollywood (for example Mary Pickford became president of 'Mary Pickford Cosmetics'), Cartier New York became the principal pioneer in this field.

[21] Poiret had already designed a model of the same name in 1905.

[22] In the 1929 exhibition in the Palais Galliéra the influence of Oriental styles was less marked than had been the case in 1925, as was apparent from the colour choice of materials: whereas then the predominant colour combination had been green-black-white (emerald-onyx-diamond), in 1929 diamond alone dominated, above all the baguette-cut, and critics spoke of the 'grand silence blanc'.

In 1929 artists including Fouquet and Templier joined the Union des Artistes Modernes, a group devoted to a strict geometrical style. These tendencies were dominant in the Colonial Exposition held in the Park of Vincennes in 1931: the strongest formal influences were Cubist experiments and the art of the African colonies such as masks and ivories. The stylistic debt to the Far East had disappeared: 'We have no more to learn from the techniques of either the Orient or the Far East.'

14. CHIMAERAS, DRAGONS AND GREAT CATS (pp. 223–37)

[1] Rock crystal differs from diamond in that it gives rise to softly modelled transitions. Its glimmering transparency had prompted mystical associations since Ezekiel's vision of 'the likeness of the firmament [which] was as the colour of the terrible crystal' [1:22]. Cartier's first used rock crystal in its new style in 1910 in spear, palm and disc shapes on hat-pins. A technical tour de force which the New York company patented was the setting of diamonds in rock crystal. The surface of the crystals was engraved with Oriental arabesques by the Berquin-Varangoz workshop.

[2] See John Boardman, *Archaic Greek Gems*, London 1964; K. R. Maxwell Hyslop, *Western Asiatic Jewellery c. 3000–612 BC*, London 1971; E. C. de La Ferté, *Les Bijoux antiques*, Paris 1956.

[3] See 'An Indian Crocodile', *Bulletin of the Museum of Fine Arts*, XXX, IV, 26.

[4] See 'Exposition d'une collection unique de perles et de bijoux de décadence antique chez Cartier', 27 May–6 June 1914.

[5] Jeanne Toussaint received a number of pieces of panther jewelry over the years, among them a wristwatch, a pearl necklace clasp and a panther shoulder brooch.

[6] In 1954 the Duchess of Windsor received a lorgnette with tiger decoration, and two years later a tiger bracelet. Bracelets in the form of stretched-out tiger skins were a Boivin speciality after the Second World War.

[7] The Princess Aga Khan's panther collection was auctioned after her death by Christie's, Geneva, on 1 May 1969.

15. THE GREAT NECKLACES · THE LONDON WORKSHOPS · GEM DEALERS (pp. 241–59)

[1] In 1928 Coco Chanel had launched a range of diamond paste jewelry designed by Comte Etienne de Beaumont. Other couture houses which produced fashion or costume jewelry were Jean Patou with necklaces of imitation gems; Madeleine Vionnet with necklaces of green feathers and crystal; and Lucien Lelong with wooden bead bracelets.

[2] Coco Chanel was an occasional customer at Cartier's from 1919, choosing, among other things, an emerald ring and a brooch with sapphire, ruby and topazes.

[3] Among the world's largest cut sapphires are the 423-carat 'Logan' sapphire (Smithsonian Institution, Washington) and a cushion-shaped sapphire of 337 carats, which Harry Winston bought in 1948 from a private collection and presented to an Eastern potentate.

[4] The sapphire sautoir passed into the family by inheritance via Queen Helena. The diamond necklace was broken up in Paris and Harry Winston sold the sapphire drop in the 1960s to a Greek collector who presented it to Queen Frederika.

[5] Ali, son-in-law of the Prophet, was the ancestral founder of the Ismaili Shi'a Muslims.

[6] The stone has recently been reduced to 33.13 carats and designated with colour 'E' and as 'flawless' by the Gemological Institute of America.

[7] Subsequently, Cartier's displayed the 107-carat emerald at exhibitions on a long diamond sautoir. In 1947 Raphael Esmerian acquired important emeralds from the Payne Whitney family and with these and two additional stones he created a necklace which he sold to Pierre Cartier; Cartier attached the 107-carat stone as a pendant. In 1954 the emerald was reduced to a drop of 75.63 carats on the advice of Esmerian. The necklace, sold meanwhile to the Rockefellers, reappeared one last time in November 1971 at a Sotheby's auction in Zurich.

[8] Roussy Sert, who embodied the chic of the 1930s, owned a Cartier bracelet of rock crystal and diamonds, which Barbara Hutton had copied. A similar model belonged to the Rani of Pudukota, and two further models to Gloria Swanson.

[9] Around 1938 classical necklaces with radiating stone motifs on the eighteenth-century model came back into vogue. Mostly they consisted of seven stones increasing in size towards the middle; Barbara Hutton had an especially valuable example of the type, which stayed in fashion up to the 1950s.

[10] In 1923, Cartier London lent jewels valued at £400,000 to the actress Alice Delysia for her 'Radiant Diamond Dress' in *Topics*. Her entrance on stage was watched over by four dogs, six policemen and three detectives.

[11] In 1927 Cartier's had created a necklace of onyx tubes and diamond roundels and suspended from it three stones from London: a square, canary-coloured diamond of 2.46 carats; an oval, amber-coloured diamond of 2.48 carats; and, below that, the 26.26-carat blue diamond.

[12] In India, the 'Queen of Holland' was rechristened the 'Ranjitsinhji'. Today the stone weighs 135.92

carats and in 1978 was designated as 'D' and 'internally flawless' by the Gemological Institute of America. The 'Queen of Holland' is second only to the 'Premier Rose', a drop diamond of 137.02 carats, which in 1978 belonged to the New York diamond dealer William Goldberg and was designated as 'D' and 'flawless' by the Gemological Institute of America.

[13] Some of the noteworthy forerunners of the geometric cuts so popular after 1900 are a hexagonal diamond, reportedly of 31.75 carats, which formed part of the 1749 'Golden Fleece', then in the French crown jewels (which later also included the 'Hope' diamond), and the pentagonal rose diamond known as 'Hortensia', which it seems already belonged to Louis XIV (now in the Louvre). In 1909 a hexagonal diamond of 16.25 carats featured as lot 4 in the Habib auction in Paris (see Chapter 18, n. 3); it could be traced back to Somaviva, a general under the First Empire; in 1933 it passed through auction to Cartier's customer the Baronne de Forest.

[14] For example, Napoleon III honoured the lapidary Grosfillex for his services in the diamond import trade. Two diamond cutters, Roulina and Goudar, were already established in Paris at the time of the 1878 Exposition.

[15] Edouard Sirakian (b. 1915) entered his father's business in 1930. Around 1960 he invented the 'Troidia' diamond cut, a triangle with convex sides. After the Second World War hexagonal diamonds were recut in the fashionable navette shapes, and pentagons into drops.

[16] Today the firm of Esmerian, New York, is headed by Ralph Esmerian (b. 1940), the fourth generation.

16. 'THE JEWELLED FLIGHT OF TIME'
(pp. 263–305)

[1] Vacheron Constantin were again supplying Cartier's between 1951 and 1972; similarly, between 1959 and 1967, Piaget's were supplying movements.

[2] Georges Verger (1884–1945), son of Ferdinand, was a jewelry and clock designer. He designed clocks with movements by Vacheron Constantin, for whom his father already held the agency. He worked for Van Cleef & Arpels, Janesich, LaCloche, Ostertag, Marz, Boucheron, Chaumet and Gübelin, and in the United States for Black Starr & Frost, Cauldwell and Tiffany. Together with Cartier, Verger was the only producer of 'mystery clocks', which he supplied to Van Cleef & Arpels, Ostertag, and to the United States. In the 1930s, Cartier ordered the *montre radiateur* ('radiator watch') from Verger, a clip-on watch with projecting strips or fins which could be attached, for example, to evening bags. Verger invented the *montre captive*, a covered pocket-watch that could be opened like a little 'altar' on a desk.

[3] In 1949 Rodanet, then president of Jaeger, spoke of the importance of Louis Cartier as 'the inspirer of the revolution in the art of the clock', in a paper entitled 'Les Méthodes de fabrication de l'horlogerie moderne'.

[4] *Recueil d'ouvrages curieux du cabinet de M. Grollier de Servières* by Grollier de Servières was published in Lyon in 1719.

[5] Tardy, *La Pendule française*, 1961–64, ill. p. 266.

[6] See Ernst von Bassermann-Jordan, *Montres, pendules et horloges*, 1964, ill. p. 194.

[7] From 1930 Coüet was established at 37 rue Réaumur in the Atelier Renault, in association with Cartier; here his assistants also did simple gold work for Cartier. During the economic crisis Coüet still employed some twenty craftsmen, including nine *orfèvres-boitiers*, one enameller and one *guillocheur*. In 1931 other workers were dismissed. In 1929 Cartier's had opened their own workshop at 17 rue Bachaumont; at the outbreak of the Second World War it moved to 9 rue d'Argenson, where Robert Linzeler had his studio. Later Coüet too moved into the studio in the rue d'Argenson, and finally moved with the other workshops to 13 rue de la Paix in 1956.

[8] In 1938 Cusin patented another invention related to the mystery clocks. This was a clock for maritime use in which two dials, without hands, moving at different speeds, represented the minutes and hours. In 1946 he invented a clock whose illuminated dial could be projected onto the wall at the press of a button.

[9] These must-haves of the late 1930s were little items of inexpensive jewelry or watches, generally produced at Christmas, and eagerly sought out by the international clientele. In 1935 it was the 'Ladybird' brooch in coral and onyx, in 1937 the 'Moor' brooch that Louise de Vilmorin loved, in 1938 the 'Sioux' brooch, and in 1939 the 'Domino' watch.

[10] See Alex Ceslas Rzewuski, *A travers l'invisible cristal*, Paris 1976, p. 171.

[11] See *La Gazette du Bon Ton*, no. 10 (1925).

[12] Various *pendules mystérieuses* were shown at the 1878 Exposition by Guilmet, Cadot, Rosset and Henri Robert. That by Jean-Eugène Robert-Houdin was the most famous of its time and was described in the *Dictionnaire encyclopédique* of 1881. The model came with either one or two hands; transmission was effected through two griffins on a crystal pillar. There is one of these Robert-Houdin clocks in the Château at Blois and another in the museum of La Chaux-de-Fonds in Switzerland. See Catherine Cardinal, *L'Horloge dans l'histoire, l'art et les sciences*, 1983, p. 108.

[13] Gold-coin watches were already being produced in the nineteenth century; the earliest model may be one of 1809 by the Swiss watchmaker Moulinie. Two coins were required for each watch – one for the case and one for the cover.

[14] The 1907 contract was renewed even before its expiry date in 1919. By that time Jaeger had been at the rue du Louvre for two years and was associated in a joint stock company with Cartier's. In the new contract the annual value of the purchases by Cartier was raised to Fr. 1,500,000. But Cartier's also had the exclusive rights to Jaeger's production both in Paris and in Switzerland (the firm of LeCoultre).

[15] There is an entry for an octagonal crystal pocket-watch in the Cartier archive as early as 1876, but not yet with the ultra-thin movement of the 1900 model.

[16] The European Watch and Clock Company looked after exports to New York, where Louis Roehrich, with eight assistants, ran the clock department. Even after the company closed, *c.* 1950, most watches and clocks came from Paris.

However certain models in 18-carat yellow gold (though not in enamel) were produced in New York. Walter Kroehnert (b. 1899), the German watchmaker at Cartier New York, was still active in the early 1980s. A contemporary of Gaston Cusin, he had, like Cusin, made his first watch at the age of fourteen. In 1936 he joined Cartier New York, where he produced Cusin's prism clock, and, as late as 1977, a series of pocket-watches with various precious stones.

[17] Ancestors of the wristwatch are recorded. In 1572 Queen Elizabeth I of England received an 'armlet or skakell of golde, all over fairely garnishedd with rubyes and dyamonds, haveing in the closing thearof a clocke'.

The *Almanach du Dauphin* for 1772 mentions a watchmaker in the rue de Buci in Paris who made ring and bracelet watches. In 1790 the inventory of Jacquet-Droz and Leschot of Geneva mentions 'une montre qui est fixée sur un bracelet'.

In 1806 the Empress Josephine presented her daughter-in-law, Princess Auguste-Amélie of Bavaria, with two bracelets of gold, pearls and emeralds made by Nitot of Paris, and a watch was mounted in one of them.

In the 1867 Paris Exposition the jeweller Rouvenat showed a wristwatch with its dial concealed beneath an emerald. In 1868 Patek Philippe sold the first Swiss wristwatch.

In 1880 the German Ministry of the Navy ordered from La Chaux-de-Fonds in Switzerland watches with metal straps for naval officers.

[18] In later years, Pierre Cartier was greatly interested in aviation. In 1928 he held a reception in the Ritz Towers, New York, for Dieudonné Coste and Joseph le Brix, who had made the first crossing of the South Atlantic in 1927. In 1930, together with Maurice Bellonte, Dieudonné Coste made the first non-stop flight from Paris to New York (Lindbergh's Atlantic crossing in the opposite direction), in the Bréguet biplane 'Question Mark'. In the following year the two were officially received in twenty-two American cities, whose mayors were later guests at an official reception given by the French President Doumergue in the Elysée Palace, Paris. Afterwards came the presentation by Bellonte at Cartier's of a silver model of the 'Question Mark' (made by Albouse and Watte after a wooden model). In 1933 the French government presented it to the Rockefeller Center in New York.

[19] The Maharaja of Kapurthala was reputed to own 250 clocks, the majority made by Cartier's. One of his servants was engaged exclusively in winding them up.

[20] A hexagonal emerald with a watch mounted in it was found in the 'Cheapside Hoard', a collection of Elizabethan and Jacobean jewels, now in the Museum of London.

[21] Princess Elizabeth was presented with this wristwatch (the world's smallest) by President Lebrun in the Elysée Palace, on the occasion of her parents' state visit to Paris in 1938. The British royal couple held a reception at the Paris Embassy for representatives of the 'Vendôme' Committee, among them Madame Ritz, Madame Charvet, Madame Boucheron and Madame Jacques Cartier.

[22] In 1929 Cartier's sold 626 watches and 86 clocks in Paris. In 1930, even after the Wall Street Crash, the figures were 423 and 69.

17. SWORDS FOR ACADEMICIANS •
CARTIER'S PATENTS • THE SECOND
WORLD WAR (pp. 309–13)

1 The five academies that make up the Institut de France have the same regulations as to dress and ceremonial swords. Most of the swords designed by Cartier were for candidates to the Académie Française.

2 Diaghilev died in 1929. In 1931 René Blum and Colonel de Basil founded the Ballets Russes de Monte Carlo, but they separated after three years. Blum and Massine retained the name 'Ballets Russes', but appeared mostly in America. De Basil's group became the Royal Covent Garden Ballets Russes and, later, the Ballets Russes de Colonel W. de Basil. In 1945 Serge Lifar founded the Nouveaux Ballets de Monte Carlo, which was taken over in 1947 by the Marquis de Cuevas.

3 Palladium is the lightest of the six members of the platinum group of metals.

18 THE GREAT TRANSACTIONS
(pp. 317–29)

1 See Evalyn Walsh McLean, *Father Struck It Rich*, London 1936, pp. 155ff.

2 See Susanne Steinem Patch, *The Blue Mystery: The Story of the Hope Diamond*, Washington 1976.

3 According to the sale catalogue for 24 June 1909, the 'Hope' had been acquired by Habib in 1908 directly from Frankel. The Habib sale comprised:
(a) A cushion-shaped, rose-coloured diamond of 5 15/16 carats
(b) A drop-shaped 'blue-white' diamond of 24 carats
(c) A cushion-shaped 'blue-white' diamond of 23 carats
(d) A hexagonal diamond of 16.25 carats. The provenance was given as Princess Mathilde, but subsequently it was traced back to General Somaviva in the early nineteenth century.
(e) An 'aquamarine-coloured', pale triangular diamond of 70 1/16 carats. This is the diamond known today as the 'Idol's Eye'; present weight 70.20 carats
(f) A cushion-shaped, rose-coloured diamond of 30½ carats
(g) The 'Mi-Régent', a drop-shaped diamond of 58 carats
(h) The 'Hope' diamond

4 The 'Star of the East' was also worn as an aigrette [397], just as the 'Hope' could be worn on either a necklace or a bandeau. Subsequently, Cartier New York created another necklace with oval diamond links on which the two stones could be worn alternately.

5 A later calculation of payments, of 1918, shows that in the end the transaction developed differently. The first payment was only $20,000, and in addition to the 'Star of the East' necklace a further diamond necklace (*cravate*) was taken into account. Payment was still not complete in 1918.

6 This 'Star of the South' is not to be confused with the 128.80-carat stone of the same name, said to be in a private collection in Bombay. The 15.46-carat 'Star of the South' had been set by Cartier's in a bracelet with sixteen rubies and sixteen diamonds. Later, Harry Winston had it recut to 14.37 carats.

7 The Sultan's jewels were auctioned during his lifetime between 27 and 29 November 1911. Catalogue nos. 234, 240 and 294 were from Cartier's.

8 See Alex Ceslas Rzewuski, *A travers l'invisible cristal*, Paris 1976, p. 250.

9 The remaining Lobanov jewels were bought for Fr. 1.4 million by the gem dealer Jacques Bienenfeld, to preempt a sale scheduled for April.

10 Unfortunately the archives do not record to whom Cartier's sold the earrings. Later Mrs Merryweather Post bequeathed them to the Smithsonian Institution, Washington.

11 The 'Polar Star' was auctioned by Christie's in Geneva on 20 November 1980 (lot 653), together with other jewels belonging to Lydia, Lady Deterding.

12 Prince Christopher of Greece, *Le Monde et ses cours*, 1939, p. 59. The Prince was the son of King George I of Greece. He married Mrs Nancy Leeds (Princess Anastasia) as his first wife, and Princess Françoise of France as his second wife.
The crown later came into the possession of Helen M. de Kays and was auctioned by Parke Bernet in 1966. It is now in the Merryweather Post collection at Hillwood, near Washington.

13 In 1898, when he was still in the boulevard des Italiens, Cartier had other pieces of historic silver: a tankard and beaker by Thomas Germain formerly in the possession of King Joseph of Portugal.

14 The 'Star of South Africa' is said to have been acquired from a young herdsman on the Zendfontein farm on the Orange River in exchange for five hundred sheep, ten oxen and a horse. It was then cut by Louis Hond, who sold it to the Countess of Dudley. From her it went to the family of J. P. Morgan. In 1971 it was sold by Christie's in Geneva.

15 For the Stotesbury wedding the Morgan diamond, 'as big as a robin's egg', was attached to a necklace. Only later did Cartier's mount it in a tiara.

16 In 1928 Cartier's were offered a further Mazarin stone of 15.88 carats.

17 Later Harry Winston sold the 'Indian Briolette' to an Indian maharani who wore it in an aigrette. Winston later bought it back and sold it in Europe in 1971.

18 The 'Bal des Pierreries' was held by Princess Jacques de Broglie in her palace in the avenue de Messine. Seven ballets were presented, one under the sign of each of the most valuable precious stones.

19 The 'Blue Heart' or 'Unzue Heart' was sold by Van Cleef & Arpels in 1953 and bought back by them in 1960. In 1964 Harry Winston sold it in a ring to Mrs Merryweather Post, who bequeathed it to the Smithsonian Institution, Washington. It had no connection with the Empress Eugénie.

20 Eugène de Beauharnais, Duke of Leuchtenberg, son of the Empress Josephine by her first marriage, had eight children. The youngest son, Maximilien-Eugène, married Marie, daughter of Nicholas I, in 1839. Their children called themselves the Princes Romanovski. The Leuchtenberg emeralds were bought in 1920 from the antique dealer Seiler's of Vevey by Bienenfeld.

21 The Diamond Dictionary of the Gemological Institute of America gives the weight of the drop as 69.80 carats.

22 Today the 'Pasha', after a further recutting, weighs 36.22 carats and is in a private European collection.

23 Subsequently, Harry Winston acquired the 'Nassak', recut it to 43.38 carats, and sold it to Trabert &

Hoeffer-Mauboussin, the New York jewellers. In 1944 Mrs William B. Leeds, daughter-in-law of Mrs Nancy Leeds, bought it. Edward Hand bought the stone at Parke Bernet in 1970 and sold it later to Bulgari's. They then sold it to a private buyer.

24 In 1912 Solly B. Joël, nephew of the diamond mine owner Barnato, had ordered a large diamond breast ornament from Cartier's; it contained a drop diamond of 34.25 carats and a navette of 23.54 carats [51].

25 The St Moritz branch was called 'JacNel' after Jacques and Nelly Cartier. At first it opened for three months in the winter and then for two months in the summer as well. In 1929 Carl Nater, son of the mayor of St Moritz, was taken on to represent the branch. Etienne Bellanger, later sales director in London, worked with him. The branch closed in 1945. In that year Nater, who had married Jacques Cartier's daughter Alice, became director in London.

26 The 'Thibaw' ruby was auctioned by Christie's in Geneva on 27 May 1971 and was subsequently recut by Van Cleef & Arpels.

27 Cartier's designed a similar flower brooch of rubies and diamonds to a commission from Dr Williamson for Princess Margaret. The jewel was later reshaped by the designer Dennis Gardner.

28 The ring and brooch of the emerald *parure* were signed by Cartier. See Jean Lanllier and Marie-Anne Pini, *Cinq siècles de joaillerie en Occident*, Paris 1971, p. 266.

29 In 1980 Elizabeth Taylor sold the diamond drop for $2 million to the New York dealer Henry Lambert.

BIBLIOGRAPHY

Abd-ul Hamid II, Sultan *Catalogue de bijoux*, Paris 1911

Abeler, Jurgen *Kronen*, Wuppertal 1976

A la Vieille Russie *The Art of the Goldsmith & the Jeweler*, New York 1968

—— *Fabergé*, exhibition catalogue, New York, 22 April–21 May 1983

Anni Trenta, exhibition catalogue, Comune di Milano, 27 January–30 April 1982

Armstrong, Nancy *Victorian Jewelry*, London 1976

Bapst, Germain *Histoire des joyaux de la couronne de France*, Paris 1889

Barten, Sigrid *René Lalique*, Munich 1977

Beaton, Cecil *Cinquante ans d'élégance et d'art de vivre*, Paris 1954

La Belle Epoque, New York 1980

Bhusan, Jamila Brij *Indian Jewellery, Ornaments and Decorative Design*, Delhi 1964

Biehn, Heinrich *Alle Kronen dieser Welt*, Munich 1974

—— *Juwelen und Preziosen*, Munich 1965

Birmingham, Stephen *The Grandes Dames*, New York 1982

Blakey, George G. *The Diamond*, London 1977

Brandau, Robert, ed. *De Meyer*, New York 1976

Brunhammer, Yvonne *1925*, Paris 1976

Cartier *Retrospective Louis Cartier: One Hundred and One Years of the Jeweler's Art*, New York 1976

—— *Retrospective Louis Cartier: Masterworks of Art Deco*, exhibition catalogue, Los Angeles County Museum of Art, 1983

Castle, Charles *La Belle Otéro*, London 1983

Charles-Roux, Edmonde *Le Temps Chanel*, Paris 1979

Chaumet *Une Pléiade de joailliers: 1780–1930*, Paris 1930

Christie's, Geneva *The H. Robert Greene Collection of Art Deco*, catalogue, 16 November 1978

—— *A Casket of Magnificent Jewels: The Collection of the late Lydia Lady Deterding*, catalogue, 20 November 1980

Demoriane, Hélène 'Les Must de Cartier 1925', *Connaissance des Arts*, April 1974

Desaultels, Paul E. *Gems in the Smithsonian*, Washington 1965

Le Diamant, Paris 1979

Fabergé 1846–1920, exhibition catalogue, Victoria and Albert Museum, London, 23 June–25 September 1977

Finestone, Jeffrey *The Last Courts of Europe*, London 1981

Flower, Margaret *Victorian Jewellery*, London 1963

Fontenay, Eugène *Les Bijoux anciens et modernes*, Paris 1887

Forster, Vanda *Bags and Purses*, London 1982

Gaal, Robert A. D. *Diamond Dictionary*, Santa Monica, Calif., 1977

Gary, Marie-Noël de *Les Fouquet: bijoutiers et joailliers à Paris, 1860–1960*, Paris c. 1983

Gautier, Gilberte *Rue de la Paix*, Paris 1980

Gere, Charlotte *Victorian Jewellery Design*, London 1972

Gernsheim, Alice *Victorian and Edwardian Fashion*, New York 1963

The Gilded Age: 1860–1968, catalogue of the Worth exhibition, Museum of the City of New York, 1983

Gold, Arthur, and Robert Fizdale *Misia*, London 1980

Golish, Vitold de *Splendeur et crépuscule des maharajas*, Paris 1963

Habsburg-Lothringen, Geza von *Fabergé: Court Jeweller to the Tsars*, London 1979

Heiniger, Ernst A. *Le Grand Livre des bijoux*, Lausanne 1974

Hendley, Thomas Holbein *Indian Jewellery*, London 1906–9

Hinks, Peter *Nineteenth-Century Jewellery*, London 1975

Howarth, Stephen *The Koh-i-Noor Diamond*, London 1980

Hughes, Graham *Modern Jewellery*, London 1963

Ileana, Princess (of Romania) *I Live Again*, New York 1951

The Indian Heritage: Court Life and Arts under Mughal Rule, exhibition catalogue, Victoria and Albert Museum, London, 21 April–22 August 1982

Jenkins, Marilyn *Islamic Jewellery in the Metropolitan Museum of Art*, New York 1983

Jourdain, Margaret *Chinese Export Art in the 18th Century*, London 1950

Jullian, Philippe *Robert de Montesquiou*, London 1967

Kochno, Boris *Diaghilev*, New York 1970

Kchessinska, Mathilda *Souvenirs de la Kschessinska*, Paris 1960

Kunz, George F. *The Book of the Pearl*, London 1908

Lanllier, Jean, and Marie-Anne Pini *Cinq siècles de joaillerie en Occident*, Paris 1971

Latif, Momin *Bijoux Moghols*, exhibition catalogue, Société Générale de Banque, Brussels, 21 January–31 March 1982

Letson, Neil 'Cartier, Sovereign Jeweller', *Connoisseur*, November 1982

Lobanov Rostovsky, Princess *Catalogue des joyaux, colliers de perles, joailleries, perles et brillants, rivières en brillants et pierres de couleurs ayant composé l'écrin de la Princesse Lobanoff de Rostoff née Princesse Dolgorouki*, sale catalogue, by Henri Baudouin et al., Lausanne 1920

Marie, Grand Duchess *The Education of a Princess*, New York 1930

Masters, Brian *Great Hostesses*, London 1982

Mathilde, Princess *Catalogue de bijoux*, Paris 1904

Menzhausen, Joachim, and Klaus G. Beyer *A la cour du Grand Mogol*, Leipzig 1965

Munn, Geoffrey *Castellani and Giuliano: Revivalist Jewellers of the Nineteenth Century*, London 1984

Nijinsky, Romola *Nijinsky*, London 1970

Nou, Jean-Louis *Les derniers Maharajahs*, Paris 1980

Paley, Princess *Souvenirs de Russie*, Paris 1923

Parke Bernet *The Magnificent Jewellery of the late Mrs John E. Rovensky*, catalogue, New York, 23 January 1957

Patch, Susanne Steinem *The Blue Mystery: The Story of the Hope Diamond*, Washington 1976

Poiret, Paul *En habillant l'époque*, Paris 1930

Ponsonby, Sir Frederick *Collections of Three Reigns*, London 1951

Pressmar, Emma *Indische Ringe*, Frankfurt am Main 1982

Princely Magnificence: Court Jewels of the Renaissance, exhibition catalogue, Victoria and Albert Museum, London, 15 October 1980–1 February 1981

Pringué, Gabriel-Louis *Trente ans de dîners en ville*, Paris 1948

Quennell, Peter *Customs and Characters*, London 1982

Reselle, Bruno du *La Mode*, Paris 1980

Rosenthal, Léonard *Au Royaume de la perle*, Paris 1920

—— *Au Jardin des gemmes*, Paris 1922

Ross, Ishbal *Silhouette in Diamonds*, New York 1975

Ross, Marvin C. *The Art of Karl Fabergé and his Contemporaries*, Norman, Okla., 1965

Seebohm, Caroline *The Man who was Vogue*, London 1983

Sinkankas, John *Emerald and other Beryl*, Radnor, Pa., 1981

Smith, Jane *Elsie de Wolfe*, New York 1982

Snowman, A. Kenneth *The Art of Carl Fabergé*, London 1955

Sondheimer, Alphonse de *Vitrine XIII*, Hamburg 1966

Spencer, Charles *The World of Diaghilev*, Harmondsworth 1974

Taburiaux, Jean *La Perle et ses secrets*, Paris 1983

Taylor, Gerald, and Diana Scarisbrick *Finger Rings from Ancient Egypt to the Present Day*, London 1978

Twining, Lord *History of the Crown Jewels of Europe*, London 1960

Van Rensselaer, Philip *Million Dollar Baby*, London 1979

Vente des diamants de la couronne, catalogue, 1887

Vever, Henri *La Bijouterie française au XIXème siècle*, Paris 1906

Vorres, Ian *The Last Grand Duchess*, London 1964

Ward, A., et al. *The Ring from Antiquity to the Twentieth Century*, London 1981

Wartski *A Thousand Years of Enamel*, exhibition catalogue, London, 18 May–5 June 1971

White, Palmer *Poiret*, London 1973

THE CARTIER FAMILY TREE

Louis-François Cartier
1755–1793/94
|
Pierre Cartier
1787–1865
|
Louis-François Cartier
1819–1904
|
[Louis-François-]Alfred Cartier
1841–1925

Louis[-Joseph] Cartier
1875–1942
= 1 Andrée Worth
daughter of Jean-Philippe Worth
|
Anne-Marie Cartier
= René Révillon
|
René-Louis
Michel

= 2 Countess
Jacqueline Almassy
|
Claude Cartier, 1925–1975
= Rita Salmona
|
Alain Véronique

Pierre[-Camille] Cartier
1878–1965
= Elma Rumsey
|
Marion Cartier
= Pierre Claudel
|
Violaine
Dominique
Marie-Pierre
Michèle
Pierre

Jacques[-Théodule] Cartier
1884–1941
= Nelly Harjes
|
Jacqueline
Alice
Jean-Jacques
Harjes

Suzanne Cartier
= Jacques Worth,
son of Gaston Worth
|
Roger
Hélène
Maurice
Gérard

CHRONOLOGY

Cartier history

1819 Birth of Louis-François Cartier

1841 Birth of Louis-François-Alfred Cartier

1847 Foundation of Cartier's, 29 rue Montorgueil,
Paris. The following mark registered on 17 April
(T. Bousquet):

1853 Cartier's move to 5 rue Neuve-des
Petits-Champs
First American client

1858 Birth of Edmond Jaeger

1859 Cartier's move to 9 boulevard des Italiens

1860 First Russian client

1869 Louis-François Cartier's Swiss voyage

1871–73 Temporary establishment of Cartier's in
London

1874 Alfred Cartier takes over the shop
1875 Birth of Louis-Joseph Cartier

1878 Birth of Pierre-Camille Cartier

1884 Birth of Jacques-Théodule Cartier
1885 Birth of Maurice Coüet

1887 Birth of Jeanne Toussaint

Cartier jewelry

1852 'Egyptian' scarab bracelet in stock
1853 First mention of platinum
       First mention of watches
1854 First hair ornaments (pearls, enamel) in stock
1855 Comtesse de Nieuwerkerke is client

1856ff. First purchase by Princess Mathilde
         Duchess of Fitz-James buys pearl and ivory
         brooch
1857 Comte de Nieuwerkerke buys imperial eagle

1859 First bandeau in silver-gilt in stock
       Empress Eugénie is client
       Count Belgiojoso buys amethyst pin
       Shirt studs in platinum in stock
1860 Prince Saltykov buys emerald bracelet
1861 Princess Mathilde buys 'Egyptian' earrings
1862 Prince Bibesco buys diamond ring

1872 Indian ear-pendants in stock
1873 Creation of 'Egyptian' châtelaine

1878 Princesse de Wagram is client

1881 'Lovebird' brooch

1883 'Chimaera' pendant

1886 Comte de Paris buys silver-gilt frames
       City of Bordeaux buys 155 medallions
       Vicomtesse de Bonnemain buys pearl bracelet
1887 Lalique sells 5 bird brooches to Cartier
       Prince of Saxe-Coburg buys 2 miniatures
       Vicomtesse de Bonnemain buys diamond
       aigrette
       Comtesse de Turenne buys peridot brooch
       Comtesse de Nattes buys diamond ring
1888 First wristwatches in stock

General events

1822 Platinum discovered in the Urals
       Champollion deciphers hieroglyphs
1831 Obelisk in Place de la Concorde, Paris

1851 Great Exhibition, London

1853 Marriage of Napoleon III to Eugénie de
       Montijo

1855 International exhibition, Paris
       Death of F. D. Froment-Meurice
       Fontenay creates blackberry tiara in platinum
1856 Birth of the Prince Imperial
       Whistler discovers Japanese woodcuts in Paris

1857 Longchamp racecourse established
1858 Charles Frederick Worth established at 7 rue de
       la Paix
       Boucheron founded
1859ff. Suez Canal built

1860 Summer Palace, Peking, destroyed
1861ff Campana Collection displayed in the Louvre
1862 International exhibition, London
1864 Chambre Syndicale de Bijouterie, Joaillerie et
       Orfèvrerie founded
       Union Centrale des Beaux-Arts appliqués à
       l'Industrie founded
1867 International exhibition, Paris
       Future Edward VII visits India and Nepal
       First major diamond find in South Africa
1869 Empress Eugénie in Egypt for inauguration of
       Suez Canal
1870 Franco-German War
       Empress Eugénie flees to England
1871 Birth of Proust
       First performance of *Aïda*
       Commune insurrection
1872 Empress Eugénie's jewels auctioned in London
       Atanik Eknayan settles in Paris

1875 Liberty's founded in London
1876 International exhibition, Philadelphia
       Peacock Room by Whistler
1877 Musée des Arts Décoratifs opens in Paris
1878 International exhibition, Paris
       Chimaera tiara by Fouquet
1879 Fouquet opens in avenue de l'Opéra
1880 De Beers Mining Co. established
       Rational Dress Society founded in England
1881 Alexander II assassinated in Moscow
       Gaillard studies Eastern lacquers and enamels
       Death of the Egyptologist Auguste Mariette
1883 Japanese exhibition, Paris
       Metropolitan Opera House, New York, opens
1884 Exhibition of French crown jewels in the
       Louvre
1886 Tonkin becomes French colony

1887 Wilson scandal in Paris
       Sale of French crown jewels
       Eugène Fontenay. *Les Bijoux anciens et modernes*

1888 Cecil Rhodes controls Kimberley Central Mine
       Sarah Bernhardt appears in Sardou's *Tosca*

Cartier history	Cartier jewelry	General events
		1889 International exhibition, Paris, with Eiffel Tower Germain Bapst, *Histoire des joyaux de la couronne de France*
	1890 Prince Pedro of Brazil is client	**1890** Société d'Encouragement à l'Art et à l'Industrie established in Paris Paul Esmerian settles in Paris
		1893 Edmond de Goncourt publishes *L'Art japonais* Eknayan opens first diamond-cutting factory
	1895 Appearance of ribbon and bow jewels	**1894** Marriage of Grand Duchess Xenia **1895** Death of Charles Frederick Worth Anna Gould marries Boni de Castellane **1896** Journal *Art et décoration* founded Coronation of Tsar Nicholas II **1897** 'Jubilee' diamond cut Vienna Secession First flights by Santos Dumont LaCloche Frères founded
		1897–99 Dreyfus Affair
1898 Louis Cartier associated with his father Alfred as 'Alfred Cartier et Fils' Louis Cartier marries Andrée Worth **1899** Cartier's move to 13 rue de la Paix	**1898** 'Japanese' and 'Chinese' buckles **1899** 'Valkyrie' aigrette 'Persian' aigrette **1900ff.** Lavallières, sévignés and cravats in fashion	**1898** Ritz Hotel opens Emile Zola publishes *J'accuse* **1899** Asscher's diamond-cutting factory established in Paris René Lalique's 'Isis and Lotus' tiara **1900** International exhibition, Paris Fouquet's shop at 6 rue Royale designed by Mucha
	1901 Prince Alexander Bariatinsky buys 6 diamond bows 'Indian' necklace for Queen Alexandra Vase-shaped clocks Duchess of Devonshire buys sunshade Princess Victoria buys belt-buckle Grand Duke Paul buys Wedgwood opera glasses Lina Cavalieri buys boa clasp Duchess of Manchester buys 'Question Mark' brooch First wheat-ear tiara	**1901** Death of Queen Victoria Flight by Santos Dumont from Saint-Cloud to Eiffel Tower Société des Artistes Décorateurs founded Birth of Harry Winston 'Hope' diamond sold in London
1902 Cartier's London branch founded at 4 New Burlington Street Alfred Cartier opens his own office at 4 rue de la Paix	**1902** Marquis of Anglesey buys charm with Santos Dumont portrait Lillie Langtry buys fancy-yellow diamond brooch Duchess of Devonshire buys pearl and diamond tiara Nellie Melba buys diamond and pearl breast ornament Countess of Essex buys diamond tiara Lady de Grey buys diamond tiara	**1902** Coronation of Edward VII Sir Ernest Cassel is the King's financial adviser Townsend develops 'twentieth-century cut' for diamonds Consuelo Vanderbilt visits Russia
1903 C & A 1903	**1903** Princesse de Polignac buys laurel tiara Countess of Warwick buys emerald tiara Mrs Keppel buys diamond tiara Grand Duke Alexis buys serpent monocle Princesse Amédée de Broglie buys ruby heart brooch Duchess of Roxburghe buys diamond bracelet Duke of Westminster buys ruby and diamond tiara Caroline Otéro buys tassel necklace Nellie Melba buys opal heart pendant Chinese jade pendants in fashion Anna Gould buys laurel tiara	**1903** 'Des Arts Musulmans' exhibition in Paris Bicentenary of foundation of St Petersburg Boyars' Ball in Winter Palace, St Petersburg Poiret opens shop in rue Pasquier, Paris
1904 Royal warrant of King Edward VII Death of Louis-François Cartier Pierre Cartier travels to Russia Royal warrant of King Alfonso XIII of Spain	**1904** Santos Dumont buys 'Merovingian' brooch Geneviève Lantelme buys diamond ring Princess George Radziwill buys statue of St Anthony Mrs Mackay buys diamond and sapphire tiara Countess Greffulhe buys laurel tiara Mrs Burns buys 'Louis XVI' thermometer Cornelius Vanderbilt buys Princess Mathilde's rose brooch Eleonora Duse buys pearl ring Vincenzo Florio buys black diamond pendant W. K. Vanderbilt buys necklace with 5 black pearls J. P. Morgan buys first sun tiara Queen Alexandra buys ruby necklace and *résille* necklace	**1904** Death of Princess Mathilde Vever moves to 14 rue de la Paix Chaumet's 'Via Vitae' exhibited in St Louis, Missouri

Cartier history	Cartier jewelry	General events
1905 Royal warrant of King Carlos of Portugal	**1905** Lilian Nordica buys briolette diamond tiara W. K. Vanderbilt buys 5 diamond combs The Aga Khan buys 6 'Louis XVI' brooches 'Marie Stuart' bandeau	**1905** Outbreak of revolution in Russia Exhibition of Fauve painters in Paris Lalique moves to Place Vendôme Chaumet moves to Place Vendôme International exhibition, Liége Einstein develops Theory of Relativity Caruso and Melba sing at Covent Garden, London, in honour of Alfonso XIII
1906 Jacques Cartier takes charge of London shop Louis and Pierre Cartier become associates as 'Cartier Frères'	**1906** First essays at Art Deco jewelry 'Renaissance' tiara in emeralds and diamonds New series of leather strap wristwatches King of Sweden buys pearl necklace	**1906** Edward VII in India International exhibition, Milan Exhibition of Russian art in Paris organized by Diaghilev Van Cleef & Arpels move to Place Vendôme Marriage of King of Spain Henri Vever, *La Bijouterie française au XIXème siècle*
1907 Fifteen-year contract with Edmond Jaeger Pierre Cartier travels to New York Dowager Empress Maria Feodorovna visits rue de la Paix shop First Cartier exhibition at Hotel d'Europe, St Petersburg Royal warrant of the King of Siam Royal warrant of Tsar Nicholas II of Russia	**1907** Chinese 'Cloud Peak' pendants Enamelled egg-shaped clocks 'Parasol' watches Baron Henri de Rothschild buys meander pattern tiara	**1907** State visit of King Haakon VII of Norway to Paris Marriage of Princess Marie Bonaparte to Prince George of Greece Picasso paints *Les Demoiselles d'Avignon* Elsie de Wolfe decorates the Colony Club, New York
1908 Temporary Cartier branch at 28 Quai de la Cour, St Petersburg Cartier received at Gatchina by Dowager Empress Maria Feodorovna Cartier received at Tsarskoe Selo by the Tsar and Tsarina Pierre Cartier marries Elma Rumsey **1908–9** Jules Glaenzer travels to the Far East	**1908** First circular clocks Onyx in fashion Grand Duchess Vladimir buys briolette diamond tiara Nellie Melba buys 'Greek' bandeau Grand Duke Paul buys pear-shaped diamond tiara 'Egyptian' choker with lotus motifs 'Star of the East' diamond sold to Mrs McLean King George of Greece buys amethyst necklace Duc d'Orléans buys 'Greek' bandeau Sultan of Zanzibar buys cigarette holder	**1908** Edward Ayrton discovers royal tomb at Thebes *Boris Godunov* staged in Paris 'La Parure Précieuse de la Femme' exhibition in Paris Poiret opens boutique, 'Chichi' Asscher cuts the 'Cullinan' diamond in Amsterdam G. F. Kunz, *The Book of the Pearl* Death of Grand Duke Vladimir
1909 Royal warrant of King George I of Greece Alfred Cartier appraises Abdul Hamid's jewels in Constantinople Charles Jacqueau joins Cartier's Transfer of London branch to 175–176 New Bond Street Cartier's opens at 712 Fifth Avenue, New York	**1909** Grand Duchess Vladimir buys sapphire kokoshnik Queen Alexandra buys fleur-de-lys tiara	**1909** Blériot flies across the English Channel Ballets Russes in Paris Lalique opens glass factory in Combe-la-Ville State visit of King Manuel of Portugal to Paris Lace exhibition at Musée des Arts Décoratifs Proust begins *A la recherche du temps perdu* Auction of 'Hope' diamond in Paris
1910 Louis Cartier and Andrée Worth divorced Louis Cartier in St Petersburg, participates in the Christmas Bazaar First record of interlocking 'C' as Cartier device **1910–11** Louis Cartier and Jacqueau travel to Moscow and Kiev	**1910** Epaulettes fashionable Onyx and diamond jewels Crystal and diamond jewels Persian influence Aigrettes Mrs Leeds buys pearl necklace for Fr. 2,850,000 Extra-flat crystal pocket-watches fashionable *Déployant* buckle invented Sale of 'Hope' diamond to Mrs McLean 'Blue Heart' 31-ct diamond sold to Mrs Unzue Marcel Proust buys opal shirt studs	**1910** Death of Edward VII State visit of Spanish sovereigns to Paris Ballet *Schéhérazade* in Paris Poiret invents the hobble skirt
1911 Exhibition of 19 tiaras at Cartier London Birth of Marion Cartier in New York **1911–12** Jacques Cartier travels to India and the Persian Gulf (to the Gulf again in 1912–13)	**1911** Mr Blumenthal buys briolette diamonds of 90.38 cts Mrs Lydig buys 43-ct pear-shaped diamond 'Santos Dumont' wristwatch Mr Stotesbury buys 10.44-ct ruby ring	**1911** Auction of the jewels of Abdul Hamid in Paris Franco-Egyptian exhibition at the Louvre George Barbier's first exhibition in Paris Coronation of George V
1912 Paris City Council presents Nicholas II with Cartier egg in Russia Cartier adds 11 rue de la Paix to no. 13 Cartier exhibition in Canada and Belgium	**1912** 'Torpedo' pendants Mrs Leeds buys emerald epaulette Queen Elizabeth of Belgium buys diamond tiara First aigrette with Indian *sarpech* motif First baguette-cut diamonds with geometric outline 'Comet' clocks Princess Nicholas of Greece buys pearl and diamond necklace	**1912** Persian Ball of the Marquise de Chabrillan Persian Ball of the Comtesse de Clermont-Tonnerre The *Titanic* sinks Auction of Doucet's collection of eighteenth-century art Lalique's last jewelry exhibition *La Gazette du Bon Ton* founded Marriage of Eva Cromwell and Edward Stotesbury in Philadelphia Dunand taught the art of Japanese lacquer by Sugawara Borchardt discovers head of Nefertiti
1913 Royal warrant of King Peter of Serbia	**1913** Mrs Leeds buys pearl and pear-shaped diamond tiara First mystery clock Mystery pendant watch Remounting of 14 bracelets for Gaekwar of Baroda	**1913** Stravinsky, *Le Sacre du Printemps* Chanel invents sport fashion Celebration of Romanov tercentenary American *Vogue*: 'Ida Rubinstein with panther'

Cartier history	Cartier jewelry	General events
1914 Royal warrant of the Duc d'Orléans	**1914** First panther motif, on watch Coloured diamond sautoir sold to Kiev Elsie de Wolfe buys 'Cantine d'automobile' Lady Randolph Churchill buys diamond pendant Jacques Doucet buys sapphire pendant Mistinguett buys pearl bracelet **1916** 'Hope' spinel mounted on necklace	**1914** First World War Marriage of Prince Felix Yusupov Crinoline Ball of Duchesse de Gramont Bal des Pierreries of Princess de Broglie Mosaic Egg by Fabergé *Woman with a Panther* by George Barbier **1916** Mikimoto patent for cultured pearls Murder of Rasputin
1917 Cartier New York move to 653 Fifth Avenue (acquired in exchange for a 2-row pearl necklace)	**1917** Emilienne d'Alençon buys ruby ring Henry Clay Frick buys 4 diamond brooches Vanity case with first complete panther	**1917** Invention of Bakelite *Garçonne* hairstyle Hollywood film *Cleopatra* Ballet *Parade* by Diaghilev Le Secq des Tournelles collection of ironwork exhibited in Rouen
	1918 Marshals' batons for Marshals Foch and Pétain King of the Belgians buys 3 brooches with royal cipher	**1918** French franc at half its pre-war value
1919 Royal warrant of King Albert I of Belgium Cartier London becomes independent of Paris Cartier exhibits 478-ct sapphire necklace at San Sebastian Coüet transferred to Cartier-owned workshop in rue Lafayette European Watch and Clock Company (EWC) founded C ⌣ C ▷ 1919	**1919** Lady Curzon of Kedleston buys diamond bandeau Caroline Otéro buys 10-row pearl 'écharpe' Arthur Rubinstein buys ring Necklace with 21.18-ct heart diamond 'Tank' watch	**1919** Treaty of Versailles Toklowsky develops brilliant cut Leopard motifs at Villa Trianon Compagnie des Arts Français opens
1920 Royal warrant of King Victor Emmanuel III of Italy Royal warrant of Prince Albert of Monaco	**1920** Cartier purchases Tsar Nicholas I pearl necklace at Lobanov auction in Lausanne Lady Granard buys diamond tiara Queen of Spain buys pearl and diamond tiara First kingfisher feathers on clock dials Mystery clocks with central axle	**1920** Death of Empress Eugénie Russian fashion starts at Chanel *Vogue* cover by Bakst Marriage of Misia with José Maria Sert Death of Peter Carl Fabergé Death of Grand Duchess Vladimir
1921 Royal warrant of the Prince of Wales 'Cartier Frères' becomes 'Cartier S.A.'	**1921** King Ferdinand of Romania buys 478-ct sapphire necklace Lady Granard buys sapphire necklace Queen Sophie of Greece buys arrow brooch Frieda Hempel buys diamond ear-pendants Queen Marie of Romania buys pearl and diamond bandeau Serge Diaghilev buys black pearl shirt studs Prince of Wales buys 'Egyptian' bracelet Mrs Leeds buys emerald necklace Historic Leuchtenberg emerald ear-pendants at Cartier New York	**1921** Chanel 'No. 5' Marriage of William Leeds to Princess Xenia of Greece Habsburg jewels for sale in Lucerne 'Salon du Goût Français' exhibition in Paris
1922 Louis Cartier travels to Spain C & P ▷ 1922	**1922** Queen Helen of Italy buys 2 diamond brooches Jeanne Lanvin buys crystal, pearl and diamond necklace First coral 'Chimaera' bangle First figurative mystery clock	**1922** Death of Marcel Proust Discovery of Tutankhamun's tomb Poincaré is President of France
1923 Exhibition of Napoleonic silver service at Cartier New York and in Boston Cartier received by King Alexander of Serbia in Belgrade	**1923** 'Egyptian' lotus bandeau Mrs Stotesbury buys emerald necklace and tiara First 'Portico' mystery clock Lady Cunard buys 'flower vase' necklace Madame Paquin buys emerald and diamond necklace King Alexander of Serbia orders emerald necklace and diamond tiara	**1923** Death of Sarah Bernhardt Steichen takes photographs for *Vogue* Death of Lord Carnarvon 'Chinese Ball' at Paris Opéra
1924 *Illustrated London News* mentions Cartier's 'Egyptian' jewels Cartier New York acquires the stock of the jeweller Dreicer for $2.5 million	**1924** Princess Helen of Serbia buys diamond necklace 'Egyptian' vanity case with pipe player Cartier buys Thiers pearls 'Trinity' ring and bracelet Fashion for long diamond sautoirs Cartier buys historic Maria Theresa ear-pendants First mother-of-pearl lacquers on vanity cases	**1924** French exhibition in Grand Central Palace, New York
1925 Death of Alfred Cartier Cartier exhibits in Exposition Internationale des Arts Décoratifs et Industriels Modernes, Paris	**1925** Zenith of Art Deco fashion Queen of Greece buys emerald and diamond bandeau Coco Chanel buys sapphire and emerald ring Baronne de Meyer buys vanity case 'Sarcophagus' vanity case Jeanne Lanvin buys spectacles with lotus motif Pendant watches fashionable Cartier's sells Prince Yusupov's black pearls	**1925** Exposition Internationale des Arts Décoratifs et Industriels Modernes in Paris 'Negro' fashion in Paris Bolsheviks discover Yusupov treasure in Moscow

Cartier history	Cartier jewelry	General events
1926 Cartier patent for handbag clasp	**1926** Ganna Walska buys coral 'Fuchsia' necklace Maharaja of Kapurthala orders emerald turban ornament	**1926** French franc falls to 240 to the pound English fashion begins at Chanel Elsie de Wolfe marries Sir Charles Mendl
1927 Patent for brooch-clip (renewed in 1934)	**1927** Madame Enrico Caruso buys handbag with turquoises Raja of Mandi orders emeraldhead ornament Queen of Spain buys laurel tiara 'Egyptian Temple Gate' clock Chinese 'Turtle' clock	**1927** Sert divorces Misia Lindbergh flies from New York to Paris Lanvin 'Arpège' First South Atlantic crossing by Dieudonné Coste and Joseph Le Brix Boucheron's 'falcon' tiara for King Fuad
1928 Royal warrant of Queen Marie of Romania Exhibition of Patiala jewels in rue de la Paix shop Pierre Cartier receives aviators Coste and Le Brix in New York Gaekwar of Baroda appoints Jacques Cartier as sole adviser on his jewels	**1928** Maria Barrientos buys emerald and diamond brooch The Glaoui buys pearl and diamond belt José Maria Sert buys ruby bead necklace State diamond necklace for Maharaja of Patiala Ganna Walska buys coral 'Chimaera' bangle 'Polar Star' diamond sold to Lady Deterding Engraved emerald Indian necklace mounted for Maharaja of Nawanagar	**1928** Death of Dowager Empress Maria Feodorovna Chanel opens in rue Cambon
1929 Cartier branch opens in Saint Moritz (closes 1945) Cartier workshop in rue Bachaumont Cartier exhibits in French Exhibition in Cairo Royal warrant of King Fuad of Egypt Aga Khan necklace exhibited in Barcelona	**1929** Maharaja of Indore buys pearl and onyx handbag 'Egyptian' cigarette case with goddess Bastet	**1929** Poincaré resigns as President Death of Diaghilev Wall Street Crash International exhibition, Barcelona Union des Artistes Modernes in Paris French exhibition in Cairo Les Arts de la Bijouterie' exhibition in Paris
S C C A 1929		
1930 Coüet workshop transferred to rue Réaumur Cartier patents for gold alloys (also 1934)	**1930** Engraved emeralds mounted for the Aga Khan Cigarette case designed as miniature motor car Necklace with 71 coloured diamonds mounted for Madame Fournier	**1930** First transatlantic flight from Paris to New York Marriage of King Umberto of Savoy to Princess Marie-José
	1931 Coloured diamond necklace with 'Queen of Holland' diamond mounted for Maharaja of Nawanagar Necklace with 6 fancy-pink diamonds First Academician's sword, for Duc de Gramont Viscountess Astor buys 'Peacock' bandeau	**1931** Colonial Exhibition, Paris Ernest Oppenheimer takes over Diamond Syndicate Ballets Russes de Monte Carlo founded Economic crisis in France
1932 Cartier received by King of Nepal in Kathmandu		**1932** Chanel presents her own jewelry collection First colour photograph in *Vogue* England legalizes 14-ct gold
1933 Exhibition of Louis Cartier's Persian miniatures in New York Marion Cartier marries Pierre Claudel 'Porter Rhodes' diamond at Cartier's Cartier patent for 'serti mystérieux' Jeanne Toussaint presides over Cartier Haute Joaillerie French government presents Cartier model of 'Question Mark' biplane to Rockefeller Center, New York	**1933** Wedding jewels for Barbara Hutton Crown designs for Gaekwar of Baroda New fashion for gold-mounted jewelry Academician's sword for François Mauriac	**1933** Hitler elected Chancellor 'A Century of Progress' exhibition in Chicago Death of Ranjitsinhji, Maharaja of Nawanagar
	1934 Purchase of Yusupov white pearls Massive crystal jewelry fashionable	**1934** Stavisky affair in France Assassination of Chancellor Dollfuss
1935 Cartier Paris designer Lemarchand works at Cartier London (until 1939) Exhibition of Historic Diamonds at rue de la Paix shop Cartier patent for lipstick holder Opening of Monte Carlo branch	**1935** First electric watches Ladybird brooches Indian emerald and ruby necklace mounted for Maharaja of Patna 20.41-ct pear-shaped diamond mounted for Queen of Spain Emerald and pearl head ornament mounted for Maharaja of Dhranghadra	**1935** Death of Paul Iribe Atlantic crossing of *Normandie* Italian troops invade Ethiopia Etienne de Beaumont's ball, 'Le Grand Siècle'
1936 Cartier's shows 'Nassak' diamond in Monte Carlo	**1936** Emperor of Annam buys diamond tiara Baroness Maud Thyssen buys ladybird bracelet	**1936** Léon Blum's 'Front Populaire' *Vogue* and *Vanity Fair* merge Edward VIII becomes King
1937 Cartier's make jewelry using 'Platinix'	**1937** Emerald necklace with cross pendant Blackamoor brooches fashionable *Sarpech* with 'Tiger's Eye' diamond for Maharaja of Nawanagar Gaston Cusin invents 'prism' clock Engraved emerald and pearl necklace mounted for Maharaja of Nawanagar	**1937** French franc taken off the gold standard and devalued Coronation of George VI Marriage of Duke of Windsor International exhibition, 'Des Arts et Techniques', in Paris
1938 Princess Elizabeth receives smallest wristwatch in the world, signed Cartier Opening of Cartier's in Cannes Jacques Cartier visits Maharaja of Nawanagar Cartier in discussion with perfume maker Pinaud Cartier exhibition in Tirana on the occasion of the marriage of King Zog I of Albania	**1938** Barbara Hutton buys diamond bandeau Jade 'drum' mystery clock Fashion for 'Sioux' brooches P. L. Weiller buys 'Jubilee' diamond Laura Corrigan buys 31.45-ct square diamond ring Mrs Horace Dodge buys 'Thibaw' ruby	**1938** State visit of English sovereigns to Paris Death of Gabriele D'Annunzio 'Mode Gitane' at Chanel's

Cartier history	Cartier jewelry	General events
1939 Designer Lemarchand goes to Jodhpur and Bahawalpur in India Royal warrant of King Zog I	**1939** Academician's sword for André Maurois Barbara Hutton buys pear-shaped and navette diamond necklace Maharaja of Jaipur buys cabochon emerald drop necklace	**1939** Outbreak of Second World War World's Fair, New York
1940 After German occupation of Paris, temporary Cartier shop in Biarritz		**1940** German occupation of Paris French gold trading prohibited French armistice under Pétain; Vichy Government (until 1944) De Gaulle escapes to London and founds the 'Free French' movement
	1941 Silver shoe created for Madame Solvay	**1941** Death of Alfonso XIII U.S.A. enters war
1942 Deaths of Louis Cartier and Jacques Cartier		**1942** Barbara Hutton marries Cary Grant
		1944 De Gaulle heads Provisional Government
1945 Pierre Cartier becomes President of Cartier International Jean-Jacques Cartier takes over Cartier London	**1945** General de Gaulle presents mystery clock to Stalin in Moscow	**1945** End of Second World War
1947 Pierre Cartier retires to Geneva	**1947** Diamond necklace and rose tiara presented by Nizam of Hyderabad to Princess Elizabeth on her wedding Remounting of emerald necklace for Barbara Hutton (Vladimir emeralds)	**1947** Dr Williamson sells Tanganjika Diamond Mine to De Beers De Gaulle's 'Rassemblement du Peuple Français' Vincent Auriol becomes President Dior 'New Look'
1948 Cartier New York presided over by Claude Cartier	**1948** Duchess of Windsor orders panther brooch	**1948** Slogan 'A diamond is forever' coined for De Beers Israel's diamond markets established
		1950 Celebration of 250 years of the Place Vendôme
	1953 Queen Elizabeth the Queen Mother orders diamond tiara	**1953** René Coty becomes President
	1954 Academician's sword for Duc de Lévis Mirepoix New 'chimaera' jewels created under Jeanne Toussaint's direction Duchess of Windsor buys tiger lorgnette	
1956 Cartier's opens workshop at 13 rue de la Paix	**1955** Academician's sword for Jean Cocteau	**1955** Synthethic diamonds made by General Electric
	1956 Duchess of Windsor buys tiger bracelet	
	1957ff. Princess Nina Aga Khan acquires panther jewels	**1957** Death of Ernest Oppenheimer
		1958 'Hope' diamond shown at the Smithsonian Institution, Washington Fifth Republic under De Gaulle International exhibition, Brussels
1959 Death of Elma Cartier	**1959** Dolphin bangle, inspired by Jeanne Toussaint	
	1960 Clock in crystal bottle inspired by Jeanne Toussaint	
1961 Cartier buys Empress Eugénie necklace in Bern	**1961** Barbara Hutton buys peacock brooch	
1962 Cartier New York sold by Claude Cartier, who remains President until 1963	**1962** Barbara Hutton buys tiger bracelet	
1965 Death of Pierre Cartier		
1966 Marion Cartier sells Cartier Paris		
	1967 Academician's sword for Maurice Druon	
	1968 Maria Félix commissions snake necklace	
1969 Cartier buys 69.42-ct pear-shaped diamond at auction and sells it to Richard Burton		
1972 A group of investors organized by Joseph Kanouï acquires control of Cartier Paris and appoints Robert Hocq as President Alain Perrin in charge of Cartier marketing		
1973 Creation of 'Les Must de Cartier' First 'Must' boutiques in Biarritz, Singapore, Tokyo		
1974 Cartier London is acquired by the owner of Cartier Paris Nathalie Hocq joins Cartier Paris		
1975 Death of Claude Cartier 'Louis Cartier' retrospective exhibition in Paris	**1975** Maria Félix commissions crocodile necklace	
1976 Another group of investors acquires Cartier New York and appoints Joseph Kanouï as Chairman Sale of the 'Louis Cartier' diamond of 107.07 cts 'Louis Cartier' retrospective exhibition in New York		
1978 Death of Jeanne Toussaint		
1979 Birth of 'Cartier World' through the merger of the groups owning the Paris, London and New York stores Death of Robert Hocq		

AUTHOR'S ACKNOWLEDGMENTS FOR THE ORIGINAL EDITION

My thanks go first to Mr Joseph Kanouï, President of Cartier, whose understanding, farsightedness and encouragement made this book possible. Equal thanks go to Mr Ralph Esmerian, who as a friend and arbiter accompanied the project right from the beginning.

At Cartier's I had the privilege of working with Mme Véronique Ristelhueber and subsequently with Mlle Betty Jais, whose assistance as archivists was at all times invaluable. Mlle Jais followed this work through to the end with practical help at all levels. In New York Mrs Bonnie Selfe opened the Fifth Avenue archives and lent all her support, as did Mr Joe Allgood at Cartier London.

Stimulating help and continued reference to literature came from Mr Frederik Schwarz, Berlin, and from Mr Nicolas Sarafis, Geneva. I am indebted to Mr Antony Derham and Mr Simon Bull who read through Chapters 13 and 16, respectively.

The following have given advice, suggestions and precious information: Jane Lady Abdy, Prince Sadruddin Aga Khan, Countess Carla Albertoni, Mr Jacques Arpels, Mr Louis Asscher, Mr Jean de Beisteigui, Mr Michael Bennett, Mr and Mme Christian Benoist, Prince Lennard Bernadotte, Mr Hans Bichsel, the late Mona Countess Bismarck, Me Suzanne Blum, Comte Bruno de Boisgelin, Mr Alain Boucheron, Mr Thierry Bousquet, Princesse Jeanne-Marie de Broglie, Mr Frédéric Brun-Theremin, Mr Paul Calmette, Mr François Canavy, Mr Robert Carlhian, Mr Alain Cartier, Mme Marion Cartier, Mlle Véronique Cartier, Mr Paul Casta (La Garantie), Mme Marguerite Carré, Mme Jutta Cassel, Countess Emmeline de Castéja, Mme Catherine Cardinal (Musée des Arts et des Métiers), Mme René Clair, Mr Peter Clayton, Mlle M. C. Commère (Bibliothèque des Commisseurs-Priseurs), Lady Diana Cooper, Mme Gilberte Cournand, Mr François Curiel, Mr Gaston Cusin, Mr Pierre Debofle (Archives de Paris), Mme Pierre Delbée, Mr André Denet, Mr Patrick Descamp, Mr Gérard Desouches, Mr Louis Devaux, the Diamond Information Center in New York, Miss Frances Dimond (Royal Archives, Photograph Collection) Mr Jean Dinh Van, Mr Daniel Du Jeannerot, Mlle Marie Du Mesnildot, the Marchioness of Dufferin and Ava, Mr Henry Duru, Miss Diana Edkins (Condé Nast Library, New York), Mr Myran Eknayan, Mme Pierre Emmanuel, Mr Rupert Emmerson, la Baronne Edwina d'Erlanger, Mme Simone Eymonaud, Mr Harry Fane, Mr Thomas Färber, Prince Jean Louis de Faucigny-Lucinge, Mr Jean Feray, Mr Christopher Forbes, Mme Claude Forêt, Mr Enrico de Franceschini, Mr Donald Fraser, Mme Tatiana Fruchaud, Mme Axelle de Gaigneron, Mr James Gardner, Mr Guillaume Garnier (Musée Galliéra), Mr Richard Garnier, Mme Marie-Noël de Gary (Musée des Arts Décoratifs) Miss Georgia Gigon, Mr David Gol, Me Blaise Grosjean, Mr H. Robert Greene, Mr Claude Guerin, Dr Géza von Habsburg, Mme P. Hebey, Mrs Gloria Hendy, Baroness von der Heydt, Fürstin Charlotte zu Hohenlohe, Mr Hanspeter Hüsistein, Mme Suzanne Jacqueau, Mr Pierre Jeannet, Messrs Johnson, Walker and Tolhurst, Mr Stephen Kahane, Photothèque Kahn, Mr Clive Kandel, Me Albert Kaufmann, Mr Lawrence Krashes, Mr Jean de Laborde Naguez, Mr Lucien Lachassagne, Mme Nicole Landolt-Sandoz, Mr Henri Larrieu, Mr Fred Leighton, Mme Marcelle Lemarchand, Mr Jacques Lenfant, Mr Jean-Marc Leri (Bibliothèque de la Ville de Paris), Mme Lévy-Strauss, Comptoir Lyon-Allemand, La Duchesse de Maillé, Mr Philippe Maitrejean, Mr Félix Marcilhac, Mlle Lucette Marson, Mr Georges Martin, Mr Paul Martini, Mr J. Martory, Mr Frederick A. Mew, Mr Albert Middlemiss, Sir Oliver Millar (the Lord Chamberlain's Office), le Comte de la Moussaye, Mr Geoffrey Munn, Miss Mary Murphy, Mr Carl Nater, Colonel Neuville (Musée de l'Armée), Mme Noetzlin, Mr Eric Nussbaum, Mr Edmond Oxeda, Mr Gaston Palewski, Mr Max Pellegrain, Mr Michel Périnet, Platingilde Frankfurt, Miss Penny Proddow, the Prince of Pudukota, Mr Corentin Quideau, Mr Nicholas Rayner, le Baron de Rédé, Mme Janine Rémy, Mr René-Louis Révillon, Mr Alexandre Reza, Me Maurice Rheims, Mr John Richardson, Prof. Frank W. Ries, Mr Peter Riva, Mr Jean Rosenthal, Mr Joël Rosenthal, la Baronne Liliane de Rothschild, la Baronne Marie-Hélène de Rothschild, Princesse Irina of Romania, Mme Geneviève Rouvrais, Mr Lionel Rouvrais, Mr Hubert Salmon, Mr Charles Schiffmann, Mrs Diana Scarisbrick, Me Pierre Sciclounoff, Mr Alexander von Solodkoff, Mr Bernard Solomon, Mme Charlotte Spoerli, H. H. Sukhjit Singh of Kapurthala, Mr Edouard Sirakian, la Comtesse Florence de Surmont, Mr Charles Spencer, Mr Karl-Hans Strauss, Miss Suzan Strong (Victoria and Albert Museum), Mr Robert Thil, Mr Jean Taburiaux, Mr Michael Tree, Mr Michel Turisk, Mr Anthony Thompson, Mr Hugh Tait (British Museum), Mr François Verger, Mr Roger Valentin (Pyramide d'Or), Mrs Diana Vreeland, Mr Gérald Van der Kemp, the Grand Duke Vladimir, Mr Guy Villeneuve, Mr David W. Wright (Pierpont Morgan Library), la Baronne Geoffroy de Waldner, Mme B. Watel, Mr Paul-Louis Weiller, Mr Paul White (Smithsonian Institution), Mr Tjerk Wicky, Mrs Cortwright Wetherill, Mrs Rosamond Wiszniewska, Mrs E. Wynkoop, Mr Maurice Worth, Princess Olga of Yugoslavia. My final thanks go to Mr Stanley Baron of Thames & Hudson.

Hans Nadelhoffer, Geneva, 1984

ACKNOWLEDGMENTS FOR ILLUSTRATIONS

Cartier Archives © Cartier 1–3, 5, 7, 8, 12, 16–24, 27, 30–38, 40–46, 49–53, 55–59, 61–70, 71 *second and bottom*, 72, 74, 75, 78, 82–89, 94–99, 101–104, 106, 107, 128, 129, 132, 135–138, 140, 145, 147, 149, 151, 152, 156–159, 163, 165, 171, 172, 175–177, 179, 180, 185–189, 194–196, 206, 207, 209, 221–230, 238–242, 250, 257, 263–266, 272, 274, 278, 282, 300, 302, 304, 305, 308–312, 318, 327, 332–334, 337, 339, 367–376, 390–392, 395–398, 400–402, 404–406, 409, 410, (photo Adolph de Meyer) 6, (photo Nadar) 4 • Cartier Collection, Photo Nick Welsh, © Cartier 9–11, 13–15, 26, 28, 29, 39, 47, 48, 60, 73, 79, 80, 81, 90–93, 105, 108–127, 133, 134, 139, 141, 144, 146, 155, 160, 162, 164, 166, 167–170, 173, 174, 178, 181, 182, 184, 190–193, 197–199, 202–204, 208, 210–213, 215–220, 231–237, 243–249, 251–256, 258–262, 267–271, 273, 275, 277, 279–281, 283–290, 292–296, 298, 306, 307, 313, 316, 317, 319–326, 328–331, 335, 336, 338, 340–366, 377–387, 389, 393, 394 • © Cartier 299 • Marcus Adams/Camera Press 408 • Courtesy of the Cecil Beaton Studio Archive, Sotheby's, London 205, 407 • © Bettmann/CORBIS 411 • C. Creutz, © Cartier 403 • Getty Images 297 • © The Metropolitan Museum of Art, New York 130, 131 • Musée des Arts Décoratifs, Paris 71 *third, fourth and fifth down* • The Royal Collection © 2007, Her Majesty Queen Elizabeth II 25 • *Vogue* © Condé Nast Inc. 100, 142, 304. Also to be thanked are Messrs Christie's; Messrs Sotheby's; Diamond Information Center, New York; Condé Nast Library, New York; Photothèque Kahn, Paris; private collections; Smithsonian Institution, Washington, D.C.; Roger-Viollet, Paris.

The line drawings were provided by the Cartier designer Jacques Diltoer.

A number of drawings by Charles Jacqueau, reproduced here as they appeared in the Cartier Archives, were presented by the designer's family in 1998 to the Petit Palais, Musée des Beaux-Arts de la Ville de Paris. Accession numbers and additional information have kindly been supplied by Monsieur Gilles Chazal, Director of the Museum: 71 *top* PPJAC00928 (graphite and black ink on the recto and blue ink on the verso of transparent vellum, 7.3 x 20 cm). 143 These drawings were subsequently unmounted, and some were presented to the Museum: *top left* PPHJAC01689, design for a pendant in diamond, sapphire, ruby, emerald, onyx and platinum, *c.* 1914–19 (graphite, ink and gouache on treated [*pellicule*] vellum, 10.6 x 6.7 cm); *top centre* PPHJAC-01685, design for a pendant in the form of a bowl with birds, in diamond, sapphire, ruby, emerald, rock crystal, onyx and platinum, *c.* 1914 (graphite and gouache on treated [*pellicule*] paper, 9.7 x 6 cm); *bottom left* PPHJAC01650, design for an 'épingle palme' (pin in the shape of a mango leaf) in diamond, emerald and platinum, *c.* 1913-19 (graphite and gouache on treated [*pellicule*] paper, 6.4 x 5 cm); *irregular sheet in the centre* PPHJAC01686, designs for five pendants in platinum and various combinations of diamond, sapphire, ruby, emerald, pearl and onyx, *c.* 1916–19 (graphite and gouache on treated [*pellicule*] paper, 20 x 8.5 cm); *far right* PPHJAC01687, design for a pendant in sapphire, ruby, emerald, amethyst, pearl, onyx and enamel, *c.* 1913 (graphite and gouache on treated [*pellicule*] paper, 12 x 1.9 cm). 148 PPJAC-00293 (graphite, black ink and gouache on transparent laid paper, 18 x 5.5 cm). 153 PPJAC03102; the drawing bears Jacqueau's signature. 154 PPJAC02158 (graphite, ink and red chalk on transparent vellum, 19 x 27.5 cm). 183 PPJAC01973 (graphite, ink and gouache on grey card, 54.2 x 47 cm); the drawing bears Jacqueau's stamp. 276 PPJAC03082; the drawing bears Jacqueau's stamp.

INDEX